Sustainable Service Marketing with Virtual Currencies

Arjun J. Nair
St. Lawrence College, Canada

Sridhar Manohar
Chitkara Business School, Chitkara University, India

Yam B. Limbu
Montclair State University, USA

Bruce A. Huhmann
Virginia Commonwealth University, USA

IGI Global
Scientific Publishing
Publishing Tomorrow's Research Today

Vice President of Editorial	Melissa Wagner
Director of Acquisitions	Mikaela Felty
Director of Book Development	Jocelynn Hessler
Production Manager	Mike Brehm
Cover Design	Jose Rosado

Published in the United States of America by
IGI Global Scientific Publishing
701 East Chocolate Avenue
Hershey, PA, 17033, USA
Tel: 717-533-8845
Fax: 717-533-7115
Website: https://www.igi-global.com E-mail: cust@igi-global.com

Library of Congress Cataloging-in-Publication Data

Names: Nair, Arjun J., 1986- editor.
Title: Sustainable service marketing with virtual currencies / [edited by] Arjun J. Nair, Sridhar Manohar, Yam Limbu, Bruce Huhmann.
Description: Hershey, PA : IGI Global Scientific Publishing, [2026] | Includes bibliographical references and index. | Summary: "This book addresses the need for businesses to integrate sustainable practices with cutting-edge virtual currency solutions. By doing so, companies can not only minimize their environmental footprint but also actively engage eco-conscious consumers, thereby fostering brand loyalty and promoting long-term sustainable growth"-- Provided by publisher.
Identifiers: LCCN 2024061707 (print) | LCCN 2024061708 (ebook) | ISBN 9798337303154 (hardcover) | ISBN 9798337303161 (paperback) | ISBN 9798337303178 (ebook)
Subjects: LCSH: Service industries--Marketing. | Service industries--Environmental aspects. | Digital currency.
Classification: LCC HD9980.5 .S933 2025 (print) | LCC HD9980.5 (ebook) | DDC 658.8--dc23/eng/20250306
LC record available at https://lccn.loc.gov/2024061707
LC ebook record available at https://lccn.loc.gov/2024061708

British Cataloguing in Publication Data
A Cataloguing in Publication record for this book is available from the British Library.

Table of Contents

Detailed Table of Contents

pieces of research tending to end up with fragmentary insights, a bibliometric analysis was designed to present innovative findings regarding undeveloped realms.

Sustainable service marketing is the integration of economic, social, and environmental dimensions followed for value-driven responsible business practice. Decentralized technologies transform the ways traditional strategies are used in marketing into new innovative ways that emphasize sustainability. These technologies redesign, deliver, and experience services but also help catalyze systemic changes within service ecosystems. The study conducts a lexicometric analysis to discuss the literature regarding sustainable service marketing and virtual currencies. It introduces key themes such as advanced technology integration, improved transparency and accountabilities with decentralized platforms, and trend towards circular economies facilitated by digital innovations. Revealing these themes outlines how virtual currencies can be instrumental in sustaining consumer behavior through optimization of the delivery of service and environmental practices in business operations. The results provide actionable implications and avenues for further research directions.

The rise of virtual currencies has created new possibilities for sustainable service marketing, offering innovative ways to enhance customer experience while promoting eco-friendly practices. This paper explores how virtual currencies can be harnessed as a transformative tool to engage consumers in sustainable behaviors, foster brand loyalty, and drive green marketing initiatives. By analyzing the challenges and

Preface

In the evolving landscape of global commerce and environmental consciousness, the convergence of green marketing, blockchain technology, and virtual currencies represents a transformational shift in how sustainable services are promoted, consumed, and financed. This edited volume, *Sustainable Service Marketing with Virtual Currencies*, explores the multi-faceted intersections of sustainability, digital financial innovation, and marketing, offering a holistic view of how businesses and consumers can engage in responsible value exchange.

As the world accelerates its digital transformation, service industries face increasing pressure to innovate sustainably while maintaining profitability and consumer trust. Virtual currencies, ranging from cryptocurrencies to central bank digital currencies (CBDCs), and the decentralized nature of blockchain offer new mechanisms for accountability, transparency, and behavioral incentivization. These technological tools are not only redefining financial ecosystems but also creating fresh opportunities for sustainable service marketing.

The contributors to this book—drawn from diverse academic and geographic backgrounds—critically assess these dynamics through empirical studies, theoretical frameworks, bibliometric analyses, and conceptual models. Together, they demonstrate how digital financial tools can catalyze sustainable practices across sectors, geographies, and consumer bases.

CHAPTER OVERVIEW

- **Chapter 1** investigates how customer experience in the Horn of Africa influences service marketing sustainability via virtual currency systems. The findings highlight the role of virtual currencies as mediators that enhance service loyalty and sustainability.

- **Chapter 2** presents a bibliometric mapping of scholarly trends in CBDCs and financial development, offering insights into the academic discourse and unexplored areas in this emerging field.
- **Chapter 3** uses lexicometric analysis to explore literature on sustainable service marketing and virtual currencies, identifying key themes like transparency, decentralization, and service redesign.
- **Chapter 4** discusses how virtual currencies can enhance customer experience and drive green marketing, addressing challenges such as regulation and technological barriers while advocating for eco-incentive systems.
- **Chapter 5** reimagines the digital economy by positioning virtual currencies as enablers of inclusive and sustainable service marketing, grounded in established theoretical frameworks.
- **Chapter 6** explores the role of virtual currencies in green service financing, proposing policy recommendations and financial ecosystem reforms to align with environmental goals.
- **Chapter 7** examines the impact of sustainable supply chain management on global service marketing, with cross-border virtual currencies acting as key mediators in emerging markets like the Horn of Africa.
- **Chapter 8** proposes a future-oriented framework for integrating blockchain and virtual currencies into green marketing, aiming to improve transparency and combat greenwashing.
- **Chapter 9** analyzes the business performance outcomes of digital currency adoption, offering practical insights through case studies and technology integration analysis.
- **Chapter 10** explores how virtual currencies are transforming sustainable service marketing in emerging economies by improving financial inclusion and access to essential services.
- **Chapter 11** conducts a bibliometric analysis on virtual currencies and green finance, revealing global trends and offering policy insights for blockchain-based environmental finance.
- **Chapter 12** focuses on the influence of social media in shaping consumer attitudes toward digital currencies, highlighting the role of influencers and trust-building mechanisms.
- **Chapter 13** introduces a conceptual model for using virtual currencies as financial incentives for sustainable service consumption, supported by real-world applications across various industries.

This volume serves as a vital resource for scholars, practitioners, and policymakers seeking to understand and leverage the synergy between digital finance and sustainability in the service economy. Through its interdisciplinary and global approach, the book aims to inform future strategies for building resilient, inclusive, and green service markets powered by innovative technologies.

Chapter 1
Customer Experience Effect on Service Marketing Sustainability Through Virtual Currency Systems in the Horn of Africa

Aynetu Terefe
https://orcid.org/0009-0003-3814-9548
Bule Hora University, Ethiopia

Shashi Kant
https://orcid.org/0000-0003-4722-5736
Bule Hora University, Ethiopia

Metasebia Adula
https://orcid.org/0000-0001-5732-2850
Bule Hora University, Ethiopia

Tafese Niguse
https://orcid.org/0009-0008-6536-6392
Bule Hora University, Ethiopia

ABSTRACT

Consequently, this research focuses on analyzing the impact of customer experience on service marketing sustainability facilitated by virtual currency in the Horn of Africa. Through the administration of questionnaires to 385 participants from the

DOI: 10.4018/979-8-3373-0315-4.ch001

service industry, the study uses the Exploratory Factor Analysis (EFA) to establish principal factors of customer experience influencing sustainable marketing practices. CFA is performed to validate these dimensions so as to have a reliable measure for the concerned dimensions. Measurement of customer experience and virtual currency system, and sustainable service marketing outcomes through SEM using AMOS is an analysis of the interconnection among them. Research outcomes suggest that improvements to customer experience help to support service marketing's sustainability, though various virtual currency systems are crucial mediators that help customers buy services and remain loyal to them.

INTRODUCTION

In an era characterized by rapid technological advancements and shifting consumer behaviors, the interplay among experience of customer (CX) and sustainability of marketing of services has emerged as a pivotal area of Investigation (Rane, 2023). This use fullness is amplified in the context of system based on currency virtually, particularly within Africa, where digital financial solutions are reshaping economic landscapes (Omeish et al., 2024). The global significance of this topic lies in its potential to drive inclusive economic growth, enhance customer engagement, and promote sustainable business practices. As economies worldwide increasingly embrace digital currencies, understanding their implications for experience of customer and service marketing becomes crucial for businesses aiming to remain competitive (Calza et al., 2023). The origin of the concept of experience of customer can be traced back to the early 2000s, when businesses began recognizing the need to focus on holistic interactions with consumers rather than merely transactional relationships (Mentari et al., 2024). Over the years, this focus has evolved to encompass various dimensions, including emotional engagement, personalization, and the use of technology. Concurrently, service marketing has shifted towards sustainability, emphasizing the use fullness of ethical practices and social responsibility in building brand loyalty and trust. The advent of virtual currencies, especially in developing markets, manifested a novel opportunity to enhance experience of customer while fostering sustainable service marketing strategies (Urdea et al., 2021).

Customer Experience defined as the overall perception and feelings a customer has during their interactions with a brand or organization. This encompasses all touch-points, including pre-purchase, purchase, and post-purchase stages (Rane, 2023). Virtual Marketing System is defined as a digital framework that utilizes online platforms and technologies to engage customers, facilitate transactions, and promote products or services. VMS often includes elements like e-commerce sites, social media marketing, and mobile applications (Mudrika, 2024). Sustainability of marketing defined as a practice of promoting and delivering services in a way that meets current consumer needs while ensuring long-term environmental, social, and economic health. This involves integrating sustainable practices into marketing strategies (Kassociation et al., 2021).

Empirical literature highlights the positive correlation among enhanced experience of customer and sustainable marketing practices. (Jabo et al, 2025). Studies demonstrate that businesses leveraging digital currencies often see increased customer loyalty and engagement, as these systems provide new avenues for rewards and incentives (Rane, 2023). Also, despite the promising findings, practical challenges remain. Many businesses face hurdles such as regulatory uncertainties, low digital literacy rates, and varying degrees of acceptance of virtual currencies among consumers. These challenges hinder the influence implementation of marketing strategies that utilize virtual currencies to enhance experience of customers (Mentari et al. 2024). Also, existing Investigation has identified notable gaps in understanding how system based on currency virtually specifically influence sustainability of marketing of services in the African context. While there is a growing body of literature on digital currencies globally, studies focusing on their implications for experience of customer and sustainable practices in Africa remain sparse. This chapter aims to fill these gaps by exploring how system based on currency virtually can be influence integrated into service marketing strategies to enhance experience of customer and promote sustainability (Omeish et al., 2024).

To guide future Investigations and policymakers, this Investigation will provide insights into best practices for utilizing virtual currencies and highlight the critical role of experience of customer in driving sustainability of marketing of services. The central Investigation question guiding this investigation is: ***"How do system based on currency virtually influence experience of customer and sustainability of marketing of services in Africa, and what strategies can businesses adopt to leverage these systems influence?"***

BACKGROUND INVESTIGATION

The integration of system based on currency virtually into service marketing strategies in Africa manifested a complex set of challenges and opportunities. System based on currency virtually, including crypto-currencies and mobile money platforms, have emerged as innovative financial solutions, offering new opportunities for enhancing experience of customer and promoting sustainable service marketing practices (Jabo et al., 2024). Also, the implementation of these concepts is fraught with challenges that require careful consideration (Rahardja et al., 2021). A real-world instance, M-Pesa in Kenya regardless of its achievement confronted substantial hurdles, such as supervisory encounters, deception, and buyer tutoring (Rane, 2023). These challenges highlighted the usefulness of customer trust in adopting digital financial solutions. While M-Pesa improved experience of customer by offering convenience and efficiency, the initial skepticism among users regarding the security of mobile transactions posed a barrier to widespread adoption. This case exemplifies how even successful implementations can encounter obstacles that influence customer engagement and overall service marketing efforts (Kassociation et al., 2021).

Another example of an amusingly-titled example is the recent emergence of crypto-currencies in the Nigerian market. However, in 2021, the CBN issued a contentious circular which banned banks from providing services to crypt-currency traders, primarily to supervise a continuously expanding sector that was considered prone to distortion the stability in the Nigerian economy. This regulatory juncture built a significant barrier for organizations seeking to incorporate crypto-currencies into their service promotional approaches (Rane, 2023). Despite the potential for increased customer engagement through virtual currency incentives, businesses in Nigeria faced challenges in navigating the restrictive regulatory environment. As a result, many potential users remained hesitant to engage with digital currencies, limiting their influence on sustainability of marketing of services (Mentari et al. 2024). Also, Investigation manifested that low levels of digital literacy in various African nations hinder the adoption of system based on currency virtually. In the same way, an Investigation focusing on the adoption of block-chain technology in South Africa revealed that many consumers lacked the necessary understanding of digital currencies, leading to reluctance in using these systems for transactions. This gap in knowledge not only influences experience of customer but also manifested a barrier to businesses aiming to leverage virtual currencies for marketing purposes. Without adequate education and support, the potential benefits of virtual currencies remain unrealized, underscoring the usefulness of addressing digital literacy as a critical factor for successful implementation (Rane, 2023).

Another outstanding proven example of such a headline is the relatively recent phenomenon of crypto-currencies in the Nigerian market. But in the year 2021, another controverted circular was issues by CBN which banned banks' engagement in supplying their services to crypt-currency traders, mainly in order to regulate a rapidly growing sector seen as capable of destabilizing the stability in the Nigerian economy. Such a regulatory conjunction created a formidable structure through which organizations desiring to integrate crypto-currencies into their service promotion strategies faced the biggest challenge (Rane, 2023).

STATEMENT OF THE PROBLEM

The ideal state for businesses is one where virtual currencies enhance experience of customer and promote sustainable marketing practices, leading to increased customer loyalty and economic inclusion (Mudrika, 2024). Also, the reality is often quite different. Despite the potential benefits, there exists contradictory evidence regarding the influence of virtual currencies in improving customer engagement and service delivery. In the same way, while some studies highlight successful implementations of digital currencies that have fostered customer loyalty, others manifested that issues such as regulatory restrictions and consumer mistrust substantially hinder adoption (Omeish et al., 2024). Further complicating the landscape are inconclusive outcomes from existing Investigation. Many studies examining the influence of virtual currencies on sustainability of marketing of services provide mixed findings, often failing to establish a clear causal relationship among the use of digital currencies and improved experience of customer. This ambiguity manifested a theoretical gap, as existing frameworks do not adequately account for the unique socio-economic contexts of African markets, where factors such as digital literacy, cultural acceptance, and regulatory environments play critical roles in shaping consumer behavior (Mentari et al., 2024).

Knowledge gaps also persist in the current literature; particularly regarding the specific mechanisms through which virtual currencies can influence enhance experience of customer in the African context. While there is a growing body of Investigation on digital currencies globally, studies focusing on their implications for sustainability of marketing of services in Africa remain limited. This lack of targeted Investigation underscores the need for a deeper understanding of how businesses can leverage virtual currencies to meet the distinct needs and preferences of African consumers (Rane, 2023). Also, context gaps are evident in the limited exploration of how local cultural norms, economic conditions, and technological infrastructures influence the adoption and influence of virtual currencies. For example, while mobile money has gained traction in countries like Kenya, similar acceptance are not universally observed across the continent. This inconsistency highlights the use fullness of context-specific studies that examine the factors contributing to successful or unsuccessful implementations of system based on currency virtually.

Finally, practical challenges continue to impede the influence use of virtual currencies in service marketing. Issues such as regulatory uncertainty, low digital literacy, and the need for robust security measures create substantial barriers for businesses seeking to adopt these systems. Without addressing these practical challenges, the potential of virtual currencies to enhance experience of customer and promote sustainability in service marketing cannot be fully realized (Omeish et al., 2024). This Investigation aims to fill these gaps by conducting a comprehensive analysis of how system based on currency virtually can be influence integrated into service marketing strategies in Africa. By examining the interplay among experience of customer, service sustainability, and digital currencies within specific African contexts, this Investigation will contribute to the theoretical understanding of these dynamics.

RELATED THEORIES

In exploring the influence of experience of customer on sustainability of marketing of services through system based on currency virtually in Africa, several theoretical frameworks provide valuable insights.

Service-Dominant Logic (SDL)

By focusing on the collaborative nature of service provision, SDL underscores the usefulness of enhancing experience of customer through personalized interactions and innovative service offerings. In the African context, where consumer relationships often drive loyalty, SDL provides a framework for understanding how virtual currencies can enhance these interactions and contribute to sustainable service marketing (Marin-Garcia et al., 2022).

Technology Acceptance Model (TAM)

By applying TAM, Investigations can analyze the barriers to adoption that may arise from concerns about security, complexity, and the overall value proposition of virtual currencies. This theory helps identify strategies for improving experience of customer by addressing these perceptions and fostering greater acceptance of digital currencies (Zaid & Patwayati, 2021).

Experience of Customer Management (CEM)

Experience of customer Management focuses on the strategies and processes that organizations use to manage and enhance customer interactions across various touch points. CEM emphasizes understanding the customer journey and leveraging technology to create meaningful experiences. In the context of virtual currencies, CEM provides insights into how businesses can design their services to align with customer expectations, thus improving satisfaction and fostering loyalty. This theory highlights the necessity of integrating customer feedback into service design, particularly when implementing new technologies like virtual currencies (Omeish et al., 2024).

Sustainable Marketing Theory

Sustainable Marketing Theory emphasizes the use fullness of ethical practices and social responsibility in marketing strategies. It advocates for aligning business goals with society al and environmental considerations. This theory is essential for examining how virtual currencies can contribute to sustainable service marketing in Africa by promoting financial inclusion and supporting local economies (Rane, et al., 2023).

Theoretical Lens

Among these theories, Service-Dominant Logic serves as the main theoretical lens for this Investigation. SDL's focus on co-creation of value through customer interactions aligns well with the objectives of integrating system based on currency virtually into service marketing. By viewing customers as active participants in the service delivery process, SDL facilitates a deeper understanding of how virtual currencies can enhance experience of customer and foster sustainable practices.

DEFINITION AND ORIGIN OF TERMS

Experience of Customer

Customer experience is defined as all organizational exchanges and interactions with customers that the customers encounter which include the pre-purchase, during-purchase and post-purchase stages of the customer journey. This is not only the physical characteristics of a product or service but also the feelings and thoughts that the buyers experiences (Omeish et al., 2024). The idea of the experience of customer came to the foreground at the beginning of the year 2000s since the gear emerged that the customer relations are not limited to the single sale (Mentari et al. 2024).

Service Marketing

Service marketing on the other hand is the process of communicating the availability of services for sale, with aim at recognizing the factors that make the marketing of services different from the marketing of goods (Zaid & Patwayati, 2021). While it is not easy to create a product that surrounds a physical tangible object, services are often created and consumed at the same time and thus the experience of the customer becomes an important aspect of the marketing mix. Some of the key concepts in service marketing involve: The nature of service quality; relationship marketing and a marketing mix that is designed specifically for service organizations as differentiated from product organizations (Morales, 2023).

Sustainability in Marketing

Marketing sustainability is the systematic incorporation of environmental/social and economic concerns into marketing operations and plans (Mentari et al. 2024). It therefore stresses on the responsibility that business organizations must apply ethical behaviors, and the impacts of the businesses on society, and the physical world. Sustainable marketing aims on satisfying the needs of the consumers in the manifest time environments without negative impacts on the future and latter part of today's generation, whereby consumers become clients in a long term relationship marketing by working with transparency (Baskaran, 2023).

EMPIRICAL LITERATURE REVIEW

Customer Experience and Service Marketing Sustainability

A positive experience of customer fosters emotional connections among consumers and brands, enhancing customer satisfaction and encouraging repeat business (Tolooee et al., 2024). In the context of service marketing where some of the interactions involve are more or less relational and not tangible the delivery of excellent service experiences becomes vital (Nair & Manohar, 2024). Customer satisfaction leads to positive word-of-mouth communication which manifested valuable, natural marketing, as well as improving a brand's reputation (Nuseir, 2023). It matters that a focus on the experience of customer as an important value also corresponds to sustainable marketing due to ethical customer engagement and social responsibility (Morales et al., 2023). When the businesses focus on the needs and demands of the customers, they are well placed to create outputs that would appeal to the market hence reducing on unnecessary production of wrong products in the market. Not only that, but this approach also covers current customer needs, which at the same time, meet future requirements and lead to the successful development of a sustainable business model for the company (Mentari et al. 2024).

Moreover, incorporating customer feedback into the actors' service design and delivery leads to sustainability of marketing of services. Through this case, organizations must take time and listen to their customers in an effort to come up with a strategy that will help them meet the needs of the market sufficiently. This cyclical process of development promotes the co-designing of the brand and customers come with a stronger bond to the brand. On the contrary adoption of the neglect experience of customer may lead to negative perceptions and customer attrition hence eradicating sustainability (Morales et al., 2023). Ultimately, the interplay among experience of customer and sustainability of marketing of services underscores the usefulness of relationship-building and ethical practices in today's competitive landscape. Companies that influence leverage experience of customer not only enhance their market position but also contribute to a more sustainable economic environment, benefiting both consumers and the broader community. These holistic approach positions businesses for long-term success demonstrating that prioritizing experience of customer is not just a marketing strategy, but a fundamental component of sustainable business practices (Tolooee et al., 2024).

> H1: Experience of customer has substantial influence on sustainability of marketing of services

Experience of Customer and System Based on Currency Virtually

A positive experience of customer can enhance trust and confidence in virtual currencies, which are often perceived as complex and risky. When users encounter intuitive interfaces, seamless transactions, and responsive customer support, they are more likely to feel comfortable engaging with these systems (Nair & Manohar, 2024). This comfort can lead to increased usage, encouraging users to explore various applications of virtual currencies, from everyday transactions to investment opportunities (Tang, 2023). Also, an exceptional experience of customer can drive word-of-mouth promotion, which is vital in the relatively nascent and evolving field of virtual currencies. Satisfied users often share their positive experiences with peers, helping to demystify virtual currencies and reduce apprehension among potential adopters. This organic promotion is particularly substantial in markets where digital literacy may be low, as personal recommendations can serve as powerful endorsements that encourage wider acceptance (Mentari et al. 2024).

Conversely, a poor experience of customer can have detrimental influences on virtual currency adoption. Issues such as complex registration processes, lack of proper educational resources, and inadequate support can deter users and foster scepticism (Manohar, 2024). If customers encounter problems that are not promptly addressed, their trust in the system diminishes, leading to negative perceptions that can stifle growth. This highlights the usefulness of investing in user-friendly platforms and comprehensive customer support services to enhance the overall experience (Morales et al., 2023). Also, as system based on currency virtually often rely on community engagement and user feedback for development and improvement, a positive experience of customer can facilitate valuable insights. Companies that prioritize experience of customer are more likely to gather and act on feedback, leading to continuous enhancements in their offerings. This iterative process not only improves the functionality and security of system based on currency virtually but also aligns them more closely with user needs, fostering a sense of community and loyalty among users (Tolooee et al., 2024).

H2: Experience of customer has substantial influence on system based on currency virtually

System Based on Currency Virtually and Service Marketing Sustainability

By integrating virtual currencies into service offerings, businesses can provide customers with greater flexibility and convenience, which can lead to increased satisfaction and loyalty (Rane, 2023). In the same way, lower transaction costs associated with virtual currencies can make services more affordable, particularly for underserved populations, thereby expanding market reach and fostering inclusivity. This accessibility aligns with sustainable marketing principles by addressing social equity and enabling a broader demographic to engage with services (Mentari et al. 2024). Also, the system based on currency virtually mostly contains services that enhance customer loyalty and incentives as they make customer to come back for more business (Manohar, 2024). These systems can help design effective loyalty programs that optimize customer motivations for their purchase as well as the development of desirable behaviours like, being environmentally conscious, or supporting local producers. This way, Morales et al., (2023) argued that, customer incentives should be given ways of making them environmentally conscious while improving on the image of businesses in the market.. Also, the successful integration of system based on currency virtually also requires a focus on experience of customer and education. Businesses must ensure that consumers understand how to use these systems influence and feel secure in their transactions. By providing clear information and support, companies can build trust and encourage adoption, which is essential for realizing the full potential of virtual currencies in service marketing (Tolooee et al., 2024).

H3: System based on currency virtually has substantial influence on Sustainability of marketing of services

Mediation of System Based on Currency Virtually

System based on currency virtually facilitate seamless transactions, reduce costs, and provide innovative ways to engage customers, which can substantially influence the sustainability of service marketing strategies (Morales et al., 2023). Firstly, virtual currencies can streamline payment processes, making transactions faster and more efficient. This efficiency not only improves customer satisfaction but also allows businesses to allocate resources more influence, reducing operational costs. When service providers can lower transaction fees and minimize overhead, they can pass these savings onto consumers, fostering loyalty and encouraging repeat business. This dynamic creates a win-win situation where both customers and businesses benefit, thereby promoting a sustainable business model (Mentari et al. 2024). Also, system based on currency virtually enables the implementation of loyalty and rewards programs that align customer behaviour with sustainable practices. The mediation influence here is substantial: virtual currencies not only facilitate transactions but also drive customer engagement in ways that support broader sustainability goals (Tolooee et al., 2024).

Also, system based on currency virtually can enhance transparency and trust, which are crucial elements for sustainable marketing. Many virtual currencies operate on block-chain technology, which provides a secure and transparent ledger of transactions (Niguse et al., 2024). This transparency can build consumer trust, as customers feel more confident in the integrity of their transactions. When businesses demonstrate ethical practices through transparent financial systems, they strengthen their brand reputation and foster long-term relationships with consumers, contributing to sustainability (Rane, 2023). Also, the successful mediation of system based on currency virtually also requires addressing challenges such as regulatory compliance, digital literacy, and consumer education. Businesses must ensure that customers understand how to use virtual currencies and the benefits they offer. By providing clear information and support, companies can facilitate smoother adoption and integration, maximizing the positive influence of virtual currencies on sustainability of marketing of services (Morales et al., 2023).

H4; The association among Experience of customer and sustainability of marketing of services is influenced by System based on currency virtually

CONCEPTUAL FRAMEWORK

Figure 1. Conceptual framework

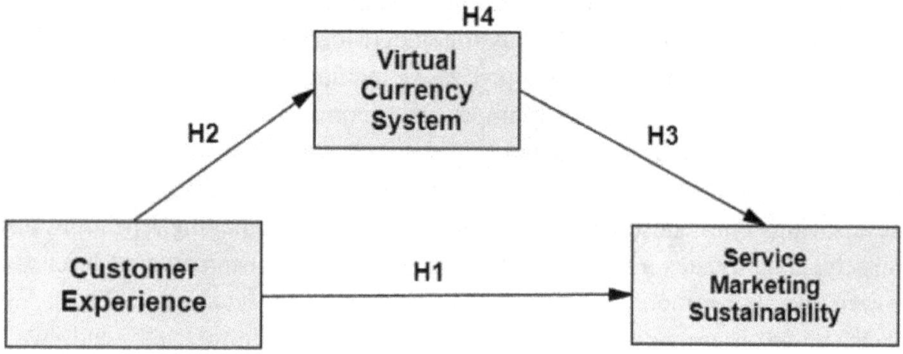

INVESTIGATION METHODOLOGY

This Investigation also used a quantitative Investigation method in analysing the effect of experience of customer and system based on currency virtually on sustainability of marketing of services. The respondents were — 390 in number to make sure there was ample data collected so that the sample size increases the reliability of the study. In the context of the Investigation, a structured questionnaire was developed aiming to assess several constructs concerning the experience of the customer, the use of virtual currency, as well as sustainable marketing practices. All the items in the questionnaire were adapted from previous literature to incorporate content validity and reliability. Kaiser's measure of sampling adequacy (KMO) as well as Bartlett's Test of Sphericity for the total set of items was also calculated before proceeding to main analyses. KMO value was computed to check the factor analysis appropriateness of the sample size and the obtained KMO value of > 0.6 were deemed as adequate sample size for sampling. The Bartlett Test of Sphericity was also used to test the null hypothesis that the correlation matrix is an identity matrix of the obtained substantial outcomes which were significant and would allow conducting EFA on the data.

After performing the KMO and Bartlett's test, Exploratory Factor Analysis was used to determine the factor solution of the constructions. They also aided in consolidating the scale's development as it tested the factor structure for appropriateness of the items and to where they best belong. These items were excluded from the Investigation in order to increase the level of clarity and convergent validity of the scales under study in which values failed to load sufficiently high. Subsequently to confirm the factor structure, structural equation modeling (SEM) was used by employing AMOS software to examine the relationships between the antecedent and consequent constructs as posited in the hypotheses. In other words, SEM enabled examination of the measurement model and the structural model at the same time and revealed about hard and soft effects of experience of customer and system based on currency virtually on sustainability of marketing of services. Adequacy of the theoretical model was assessed with the help of fit indices such as Chi-square, Comparative Fit Index (CFI), and Root Mean Square Error of Approximation (RMSEA) tests so that the model may correctly depict the reality.

Overall, the Investigation methodology employed in this Investigation facilitated a comprehensive analysis of the relationships among experience of customer, system based on currency virtually, and sustainability of marketing of services. By utilizing rigorous statistical techniques such as KMO, EFA, and SEM through AMOS, the Investigation contributed valuable insights into the dynamics of these constructs within the context of the African market. The systematic approach to scale development and validation further strengthened the reliability and validity of the findings, providing a solid foundation for future Investigation in this area.

Table 1. KMO and Bartlett's Test

Kaiser-Meyer-Olkin Measure of Sampling Adequacy.		**.840**
Bartlett's Test of Sphericity	Approx. Chi-Square	1419.718
	df	93
	Sig.	.000

Source: Authors

The KMO value obtained in Table 1 is 0.840, which manifested a high level of sampling adequacy. KMO values range from 0 to 1, with values closer to 1 suggesting that the data is suitable for factor analysis. A KMO value above 0.8 is generally considered meritorious, indicating that the variables share a substantial amount of variance and that factor analysis is appropriate for the dataset. This high KMO value suggests that the correlations among the variables are strong enough to justify the use of factor analysis. Bartlett's Test of Sphericity yielded an approximate Chi-Square value of 1419.718 with 93 degrees of freedom and a significance level (Sig.) of 0.000. This result is highly substantial, as it is well below the conventional alpha level of 0.05.

Table 2. Total variance explained

Component	Initial Eigenvalues			Extraction Sums of Squared Loadings			Rotation Sums of Squared Loadings		
	Total	% of Variance	Cumulative %	Total	% of Variance	Cumulative %	Total	% of Variance	Cumulative %
1	4.51	32.233	32.235	4.51	32.233	32.233	3.00	21.450	21.450
2	1.37	9.787	42.022	1.37	9.787	42.022	2.16	15.491	36.942
3	1.27	9.087	51.110	1.27	9.087	51.110	1.98	14.168	51.110
4	.946	6.781	57.891						
5	.873	6.221	64.117						
6	.775	5.518	69.635						

Extraction Method: Principal Component Analysis.
Source: Authors

Table 2 manifested the underlying structure of the data. The initial eigenvalues manifested that the first component accounts for 4.51 of the variance, manifesting 32.233% of the total variance. This suggests that the first factor captures a substantial portion of the information contained in the dataset. The cumulative percentage at this stage reaches 32.235%, indicating that the first component alone is sufficient to explain a considerable amount of the variance. The second component, with an eigenvalue of 1.37, accounts for an additional 9.787% of the variance, bringing the cumulative percentage to 42.022%. This pattern continues with the third component, which has an eigenvalue of 1.27 and explains an additional 9.087%, resulting in a cumulative variance of 51.110%. The extraction sums of squared loadings also reflect the same components, with the first three components retaining their significance. The first component remains at 4.51, confirming its strong influence, while the second and third components continue to support the structure with values of 1.37 and 1.27, respectively. The cumulative variance explained by the first three components reaches 51.110%, indicating that these factors collectively account for over half of the variance in the data.

The outcomes of the total variance explained manifested that the first three components play a crucial role in capturing the underlying structure of the data, with a cumulative explained variance of over 51%. This analysis highlights the influence of the principal component analysis in identifying key factors, setting the stage for further examination of these components in relation to experience of customer, system based on currency virtually, and sustainability of marketing of services. The findings underscore the usefulness of these factors in understanding the dynamics within the dataset, providing a solid foundation for subsequent analyses and model development.

Confirmatory Principle Component Examination

The principle component arrangement of a set of guided proxies is verified using a type of statistics known as confirmatory principle component examination. Based on the underlying frame job and correlatives among observed proxies, investigations can evaluate hypotheses utilizing CFA. To evaluate the hypothesis that there is a association among the proxies that are being steered and the latent conceptions that underpin them, the inquiry employed CFA under table 3.

Table 3. Co-variances

Covariance			**Approximation**	**S.E.**	**C.R.**	**P**	**Hy.**
System based on currency virtually	**<-->**	**Experience of customer**	**.242**	**.021**	**8.230**	**.00**	**H2**
Virtual Marketing System	<-->	Service Marketing Strategy Sustainability	.301	.030	7.692	.00	**H3**
Experience of customer	<-->	Sustainability of marketing of services	.253	.21	7.831	.00	**H1**

Source: Authors

Table 3 manifested the co-variances among the key constructs examined in this Investigation, providing substantial insights into the relationships among system based on currency virtually, experience of customer, and sustainability of marketing of services. The co-variances reflect the strength and direction of the associations among these variables, which are critical for understanding how they interact within the proposed model. The covariance among the "System based on currency virtually" and "Experience of customer" is reported at 0.242, with a standard error (S.E.) of 0.021. The critical ratio (C.R.) for this relationship is 8.230, with a significance level manifested by ".00", suggesting that this relationship is statistically substantial. This finding highlights that enhancements in system based on currency virtually are positively associated with improvements in experience of customer, reinforcing the idea that influence virtual currency implementations can lead to more satisfactory customer interactions. Similarly, the covariance among the "Virtual Marketing System" and "Service Marketing Strategy Sustainability" shows a value of 0.301, with an S.E. of 0.030 and a C.R. of 7.692, also marked with ".00". This substantial covariance manifested a strong positive relationship, suggesting that influence use of virtual marketing systems contributes to the sustainability of service marketing strategies. This relationship underscores the potential for virtual marketing systems to not only engage customers but also to promote sustainable practices in marketing.

Lastly, the covariance among "Experience of customer" and "Sustainability of marketing of services" is reported as 0.253, with an S.E. of 0.21 and a C.R. of 7.831, marked substantial with ".00". This result highlights the usefulness of experience of customer as a mediating factor in achieving sustainable service marketing practices. The positive covariance manifested that improved experience of customers are associated with greater sustainability in marketing strategies, emphasizing the critical role of customer satisfaction in fostering long-term brand loyalty and responsible marketing approaches.

Table 4. Validity concern

	CR	AVE	MSV	MaxR(H)	CE	VMS	SMSS
CE	0.712	0.623	0.219	0.852	**0.654**		
VMS	0.738	0.637	0.132	0.763	0.172	**0.667**	
SMSS	0.773	0.613	0.274	0.797	0.381	0.191	**0.683**

Note: CE= Experience of customer; VMS= Virtual Marketing System; SMSS=Service Marketing Strategy Sustainability

Source: Authors

The Average Variance Extracted values depicted in table 4.. CE has an AVE of 0.623, VMS has an AVE of 0.637, and SMSS has an AVE of 0.613. An AVE value above 0.5 suggests that more than half of the variance in the indicators is captured by the construct, confirming adequate convergent validity. All three constructs meet this criterion, reinforcing their validity as manifestation measures of the underlying concepts. The Maximum Shared Variance values, which manifested the maximum squared correlation among two constructs, are also critical for evaluating discriminant validity. CE has an MSV of 0.219, VMS has an MSV of 0.132, and SMSS has an MSV of 0.274. The MSV values are notably lower than the AVE values for each construct, suggesting that the constructs are sufficiently distinct from one another. This supports the notion that each construct captures a unique aspect of the theoretical framework being studied. The Maximum Reliability values further echo the reliability of the constructs, with CE at 0.852, VMS at 0.763, and SMSS at 0.797. These values manifested that the constructs have high reliability under the maximum loading of items, further affirming their robustness.

MEDIATION EXAMINATION

Figure 2. Structural equation model

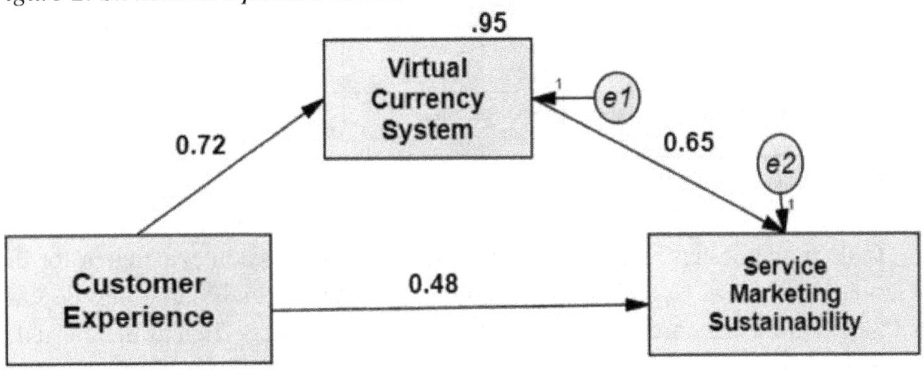

Model Fit Indices

Table 5. Model fit

Sig.	Chi-Sq	RMR	Fitness Goodness	Fitness Confirmatory	TLI	RMSEA
0.002	1.956	.037	0.931	0.910	0.913	.026

Source: Authors

Table 5 manifested the model fit indices. The Chi-Square value is 1.956. A lower Chi-Square value relative to the degrees of freedom manifested a better fit. In this case, the relatively low value suggests minimal deviation among the observed data and the model predictions, reinforcing the model's validity. The RMR is 0.037, which is substantially below the acceptable threshold of 0.08. This low RMR manifested that the average discrepancy among the observed and predicted values is small, further supporting the model's fit. The GFI is reported at 0.931, exceeding the recommended threshold of 0.90. This value manifested a strong fit of the model to the data, suggesting that the model explains a substantial proportion of the variance in the observed data. The CFI value is 0.910, also above the acceptable threshold of 0.90. This index compares the fit of the specified model with that of a baseline model, indicating that the proposed model performs well in capturing the relationships among the constructs. The TLI is 0.913, which further supports the model's fit.

Table 6. Regression examination

Relative			Approx.	S.E.	C.R.	P	Ass.
Virtual Marketing System	<---	Experience of customer	.861	.142	7.585	.00	H2
Sustainability of marketing of services	<---	Virtual Marketing System	.328	.134	2.851	.00	H3
Sustainability of marketing of services	<---	Experience of customer	.958	.191	7.959	.00	H1

Source: Authors

Table 6 manifested regression examination. The regression coefficient for the relationship among "Experience of customer" and the "Virtual Marketing System" is 0.861, with a standard error (S.E.) of 0.142. This high coefficient manifested a strong positive influence of experience of customer on the virtual marketing system, suggesting that improvements in experience of customer substantially enhance the influence of virtual marketing strategies. The critical ratio of 7.585 is well above the threshold for significance, and the p-value is marked as ".00", indicating that this relationship is statistically substantial. This finding supports Hypothesis 2 (H2), confirming that experience of customer is a crucial driver of virtual marketing system influence.

In the next pathway, the regression coefficient for the "Virtual Marketing System" influencing "Sustainability of marketing of services" is 0.328, with an S.E. of 0.134. This coefficient manifested a moderate positive relationship, suggesting that enhancements in the virtual marketing system contribute to the sustainability of service marketing strategies. The critical ratio of 2.851, along with a substantial p-value, supports Hypothesis 3 (H3), demonstrating that influence virtual marketing practices are essential for achieving sustainable service marketing outcomes.

Finally, the regression coefficient for the direct relationship among "Experience of customer" and "Sustainability of marketing of services" is notably high at 0.958, with an S.E. of 0.191. This result manifested a very strong positive influence, suggesting that improving experience of customer directly correlates with enhanced sustainability in service marketing. The critical ratio of 7.959 and the substantial p-value further reinforce the validity of this relationship, supporting Hypothesis 1 (H1).

Table 7. Mediating role influence

	Influence	worth	Path Influence
Experience of customer → Sustainability of marketing of services	Direct Influence	.48	Direct influence stated
Experience of customer → Virtual Marketing System → Sustainability of marketing of services	Indirect Influence	.72*.65=.47	Indirect Influence Ensued
	Whole influence	.95	Partial mediation

Source: Authors

Table 7 manifested the mediating role of the Virtual Marketing System (VMS) in the relationship among Experience of customer (CE) and Sustainability of marketing of services (SMS). The table distinguishes among direct and indirect influences, providing a comprehensive view of how these constructs interact. The "direct influence" of Experience of customer on Sustainability of marketing of services is quantified at 0.48. This value manifested a substantial direct relationship, suggesting that improvements in experience of customer substantially enhance sustainability in service marketing strategies. This direct influence underscores the usefulness of customer satisfaction as a primary driver of sustainable practices within organizations.

In addition to the direct influence, the "indirect influence" of Experience of customer through the Virtual Marketing System is calculated as follows: 0.72 (the influence of experience of customer on the virtual marketing system) multiplied by 0.65 (the influence of the virtual marketing system on sustainability of marketing of services), yielding an indirect influence of 0.47. This calculation manifested that while there is a substantial pathway from experience of customer to sustainability via the virtual marketing system, the direct influence remains notable.

The "whole influence" of Experience of customer on Sustainability of marketing of services, combining both direct and indirect influences, totals 0.95. This high cumulative value demonstrates that the overall influence of experience of customer on sustainability is substantial, emphasizing the interconnectedness of these constructs.

The analysis manifested in Table 7 illustrates a "partial mediation" influence, where the Virtual Marketing System acts as a mediator in the relationship among Experience of customer and Sustainability of marketing of services. While Experience of customer has a strong direct influence on sustainability, the mediating role of the virtual marketing system also contributes substantially to this relationship. These findings highlight the use fullness of both enhancing experience of customer and influence leveraging virtual marketing strategies to promote sustainable service marketing practices. Organizations can benefit from focusing on these areas to achieve optimal outcomes in their marketing efforts.

DISCUSSION

The findings of this Investigation underscore the substantial interrelationships among experience of customer, system based on currency virtually, and sustainability of marketing of services. The outcomes reveal that enhancing experience of customer directly influences the influence of virtual marketing systems, which in turn contributes to sustainable marketing strategies. This relationship highlights the critical role that customer satisfaction plays in driving not only immediate business outcomes but also long-term sustainability in marketing practices. By prioritizing experience of customer, organizations can foster more influence virtual marketing initiatives that resonate with consumers and promote loyalty. Also, the Investigation demonstrates that system based on currency virtually can serve as powerful tools in enhancing customer engagement and facilitating transactions. As customers become more familiar with these systems, their positive experiences can lead to increased acceptance and use, further reinforcing the relationship among experience of customer and sustainability of marketing of services. The mediation analysis manifested that while there is a strong direct influence of experience of customer on sustainability, the virtual marketing system also plays a crucial role in this dynamic, suggesting that businesses should strategically integrate these components to maximize their influence.

The implications for practitioners are clear: organizations should invest in improving experience of customers across all touch points, particularly in their interactions with virtual marketing systems. This investment not only enhances customer satisfaction but also supports broader sustainability goals by promoting responsible consumption and engagement. As businesses navigate an increasingly digital landscape, leveraging system based on currency virtually and improving customer interactions will be essential for achieving sustainable competitive advantages.

CONCLUSION

In conclusion, this Investigation provides valuable insights into the relationships among experience of customer, virtual marketing systems, and sustainability of marketing of services. The outcomes demonstrate that experience of customer is a vital driver of both the influence of virtual marketing strategies and the sustainability of service marketing practices. The substantial direct and indirect influences identified in the analysis highlight the interconnectedness of these constructs, emphasizing the usefulness of a holistic approach to marketing strategy development. As organizations seek to navigate the complexities of modern markets, focusing on enhancing experience of customers while influence utilizing system based on currency virtually will be crucial.

MANAGERIAL INFERENCES

The findings of this Investigation offer several substantial managerial implications for organizations seeking to enhance their marketing strategies through improved experience of customer and system based on currency virtually. The Investigation highlights the significance of integrating virtual marketing systems into broader marketing strategies. Managers should leverage these systems to facilitate seamless transactions and enhance customer engagement, as the analysis demonstrates their positive influence on sustainability of marketing of services. Training staff on the influence use of these systems and ensuring that all marketing communications reflect their benefits can further support this integration. Also, managers should consider utilizing customer feedback to continuously refine their virtual marketing strategies, ensuring they remain aligned with evolving consumer expectations.

Finally, organizations should adopt a holistic approach to sustainability in marketing by connecting experience of customer initiatives with broader corporate social responsibility goals. This alignment can enhance brand reputation and attract socially conscious consumers, ultimately driving long-term success.

PRACTICAL INFERENCES

The practical implications of this Investigation extend to various facets of marketing and customer relationship management. Organizations should implement strategies that enhance experience of customer across all touch points, particularly in digital environments where system based on currency virtually are utilized. This may involve investing in technology that streamlines the user experience, ensuring that transactions are quick, secure, and easy to navigate. Training employees to be knowledgeable about these systems and responsive to customer inquiries can substantially improve the overall experience. Also, businesses should consider developing targeted marketing campaigns that emphasize the benefits of system based on currency virtually. Educating consumers about how these systems work and their advantages—such as lower transaction costs and enhanced security—can drive adoption and increase customer engagement. Also, organizations should actively seek customer feedback regarding their experiences with virtual currencies and virtual marketing systems. This information can be invaluable for making informed adjustments to improve both the technology and the marketing approaches used.

Lastly, companies should integrate sustainability into their marketing narratives, demonstrating how improved experience of customers and virtual marketing strategies contribute to broader environmental and social goals.

THEORETICAL INFERENCES

The identification of a substantial direct relationship among experience of customer and sustainability of marketing of services reinforces the notion that positive customer interactions are fundamental to achieving sustainable marketing outcomes. This aligns with existing theories that emphasize the usefulness of customer satisfaction and loyalty in driving business success. Also, the Investigation's exploration of the mediating role of virtual marketing systems provides a new perspective on how technology can enhance traditional marketing frameworks. By demonstrating that virtual marketing systems not only influence experience of customer but also serve as a conduit for promoting sustainability, this Investigation extends the application of technology acceptance models and customer relationship management theories. It suggests that integrating technological advancements into marketing strategies can lead to more sustainable practices, thereby enriching theoretical discussions around the intersection of technology, customer behaviour, and sustainability. Also, this Investigation highlights the need for a more nuanced understanding of the mechanisms through which experience of customer influences marketing sustainability..

RECOMMENDATIONS

Based on the findings and implications of this Investigation, several recommendations can be made for practitioners and Investigations alike. First, organizations should prioritize the enhancement of experience of customer as a strategic focus, ensuring that all marketing efforts are aligned with the goal of increasing customer satisfaction. Second, businesses are encouraged to implement and promote virtual marketing systems that facilitate smoother transactions and improve customer engagement. Training employees to influence utilize these systems and continuously gathering customer feedback will enable organizations to adapt and refine their approaches, ensuring they meet evolving consumer needs.

Also, organizations should consider developing comprehensive marketing campaigns that educate consumers about the benefits of system based on currency virtually and their role in promoting sustainability. By clearly communicating how these systems contribute to a more efficient and responsible marketplace, businesses can foster greater acceptance and utilization among their customer base.

Lastly, Investigations are encouraged to explore the broader implications of these findings by examining the influence of various external factors, such as market trends and regulatory changes, on the relationships identified in this Investigation. By broadening the scope of inquiry, future Investigation can provide deeper insights into the interplay among experience of customer, technology, and sustainability in marketing practices.

FUTURE DIRECTIONS

Future Investigation in the realm of experience of customer, virtual marketing systems, and sustainability of marketing of services should explore several promising avenues to deepen understanding and enhance practical applications. First, longitudinal studies could provide insights into how experience of customers and perceptions of virtual marketing systems evolve over time, particularly as technology continues to advance. This approach would allow Investigations to examine the long-term influences of these systems on customer loyalty and brand perception, offering a more comprehensive view of their influence on sustainability. Also, Investigations could investigate the role of demographic and cultural factors in shaping consumer attitudes toward system based on currency virtually and their relationship with sustainability of marketing of services. Understanding how different consumer segments respond to these systems could help organizations tailor their marketing strategies more influence, ensuring that they resonate with diverse audiences. Another substantial direction for future Investigation is the exploration of the psychological mechanisms underlying experience of customer and its influences on sustainability. Also, Investigation could benefit from examining the integration of artificial intelligence and machine learning in virtual marketing systems. Investigating how these technologies can personalize experience of customers and optimize marketing strategies may reveal new opportunities for enhancing service sustainability. Finally, collaborative studies involving multiple industries could enrich the understanding of how virtual marketing systems function across different contexts.

REFERENCES

Baskaran, K. (2023). Experience of customer in the E-commerce market through the virtual world of metaverse. In *Handbook of Investigation on consumer behavioral analytics in metaverse and the adoption of a virtual world* (pp. 153–170). IGI Global. DOI: 10.4018/978-1-6684-7029-9.ch008

Calza, F., Sorrentino, A., & Tutore, I. (2023). Combining corporate environmental sustainability and experience of customer management to build an integrated model for decision-making. *Management Decision*, *61*(13), 54–84. DOI: 10.1108/MD-05-2022-0613

Chen, S. C., Chou, T. H., Hongsuchon, T., Ruangkanjanases, A., Kittikowit, S., & Lee, T. C. (2022). The mediation influence of marketing activities toward augmented reality: The perspective of extended experience of customer. *Journal of Hospitality and Tourism Technology*, *13*(3), 461–480. DOI: 10.1108/JHTT-03-2021-0093

Jabo, B., & Kant, S. "Impact of Technical CRM on Ethiopia Bank Human-Computer Interface and Competitive Advantage as Mediators of Performance," *2024 IEEE International Conference on Computing, Power and Communication Technologies (IC2PCT)*, Greater Noida, India, 2024, pp. 679-682, https://doi.org/DOI: 10.1109/IC2PCT60090.2024.10486237

Jabo, D., Kant, S., & Borji, B. (2025). Customer Orientation and Ethiopian Bank Performance With Mediation of Competitive Advantage. In *Leveraging AI for Effective Digital Relationship Marketing* (pp. 459–482). IGI Global., DOI: 10.4018/979-8-3693-5340-0.ch015

Kassociation, R. R., Zhang, J. Q., & Athaide, G. A. (2021). Measuring experience of customer management and its influence on financial performance. *European Journal of Marketing*, *55*(3), 840–867. DOI: 10.1108/EJM-07-2019-0592

Manohar, S. (2024). Cryptocurrency as a Slice in Investment Portfolio: Identifying Critical Antecedents and Building Taxonomy for Emerging Economy. *Asia-Pacific Financial Markets*, •••, 1–26. DOI: 10.1007/s10690-024-09490-7

Manyanga, W., Makanyeza, C., & Muranda, Z. (2022). The influence of experience of customer, customer satisfaction and word of mouth intention on customer loyalty: The moderating role of consumer demographics. *Cogent Business & Management*, *9*(1), 2082015. DOI: 10.1080/23311975.2022.2082015

Marin-Garcia, A., Gil-Saura, I., & Ruiz-Molina, M. E. (2022). Do innovation and sustainability influence customer satisfaction in retail? A question of gender. Economic Investigation-. *Ekonomska Istrazivanja, 35*(1), 546–563. DOI: 10.1080/1331677X.2021.1924217

Mentari, T., Setiawan, R. Y., Wiriatmaja, N. U., Hutauruk, J. R., Muhyiansyah, A. R., & Rahman, N. (2024). The Influence of Financial Technology and Virtual Customer Service on Customer Satisfaction. *International Journal of Business, Law, and Education, 5*(2), 2694–2614. DOI: 10.56442/ijble.v5i2.916

Morales, J., Cornide-Reyes, H., Rossel, P. O., Sáez, P., & Silva-Aravena, F. (2023, July). Virtual reality, augmented reality and metaverse: experience of customer approach and user experience evaluation methods. Literature review. In International Conference on Human-Computer Interaction (pp. 554-566). Cham: Springer Nature Switzerland. DOI: 10.1007/978-3-031-35915-6_40

Mudrika, S., Suharjo, D., Deni, D., & Wiadi, I. (2024). Sustainability in Marketing: Exploring the Influence of Green Marketing on Environmental Concern and Customer Satisfaction. *International Journal of Multicultural and Multireligious Understanding, 11*(2), 97–112. DOI: 10.18415/ijmmu.v11i2.5431

Nair, A. J., & Manohar, S. (2024). Green Service Consumption: Unlocking Customer Expectations on Technological Transformations Enhancing Purchase Experience in Retail Store. *International Journal of Information Management Data Insights, 4*(2), 100277. DOI: 10.1016/j.jjimei.2024.100277

Niguse, T., Kant, S., & Adula, M. (2025). Mediation Effect of Customer Loyalty in Relationship Between Market Orientation, Entrepreneurial Orientation, and Firm Performance in Ethiopia. In *Leveraging AI for Effective Digital Relationship Marketing* (pp. 419–458). IGI Global., DOI: 10.4018/979-8-3693-5340-0.ch014

Nuseir, M. T., El Refae, G. A., Aljumah, A., Alshurideh, M., Urabi, S., & Kurdi, B. A. (2023). Digital marketing strategies and the influence on experience of customer: A systematic review. The Influence of Information Technology on Business and Marketing Intelligence Systems, 21-44.

Omeish, F., Al Khasawneh, M., & Khair, N. (2024). Investigating the influence of AI on improving experience of customer through social media marketing: An analysis of Jordanian Millennials. *Computers in Human Behavior Reports, 15*, 100464. DOI: 10.1016/j.chbr.2024.100464

Rahardja, U., Hongsuchon, T., Hariguna, T., & Ruangkanjanases, A. (2021). Understanding influence sustainable intention of s-commerce activities: The role of experience of customers, perceived value, and mediation of relationship quality. *Sustainability, 13*(20), 11492. DOI: 10.3390/su132011492

Rane, N., Choudhary, S., & Rane, J. (2023). Metaverse marketing strategies: enhancing experience of customer and analysing consumer behaviour through leading-edge Metaverse technologies, platforms, and models. Platforms, and Models (November 3, 2023).

Tang, Y. M., Lau, Y. Y., & Ho, U. L. (2023). Empowering digital marketing with interactive virtual reality (IVR) in interior design: Influences on customer satisfaction and behaviour intention. *Journal of Theoretical and Applied Electronic Commerce Research, 18*(2), 889–907. DOI: 10.3390/jtaer18020046

Tolooee, K., Budaghi Khajeh Noubar, H., Gharehbiglo, H., & Ramazani, M. (2024). Providing a model of purchase intention and experience of customer on customer behavior in virtual networks. Journal of value creating in Business Management, 4(3), 274-297.

Urdea, A. M., Constantin, C. P., & Purcaru, I. M. (2021). Implementing experiential marketing in the digital age for a more sustainable customer relationship. *Sustainability (Basel), 13*(4), 1865. DOI: 10.3390/su13041865

Wibowo, A., Chen, S. C., Wiangin, U., Ma, Y., & Ruangkanjanases, A. (2020). Customer behavior as an outcome of social media marketing: The role of social media marketing activity and experience of customer. *Sustainability, 13*(1), 189. DOI: 10.3390/su13010189

Zaid, S., & Patwayati, P. (2021). Influence of experience of customer and customer engagement on satisfaction and loyalty: A case Investigation in Indonesia. *The Journal of Asian Finance, Economics and Business, 8*(4), 983–992.

Chapter 2
Decoding Scholarly Trends in CBDC and Financial Development:
An Intellectual Mapping Through Bibliometric Analysis

Tanya
Chandigarh University, India

Nitin Pathak
https://orcid.org/0000-0002-8062-0554
Chandigarh University, India

Priyanka Chugh
https://orcid.org/0009-0004-9553-1329
Chandigarh University, India

ABSTRACT

Central Bank Digital Currencies (CBDCs) are on the rise as major financial innovations, making use of technologies such as Distributed Ledger Technology (DLT) to transform monetary systems. India, under the Reserve Bank of India (RBI), is working on a number of CBDC projects to evaluate their feasibility, although a conclusive position on their adoption remains to be formulated. In this chapter, an organized summary of current literature covering CBDCs and their capacity to advance economic development has been presented. To address the prominence of individual pieces of research tending to end up with fragmentary insights, a bibliometric analysis was designed to present innovative findings regarding undeveloped realms.

DOI: 10.4018/979-8-3373-0315-4.ch002

1. INTRODUCTION

In 2025 the Decentralized Finance (DeFi) and Artificial Intelligence (AI) landscapes in 2025 are rapidly expanding with technology and increased institutional adoption. The global DeFi market is forecasted to grow from USD 32.36 billion in 2025 to USD 1,558.15 billion by 2034 with a compound annual growth rate (CAGR) of 53.80% (Precedence Research, 2024). North America alone accounted for over USD 7.78 billion DeFi market share in 2024, and illustrates that regions are beginning to establish digital finance ecosystems (Precedence Research, 2024). Similarly, generative AI is emerging as a unique aspect of the approximately USD 279.22 billion global AI market in 2024 that is expected to grow in 2025 to USD 390.90 billion with a project CAGR of 35.9% reaching in USD 1.81 trillion by 2030 (Grand View Research, 2024) and as sector, will grow in the US from USD 25.86 billion in 2024 to USD 803.90 billion in 2033 (GlobeNewswire, 2025). Additionally, Saudi Arabia is establishing advancements in AI via investments in capacity with AI infrastructure that can manage increase to 500 megawatts of the computing capacity, potentially realizing in the range of $3–$5 billion annually in chip sales (Investor's Business Daily, 2025). There are compelling ways to operationalize DeFi digital currencies and virtual assets to undertake trade in new ways based on the expanding scope of AI applications. with the DeFi and AI forecasts demonstrating the rapid trends for DeFi and AI as integrators of hosting an increased selection of actors in socioeconomics is simultaneously but never as nuanced as what AI imagines socioeconomics inclusive of bias. Financial Technology (Fintech) brings transformative effects to financial products and services by employing technology as per the research of Arner et al. (2016). The financial industry went through a seismic change through Fintech which enabled consumers and businesses to have new ways of dealing with financial institutions. The payment system modernization efforts of central banks worldwide now focus on developing Central Bank Digital Currencies (CBDCs) as per Auer et al. (2020). Digital currency services can be seen as, and involve, technology-enabled platforms to facilitate the exchange of digital value (e.g., central bank digital currencies, cryptocurrencies, stablecoins, e-wallets). These CBDCs are not cryptocurrencies but are regulated and issued by central banks to develop secure, efficient, and inclusive financial systems (BIS, 2021). The Reserve Bank of India (RBI) has launched the pilots of the Digital Rupee to develop digital financial infrastructure (RBI, 2023). In parallel, a social media ecosystem like Twitter, Reddit, and YouTube are reshaping the public's perceptions, behaviors, and market sentiments towards digital currencies, while facilitating peer learning, jointly created and community-driven financial conversations, and spreading of live sentiment, sometimes associated with irrational imitation (or herding) and speculation (Zhang et al., 2020; Ante, 2021). In particular, social media in developing economies are not formally sanctioned, but are a powerful forms of informal financial education and dissemination towards the potential adoption of digital currency technologies. The authorities at central banks regulate and issue CBDCs which serve as digital currencies that provide digital payment advantages while preserving the secure features of fiat money (BIS, 2021). The Reserve Bank of India (RBI) through its Digital Rupee pilot programs works to integrate the nation into digital financial services and achieve cheaper transactions and stronger payment system reliability (RBI, 2023). CBDC states to the digital method of a nation's fiat money (e.g., Indian Rupee). Grounded on DLT, CBDC is distributed by the Chief Bank of a country. Contrasting cryptocurrencies, CBDC is controlled by a Central Authority. In India, RBI is presently studying the probability of CBDCs through experimental project, Yet the position of official CBDC is uncertain. This chapter examine the potential of CBDC as a fuel for economic development in India. Development of financial technologies and increasing digitization of nation are the givers in CBDCs emergence. Satoshi Nakamoto, the father of blockchain, created the public distributed ledger for bitcoin cryptocurrency transactions. DLT contains various technologies or conventions that harness distributed members to preserve a distributed digital index without a dominant authority. DLT proposals a viable outline for implementing CBDC, enabling the execution and settlement of peer-to-peer transactions (Sethaput & Innet, 2023). The growing attention in CBDC highlights the necessity for improved security procedures within blockchain outlines to protect user privacy (Lee et al., 2021). A rapid digital transformation is driven by the advancement in financial technology. The RBI is initiating the pilot programs for digital rupee, the concept of CBDCs is gaining momentum as a potential tool for inclusive finance, reduction in cost and enhancement of the efficiency in the payment infrastructure (RBI, 2023). Despite thwarted efforts, there remains limited empirical evidence regarding the full-scale implementation and policy clarity regarding the full-scale implementation, impacts and challenges faced in Indian context (Lee et al., 2021). Given the scale of India's economy and its large unbanked population, studying the potential of CBDC as an instrument for the economic development, financial inclusion and digital innovation. Therefore, the present study aims to examine the following research questions

RQ1 Analysis of the publication trends to identify peak research activity and key contributing academic journals.

RQ2 Evaluation of influential contributions through citation analysis and identification of leading authors in the field.

RQ3 Exploration of collaboration patterns through co-authorship networks and international research partnerships.

RQ4 Investigation of recurring keywords to uncover prevailing themes and research focus areas within the field.

Section 2 outlines the background and contextual framework of the study. Section 3 describes the procedure and methodological approach adopted. Section 4 presents the results, highlighting the key findings. Section 5 provides a detailed discussion and offers final interpretations of the outcomes.

2. EVOLUTION OF CBDC

The history of Central Bank Digital Currencies (CBDCs) begins in the early 1990s, with the launch of the Avant smart card in Finland in 1993—the world's first CBDC according to most sources. Over the past few years, especially throughout the COVID-19 pandemic, the development of payment systems has accelerated exponentially. The pandemic saw a significant decrease in the use of cash and increased interest in digital currency-based solutions across the world (Srouji & Torre, 2022). Among the pioneers, China has been a trailblazer with its digital yuan. Large-scale pilot projects have enabled the digital currency to grow massively, serving as a benchmark for other countries (Xu & Jin, 2022). At the international level, CBDCs are now seen as tools that can boost economic well-being by promoting competition in payment systems and maximizing the deployment of safe, central bank-guaranteed assets in the financial system (Williams, 2022). India's entry into CBDCs, indicated by the introduction of the digital rupee (e), has both promising prospects and crucial challenges. The Reserve Bank of India (RBI) is exercising caution addressing challenges like cybersecurity, data protection, and widespread adoption by the public (Haque & Shoaib, 2023). The central bank is focused on enhancing financial stability and enhancing operational efficiency across the country's financial infrastructure (Banerjee & Sinha, 2023). Recent literature reflects increasing scholarly attention on the interrelation between services related to digital currencies and communication platforms that facilitate the exchange of social perspectives. Central bank digital currencies (CBDCs), in particular, are increasingly viewed as a mechanism for improving financial inclusion, payment efficiency, and monetary sovereignty (Genc & Takagi, 2024; Le et al., 2023) in developing countries. Research indicates that successful implementation of CBDCs includes considerations around technological readiness (including user access), regulatory direction, and consumer trust. Similar to the ever-changing social media landscape, social media continues to impact the behavior of investigators. Ante (2021) and Swartz and Westermeier (2023) indicate that social media platforms like Twitter and Reddit shape market sentiment and are social resources for many retail users, solidifying an online community that can foster or inhibit the acceptance of digital currencies. More recently, research is exploring if social media can educate or misinform retail users and integrating consideration of emerging media literacy as well as regulation. Overall, these studies indicate that the progress of digital currency technologies is not only about the physical infrastructure but is also bound up with narrative, social influence, and participation.

2.1 India's Policy and Regulatory Readiness

The status of India's trek towards a Central Bank Digital Currency (CBDC) is one of an undefined and developing regulatory context. While pilots were initiated for the Digital Rupee through the Reserve Bank of India (RBI) in 2022, the overall legal infrastructure is still being established (Reserve Bank of India [RBI], 2022). Significant regulatory questions; namely, digital privacv, anti-money laundering (AML), know-your-customer (KYC) obligations, and the question of legal tender status, are still outstanding. The absence of any final legislation creates uncertainty for the respective financial institutions and fintech firms to operate from. Kiff et al. (2020) articulated how necessary regulatory clarity is to ensure legal soundness, institutional trust and consumer protection in any CBDC ecosystem. If these factors are not present, scalability and user adoption are at risk of facing substantial hinderance.

2.2 Technological Infrastructure and Cybersecurity

India has a quite solid digital environment, as evidenced by the popularity and success of the Unified Payments Interface (UPI), with over 10 billion monthly transactions in August 2024, alone (National Payments Corporation of India, 2024). But this is just an example of one digital system, and ultimately a secure and scalable CBDC will require a stronger technology base, in particular a blockchain or distributed ledger platforms that allows for high transactions and secure data. Furthermore, there has been many cyber intrusions, with close to 50,000 cybersecurity breaches in the financial services sector in 2024 (Indian Computer Emergency Response Team [CERT-In], 2024). In their account, Arner, Auer & Frost (2020) explained that any vulnerabilities in the CBDC technology would significantly decrease public confidence in the CBDC and national financial stability. Therefore, building a tech-specific cybersecurity framework is not a choice but a requirement.

2.3 Consumer Behavior, Trust, and Financial Literacy

Factors such as trust, awareness, and digital financial literacy affect consumer readiness to adopt a Central Bank Digital Currency (CBDC) in India. The level of uptake of digital payments has increased significantly, however, a large section of the population is still worried about moving from cash to digital currency backed by the government. A survey by Deloitte (2023) found that although 58% of Indian consumers use digital wallets, 42% are concerned about fraud and misuse of data. In addition, the National Centre for Financial Education (2022) reported that only 27% of Indian adults have the capability to be financially literate. Trust in digital currencies has also been negatively impacted by the lack of public knowledge regarding the Digital Rupee, with only 18% of respondents to a YouGov (2024) survey aware of its existence. These figures highlight the need for public education campaigns and trust building strategies to facilitate fair and informed adoption.

2.4 Theoretical Background

This study applies an integrated theoretical framework to understand user behavior in relation to the adoption of digital currency, especially in terms of a social media influenced context. This research begins with the framework developed in Davis' (1989) Technology Acceptance Model (TAM) which argues that an individual's intention to use new technologies, such as Central Bank Digital Currencies (CBDCs), originates from their perceptions of usefulness and perceived ease of use of the new technologies. Moreover, the research incorporates Venkatesh & Morris' (2003) Unified Theory of Acceptance and Use of Technology (UTAUT) to address additional factors surrounding what constitutes an adoption decision. The UTAUT framework identified performance expectancy, effort expectancy, and social influence while introducing social influence as a potentially critical determinant in adoption decisions, by including the influence of peers and online community concept of social media while making adoption decisions. The research incorporates Rogers (2003) Diffusion of Innovations Theory, which seeks to understand how innovations spread over a period of time throughout social systems, including the types of adopter categories, and the communication channels to get information, which is now social media platforms. Finally, the research integrates Katz, Blumler, and Gurevitch's (1973) Uses and Gratifications Theory, to look at user motivations and how they engage with financial content through social media, to study because users seek and trust financial content for informational, social or emotional purposes. Collectively, these four theoretical perspectives provide a comprehensive, multi-faceted view that addresses individual user perceptions, social influences, and communication settings underlying the diffusion and downward process of digital currencies in today's digital ecosystems.

2.5 Research Gap

While the foundational theories, such as Technology Acceptance Model (TAM), the Unified Theory of Acceptance and Use of Technology (UTAUT), the Diffusion of Innovations (DOI), and Uses and Gratification theories that have been widely used in studying digital currency adoption, there is a still a gap in the literature in terms of a comprehensive bibliometric analysis to map the evolution, trends, and interdisciplinary connections of these paradigms in the area of digital currency studies. While a number of studies are empirical validations of specific constructs or extensions of a theory, the vast majorities of studies tend to ignore the structure of knowledge or how social media influences, as well as more holistic research agendas, shape the research dynamics, or identify how research agenda intersects with behavioral finance, and there are limited exploration ns of bibliometric approaches specifically on how the intersection of these theories in order to apply the emergent theoretical structures to topics of digital currency adoption, inclusive of convergence Theories of CBDC and the role of social media in the processes of diffusion and communication. A systematic review of the literature is useful to address the gap in next generation bibliometric literature to show how a research cluster formation occurred, focused research themes highlighted, collaboration networks represented to be useful in guiding future interdisciplinary study and practical implications, which progresses the ecosystem of digital financial interactions.

3.RESEARCH METHODOLOGY

This study used the Scopus database to answer the research questions posed above. Zhu and Liu (2020) remark that Scopus has significant coverage of academic publications. Initially, 189 articles were found with the aid of this database. The search was directed towards titled publications with the phrases "CBDC", "central bank", "financial development", and "distributed ledger technology" as keywords within the title. The search was also limited to journal articles written in English in the domains of Economics, Business, Management, and Accounting published as journals. Data was collected, and further, an abstract review was conducted manually to remove out of scope articles aligned with the core themes of the research. After this, a total of 101 articles were selected for analysis. A bibliometric approach was conducted to analyze the current trends, major journals, research results, collaboration patterns, and dominant themes in the research area. This approach is often used for mapping the scholarly research landscape through the identification of the author, co-authors, cited and citing journals and keywords. For the first search, Boolean combinations: "CBDC" AND "Financial AND Development" and "CBDC" AND "Financial AND Inclusion" were used in Scopus with the aim of finding relevant literature. Data collection also included related fields within Economics and Econometrics.

4. ANALYSIS AND FINDINGS

4.1 Publication Trends (Year wise Analysis)

The bar chart above shows the annual breakdown of Central Bank Digital Currency (CBDC) and financial development publications from 2019 to 2024. It clearly illustrates the increasing academic interest in this topic over time, with numbers of publication rising steeply over the years and most recently decreasing slightly. Overall, the figure represents the emergence and subsequent institutionalization of cbdc-related discourse within both academic and institutional context. In 2019, the field was effectively still nascent, evidenced by a paltry 2 publications. The emerging field refers to the early stage of ideas and exploratory research considering digital currency as a feasible economic concept, technological arrangement, or macroeconomic practice. A publication count of 2 suggests a limited circumscription of a global awareness and only minor institutional commitment to experiments of digital currency at the time. By 2020, the number of publications rose to a modest 5, which may correspond to the increasing concern of central banks about the idea of digital legal tender. The catalyzing factor, with respect to publications, may also have been the early incidents of the COVID-19 pandemic as digital payment systems became increasingly used, while traditional cash usage, although stable, was on the decline. The year 2020 probably represents the juncture in which expanded conceptual considerations transition into research activities that were as often applied to financial considerations (including inclusion and accessibility). There was a significant spike in 2021, with 16 publications, three times the number from just one year before which marks a key moment of upward epistemic trajectory, where CBDC research gained considerable attention in academia. This uptick coincides with the public announcements from key institutions including the People's Bank of China, the European Central Bank, and the Bank for International Settlements, which put more pressure on discussions of design, pilots, and implications than ever before. The rise also reveals a widening field of research, which included dimensions of law, cybersecurity, governance, and ethics.

The upward trend continued into 2022 with 25 publications. The increase of publications reflects a maturing field. More contributors started to delve into particular facets of CBDCs, inclusive of financial stability, monetary transmission channel, and international remittance use. This phase of CBDC research started to see more interdisciplinary engagement, which opened the door for research agendas to be shared among economists, computer science, legal scholars, and public policy experts.

In 2023 there was another peak, with 37 publications reported, the highest in the study window. This peak represents what had been built prior, and coincided with real pilot implementations and regulatory debates in multiple countries. Additionally, it might indicate that CBDCS are becoming more relevant in academic syllabus and think tank priorities and international networks. All the increases in publications suggested a high level of global agreement on CBDCs in academia and policy.

Figure 1. Graphical representation of year -wise no. of publications

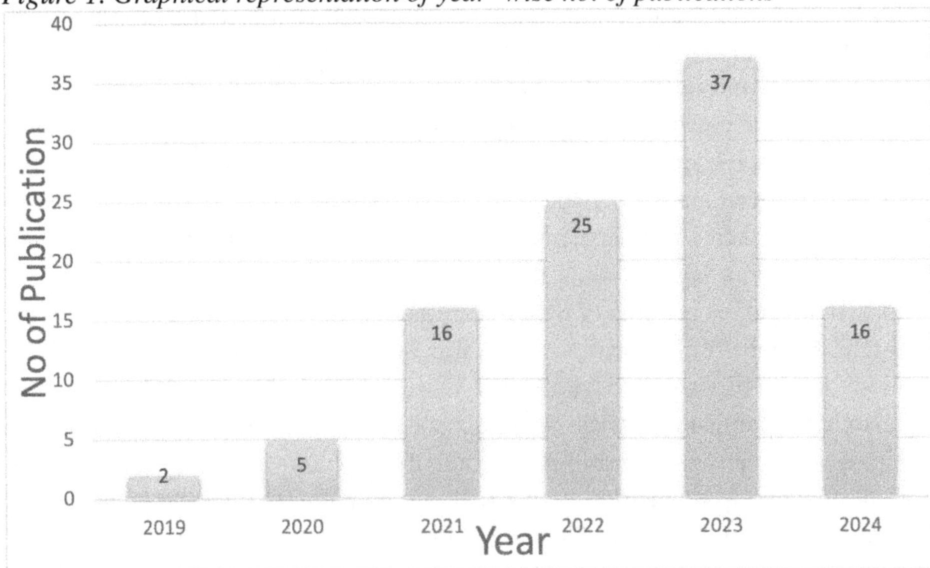

Notably, 2024 shows a decline to 16 total publications, which is the same as in 2021. This decline might be attributable to a number of factors. Perhaps firstly, the initial hype and novelty effects have settled down, and the field is more likely to route itself toward more specific or technical sub-topics. Or, it is like we are encountering publication lags or momentum surrounding evaluation and impact rather than exploration.

In summary, the chart is a representation of a rapid evolution and institutionalization of CBDC literature over the span of six years. It shows the dynamism of the field, particularly as it responds to geopolitical changes, regulatory conversations, and technology. While 2023 appears to be the peak of publications the future probably involves more focused and contextual studies, as the digital currency moves from idea to operationalization.

4.2 Journal Dispersal

Digital currency literature started in 1983 by David Chaum entitled "Blind Signatures for Untraceable Payments". However, the literature started getting attention of research community post Covid-19 in 2020. Articles related to the literature started getting published in Management/economics and non-Management/economics journals. In our study, 65 journals published the total 101 Articles interconnecting CBDC, Central bank, Financial Inclusion and Financial Development parameters. Sustainability (Switzerland), One survey results showed that research in international business and finance, Latin American journal of central banking, research in international business and finance, journal of banking regulation, economics and business letters, and finance: theory and practice each obtained the most document publications. The journals technological forecasting and social change along with journal of political economy, international review of financial analysis, technology in society, financial innovation, journal of business ethics, research in international business and finance, sustainable futures earned the most citations. **Table 1.** Presents the leading 15 journals, detailing their total number of published papers, impact factors (IFs), and the quantity of SCOPUS citations garnered by each. Journal with the highest number of Publications i.e. 4 was Sustainability (Switzerland) with 70 citations and 3.9 IF associated with MDPI. Latin American Journal of Central Banking also has 4 publications with 21 citations and 0.7 IF. Research in International Business and Finance with 6.143 IF, Journal of Monetary economics with 4.63 IF, Journal of Banking Regulation with 1.6 IF, Economic and Business Letters with 0.9 impact factor and Finance: Theory and Practice with 0.612 IF have published 3 Articles each. Whereas, Journal of Political Economy with 9.637 IF, International review of Financial Analysis with 8.235 IF, Financial Innovation with 6.793 impact factor, Public Finance Quarterly with 4.51 IF, Journal of Financial Stability with 3.554, Journal of Banking Theory and Practice with 1.4 IF, China Economic Journal with 3.3 impact factor and Journal of Economic Dynamics and Control with 1.87 IF have published 2 Articles. Out of 15 papers 4 are associated with Elsevier B.V, and rest with Elsevier Inc., MDPI, Elsevier LTD., Palgrave Macmillan, Oviedo University Press, Financial University under The Government of Russian Federation, University of Chicago Press, Springer Science and Business Media Deutschland

GmbH, State Audit Office of Hungary, Sciendo, University of Pennsylvania Press each. Majority of the studies focused on Monetary policy, Financial Inclusion, Financial Stability, Banking CBDC and Electronic money. From **Table 1.** We can easily say that out of 15 journals Journal of Political Economy has the maximum IF 9.637 with 41 citations, Rest of the journals with IF of 5 or less than that, find it difficult to publish articles in top-quality journals. Thus, the future scholars are required to focus on delivering high quality research in the domain.

Table 1. Journal distribution along with the number of papers, citation and impact factor

S.No	Source	No. of Publications	citations	Publisher	Impact Factor
1	Sustainability (Switzerland)	4	70	MDPI	3.9
2	Latin American Journal of Central Banking	4		Elsevier B.V.	0.7
3	Research in International Business and Finance	3	13	Elsevier Ltd	6.143
4	Journal of Monetary Economics	3	194	Elsevier B.V.	4.63
5	Journal of Banking Regulation	3	21	Palgrave Macmillan	1.6
6	Economics and Business Letters	3	9	Oviedo University Press	0.9
7	Finance: Theory and Practice	3	18	Financial University under The Government of Russian Federation	0.612
8	Journal of Political Economy	2	41	University of Chicago Press	9.637
9	International Review of Financial Analysis	2	0	Elsevier Inc.	8.235
10	Financial Innovation	2	22	Springer Science and Business Media Deutschland GmbH	6.793
11	Public Finance Quarterly	2	0	State Audit Office of Hungary	4.51
12	Journal of Financial Stability	2	13	Elsevier B.V.	3.554
13	Journal of Central Banking Theory and Practice	2	1	Sciendo	1.4

continued on following page

Table 1. Continued

S.No	Source	No. of Publications	citations	Publisher	Impact Factor
14	China Economic Journal	2	67	University of Pennsylvania Press	3.3
15	Journal of Economic Dynamics and Control	2	20	Elsevier B.V.	1.87

Source: Author's own work

4.3 Most Outstanding Article in the Domain

The study demonstrates superior research work in "On the equivalence of private and public money" (Brunnermeier and Neiplet.,2019). This paper identifies a scenario where private cryptocurrencies could potentially be exchanged with CBDC and preserves balanced price distribution avoidance of financial instability and credit crises. The research paper has gathered 89 citations. "Fintech, Cryptocurrencies, and CBDC: Financial Structural Transformation in China "(Allen et al.,2022) is the second most cited paper with the citation score of 84. The paper explores the significant impact of stablecoins, Fintech and CBDCs in the financial inclusion focusing, China's initiatives in the fintech to address the potential of e-CNY and to address traditional financial challenges. "Central bank digital currency: Central banking for all?" (Fernåndez et al., 2021) is the third most prominent article in the domain with a citation score of 82. The paper investigates the possible implications of Central Bank Digital Currency for Financial intermediaries. Furthermore, the fourth most influential article is "Designing central bank digital currencies" with a citation score of 69. This paper focused into designing a CBDC considering the various factors such as anonymity, security and network effects. Our analysis focused on most prominent articles in the domain of CBDC. "Development of Friedrich von Hayek's theory of private money and economic implications for digital currencies" (Mikhaylov, A.Yu.,2021) is the fifth most influential article in the domain with a citation score of 67. The Paper probe into Hayek's private money theory in the information age, supporting CBDCs and basic income for distributional equity. The study warns in case of "digital dollarization," emphasizing firm digital currencies for healthy monetary policy in cashless economies. We identified top 10 articles in the domain with high citations from 2019-2024. The articles explore the literature related to designing and challenges of CBDC. In addition to that, the articles also focused on the implications of CBDC and its role in financial inclusion. This investigation also reveals the creative thinkers in the domain. Journal of Monetary Economics, Journal of International Money, Finance Review of Economic Dynamics and Terra Economics are the top four journals associated with the most outstanding articles in the domain.

Table 2. Paper distribution along with the journal and citation

S.No.	Title	Source title	Citation
1	On the equivalence of private and public money	Journal of Monetary Economics	89
2	Fintech, Cryptocurrencies, and CBDC: Financial Structural Transformation in China	Journal of International Money and Finance	84
3	Central bank digital currency: Central banking for all?	Review of Economic Dynamics	82
4	Designing central bank digital currencies	Journal of Monetary Economics	69
5	Development of Friedrich von Hayek's theory of private money and economic implications for digital currencies	Terra Economics	67
6	The Effects of Central Bank Digital Currencies News on Financial Markets	Technological Forecasting and Social Change	58
7	A global perspective on central bank digital currency	China Economic Journal	54
8	Ethical Marketing in the Blockchain-Based Sharing Economy: Theoretical Integration and Guiding Insights	Journal of Business Ethics	45
9	Central banks digital currency: Detection of optimal countries for the implementation of a CBDC and the implication for payment industry open innovation	Journal of Open Innovation: Technology, Market, and Complexity	44
10	Reasons fostering or discouraging the implementation of central bank-backed digital currency: A review	Economies	40

Source: Author's Own Work

4.4 Most Contributors Authors of the Domain

Figure 1 shows the scholarly impact of the 10 most-cited authors in CBDC and financial development, using total citations (gold columns, left axis) versus number of documents (peach line, right axis). In the data, all 10 authors reported data for only one paper (the bars all post a value of "1" on the document axis) but had a considerable variation in citations, which implies that one influential article could dominate conversations in an emergent field. Brunnermeier M.K. is on the extreme left with 89 citations, next is Allen F. (84) and then Fernández-Villaverde J. (82). These three authors occupy a first tier of citations (>80) which is reflective of the foundational nature of their papers - conceptually or methodologically, subsequently referring to the paper frequently in framing CBDC design, monetary-policy transmission or macro-financial stability. Since they evidence the same document count (one paper each), it showcases a distinct characteristic of new and high-velocity topics - the early seminal paper(s) accrue citations faster than later multiple-paper portfolios. The second tier appears and includes two authors who received citations from the range of between 67 and 69 - Agur I. (69) and Mikhaylov A.Y. (67). Even though these papers are a little less influential than the first tier, both papers are clearly engaging sub-communities across disciplines potentially evaluating implementation mechanisms or comparative case studies, hence broadening the theoretical story.

There is a drop in citation counts after this point to the mid-50s for Wang Y. (58) and Lee D.K.C. (54), then to the mid-40s for Tan T.M. (45). These values establish a third layer of distribution indicating significant reach but diminishing impact. Notably, the orange line takes a jump at Ozili P.K. whose one article has 37 citations but is the fourth paper-author combination in the data set—a reminder that citation hierarchies are not linear and sensitive to audiences in sub-fields; Ozili may have a specialized audience (e.g., financial-inclusion or ethics scholar), not an international CBDC community. Beyond Ozili, numbers tail off to 36 for Ferrari Minesso M., 34 for Gupta M., and 27 for Williamson S., a long tail distribution typical of bibliometric maps: with influence that declines gradually rather than abruptly reflecting an incremental influence that is less frequently cited in subsequent works. The gold bars notably decline in size while the peach line remains constant—again emphasizing that the impact of each author derives only from one highly cited document and not from a large collective output.

From an intellectual-structure perspective, two important insights are apparent. One, citation leadership does not necessarily accompany productivity; quality and timing outweigh quantity for the more current subjects. Two, it is important to note the lack of multi-document authors in the top 10 authors; most are singular citations.

Figure 2. Journal distribution along with the number of papers, citation and impact factor

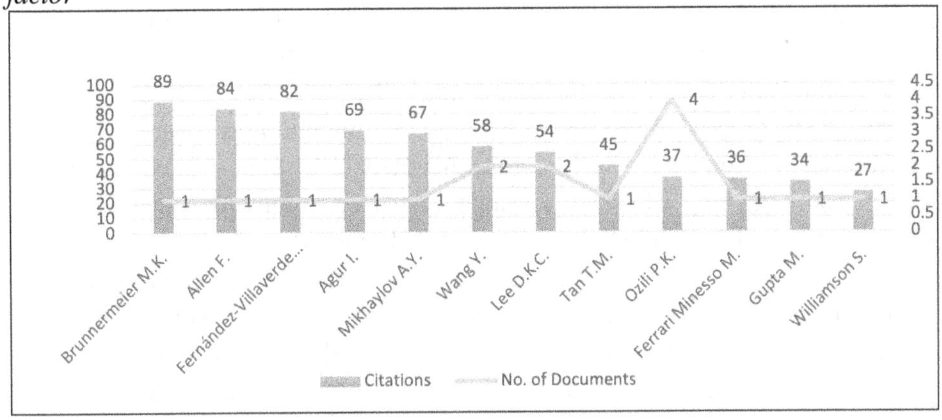

Source: Author's Own Work

The next significant authors in the area Allen Franklin, Gu Xian and Jagtiani Julapa have published one article in the journal of International Money and Finance with the citation of 84. Their study "Fintech, Cryptocurrencies, and CBDC: Financial Structural Transformation in China" (Allen et al.,2022) focused on the significant impact of stablecoins, Fintech and CBDCs in the financial inclusion focusing, China's initiatives in the fintech to address the potential of e-CNY and to address traditional financial challenges. Allen Franklin and Gu Xian are from United Kingdom and Jagtiani Julapa is from The United States. Another prominent author in the domain are Jesus Fernandez Villaverde, Danial Sanches, Linda Schilling and Harald Uhlig. Jesus Fernandez Villaverde, Danial Sanches and Harald Uhlig are from The United Sates of America and Linda Schilling is from France. Their study Central bank digital currency: Central banking for all?" (Fernández et al., 2021) investigated all the possible implications of Central Bank Digital Currency (CBDC) for financial intermediaries.

4.5 Analysis of Analysis of Co-Authorship Structured Among the Researchers

Figure 3. represents a visualization of co-authorship of scholars within this area of research on Central Bank Digital Currencies (CBDC) and financial development. Each node indicates an author, while the links (edges) indicate that at least one paper had co-authorship between the two nodes that are connected. The clusters, which are in different shades of gray, indicate groups of authors that have a tighter relationship with each other than with other groups.

The network demonstrated a collaboration structure that is relatively sparse. This indicates that although there are many researchers in the field, the majority are working alone or as part of small isolated teams. This is typical of emerging fields such as CBDC research because specialization within domains is often high, and shared research agendas are still being formulated. Where there is co-authorship that links authors, only a few authors appear to share common associations; most authors appear to be loosely linked, or isolated through their research. The largest and most connected cluster on the map appears in the top-center of the image and consists of authors such as Sergio Luis Náñez Alonso, Miguel Ángel Fernández, and Javier Jorge-Vázquez. The relationships among these authors suggest active collaborations over several papers and strong ties that may indicate a stable research team, or institutional affiliation, that is actively generating coordinated CBDC-related research. Given the prominence and centrality of their node, they also may have higher productivity or influence or other collaborative advantages. Evidence of another minor collaborative link exists between Jonathan Chiu and Seyed Mohammad Davoodalhosseini, which also look to be an independent unit. Each author's work, which may fall into a collaborative category (such as co-authored works or macroeconomic modeling or central banking policy), is an area of research both author's monitor. They are representing another isolated pair of research undertaken independently, without ties to other nodes. It is also interesting that other authors look completely isolated, demonstrating no connection with any other author, such as David Kuo Chuen Lee, Peters O. Ozili, Raúl Morales-Reséndiz, Larisa Yarovaya, and Samuele Bibi. The isolated nodes in this example indicate either a single authored work or contributor's work who has contributed independently of any other work, which may have become roles adopted because of expertise in the subject matter, or by contribution within a specified niche subfield. The evidence shows they could be available for future collaborations across types of expertise, fields, geographic origin and disciplines.

The figure includes a legend for eight clusters, even though most have little to no representation or intermixed data for interlinkages at present. This might suggest a fragmentation of the academic areas of to coincide with the timing of developing literature in CBDC, as well as the geographical, institutional, and discipline division is typical of the field. Ultimately, the visualization highlights an important realization: the research on CBDCs and financial development is growing, but remains very heterogenous with weak collaborative ties. Strengthening co-authorship ties and interdisciplinary collaboration would allow research outputs to be more robust and relevant. For both policymakers and academic institutions, creating, or investing in collaborative platforms (or thematic research consortia) can be a way to help fill these gaps and build intellectual cohesion within the field.

Figure 3. Co-authorship network among authors

Source: *Figure extracted from VOS Viewer*

4.6 Level of International Participation and Collaboration Among Countries in this Field

The above table provides a quantitative analysis of the academic contributions to the area of Central Bank Digital Currency (CBDC) and financial development by country. The measures include documents (publications), citations (a measure of the academic impact), and total link strength (TLS) which reflects how strongly countries collaborated internationally in co-authorship networks. This data provides insight as both a productivity and influencing factor, as well as how globally connected the different countries are in their scholarly endeavor.

The United States is clearly the most dominant contributor with 11 publications, 361 citations, and a TLS of 13. Although the United States does not contribute the most publications, its citation total is markedly higher than the other countries—suggesting that the visibility and impact of its research output are high. The TLS is also high, indicating that United States-based scholars are entrenched in other international collaborative networks where they are well-positioned both as a producer of knowledge but also as a global research partner.

The United Kingdom also provides the highest volume of contributions with 14 documents, and had the second most citations at 185 with the same TLS of 13. This indicates a strong balanced performance—both prolific but impactful contributions—while also having strong international linkages. Overall, the United States and the United Kingdom appear to be the centres of activity.

Despite fewer publications, both Spain and Switzerland are also strong on citations. Spain (6 documents) received 148 citations. Switzerland (7 documents) received 125 citations. They both have very low TLS scores (3 and 1), indicating that working with foreign scholars is less common, or perhaps less intense, than in other countries or geographically clustered. Their research may be more regionally focused or institutional focused.

China stood out with 9 publications, 111 citations, a comparatively high number of articles and citations for Amanda's paper. However, China also had a TLS score of 11, which suggests that Chinese scholars value using this discussion across borders, and are increasingly likely to participate in cross-border academic work. China's increasing significance in global finance (due to global monetary policy changes) and digital technology (particularly its role in the ongoing innovation and development of CBDCs) likely influences its interest in CBDC discussions.

Patterns were also present for France and the Russian Federation, who had moderate publication counts (4 each) and high citation counts (99 and 85), and very low TLS scores (1 and 0). This information seems to indicate their research is well regarded, but much of the research is done either individually or domestically, not through partnerships across the globe.

Canada, Singapore, and Germany present a more balanced profile with 5–6 documents; every country with citations between 54–71, and moderate TLS values (5–6). Each of these countries are medium-level contributors with a respectable level of academic visibility and productive collaborative links.

Countries such as Italy, Nigeria, and Australia are also meaningful contributors but have lower TLS scores (≤ 4) and thus indicate their research is not yet as internationally integrated. Lastly, the Netherlands has the lowest TLS (0) despite producing 4 documents, and has limited citation impact (13), this suggests their research in this area is nascent or isolated.

Table 3. Level of international participation and collaboration among countries in this field

Country	Document	Citations	Total Link Strength
Australia	4	12	4
Canada	5	54	6
China	9	111	11
France	4	99	1
Germany	6	60	5
Italy	5	73	3
Netherlands	4	13	0
Nigeria	4	59	2
Russian Federation	4	85	0
Singapore	5	71	6
Spain	6	148	3
Switzerland	7	125	1
United Kingdom	14	185	13
United States	11	361	13

Source: Author's Own Work

Figure 4 to demonstrate country-level collaboration. Co-authorship between different countries can be viewed through the presented network diagram. The network diagram displays large and small circles which connect through drawing lines. Bigger circles in the figure represent countries with a higher number of collaborations. Colors in the visualization represent the membership of a respective nation to its designated cluster. The connected lines in the network correspond to the data about country collaborations detailed in **Table 3**. The network display helps identify which countries form the most partnerships. The results indicate that the UK participates in the most collaborative relationships with 5 different linkages of total strength amounting to 13. The United States follows the UK as it maintains 6 links which add up to 13 in total link strength. China belongs in the third position and Switzerland stands as the fourth position since they each share relationships with 6 and 1 other countries. The two nations share a total link strength of 11 and 1.The network of Spain connects with six other nations while its total network strength amounts to 3. The collaborative networks of Germany include three countries and achieve seventh rank through a total link strength of seven points whereas Canada and Italy share four links each to reach sixth position keeping Singapore at the same rank with six points. Cited publications mainly emerge from collaborative research work. The maximum number of cited articles comes from countries which are part of the UK cluster as per analysis.

Figure 4. Co-authorship network among authors

Source: Figure extracted from VOS Viewer

4.7 The Most Commonly Used Keywords

The term co-occurrence indicates the number of times keywords appear together in a context. The statement reflects previous distribution patterns found in published documents. Out of the keywords subjected to a minimum occurrence threshold (5), 18 out of 356 keywords exceeded this threshold. VOSviewer client produced the keyword co-occurrence network visualized in **Figure. 5.** A network map displays high-frequency keywords which measure their relation through distance between them. Two keyword terms connect through this virtual line which indicates their shared working environment. The closer the two, the more the relationship. The data includes keywords which appear at least five times and these phrases are showcased in **Table 4**. The sample contains two main keywords starting with cbdc (f=38) which has 89 total link strength and central bank digital currency (f = 30) with 59 total link strength. This knowledge intersection renders the investigation results vital for exploring multiple research directions which belong to the research domain. **Figure 5** shows the visual representation of keywords which occur together throughout the content. Analysis revealed that most prominent keywords preferably appeared alongside "cbdc" and "central bank digital currency." The identified keywords allow researchers to discover newly emerging research topics between them. Research discovered both "Central Bank" and "Digital Currency" stand as major topics of investigation. VOSviewer identifies three clusters which contain the research keywords. Different colour schemes represent the clusters throughout the bibliometric network. Every keyword represents a color which matches its assigned cluster. The literature within each cluster designates separate groups which belong to distinct themes within the field of study where cluster 1 uses “cbdc” as its most prevalent keyword. Keywords in the second cluster appear most frequently with “central bank”. The keyword “monetary policy” appears most frequently within the contents of cluster 3. Research field development appears through keyword data.

Figure 5. Keywords co-occurrences network map Source: Figure extracted from VOS Viewer

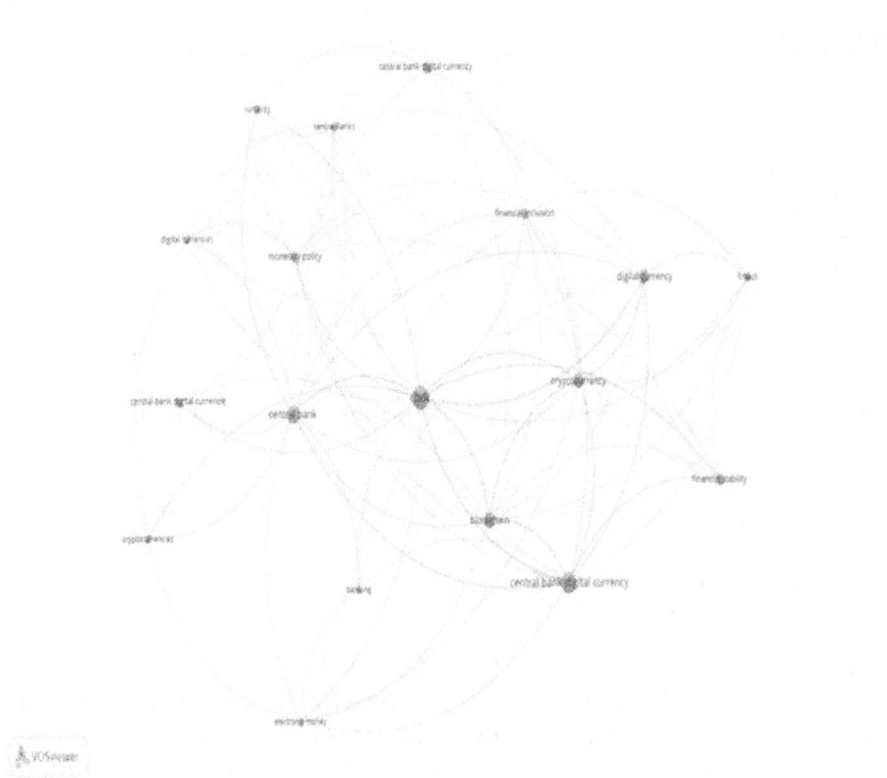

Table 4. Maximum occurring keywords

Keyword	Occurrences	Total Link Strength
banking	5	13
blockchain	15	44
cbdc	38	89
central bank	21	54
central bank digital currencies	7	10
central bank digital currency	30	59
central banks	5	11
cryptocurrencies	6	8
cryptocurrency	14	41
currency	6	16
digital currencies	6	12
digital currency	14	33
electronic money	5	12
financial inclusion	7	22
financial stability	8	19
fintech	6	11
monetary policy	8	19

Source: Author's Own Work

5. CONCLUSION

A growing amount of research now focuses on CBDC implementation due to its current necessity. CBDCs and stock market to some extent influence each other. The main objective of CBDCs to absorb stock market volatility demonstrates that these currencies have the capability to reduce market instabilities. (Frolov et al., 2023). The adoption of CBDC depends on both Anti-money laundering and terrorist financing protocols together with financial market enhancement as well as inflation and technological transformation (Le et al. 2023). Another essential aspect of central bank digital currency (CBDC) implementation showcases that reducing specific threats such as cashless societies or currency swapping leads to increased possibilities of structural bank disintermediation (Viñuela et al., 2020). Digital payment growth has emerged because of COVID-19 which demonstrates the requirement of breaking down digital payment frameworks into separate regional systems. (Srouji J., Torre D.,2022). The leading economic journal for quantitative research titled Journal of Monetary Economics maintains a relationship with Elsevier B.V. whereas it publishes

3 articles in its field accumulating 194 citations. Article "On the equivalence of private and public money" by Brunnermeier Markus K. and Niepelt Drik achieved 89 citations to become the most-read piece in the domain (Brunnermeier and Niepelt. 2019). Both authors Brunnermeier Markus K. with The United States heritage and Niepelt Drik with Swiss roots place their nations among the top second and fourth positions for maximum articles in this field. The visual representation of author partnerships indicates that research teams typically consist of two or three members who lead the field in terms of productivity. Authentic paper quality enhancement alongside thorough domain understanding drives authors to work together more frequently among their own peer networks. Worldwide collaboration shows that The UK together with The USA hold the record for having 13 international connections. The digital currency terms "cbdc" and "central bank digital currency "appear as the two most used keywords. The research indicates that numerous scholars analyze both CBDCs and their impact on financial inclusion and monetary policy through keyword analysis. The research examined both Blockchain as the base technology of CBDC and its parent role. Research had shown limited publication in the field which means additional studies must be done on how CBDC affects economic financial development. Additional research about digitalization in India needs to be done because it represents the world's fastest expanding economy. This article completes the current body of research within this subject domain.

6. LIMITATION

While this bibliometric analysis provides rich insights into the intellectual structure and developing patterns in Central Bank Digital Currency (CBDC) and financial development research, there are a few limitations:

Database Limitation: The database used is limited to the resources in one bibliographic database (i.e. Scopus/Web of Science). This study may miss key works that are published in non-indexed journals, local journals, and grey literature.

Time Horizon: The analysis includes publications above a cut-off year, but due to the dynamic and fast-changing nature of CBDC research, the landscape or the availability of works is too fast for any one analysis to capture.

Language Constraint: The study primarily includes English-language works, which may overlook important works published in other languages, particularly in parts of the world that are piloting or implementing CBDCs.

Keyword Choices: As bibliometric mapping is query based, the interpretation of mapping is based on the queries alone, and any relevant works that do not use the selected keywords in the title, abstract, or keywords might not have been included.

Citations Based: This study relies on citation-based indicators, which will advantage older papers and authors in established research networks, but exclude newer authors and recent publications.

7. FUTURE IMPLICATION

The findings from this bibliometric review will serve as a building block and many opportunities for the suggestions for future research and policies in the swiftly changing and multidisciplinary area of Central Bank Digital Currencies (CBDC) and financial development. The digital monetary ecosystem is changing, creating urgency for researchers to explore new topics, notably the socio-economic implications or use of CBDCs to promote financial inclusion of disadvantaged segments of the population and unbanked individuals. There is a need to understand the different geographical circumstances related to the adoption and use of CBDCs, including the challenges posed by infrastructure, in a culture, and the economic situation relevant for disparities between developed and developing economies. Moreover, digital currencies are complementary to established systems meaning, from a research standpoint, it is also important to check factors such as public trust, digital literacy, and institutional credibility and their effect on adoption and usage. From a policy perspective, the implications of these findings highlight the importance of developing an evidence-based, forward-looking regulatory framework capable of supporting innovation balanced by governance. While microeconomic effects of CBDC adoption may include shifts in consumer payment choices and spending behavior driven by ease and perceived trust, CBDC may also impact the cost structures and competitive standing of banks and fintech companies in the retail payments ecosystem. Policymakers should utilize academic research to forward emerging questions of concern, such as; data privacy, cybersecurity, monetary sovereignty, and interoperability with existing financial infrastructures to address key questions of concern. Finally, given the emergent nature of the field, it is important that we take a more holistic, trans-disciplinary approach. Economists, technologists, legal scholars, and public policy actors should all work together to make sure we are giving ourselves a chance to foster the ethical designs of solutions so that we can mitigate negative consequences of digital currency designs. A significant omission present within the literature is the reliance on English-language, Anglo-centric research, that may not take into account context-specific dynamics relevant to the Global South.

Future research should therefore aim to develop multilingual, culturally grounded, and regionally specific approaches to CBDCs to promote extent and representation of CBDC discourse. Engaging with a comprehensive array of voices and experiences will ensure better assessments of the respective benefits and risks posed by CBDCs, aimed towards global but locally-relevant solutions. In addition, the future of bibliometric analysis within this discipline is promising. More sophisticated and contemporary bibliometric approaches including text mining, machine learning, and semantic analysis will, in the hands of scholars, mean greater thematic detail by tracking innovative research fronts, new policy dynamics, and shifting forms of intellectual leadership. They can also help researchers chart the ongoing interplay between regulatory pressure, technological innovation, and economic behavior in real time. This will ultimately allow academic discourse to objectively track the shift of discussion on CBDCs from theoretical exploration to applied policy.

REFERENCES

Allen, F., Gu, X., & Jagtiani, J. (2022). Fintech, Cryptocurrencies, and CBDC: Financial Structural Transformation in China. *Journal of International Money and Finance, 124*, 102625. Advance online publication. DOI: 10.1016/j.jimonfin.2022.102625

Alonso, S. L. N., Fernández, M. Á. E., Bas, D. S., & Kaczmarek, J. (2020). Reasons fostering or discouraging the implementation of central bank-backed digital currency. *A review Economies*, *8*(2), 41. Advance online publication. DOI: 10.3390/economies8020041

Ante, L. (2021). How Elon Musk's Twitter activity moves cryptocurrency markets. *Finance Research Letters, 38*, 101534. DOI: 10.1016/j.frl.2020.101534

Ante, L. (2021). How Elon Musk's Twitter activity moves cryptocurrency markets. *Finance Research Letters, 38*, 101534. DOI: 10.1016/j.frl.2020.101534

Arner, D. W., Auer, R., & Frost, J. (2020). *Stablecoins: Risks, potential and regulation*. Bank for International Settlements. https://www.bis.org/publ/bisbull05.htm

Arner, D. W., Barberis, J., & Buckley, R. P. (2016). The Evolution of Fintech: A New Post-Crisis Paradigm? *University of Hong Kong Faculty of Law Research Paper No. 2015/047*.

Auer, R., & Böhme, R. (2020). *The technology of retail central bank digital currency*. BIS Quarterly Review, March 2020, 85–100. https://www.bis.org/publ/qtrpdf/r_qt2003j.pdf

Auer, R., Cornelli, G., & Frost, J. (2020). Rise of the Central Bank Digital Currencies: Drivers, Approaches, and Technologies. *BIS Working Papers*.

Banerjee S. and Sinha M., (2023). Promoting Financial Inclusion through Central Bank Digital Currency: An Evaluation of Payment System Viability in India Australasian Accounting, Business and Finance Journal https://doi.org/DOI: 10.14453/aabfj.v17i1.14

Bank for International Settlements. (2021). *Central Bank Digital Currencies: Financial Stability Implications*. BIS Quarterly Review.

Bank for International Settlements. (2021). *Central bank digital currencies: Financial stability implications*. BIS Quarterly Review. https://www.bis.org

Bank for International Settlements (BIS). (2021). *CBDCs: Financial stability implications*. https://www.bis.org/publ/bppdf/bispap117.pdf

Belke, A., & Beretta, E. (2020). From cash to central bank digital currencies and cryptocurrencies: A balancing act between modernity and monetary stability. *Journal of Economic Studies (Glasgow, Scotland)*, *47*(4), 911–938. Advance online publication. DOI: 10.1108/JES-07-2019-0311

Brunnermeier, M. K., & Niepelt, D. (2019). On the equivalence of private and public money. *Journal of Monetary Economics*, *106*, 27–41. Advance online publication. DOI: 10.1016/j.jmoneco.2019.07.004

CERT-In. (2024). *Annual report on cyber security incidents*. Ministry of Electronics and Information Technology, Government of India.

Cheng, P., (2022), Decoding the rise of Central Bank Digital Currency in China: designs, problems, and prospects Journal of Banking Regulation (2023) 24:156–170 https://doi.org/DOI: 10.1057/s41261-022-00193-5

Danvila-del-Valle, I., Estévez-Mendoza, C., & Lara, J. (2019, August). F., Human resources training: A bibliometric analysis. *Journal of Business Research*, *101*, 627–636. Advance online publication. DOI: 10.1016/j.jbusres.2019.02.026

Davis, F. D. (1989). Perceived usefulness, perceived ease of use, and user acceptance of information technology. *Management Information Systems Quarterly*, *13*(3), 319–340. DOI: 10.2307/249008

Deloitte. (2023). *Digital payments in India: Navigating trust and security*. Deloitte Insights. https://www2.deloitte.com/in/en.html

Donthu, N., Pattnaik, D., Pandey, N., and Kumar, s., (2020), A Bibliometric Review of International Marketing Review (IMR): Past, Present, and Future International Marketing Review http://dx.doi.org/DOI: 10.1108/IMR-11-2020-0244

Eck, N., & Waltman, L. (2010). oftware survey: VOSviewer, a computer program for bibliometric mapping. *Scientometrics*, *84*(2), 523–538. DOI: 10.1007/s11192-009-0146-3 PMID: 20585380

Eck, N., & Waltman, L. (2010). oftware survey: VOSviewer, a computer program for bibliometric mapping. *Scientometrics*, *84*(2), 523–538. DOI: 10.1007/s11192-009-0146-3 PMID: 20585380

Fernández, M. A. E., Alonso, S. L. N., Jorge-Vázquez, J., & Forradellas, R. F. R. (2021). *Central banks' monetary policy in the face of the COVID-19 economic crisis: Monetary stimulus and the emergence of CBDCs*. Sustainability., DOI: 10.3390/su13084242

Fernández-Villaverde, J., Sanches, D., Schilling, L., & Uhlig, H. (2021, July). Fernández-Villaverde, j.,Daniel, S., Linda, S., and Harald, U, (2020), Central bank digital currency: Central banking for all? *Review of Economic Dynamics, 41*, 225–242. Advance online publication. DOI: 10.1016/j.red.2020.12.004

Frolov, S., Ivasenko, M., Dykha, M., Heyenko, M., & Datsenko, V. (2023). *Analysis of the impact of central bank digital currency on stock markets: Dynamics and implications*. Banks and Bank Systems., DOI: 10.21511/bbs.18(4).2023.14

Frolov, S., Ivasenko, M., Dykha, M., Heyenko, M., Datsenko, V., (2023), Analysis of the impact of central bank digital currency on stock markets: Dynamics and implications Banks and Bank Systems, 18(4), 149-168. DOI: 10.21511/bbs.18(4).2023.14

Garfield, E., (2004), Historiographic Mapping of Knowledge Domains Literature Journal of Information Science 30(2):119-145 DOI: and Simoes, R., Quieroz, G., Ferreira, K.,Vinhas, L., postgis-t: toward a spatiotemporal postgresql database extension Revista Brasileira de Cartografia 69(5) DOI:DOI: 10.1177/0165551504042802

Genc, H., & Takagi, S. (2024). A literature review on the design and implementation of central bank digital currencies. *International Journal of Economic Policy Studies, 18*(1), 197–225. DOI: 10.1007/s42495-023-00125-9

Genc, H., and Takagi,S., (2024), A literature review on the design and implementation of central bank digital currencies International Journal of Economic Policy Studies (2024) 18:197–225 https://doi.org/DOI: 10.1007/s42495-023-00125-9

Gerard, D. (1993), Avant Card —(Online) a central bank digital currency from 1990s Finland https://davidgerard.co.uk/blockchain/2020/01/25/avant-card-a-central-bank-digital-currency-from-1990s-finland/

GlobeNewswire. (2025, April 10). *Generative AI market size expected to reach USD 1,005.07 Bn by 2034*. https://www.globenewswire.com/news-release/2025/04/10/3059463/0/en/Generative-AI-Market-Size-Expected-to-Reach-USD-1-005-07-Bn-By-2034.html

Grand View Research. (2024). *Artificial intelligence (AI) market size, share & trends analysis report*. https://www.grandviewresearch.com/industry-analysis/artificial-intelligence-ai-market

Haque M.A.; Shoaib M., (2023), e —The digital currency in India: Challenges and prospects *BenchCouncil Transactions on Benchmarks, Standards and Evaluations* DOI:DOI: 10.1016/j.tbench.2023.100107

Horvath, D. (2023). Money in the Digital Age: Exploring the Potential of Central Bank Digital Currency with a Focus on Social Adaptation and Education. *Sustainable Futures : An Applied Journal of Technology, Environment and Society*, *6*, 100136. Advance online publication. DOI: 10.1016/j.sftr.2023.100136

Investor's Business Daily. (2025, April). *AI stocks: Saudi Arabia's AI expansion could boost Nvidia, AMD.* https://www.investors.com/news/technology/ai-stocks-saudi-deals-nvidia-amd-supermicro/

Jun, J., & Yeo, E. (2021). Central bank digital currency, loan supply, and bank failure risk: A microeconomic approach. *Financial Innovation*, *7*(1), 81. Advance online publication. DOI: 10.1186/s40854-021-00296-4 PMID: 35024292

Katz, E., Blumler, J. G., & Gurevitch, M. (1973). Uses and gratifications research. *Public Opinion Quarterly*, *37*(4), 509–523. DOI: 10.1086/268109

Kiff, J., Alwazir, J., Davidovic, S., & Farias, F. (2020). *A survey of research on retail central bank digital currency*. International Monetary Fund. https://www.imf.org/en/Publications/WP/Issues/2020/06/26/A-Survey-of-Research-on-Retail-Central-Bank-Digital-Currency-49517

Kochergin, D., & Yangirova, A. (2019). Central bank Digital Currencies: Key Characteristics and Directions of Influence on Monetary and Credit and Payment Systems *Finance. Theory into Practice*, *23*(4), 80–98. DOI: 10.26794/2587-5671-2019-23-4-80-98

Kochergin, D. A., & Yangirova, A. I. (2019). Central bank Digital Currencies: Key Characteristics and Directions of Influence on Monetary and Credit and Payment Systems. *Finance: Theory and Practice*, *23*(4), 80–98. DOI: 10.26794/2587-5671-2019-23-4-80-98

Kumhof, M., & Noone, C. (2018). *Central bank digital currencies—Design principles and balance sheet implications*. Bank of England Staff Working Paper No. 725. DOI: 10.2139/ssrn.3180713

Le, T., Tran, S., Nguyen, D. Q. A. T., & Ngo, T. (2023). The degrees of central bank digital currency adoption across countries: A preliminary analysis. *Economics and Business Letters*, *12*(2), 97–104. DOI: 10.17811/ebl.12.2.2023.97-104

Lee,Y., Son,B., Park,.S Lee, J., Jang, H., (2021), A Survey on Security and Privacy in Blockchain-based Central Bank Digital Currencies journal of Internet Services and Information Security (JISIS), volume: 11, number: 3 (August 2021), pp. 16-29 DOI:DOI: 10.22667/JISIS.2021.08.31.016

Miernicki, M. (2024). Cash, accounts, and central bank digital currencies: a legal view on the introduction of account- and token-based digital central bank money Law and Financial Markets Review https://doi.org/DOI: 10.1080/17521440.2024.2308800

Miernicki, M., & Ying, H., (2024), Artifcial intelligence and moral rights *AI & SOCIETY* (2021) 36:319–329 https://doi.org/DOI: 10.1007/s00146-020-01027-6

Mikhaylov, A. (2021), Development of Friedrich von Hayek's theory of private money and economic implications for digital currencies. http://dx.doi.org/DOI: 10.18522/2073-6606-2021-19-1-53-62

Mikhaylov A.Y., (2021), Development of Friedrich von Hayek's theory of private money and economic implications for digital currencies; *Terra Economicus* http://dx.doi.org/DOI: 10.18522/2073-6606-2021-19-1-53-62

Nakamoto, S. (Online). Available: (2008), https://bitcoin.org/ bitcoin.pdf. Accessed 15 May 2020

National Centre for Financial Education (NCFE). (2022). *Financial literacy and inclusion survey report.* https://www.ncfe.org.in/

National Payments Corporation of India (NPCI). (2024). *UPI statistics.* https://www.npci.org.in/

Omotubora, A. (2024). 2024 Same Naira, More Possibilities! Assessing the Legal Status of the eNaira and Its Potential for Privacy and Inclusion. *Journal of African Law*, *68*(2), 1–18. DOI: 10.1017/S0021855324000044

Pelagidis, T., & Kostika, E. (2022). Investigating the role of central banks in the interconnection between financial markets and cryptoassets. *Economia e Politica Industriale*, *2022*(49), 481–507. DOI: 10.1007/s40812-022-00227-z

Precedence Research. (2024). *Decentralized finance market size, share, growth 2024 to 2034.* https://www.precedenceresearch.com/decentralized-finance-market

Rennie, E., & Steele, S. (2021). Privacy and emergency payments in a pandemic: How to think about privacy and a central bank digital currency. Law. *Technology and Humans*, *3*(1), 6–17.

Reserve Bank of India (2023). Concept Note on Central Bank Digital Currency.

Reserve Bank of India. (2023). *Concept note on Central Bank Digital Currency.* https://www.rbi.org.in

Reserve Bank of India (RBI). (2022). *Concept Note on Central Bank Digital Currency.* https://www.rbi.org.in/Scripts/PublicationReportDetails.aspx?UrlPage=&ID=1210

Rogers, E. M. (2003). *Diffusion of innovations* (5th ed.). Free Press.

Sarmiento A., (2022), Seven lessons from the e-Peso pilot plan: The possibility of a Central Bank Digital Currency Latin American Journal of Central Banking https://doi.org/DOI: 10.1016/j.latcb.2022.100062

Sethaput, V., & Innet, S. (2023). Blockchain application for central bank digital currencies (CBDC). *Cluster Computing*, *26*(4), 2183–2197. DOI: 10.1007/s10586-022-03962-z PMID: 36686339

Singh, A., Rupeika-Apoga, R., & Jangir, K. (2023). Does Previous Experience with the Unified Payments Interface (UPI) Affect the Usage of Central Bank Digital Currency (CBDC)? *Journal of Risk and Financial Management*, *16*(6), 286. Advance online publication. DOI: 10.3390/jrfm16060286

Srouji J., Torre D., (2022), The Global Pandemic, Laboratory of the Cashless Economy? *International Journal of Financial Studies*https://doi.org/DOI: 10.3390/ijfs10040109

Swartz, L., & Westermeier, C. (2023). The money tree: Exploring central bank digital currency blockchain imaginaries. *Anthropology Today*, *39*(4), 13–16. Advance online publication. DOI: 10.1111/1467-8322.12827

Venkatesh, V., Morris, M. G., Davis, G. B., & Davis, F. D. (2003). User acceptance of information technology: Toward a unified view. *Management Information Systems Quarterly*, *27*(3), 425–478. DOI: 10.2307/30036540

Vinuella, C., Sapena, J., & Wandosell, G. (2020). The Future of Money and the Central Bank Digital Currency Dilemma. *Sustainability (Basel)*, *12*(22), 9697. DOI: 10.3390/su12229697

Williams, S. (2022). Central Bank Digital Currency: Welfare and Policy Implications. *Journal of Political Economy*, *130*(11), 2829–2861. Advance online publication. DOI: 10.1086/720457

Xu, C., & Jin, B. (2022). Digital currency in China: Pilot implementations, legal challenges and prospects. *Juridical Trib.*, *12*, 177.

YouGov. (2024). *CBDC awareness and public sentiment survey—India.* https://yougov.in/

Zhang, Y., Xie, J., & Xu, Z. (2020). The role of social media in the cryptocurrency market: Evidence from sentiment analysis. *Applied Economics Letters*, *27*(18), 1489–1494. DOI: 10.1080/13504851.2019.1704674

Chapter 3
Exploring Sustainable Service Marketing and Virtual Currencies:
A Lexicometric Analysis

Nitika Sharma
https://orcid.org/0009-0008-6437-2539
Chitkara Business School, Chitkara University, Punjab, India

Paras Sarjolta
HyperBizz Global, India

ABSTRACT

Sustainable service marketing is the integration of economic, social, and environmental dimensions followed for value-driven responsible business practice. Decentralized technologies transform the ways traditional strategies are used in marketing into new innovative ways that emphasize sustainability. These technologies redesign, deliver, and experience services but also help catalyze systemic changes within service ecosystems. The study conducts a lexicometric analysis to discuss the literature regarding sustainable service marketing and virtual currencies. It introduces key themes such as advanced technology integration, improved transparency and accountabilities with decentralized platforms, and trend towards circular economies facilitated by digital innovations. Revealing these themes outlines how virtual currencies can be instrumental in sustaining consumer behavior through optimization of the delivery of service and environmental practices in business operations. The results provide actionable implications and avenues for further research directions.

DOI: 10.4018/979-8-3373-0315-4.ch003

1. INTRODUCTION

Sustainable service marketing is a combination of the goals of economic development, environmental concerns, and welfare benefits to achieve service innovations using responsible business techniques (Fernando et al. 2019). With the growing head turns of more and more economic markets toward embracing digital transformation, virtual currencies with the technologies involved have been introduced, shifting how services get marketed, distributed, and felt. These are certainly not enriching forms of tradition; instead, they are in effect leading toward systemic changes affecting service design and delivery as well as consumption that disrupt and reinterpret well-established long-term paradigms (Golinelli et al. 2012). There's a plethora of unprecedentedly enhanced opportunities from blockchain and other decentralized systems for sustainability through openness, accountability, and consumer-level participation. More importantly, they enable businesses to establish practices of marketing that are ethical and sustainable and thus address important concerns about the environment and society. For instance, more firms now use tokens and blockchain systems as a means of rewarding responsible practices, enhancing traceability, and conserving resources.

In discussing this chapter, the paper applies lexicometric analysis in unearthing the existing trends of literature surrounding sustainable service marketing and virtual currencies. It allows for a systematic observation on the different ways in which those technologies impact upon the service marketing - from personal at consumer-level engagements all the way up to that point of much more dynamic systems. Conclusions would focus around themes relevant to old models transformations with integration into innovation technologies and towards design of novel models for interactions that are more sustainable. This chapter aims to add contribution towards an understanding of how virtual currencies may come in support of realizing sustainable service marketing, setting future avenues for elaborating on changes within this realm.

2. LITERATURE BACKGROUND

Sustainable service marketing acts as a pathway to fulfil environmental and economical goals to create values that are in alignment with the sustainability principles (Peterson et al. 2021). Sustainable marketing is not only a solution for tackling environmental issues, however it also offers novel opportunities in supporting circular economy models. The literature background highlights the state of literature in sustainable service marketing and virtual currencies.

2.1. Technology and Marketing Practices

Technological innovation in blockchain and artificial intelligence has opened new pathways in achieving optimized and sustainable solutions in the field of marketing (Singh et al. 2020). Blockchain technology provides safe and transparent transactions, hence business and consumers gain confidence from this technology (Laroiya et al. 2020). Köhler et al. (2022) found out that applications of blockchain-based services on marketing platforms reduced the environmental footprint by a significantly large margin compared to paper-based traditional campaigns. Therefore, this innovation is supporting businesses to save costs while advancing accountability towards sustainable marketing strategies.

This AI-based technology would considerably aid in the sustenance of service marketing. Predictive analytics and machine learning algorithms would help the companies in reducing waste while implementing proper marketing campaigns as per the requirements of the consumers who look forward to green environment-friendly products (Hasan et al. 2024). Literature also reflected evidence about handling big datasets and the consequent application of suitable, sustainable solutions through AI (Bibri et al. 2023). This scenario points out how transformative AI can be for service marketing.

2.2. Consumer Empowerment and Transparency

The most prominent theme of the literature was consumer empowerment, with decentralized platforms and transparent marketing processes. Concerning this area, blockchain, a decentralized ledger, plays an important role in giving an equal playing field by attesting to verifiability of the marketing claims over sustainability rather than greenwashing. The researchers have continued to understand how the companies with blockchain can make their supply chains become more transparent to the consumers, and through this information, they can make purchasing decisions on the products (Francisco and Swanson 2018).

Additionally, customers can also be empowered through smart contracts. These are self-enforcing contracts, which enforce the agreement automatically between the parties with minimum involvement of the intermediaries for ensuring that the companies respect their commitment to sustainability (Sharma and Manohar 2024). Other literature goes ahead to explain that such innovation is linked to consumer trust and participation in sustainable ecosystems (Ciasullo et al. 2020). Decentralized technologies stimulate the consumer to be more engaged with the tools that are provided to him so that he assumes ownership of the decision made at the time of purchase and ensures that it goes well with the value of sustainability.

2.3. Role of Virtual Currencies

Virtual currencies have now emerged as a new model of marketing and incentives for sustainable consumer behavior. For instance, NFTs can be gamified through such sustainability practices (Kotha et al. 2024). Companies are rewarding NFTs to people who recycle or buy environment-friendly products. Such consumers are rewarded with exclusive benefits attached to such NFTs. Consumers find motivation in the fact that they are included in the community and maintain loyalty to it (Hur et al. 2011). In addition, newer cryptocurrencies have incorporated sustainability incentives directly into their protocols. For instance, "green coins" are coins that finance renewable energy projects or carbon offset each transaction. Literature continues to elaborate how businesses leverage these innovative currencies for repeat interactions with environmentally responsible brands, which is a mutually reinforcing relationship between marketing and sustainability.

2.4. Marketing and Circular Economies

Much literature outlines synergies between marketing strategies and circular economy principles, especially with virtual currencies and blockchain technologies. The circular economy model supports the aspects of less waste and greater resource reuse and value created over a more extended period. Blockchain technology promotes these principles by enhancing lifecycle tracking and the accountability of claims concerning the sustainability of companies.

For example, detailed research has further explained how blockchain technologies can be used for returning and re-use of products using ownership histories as well as composition of materials involved in the production of products (O'Dair 2018). This encourages the firms to incorporate more sustainable designs as well as engaging consumers with sustainable consumption. Virtual currencies that are part of circular economy approach help the firms to facilitate recycling or returning back the used products by enabling consumers to close the circle of services delivery in an environmentally friendly way.

3. METHODOLOGY

3.1. Data Collection

The intention of this study is to be comprehensive, conducting an inter-domain based research to extensively review the current state of literature in service marketing and virtual currencies. To obtain information on the literature, Systematic

Procedures and Rationales for Systematic Literature Review (SPAR-4-SLR) by Paul et al. (2021) was used. SPAR-4-SLR undergoes 3 stages in order to comprehensively enhance the quality of literature reviews (Figure 1). The stages are as follows:

Assembling: This stage comprises identifying and acquiring the documents to be included in the study. Data was extracted from Scopus which provides a comprehensive collection of scholarly articles, books, etc. to gain deeper understanding of the subject area. The period for the study was set up to January, 2025. The search keywords finalized for the string were *("sustainable") AND ("marketing") AND ("virtual currenc*" OR "digital asset*" OR "digital currenc*" OR "metaverse")* wherein 43 documents were retrieved after removing the duplicate documents.

Arranging: For the purpose of this stage, organization and purification of the documents was done. Careful consideration was given to the following factors:

- Subject area was limited to: Business Management & Accounting; Social Sciences; Economics, Econometrics & Finance; Decision Sciences; Psychology; Arts and Humanities; and Multidisciplinary.
- Publication stage was set to: Final stage
- Language was limited to: English language

Subsequently, the documents were narrowed down to 25.

Figure 1. Review procedure using SPAR-4-SLR

Assembling
Identification

- Domain: Marketing and Digital Finance
- Source type: Journals
- Source quality: Scopus

Acquisition

- Search mechanism and material acquisition: Scopus
- Search period: Up to January, 2025
- Search keywords: ("sustainable") AND ("marketing") AND ("virtual currenc*" OR "digital asset*" OR "digital currenc*" OR "metaverse")
- Source quality: Scopus
- Total articles returned from the search: 43

Arranging
Organization

- Organizing codes: Subject area, publication stage, and language

Purification

- Subject area: Business Management & Accounting; Social Sciences; Economics, Econometrics & Finance; Decision Sciences; Psychology; Arts and Humanities; and Multidisciplinary.
- Publication Stage: Final
- Language: English
- Total documents retained: 25

Assessing
Evaluation

- Total documents for analysis: 25 documents
- Science mapping: Lexicometric analysis for Descriptive statistics, Factorial Correspondence, Similarity and Word Cloud Analysis

Softwares used: Iramuteq

[Source: Paul et al. 2021]

Assessing: Last stage of the SPAR-4-SLR is assessing wherein the data is evaluated. The data of 23 documents was analyzed through techniques of lexicometric analysis to identify latent meaning of texts and make inferences from it. The analysis was based on the abstracts, titles, and keywords of the data. Lexicometric analysis processes corpus of text efficiently, enabling the identification of essential themes within the subject area. Open-source software named Iramuteq (Ratinaud 2014) was used which segments the input data based on similarities. Further, the software clusters the texts into different themes which calculates the statistical distribution of lexical elements (Reinet's 1990).

The first analysis conducted was descriptive statistics which gives the details of texts, occurrences, forms, hapax, and mean of occurrences. Next, factorial correspondence analysis was undertaken to reveal the intersections between key terms and their distribution. Visualization of major research themes was done through similarity analysis followed by a word cloud analysis for a condensed view of prominent themes and clusters identified.

4. FINDINGS

4.1. Descriptive Statistics

The rank frequency plot (Figure 2) depicts the distribution of word frequencies inside the corpus, demonstrating a power-law relationship, reoccurring with Zipf's Law. The steep initial decline indicates the dominance of persistent terms throughout the discourse, most likely to be foundational terms such as, "marketing", "technology" and "sustainability". These commonly used terms form the backbone of the corpus and are mostly used as anchor terms for the discussion. On the contrary, the tail end of the curve represents the less frequent, more niche-specific terms that are used throughout the discourse like, "metaverse", "gamification", and 'artificial intelligence", which offer deeper insights into the discussion where more light gets shed on the integration of advanced technologies for sustainable service marketing strategies.

Figure 2. Zipf diagram of descriptive statistics

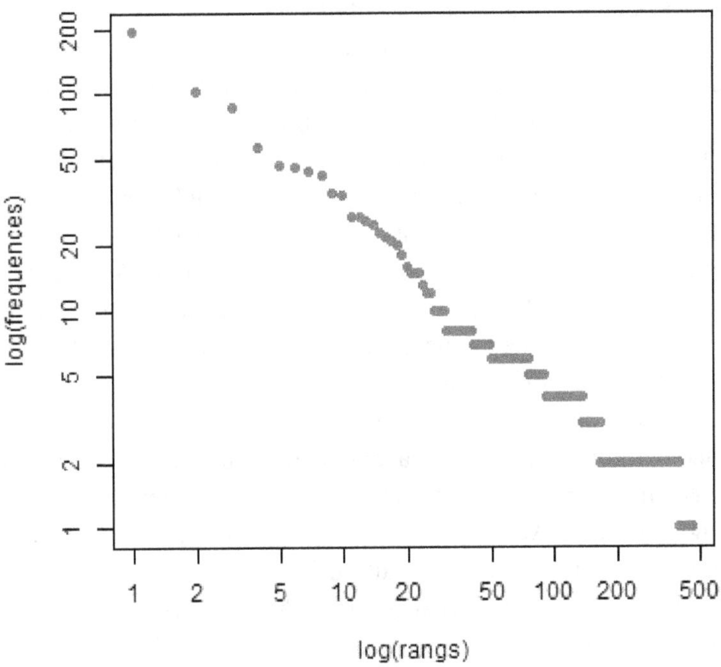

[Source: Author's own work]

This distribution not only reflects the thematic concentration but also highlights its diversity throughout the corpus. By interpreting the relationship between frequent and infrequent terms, the plot illustrates how the main themes of sustainability and technology are interconnected with sprouting trends and major advancements, substantially enriching the overall discussion.

4.2. Factorial Correspondence Analysis

The factorial correspondence analysis in Figure 3 represents the relation of key terms in the corpus on two dimensions of variance so that there is a clear distinction in the pattern of association and thematic clustering. The horizontal axis, Factor 1, plots a spectrum from abstract, conceptual discussions to concrete, domain-specific studies. Towards the further end of the spectrum, abstruse words such as "economy," "virtual," and "paradigm" imply much greater theoretical frameworks as well as extraordinary ideas. Larger ideas direct sustainable service marketing and digital currencies toward wider structural and philosophical considerations. While on the other axis, more concrete terms such as "research," "analysis," and "datum" indicate methodological and empirical work that directly involves particular case studies, data sets, or industry contexts. This axis thus captures, then, the tension between generalization and specificity, underlining how the corpus covers the entire scope from broad conceptual exploration to a level of very focused inquiry.

The vertical axis, Factor 3, distinguishes between theoretical insights and practical implementations. Terms such as "experience" and "transformation" reflect a theoretical approach since they encompass consumer behavior, market fluidity, and technological change. Vocabulary, in this case, reflects the imagination that reflects the interaction of these concepts between sustainability and technology in service marketing. Conversely, terms such as "city," "wellbeing," and "tool" suggest practical application and real implementations that reflect how these ideas materialize in particular contexts such as urban development, public health, and any technological tool. The axis thus speaks to the implications of theoretical insight and how abstract concepts are made into action-oriented strategies.

Together, these two axes make it clear how there is interplay between the abstract conceptual theories and the real empirical applications and vice versa, which is specifically relevant in this area of sustainable service marketing and virtual currencies by virtue of metaverse and AI technologies. This would further mean that not only are technologies changing the more traditional service marketing strategies but they also influence larger systemic changes about how services might be designed, delivered, and experienced.

Figure 3. Factorial correspondence plot

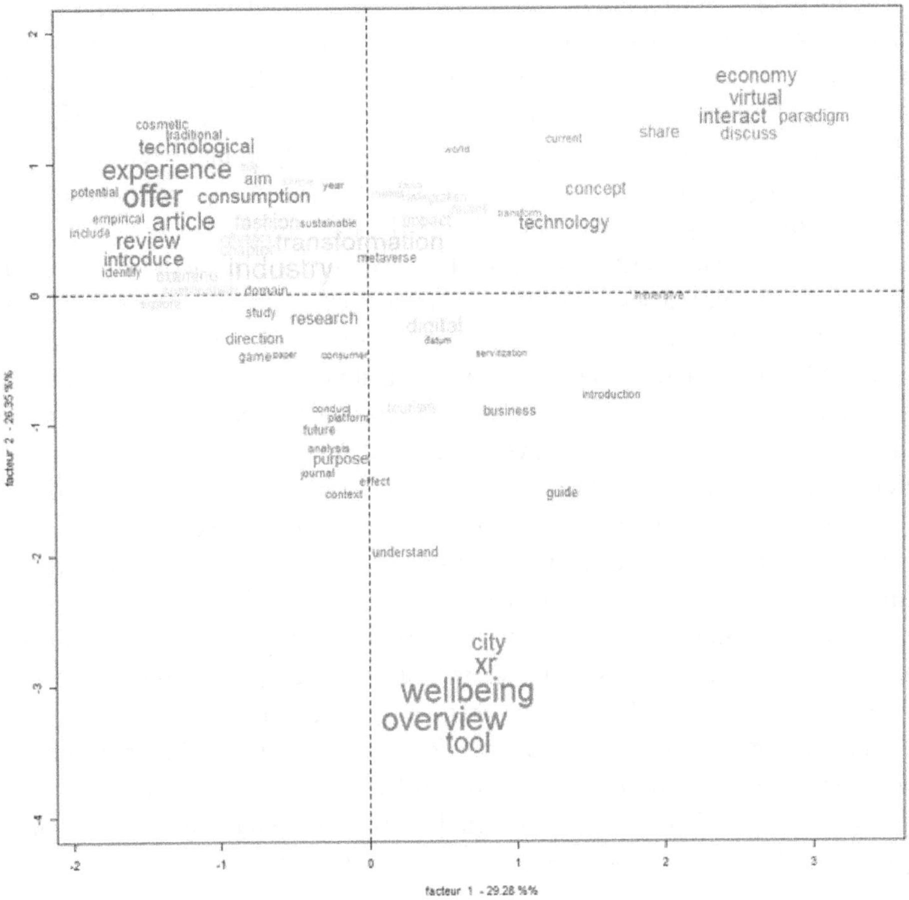

[Source: Author's own work]

Furthermore, in the distribution of terms across the quadrants, interdisciplinarity is indicated and varied by perspectives in the corpus. While the whole cluster containing "economy" and "virtual" refers to discussions of the metaverse in terms of a paradigm shift from the existing economic models, on the other hand, the grouping of "city" and "wellbeing" reflects localized and practical concerns, for example, how virtual technologies can enhance urban living and community health. This visualization ultimately emphasizes the dual focus of the corpus: advancing theoretical knowledge while addressing practical challenges, thus bridging the gap between academic inquiry and industry relevance.

4.3. Similarity Analysis

The network map, Figure 4, illustrates the complex relationships of various themes and concepts related to sustainable service marketing and virtual currencies, which creates a clear distinction of thematic clusters that define this new field of study. Nuclei on the map are terms such as "sustainable," "marketing," "metaverse," and "technology" in order to emphasize how they are important nodes in modern marketing strategies. Such terms therefore, underscore integration of sustainability and technology as key drivers of innovation and transformation.

One of the thematic clusters addresses the academic and research basis; here, a systematic study, bibliometric analysis, and theoretical review are underlined. The three words "study," "review," and "bibliometric" - all enforce the evidence-based research reliance on setting up the frameworks, making trend detection, and building a solid platform for sustainable practice. Therefore, the thematic cluster stands as a sign of intellectual work not directly needed, but needful for the assistance of action strategies inside the field.

The second cluster is the change to be brought about by the emergent technologies, namely artificial intelligence and the metaverse. The terms "artificial intelligence, business, paradigm" really signal a kind of new technology type of rethinking toward the old marketing models. The approach is in relation to the disruption technology can offer to totally new and sustainable ways to both companies and consumers. The main theme of digitalization provides an essential part and emphasizes the influence on consumer behavior and decision-making while underlining its importance in industries like tourism. The terms, "behavior", "strategy", "tourism", and "transformation", indicate the role of digital instruments and ecosystems for inter-organizational cooperation, greater experience for the customer, and sustainability in operations.

The second most prominent theme is the integration of sustainability in day-to-day activities and customer engagement. This would include terms like supply chain management, gamification, and experiential marketing. Keywords like "supply," "experience," "transform," and "gamification" reveal how sustainability can be smoothly integrated into daily operations but still be effective in customer interactions and eco-friendliness. Much broader, systemic is how sustainability is integrated into larger market systems. Words like "economy," "framework," and "scheme" create a perception that there are industry or market level strategies to put into action the principles of sustainability. This theme reflects how systemic change addresses the issues of sustainability in a global environment and, simultaneously, creates value in the long term.

Figure 4. Similarity analysis

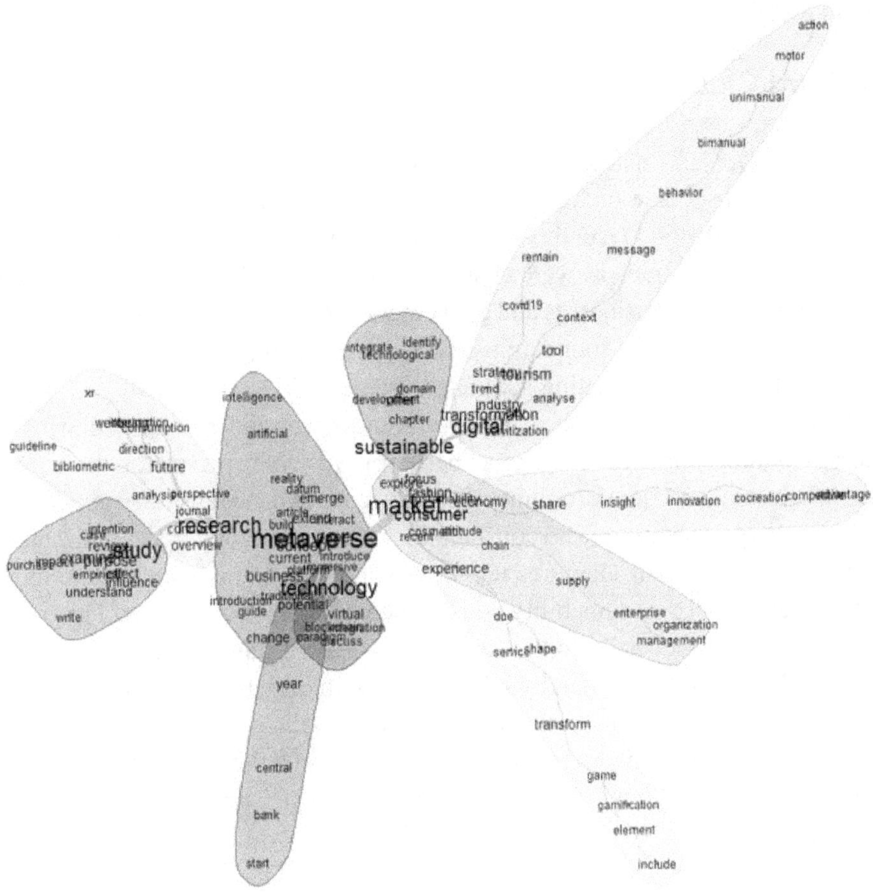

[Source: Author's own work]

The last, a forward-looking theme, represents the trends of tomorrow and tomorrow's innovations: words like "guideline," "future," and "xr" for extended reality. This thematic area reveals an aspect of future immersion technology trends and will redefine the marketing experiences while paving new sustainable approaches into this field, demonstrating the power of knowing when to prepare ahead for what would change the direction of the business in the industry. Altogether, the network map represents the interlinked and interdisciplinary gravy of sustainable service marketing and virtual money. It manifests how original research, technological advancement, digital activity, practical usage, systemic integration, and future-looking innovation are linked together in order to build a comprehensive and dynamic framework. It illustrates the need for collaboration across industries and domains to resolve the challenges now and to grab the future opportunities in marketing normally spurred by sustainability.

4.4. Word Cloud

The "metaverse," "market," "sustainable," and "technology" would be central themes to the discourse on sustainable service marketing and virtual currencies through this word cloud visualization. These major terms thus indicate integration of emerging technologies as well as sustainability in marketing strategies toward the evolving needs of businesses and consumers. "Research" and "study" are major terms, thereby indicating foundational roles for academic inquiry and empirical analysis in the dynamics, setting actionable frameworks.

The word "digital" emphasizes the pervasiveness of digital transformation in most sectors, including tourism and consumer behavior, with concepts such as "consumer," "transformation," and "tourism" hinting at the need to enhance customer experiences and technology adaptation. The consonance with "technology," "artificial intelligence," and "blockchain" captures the increasing reliance on innovative tools and systems that push for sustainability and efficiency in service delivery. The themes "wellbeing," "experience," and "co-creation" suggest a human-centric orientation of sustainable marketing, whereby interactions with consumers, value-driven both in terms of satisfaction and social responsibility, are valued. Words like "economy", "integration" and "framework" also indicate that sustainability is being embedded in the larger economic systems and organizational strategies for longer term practical sustenance relevance.

Figure 5. Word cloud

[Source: Author's own work]

It is also forward-looking in its visualization, as the adjectives future, guideline and explore all suggest the hope of trends and being in front of/anticipating future strategies to confront them. This goes hand in hand with the more general objective of aligning technological advancements, like the metaverse, with sustainable principles to further innovation while being mindful of the global environmental and social concerns. The word cloud in short sums up the holistic view of interplay among research, technology, consumer behavior, and sustainability to define the field's interdisciplinary nature as well as the ability of this field to redefine the old paradigms of marketing. The interlinking aspect speaks for the necessity of balancing theory and practice toward impact and sustainability in a world in rapid motion.

5. DISCUSSION

Study on sustainable service marketing and virtual currencies illuminated how technological advancement co-evolves with sustainable business practices among those industries that are now accelerating into digital transformation (Mora et al. 2021). As one example, the metaverse and virtual currencies could redefine customer engagement and operational models in realms like the hospitality industry. To get to these customers, luxury hotel chains like Marriott are now making inroads in virtual spaces that allow potential guests to "walk through" rooms and facilities within the metaverse before making a reservation. Thus, this highlights how emerging technologies fill the gaps that link the abstract with tangible outcomes; that is, where digital transformation and enhanced customer experience meet. Moreover, blockchain for transparent loyalty programs and virtual currencies for cross-border payments without friction reinforce these applications. Word cluster analysis further confirms this by showing the amalgamation of theoretical constructs-in this case, sustainability and co-creation-better understood by their relationship with industry-specific solutions-gamification and enterprise tools. This confines not only to consumer demands based on ease and personalization but also to broader purposes such as making carbon footprints smaller through the virtualization process (Schulz 2016). This discussion brings out how business houses must change with consumer expectation and transform technology to evolve sustainable, effective, and foresighted service models.

6. FUTURE RESEARCH DIRECTION

Interestingly, virtual currencies and blockchain pose some critical challenges for sustainable marketing. The main challenges dealt with in the literature include regulatory uncertainty, technological constraints, and barriers to consumer acceptance. For instance, regulations relating to standardized usage of virtual currencies in marketing programs are available in very few countries only. Some other blockchain-based systems consume a lot of energy, making them unsustainable, which contradicts what is anticipated through blockchain-related sustainability. Problems, however, are also innovation opportunities. Such problems would necessitate blockchain solutions with extremely low energy levels, much more open and accessible policy frameworks, and also make the consumer far more educated about both the advantages and the ethics behind VCs and blockchain use. Therefore, all these problems, therefore, require a multidisciplinary engagement of policymakers, technologists, and marketers in search of a way forward on such issues.

Future studies in sustainable service marketing and digital currencies should focus further on the metaverse, blockchain technology, AI in service ecosystem integrating technology with long term consequences. With current research as well raising frameworks for the transformation impacts, both further outlines attention to key issues on scale, ethics and alter in consumer behaviour in different landscapes while accessing economic contexts. Future studies can approach DeFi as well as virtual currencies and investigate in depth what decentralized finance does to consumer trust, adoption in developing economies that are largely unbanked. Then the other kind of research is gamification and immersion in sustainable tourism, retail consumer behaviour. Another direction the researchers could address are environmental consequences of these technologies as well. They may debate how blockchain networks consume energy, while offering ways to reduce the carbon output Holda The inter-disciplinary answer from marketing and technology won even provide novel frameworks for co-creation value in both, digital as well as physical places is likely. It will bridge the gaps and be incredibly beneficial to future research by clarifying directions for policy-makers, business and technologists to develop sustainable, equitable and technologically advanced service ecosystems.

7. CONCLUSION

This study on sustainable service marketing and virtual currency shows that the future marketing strategies have to cope with emerging technologies like metaverse, blockchain and artificial intelligence are expected to upend industry and experiences at scale. Using lexicometric and factorial correspondence analysis, the study investigated how theoretical concepts link to applied cases in order to make explicit the complex and interdisciplinary nature of this research domain. The results highlight that there is an opportunity to bridge their gap via incorporation of digital tools in order market sustainably, engage consumer and create value co-creation from one side to another such as tourism, retail, finance etc. Yet, at the same time we also have to do this in a responsible way balancing ethical, cultural and environmental implications. Through future research to solve these challenges, business and policymakers can unlock the systematic potential of these technologies that lead into a more inclusive and ecologically sustainable global service ecosystem. This paper represents a foundational study that helps explore the nexus of technology, marketing, and sustainability and provides a compass for future exploration with innovation.

REFERENCES

Bibri, S. E., Alexandre, A., Sharifi, A., & Krogstie, J. (2023). Environmentally sustainable smart cities and their converging AI, IoT, and big data technologies and solutions: An integrated approach to an extensive literature review. *Energy Informatics*, *6*(1), 9. DOI: 10.1186/s42162-023-00259-2 PMID: 37032812

Ciasullo, M. V., Troisi, O., Grimaldi, M., & Leone, D. (2020). Multi-level governance for sustainable innovation in smart communities: An ecosystems approach. *The International Entrepreneurship and Management Journal*, *16*(4), 1167–1195. DOI: 10.1007/s11365-020-00641-6

Fernando, Y., Jabbour, C. J. C., & Wah, W. X. (2019). Pursuing green growth in technology firms through the connections between environmental innovation and sustainable business performance: Does service capability matter? *Resources, Conservation and Recycling*, *141*, 8–20. DOI: 10.1016/j.resconrec.2018.09.031

Francisco, K., & Swanson, D. (2018). The supply chain has no clothes: Technology adoption of blockchain for supply chain transparency. *Logistics (Basel)*, *2*(1), 2. DOI: 10.3390/logistics2010002

Golinelli, G. M., Barile, S., Saviano, M., & Polese, F. (2012). Perspective shifts in marketing: Toward a paradigm change? *Service Science*, *4*(2), 121–134. DOI: 10.1287/serv.1120.0015

Hasan, M. R., Islam, M. Z., Sumon, M. F. I., Osiujjaman, M., Debnath, P., & Pant, L. (2024). Integrating artificial intelligence and predictive analytics in supply chain management to minimize carbon footprint and enhance business growth in the USA. *Journal of Business and Management Studies*, *6*(4), 195–212. DOI: 10.32996/jbms.2024.6.4.17

Hur, W. M., Ahn, K. H., & Kim, M. (2011). Building brand loyalty through managing brand community commitment. *Management Decision*, *49*(7), 1194–1213. DOI: 10.1108/00251741111151217

Köhler, S., Bager, S., & Pizzol, M. (2022). Sustainability standards and blockchain in agro-food supply chains: Synergies and conflicts. *Technological Forecasting and Social Change*, *185*, 122094. DOI: 10.1016/j.techfore.2022.122094

Kotha, T., Amadae, S., & Rossi, M. (2024). Engaging consumers in sustainable behaviors using blockchain applications. In *Scandinavian Conference on Information Systems*. Association for Information Systems. DOI:https://research.aalto.fi/en/publications/engaging-consumers-in-sustainable-behaviors-using-blockchain-appl

Laroiya, C., Saxena, D., & Komalavalli, C. (2020). Applications of blockchain technology. In *Handbook of research on blockchain technology* (pp. 213–243). Academic press., DOI: 10.1016/B978-0-12-819816-2.00009-5

Mora, H., Morales-Morales, M. R., Pujol-López, F. A., & Mollá-Sirvent, R. (2021). Social cryptocurrencies as model for enhancing sustainable development. *Kybernetes, 50*(10), 2883–2916. DOI: 10.1108/K-05-2020-0259

O'Dair, M. (2018). Distributed creativity: How blockchain technology will transform the creative economy.

Paul, J., Lim, W. M., O'Cass, A., Hao, A. W., & Bresciani, S. (2021). Scientific procedures and rationales for systematic literature reviews (SPAR-4-SLR). *International Journal of Consumer Studies, 45*(4), O1–O16. DOI: 10.1111/ijcs.12695

Peterson, M., Minton, E. A., Liu, R. L., & Bartholomew, D. E. (2021). Sustainable marketing and consumer support for sustainable businsses. *Sustainable Production and Consumption, 27*, 157–168. DOI: 10.1016/j.spc.2020.10.018

Ratinaud, P. (2014). IRaMuTeQ: Interface de R pour les Analyses Multidimensionnelles de Textes et de Questionnaires (Version 0.7 alpha 2). En ligne: http://www. iramuteq. org (consulté le 8 janvier 2024).

Reinert, M. (1990). Alceste une méthodologie d'analyse des données textuelles et une application: Aurelia De Gerard De Nerval. *Bulletin of Sociological Methodology. Bulletin de Methodologie Sociologique, 26*(1), 24–54. DOI: 10.1177/075910639002600103

Schulz, G. (2016). *The green and virtual data center*. CRC Press. DOI: 10.1201/9781420086676

Sharma, N., & Manohar, S. (2024). Unlocking the Metaverse and Navigating Legal Implications in the NFT Landscape. In *Exploring the Use of Metaverse in Business and Education* (pp. 193–209). IGI Global., DOI: 10.4018/979-8-3693-5868-9.ch011

Singh, S., Sharma, P. K., Yoon, B., Shojafar, M., Cho, G. H., & Ra, I. H. (2020). Convergence of blockchain and artificial intelligence in IoT network for the sustainable smart city. *Sustainable Cities and Society, 63*, 102364. DOI: 10.1016/j.scs.2020.102364

Chapter 4

Harnessing Virtual Currencies to Transform Customer Experience:
Challenges and Opportunities in Sustainable Service Marketing

Manoj Govindaraj
https://orcid.org/0000-0003-2830-7875
VelTech Rangarajan Dr. Sagunthala R&D Institute of Science and Technology, Chennai, India

Ravishankar Krishnan
VelTech Rangarajan Dr. Sagunthala R&D Institute of Science and Technology, Chennai, India

L. Anitha
https://orcid.org/0009-0006-1868-2048
Saveetha Engineering College, Chennai, India

G. M. Shaju
MIANZ International College, Male', Maldives

Chandramowleeswaran Gnanasekaran
https://orcid.org/0000-0002-1293-1043
VelTech Rangarajan Dr. Sagunthala R&D Institute of Science and Technology, Chennai, India

Jenifer Lawrence
https://orcid.org/0000-0002-4115-1521
Woldia University, Ethiopia

ABSTRACT

The rise of virtual currencies has created new possibilities for sustainable service marketing, offering innovative ways to enhance customer experience while promoting eco-friendly practices. This paper explores how virtual currencies can be harnessed as a transformative tool to engage consumers in sustainable behaviors, foster brand loyalty, and drive green marketing initiatives. By analyzing the challenges and opportunities presented by virtual currencies in this domain, we highlight potential

DOI: 10.4018/979-8-3373-0315-4.ch004

strategies for overcoming obstacles such as regulatory uncertainty, trust issues, and technological barriers. Furthermore, we discuss the role of virtual currencies in promoting transparency, supporting circular economy models, and enabling eco-friendly rewards systems. This paper aims to provide insights into the integration of virtual currencies within sustainable service marketing frameworks, ultimately contributing to a greener and more customer-centric marketplace.

INTRODUCTION

Virtual currencies are bringing about a change in the course of service marketing. Through them, there are many ways to enhance customer experience but sustain it at the same time. Virtual currencies differ from the traditional monetary system as brands are provided with unique tools through which they can encourage sustainable behavior, foster greater customer loyalty, and incorporate more green initiatives into their business model. As consumers increasingly turn the corner towards sustainability, virtual currencies enable companies to connect with customers based on common values in the environment. The metaverse represents a new era of digital interaction, integrating extended reality technologies that offer immersive experiences with vast implications for various sectors, including marketing and retail (XVI International Scientific Conference, 2024).

Virtual currencies, based on blockchain technology, assure a transparent and secure transaction and are, therefore, imperative for building trust and responsibility. Virtual currencies support the idea of circular economy models that are sustainable in consumption and generate eco-friendly rewards; and businesses can differentiate themselves as part of a competitive green marketing environment. However, the challenges lie in unlocking virtual currencies to their full potential in sustainable service marketing. All these initiatives, therefore, require careful navigation in terms of regulatory uncertainty, technological barriers, and trust issues for such initiatives to be impactful and ethical.

This paper discusses the opportunities and barriers virtual currencies introduce into sustainable service marketing. Strategies in overcoming these barriers to create a greener and more customer-centric marketplace are discussed here.

BACKGROUND OF THE STUDY

This is the way digital technologies, sustainability, and customer experience are essentially transforming business operations across industries. Virtual currencies have become mighty instruments in this change to facilitate customer interaction and for businesses to push forward an eco-friendly practice. While digital assets increase, the firm can devise new offerings that encourage customer loyalty within the framework of sustainability strategies and thus establish a differential advantage in a competitive marketplace (Mora & Mollá-Sirvent, 2019; Buhalis et al., 2022). As innovations such as virtual currencies shape new avenues for customer engagement, understanding diverse stakeholder perspectives becomes essential for driving sustainable practices in service marketing (Krishnan et al., 2024).

Virtual currencies, thus connecting digital, physical, and social realms, are thereby challenging and providing opportunities to an organization to bridge different realities. According to the calls of Bolton et al., 2018 research that seeks reconciliation of the several different realms in developing experiences that are superior to customer perceptions, virtual currencies allow business house to design hybrid experiences. These improve customer interaction on every touch point, making brand loyalty and customer satisfaction more sustainable. Virtual currencies thus are employed to foster positive behaviors for the environment with the view of making a consumer align with brands with environmental stewardship. According to a World Economic Forum survey, demand for sustainable product purchases by consumers has risen 71% over the past decade. This trend actually reflects an increase in consumer preference for green products and services. Service innovation, when aligned with a positive corporate reputation, significantly enhances word-of-mouth impact, a dynamic applicable to the adoption of virtual currencies in sustainable service marketing (Manohar et al., 2020).

In the recent past, technology advancement has changed the entire customer experience landscape. On the one hand, increasing consumer expectations have been responding to the pace of this technological advancement. According to Purcărea and Purcarea (2017), successful service firms engage in the development of a relationship and loyalty through services marketing strategies. This marks the most important point for maximizing customer experience through the capture of data and its use to provide insights. The "Digital Transformation Initiative" (DTI) by the World Economic Forum reports that how an organization connects with its customers is changing, not just in the case of companies related to aviation and tourism but for any business firm across the globe. Organizations, according to the initiative, are turning to data-driven strategies as a means of strengthening their interaction with customers (2017).

The new technologies are including the Internet of Things, augmented reality, virtual reality, and artificial intelligence transforming the customer experience. The new journey of shopping creates an immersion of customer experiences and more personalisation appealing to their preferences according to Hoyer et al. (2020). When such technologies combine with virtual currencies, personalisation and the efficiency of the marketing approach will add a significant impetus toward co-creating value through increased engagement.

Nevertheless, acceptance of virtual currencies in sustainable service marketing does not come without challenges. Organizations face uncertainty in regulatory frameworks and must build trust with consumers while being certain of data privacy and ethical transparency. With consumers now increasingly aware of how their data is being used, business organizations must concentrate on being transparent in their practices in order to establish trust and loyalty (Kumar et al., 2019)

This study attempts to explore the role virtual currencies play in transforming sustainable service marketing by considering the opportunities and challenges. It advances knowledge on how virtual currencies may be used to create a more sustainable, customer-centric marketplace by investigating the nexus between digital currencies and experience of the customer.

EMPOWERING SUSTAINABLE CHOICE: THE ROLE OF VIRTUAL CURRENCIES IN SERVICE MARKETING

The virtual currency will shake the service marketing landscape since new avenues to interact with the customers are brought forth regarding sustainable practice. Virtual currencies refer to digital representations of value, which exist only in electronic environments; they can dramatically reduce the costs of transactions and increase the efficiency of service marketing. Business can offer better pricing and decrease environment impact that goes with traditional methods of payment processing if the intermediaries could be removed. This high efficiency is highly beneficial for small businesses and start-ups promoting sustainability through a low cost of operations. The transformative nature of digital currencies parallels other sectors where technology has driven fundamental changes, indicating a similar potential for revolutionizing sustainability in service marketing (Govindaraj et al., 2024).

Besides, through marketing virtual currencies, companies can directly reach their consumers. Companies can encourage customers by offering loyalty rewards and discounts for use of virtual currencies. Such approaches favor sustainably purchasing behavior, and also users who share the same values in regard to sustainability and innovation can develop social links. This provides underbanked populations with a source of finance in cases where they lack the banking infrastructure, thereby affording them participation in the economy and broadening the customer base for businesses committed to inclusive practices.

The second is that firms embracing virtual currencies can provide new service models that are sustainable. Companies using blockchain can show the sustainability characteristics of their products or services publicly and therefore build consumers' trust and compel other firms to follow a similar approach. However, though the benefits are tremendous, there are several issues. The unregulated status of virtual currencies poses a threat related to security and legality issues, which companies must resolve. Many virtual currencies are volatile; hence they may discourage people from adopting them as steady payment systems. Companies therefore have to think about this fact when formulating their marketing strategies. Additionally, virtual currencies are forms of digital assets and can be hacked easily and fraudulent activities may be performed upon them; therefore, such currencies require more security measures regarding assets and customer information. Resilient and adaptable service organizations are better positioned to integrate sustainable practices, such as virtual currency incentives, to meet evolving consumer demands for environmental responsibility (Nair et al., 2024). Combine repeated ideas about how virtual currencies promote green loyalty and consumer engagement. For instance, consolidate the points on how brands like H&M and Natura use these strategies into a single cohesive paragraph within the subsection on "Case Examples: Brands Utilizing Virtual Currencies for Green Loyalty."

Virtual currencies hold much potential in empowering responsible choices in service marketing. They help transform the marketing landscape into a responsible practice through efficient transactions, enhanced consumer engagement, financial inclusion, and sustainability of business models. Businesses will have to face such challenges related to regulation, volatility, and cyber security before unlocking the full potential of virtual currencies in their marketing strategy.

RESEARCH QUESTION

Determine how virtual currencies can be best utilized in the development of customer experience through sustainable practices in service marketing in the face of challenges

Objective

This article pursues the exploration of how virtual currencies can be harnessed to transform customer experience and promote sustainable service marketing. Specific objectives include:

- Analyze how virtual currencies can be used to change customer experiences and develop engagement and loyalty in sustainable service marketing initiatives.

- To identify the regulatory uncertainty and trust issues with technological problems that will constrain the acceptance of virtual currency in sustainable marketing practices, and then evaluate these factors.
- Research and explore the use of virtual currencies to promote green loyalty and transparent marketing initiatives aligned with the principles of the circular economy.
- Whether virtual currencies can influence consumer behavior towards sustainability through an increased level of participation in green marketing and eco-friendly practices.

METHODOLOGY

This paper, "Exploring the Role of Virtual Currencies in Promoting Green Loyalty and Sustainability: Implications for Consumer Behavior and Business Strategy," uses an elaborative review of current literature, research articles, and case studies to achieve its objectives. Virtual currencies in business usage may promote sustainable consumer behavior, enhance loyalty, and encourage environmentally responsible marketing campaigns. The key areas of research are to investigate how virtual currencies may be integrated into green loyalty schemes and the regulatory and trust-related issues that influence adoption.

This real-world case study has opportunities and challenges in the application of incentives that are digital for favorable action. The study focuses significantly on blockchain in transparency, data analytics in consumer engagement tracking, and gamification as a push towards higher participation. As a result, this approach gives an all-inclusive view of how virtual currencies affect green loyalty and sustainable marketing strategies, offering insights that can be handy to businesses and policymakers alike.

LEVERGING VIRTUAL CURRENCIES TO ENHANCE CUSTOMER EXPERIENCE AND LOYALITY IN SUSTAINABLE SERVICE MARKETING

Virtual currencies refer mostly to digital assets or tokens designed to be used in a fully networked environment as representations of value. Relations between businesses and customers are significantly changed with the use of this new medium. Virtual currencies are indeed a new source of rewarding and engaging with people in innovative ways: they are being used, for example, as part of a new medium toward loyalty and personalized consumer experiences in a brand. Virtual currencies are an attractive tool to support this alignment between the brand and sustainable practice in the realm of sustainable service marketing, as these digital assets can help enhance deeper customer relationships and raise engagement and loyalty, together with sustainable values. Aligning innovative strategies in customer loyalty with sustainability goals requires a forward-thinking approach, as seen in the development of leadership strategies for the innovation economy (Krishnan et al., 2024).

Building Customer Experience through Virtual Currencies

Virtual currencies will allow a high level of elevation in customer experience through the unique value provision in an interactive way. For instance, digital money helps execute cashless transactions fluently so that the consumer could carry on with the transaction quite smoothly and easily. Virtual money could be designed for the purposes of incentive schemes, rewards, exclusive access, or access that would appeal to customer's interests-so customers could develop a more personalized affinity to a brand. This unique value proposition improves the customer's experience, differentiates brands in competitive markets, and makes them prominent, especially for those businesses that emphasize service initiatives aligned with sustainability.

Virtual Currencies for Encouraging Customer Loyalty

Offering virtual currencies as incentives for loyalty can encourage greater engagement from customers through programs promoting environmentally responsible behaviors or patronage loyalty. With digital loyalty programs, customers earn virtual currency points or tokens through recycling, purchasing sustainable products, or participating in green initiatives. Those points can be redeemed for discounts, exclusive offers, or even donations to environmental causes. Brand values are thus matched with customer incentives. This approach encourages loyalty but forces customers to behave in ways that are pro-environmental, thereby establishing a virtuous circle both for the business and for the environment. Ganesan, P., & Sridhar, M. (2016). Service innovation and customer performance of telecommunication service provider: A study on mediation effect of corporate reputation. Corporate Reputation Review, 19(1), 77-101.

Role of Virtual Currencies in Sustainable Service Marketing

Sustainable service marketing helps in responsible consumption and minimizes environmental effects as well as supports ethical conducts. Virtual currencies present brands with a chance to tie sustainability into their engagement of customers through rewarding them with eco-friendly behavior. By giving virtual currencies to the consumers for their sustainability behavior, such as selecting an alternative that is more environmentally friendly or reducing waste, brands can encourage positive consumption and enforce their agenda of sustainability. This linkage of virtual currency rewards and sustainable goals sets a brand equity based on environmental stewardship and attracts customers who feel aligned with the concept of living sustainably. The metaverse represents a new era of digital interaction, integrating extended reality technologies that offer immersive experiences with vast implications for various sectors, including marketing and retail (XVI International Scientific Conference, 2024). Different typologies of service innovation, such as virtual currency rewards, can serve as powerful tools for enhancing consumer engagement within the framework of sustainable service marketing (Manohar & Kapur, 2019).

Advantages and Disadvantages of Virtual Currencies for Sustainable Marketing

The use of virtual currencies in sustainable marketing may bring about several benefits, such as customer loyalty, brand differentiation, and positive brand perception. However, there are challenges, including regulatory uncertainty, trust issues, and technological barriers. Some customers may not be willing to adopt virtual currencies because they do not know them or fear data privacy. Transcending these issues will be made possible by the transparency of virtual currency programs by brands, a clear value proposition, and educating customers about the merits of participation in such an innovative loyalty systems. AI and big data analytics, integrated with decision support systems, are transforming finance and customer service by delivering data-driven decision-making capabilities crucial to the digital economy (Priyanka et al., 2024)."

Successful Integration in Customer Experience and Loyalty Examples

Many companies have successfully utilized virtual currencies to develop customer engagement and loyalty. For instance, fashion and electronics brands have created virtual currency programs that reward consumers for activities such as recycling old products or selecting environmentally friendly packaging. The case studies will be of interest and practice, demonstrating that a thoughtful integration of virtual currencies will result in greater loyalty, stronger customer relationships, and a more dominant brand presence in the sustainable market.

Future Virtual Currencies in Sustainable Marketing

Virtual currencies, no matter how mainstream they have been growing into, are very likely to gain more and further speed into sustainable service marketing. For instance, it has increased the transparency as well as the security that it offers with the help of the blockchain technology, which is said to foster more usage as well as trust on the virtual currencies by customers in the future. Virtual currencies, for instance, would most likely play the lead role in encouraging higher participation of customers in such a new loyalty program on behalf of the eco-friendly activities that can be done in the near future. This can help brands build a foundational loyalty that supports both satisfaction and sustainability goals by following the changing values of these environmentally-conscious consumers.

Virtual currencies are going to change customer engagement and loyalty through sustainable marketing frameworks. This will attract customers to such brands who want to create a positive impact on the environment by rewarding them with digital rewards, which are eco-friendly in nature. Therefore, customer values, transparency, and compliance with regulatory requirements would become vital to the successful implementation of virtual currency programs. As business innovation continues, virtual currencies may become the cornerstones of sustainable service marketing, resulting in a win-win situation for businesses, customers, and the environment. Strategic innovation planning is crucial for aligning sustainability with consumer incentives, as firms navigate complex new loyalty frameworks (Krishnan et al., 2024).

ADDRESSING REGULATORY UNCERTAINTY AND TRUST ISSUES IN THE ADOPTION OF VIRTUAL CURRENCIES FOR SUSTAINABLE MARKETING

Virtual currencies refer mostly to digital assets or tokens designed to be used in a fully networked environment as representations of value. Relations between businesses and customers are significantly changed with the use of this new medium. Virtual currencies are indeed a new source of rewarding and engaging with people in innovative ways: they are being used, for example, as part of a new medium toward loyalty and personalized consumer experiences in a brand. Virtual currencies are an attractive tool to support this alignment between the brand and sustainable practice in the realm of sustainable service marketing, as these digital assets can help enhance deeper customer relationships and raise engagement and loyalty, together with sustainable values.

Building Customer Experience through Virtual Currencies

Virtual currencies will allow a high level of elevation in customer experience through the unique value provision in an interactive way. For instance, digital money helps execute cashless transactions fluently so that the consumer could carry on with the transaction quite smoothly and easily. Virtual money could be designed for the purposes of incentive schemes, rewards, exclusive access, or access that would appeal to customer's interests-so customers could develop a more personalized affinity to a brand. This unique value proposition improves the customer's experience, differentiates brands in competitive markets, and makes them prominent, especially for those businesses that emphasize service initiatives aligned with sustainability.

Virtual Currencies for Encouraging Customer Loyalty

Offering virtual currencies as incentives for loyalty can encourage greater engagement from customers through programs promoting environmentally responsible behaviors or patronage loyalty. With digital loyalty programs, customers earn virtual currency points or tokens through recycling, purchasing sustainable products, or participating in green initiatives. Those points can be redeemed for discounts, exclusive offers, or even donations to environmental causes. Brand values are thus matched with customer incentives. This approach encourages loyalty but forces customers to behave in ways that are pro-environmental, thereby establishing a virtuous circle both for the business and for the environment.

Role of Virtual Currencies in Sustainable Service Marketing

Sustainable service marketing helps in responsible consumption and minimizes environmental effects as well as supports ethical conducts. Virtual currencies present brands with a chance to tie sustainability into their engagement of customers through rewarding them with eco-friendly behavior. By giving virtual currencies to the consumers for their sustainability behavior, such as selecting an alternative that is more environmentally friendly or reducing waste, brands can encourage positive consumption and enforce their agenda of sustainability. This linkage of virtual currency rewards and sustainable goals sets a brand equity based on environmental stewardship and attracts customers who feel aligned with the concept of living sustainably.

Advantages and Disadvantages of Virtual Currencies for Sustainable Marketing

The use of virtual currencies in sustainable marketing may bring about several benefits, such as customer loyalty, brand differentiation, and positive brand perception. However, there are challenges, including regulatory uncertainty, trust issues, and technological barriers. Some customers may not be willing to adopt virtual currencies because they do not know them or fear data privacy. Transcending these issues will be made possible by the transparency of virtual currency programs by brands, a clear value proposition, and educating customers about the merits of participation in such an innovative loyalty systems.

Successful Integration in Customer Experience and Loyalty Examples

Many companies have successfully utilized virtual currencies to develop customer engagement and loyalty. For instance, fashion and electronics brands have created virtual currency programs that reward consumers for activities such as recycling old products or selecting environmentally friendly packaging. The case studies will be of interest and practice, demonstrating that a thoughtful integration of virtual currencies will result in greater loyalty, stronger customer relationships, and a more dominant brand presence in the sustainable market

Example from Hospitality Industry: Marriott's pilot program offering guests rewards for sustainable behavior, such as choosing eco-friendly housekeeping options.
Example from Food Industry: Starbucks Rewards allowing consumers to earn points for sustainable purchases like reusable cup usage.

Future Virtual Currencies in Sustainable Marketing

Virtual currencies, no matter how mainstream they have been growing into, are very likely to gain more and further speed into sustainable service marketing. For instance, it has increased the transparency as well as the security that it offers with the help of the blockchain technology, which is said to foster more usage as well as trust on the virtual currencies by customers in the future. Virtual currencies, for instance, would most likely play the lead role in encouraging higher participation of customers in such a new loyalty program on behalf of the eco-friendly activities that can be done in the near future. This can help brands build a foundational loyalty that supports both satisfaction and sustainability goals by following the changing values of these environmentally-conscious consumers.

Virtual currencies are going to change customer engagement and loyalty through sustainable marketing frameworks. This will attract customers to such brands who want to create a positive impact on the environment by rewarding them with digital rewards, which are eco-friendly in nature. Therefore, customer values, transparency, and compliance with regulatory requirements would become vital to the successful implementation of virtual currency programs. As business innovation continues, virtual currencies may become the cornerstones of sustainable service marketing, resulting in a win-win situation for businesses, customers, and the environment.

Fostering Green Loyalty: Virtual Currencies as Drivers for Transparent and Circular Economy-Aligned Marketing Initiatives

Green loyalty programs reward customers for sustainable behavior in support of broader environmental goals. Virtual currencies, as digital tokens or points, have emerged as a valuable tool for such programs, encouraging consumers to adopt sustainable practices. With virtual currencies integrated into green loyalty initiatives, brands can establish long-term relationships with customers based on shared values around the environment and help to support circular economy principles through transparent, impactful engagement.

Alignment of Virtual Currencies with the Principles of the Circular Economy

The circular economy is meant to promote waste reduction, longer lives for products, and higher recycling rates-all objectives which are in tune with incentives offered by virtual currencies for green loyalty programs. This includes rewarding a consumer for recycling used products, making sustainable packaging choices, or buying refurbished products. These incentives not only encourage circular behavior but also enable consumers to directly participate in sustainable consumption practices. As the Ellen MacArthur Foundation puts it, aligning business practices with the circular economy may lead to waste reduction and increased resource efficiency, making virtual currencies a practical tool for promoting such objectives.

Transparency in Green Loyalty Programs Using Virtual Currencies

The key benefits of virtual currencies in green loyalty programs include transparency, especially in blockchain-based virtual currencies. These enable the tracking of customers' actions and rewards for their environmentally friendly actions, thus maintaining a verifiable record of efforts towards sustainability. Transparency generates trust because customers can observe the direct impact of participation. For instance, a brand might utilize blockchain to verify the reward points generated from recycling or green purchases a customer has made. The customer should, therefore be able to redeem them at will. In 2022, PwC published a report showing 70% of consumers claim transparency matters when purchasing products hence the use of virtual currency may help instill confidence in this respect.

Case Examples: Brands Utilizing Virtual Currencies for Green Loyalty

Some companies have added virtual currencies to their green loyalty programs and have been successful with them. For example, H&M's "LoopThe author commends H&M's 'Loop' program for seamlessly integrating virtual currencies into its sustainability initiatives. By aligning consumer incentives with environmental goals, H&M demonstrates a practical and scalable model for fostering green loyalty." rewards customers with virtual points when they recycle old clothes, and those points are redeemable for discounts on sustainable products. Natura, a cosmetics company, encourages its customers to fill up their containers and recycle the plastics by giving them virtual tokens for future purchases. The author appreciates Natura's innovative approach in incentivizing eco-friendly consumer behaviors through refillable packaging. This not only reduces plastic waste but also reinforces the brand's commitment to sustainability. All case studies will show the feasibility of virtual currencies to create sustained consumer behavior and hence induce brand loyalty as well as encourage the circular economy.

The Advantages of Virtual Currencies Lie in the Following Respects

Virtual currencies are relatively simple to use as a factor for green loyalty by their convenience in earning, tracking and redeeming points of ecological actions that will facilitate stronger customer engagement. Virtual currencies can also boost the brand image through showing care about the environment, thereby attracting environmental-sensitive consumers. In fact, a recent Deloitte survey has indicated that

63% of millennials would support brands that could clearly show their commitment to sustainability, and as such, virtual currency programs could greatly influence customer loyalty and branding perception.

Challenges in the Adoption of Virtual Currencies for Green Loyalty

Indeed, virtual currencies represent promising tools for green loyalty, though there is considerable challenge in putting it to work in practice. The author commends ongoing research efforts that bridge consumer behavior and virtual currency adoption, emphasizing the critical role of education in fostering greater participation in green loyalty programs." Brands are going to require significant system infrastructure to track and cash in on their rewards while also investing considerable money on technology and data management infrastructure. Regulatory barriers and distrust will be two of the challenges brands must look beyond because consumers will hesitate to engage with new digital assets. "Blockchain, while crucial for ensuring transparency, poses challenges related to energy consumption and scalability. Recent studies highlight the need for energy-efficient blockchain solutions to reduce the carbon footprint associated with virtual currencies. Metrics such as energy consumption per transaction and lifecycle impact assessments could guide businesses in selecting sustainable blockchain technologies." All these issues require proper planning, open communication, and sometimes third-party partners to ensure safe transactions.

Virtual Currencies in Green Marketing: Future Prospects

Virtual currencies are going to play an increasingly important role in green loyalty and marketing programs as the pressure from consumers on companies to adopt more sustainable practices increases. Technology will advance with the use of blockchain, and virtual currencies can be even more transparent, accountable, and scalable for green initiatives. Further, as more brands embrace the circular economy, virtual currencies could standardize across industries, making it possible for customers to earn and redeem green loyalty points across several eco-conscious brands. This future potential speaks to the value of virtual currencies in enabling sustainable behavior on a broader scale.

Virtual currencies are a powerful path toward green loyalty and concomitant alignment with principles of the circular economy for brands. Rewarding environmentally positive actions in a clear way and engaging customers into pro-environmental practice help strengthen customer relationships through a responsible consumption process, leading to responsible consumption processes, while still leaving areas that need improvement. There will always be challenges involved. However, early movers will create a new paradigm regarding their impacts on green marketing processes to be used by many environmental-conscious consumers today.

INFLUENCING CONSUMER BEHAVIOR TOWARDS SUSTAINABILITY: THE ROLE OF VIRTUAL CURRENCIES IN PROMOTING ECO-FRIENDLY PRACTICES

Because more and more people are conscious of the effects of their behavior, business is in a hunt for innovative means of supporting sustainable behavior. Virtual currencies can be the next effective tool to inspire the customers towards sustainable behaviors because, like digital tokens or points, they represent the cash of loyalty programs. With incentives for good ecological action, virtual currencies have the ability to steer customer behavior toward better sustainable options. This model covers how virtual currencies apply incentives to encouraging eco-friendly behavior, the effectiveness of this method in altering the purchase habits of consumers, and its relevance to bigger sustainability goals.

Virtual Currencies and Sustainability: Conceptualization

Virtual currencies in the sustainable marketing realm have been defined as electronic tokens or points that consumers can earn and redeem based on their activities in alignment with environmental values. For example, for recycling, the use of fewer plastics, or choosing green products, customers can gain virtual tokens to be used for discounts or rewards. Virtual currencies do not only make sustainable choices appealing but also make customers believe environmental responsibility as a rewarding experience. The approach taps into behavioral economics, using rewards to positively reinforce green actions, and ultimately fosters loyalty and habit formation.

Incentives to Shape Consumer Behavior

Virtual currencies are a pragmatic incentive for a greener behavior. The direct, tangible rewards provided by virtual currencies do indeed shape consumer behavior. According to research in behavioral psychology, incentives are essential for habit formation because people tend to acquire new behaviors only when they are rewarded meaningfully. Attach a value to sustainable actions, for instance, reusing materials or buying eco-friendly products and brands will entice customers to adopt those behaviors as part of their personal habits. According to Accenture, 72% will continue to use the same brands if they find that said brands reflect their environmental values, making virtual currency-based rewards a very strong platform on which to base behavior changes. "Behavioral economics principles, such as those outlined by Richard Thaler, emphasize the importance of immediate, tangible rewards in encouraging sustainable behaviors. Virtual currencies align with these principles by making eco-friendly actions more appealing and habitual."

Cases of businesses that have already taken action, using virtual currencies in programs to promote the transition of consumers toward more responsible practices. Examples include a few companies: Recyclebank, for instance, lets people earn points when people recycle and can later cash it in at local businesses and outlets. Allbirds established a "Tree Token," which gives digital awards from purchases of low-carbon items, thus encouraging responsible decisions. Natura is also a brand in the cosmetics company that promises virtual rewards if customers can refill their containers or stop producing plastic wastes. As it is witnessed, those kinds of initiatives have actually helped encourage some aspects of consumers to go about their businesses in a cleaner way; hence, proving that virtual currencies are one useful tool when a brand considers sustainability part of the customer's life.

Virtual Currencies and Environment

Virtual currencies, therefore, not only induce personal actions but also bring a reduction in the aggregate environment impact by encouraging sustainable consumption. Rewarding action in recycling, eco-friendly product purchases, and waste reduction ensures that customer incentives align with environmental benefits. The World Economic Forum also highlighted in a report that the consumer demand to have sustainable products has already gone up 71 percent from the past decade alone. This will surely be beneficial to any programs that couple ecological behavior with customer loyalty.

Virtual currencies can offer rewards to consumers that lower their carbon footprints as well as minimize the amount of wastes and pollutants released into the environment. As such, the larger objectives of supporting a cleaner and greener planet can be achieved within a program designed to answer consumer expectations.

Virtual Currency Marketing Strategies End

Virtual currencies should be incorporated as a part of a brand's overall eco-friendly marketing program for peak performance. In this way, alignment enables virtual currency programs to be in line with the customer's mindset, serving as a reiteration of the brand's environmental values at each touchpoint. For example, brands can establish green messaging within their virtual currency programs and how customer activities relate to sustainability goals. In addition, the brands could use this program to display certain eco-friendly products being sold to the consumer and make a better-informed choice. According to secondary data from PwC, 65 percent of consumers prefer companies that are clear and transparent regarding their efforts related to the environment; it brings to focus how imperative it is for the programs of virtual currency to be in sync with pure, eco-friendly messages.

Virtual Currency Programs and Trust and Transparency

For virtual currencies to influence the behavior of consumers, brands must have trust and transparency in the way that the programs function. A blockchain technology applied to trace virtual currency transactions can, therefore, transparently follow customer actions as well as reward allocations, thus being reassuring to the customers regarding their eco-friendly actions to contribute to efforts toward sustainability and preventing a problem such as point inflation or rewards mismanagement. A report by Deloitte shows that 68 percent of consumers feel confident more in brands that are transparent during their operations, meaning therefore that trust is an excellent determinant of the success and failure of virtual currency schemes for sustainable marketing.

Opportunities and Challenges when Implementing Virtual Currencies for Sustainable Behavior Change. Technical barriers may also be imposed on brands as blockchain or other tracing technologies might be needed to provide protection and transparency. Customers might, however also despise virtual currencies because of un-familiarity or lack of knowledge regarding data privacy. Brands will need to enlighten consumers on the advantages of virtual currencies but provide full disclosure of data security guarantees. Moreover, brands will have to invest in collaborations with fintech or blockchain companies that can create robust, scalable virtual currency systems that handle massive customer bases and sustain long-term engagement.

Consumer Acceptance and Behavioral Understanding

Research indicates that consumers are receptive to virtual currency programs, especially within the environmentally conscious demographic. Millennials and Gen Z prefer brands that support the cause of sustainability and rewards them for eco-friendly actions. Nielsen's report shows that 73 percent of Gen Z consumers agreed to pay more for sustainable products-an indication of will in terms of virtual currency programs that prefer environmentally friendly behavior. In terms of these values, virtual currencies place themselves at the crux of brands' sustainability efforts to win the affection of younger audiences adopting sustainability as a core determinant when making purchase decisions.

Extended Impact of Virtual Currencies on Sustainable Consumer Behavior

Virtual currencies can thus trigger a positive feedback mechanism that promotes sustainable behavior change. For example, when customers are rewarded for repeating their eco-friendly actions, they will be motivated to continue the same behavior, and as time goes by, they begin to develop sustainable habits. Eventually, this practice could lead to considerable behavioral modification in consumers, which further supports a responsible consumption culture. The findings of behavioral studies recommend that incentives have to be consistently meaningful for long-lasting habits, meaning virtual currencies are continuous adaptive rewards, not one-time incentives.

Future of Virtual Currencies in Eco-Friendly Marketing

Virtual currencies will gradually become more integral to the eco-friendly marketing and the involvement of consumers. Advances in blockchain and fintech technologies will make virtual currencies more accessible, more transparent, and much safer for consumers. Consumer confidence in the programs further solidifies due to these same reasons. "Expanding interoperable virtual currency systems that work across industries could foster a circular economy on a broader scale. By integrating blockchain technologies designed for minimal energy consumption, brands can align their virtual currency programs with global sustainability goals. This approach addresses the dual challenges of consumer trust and environmental impact." As sustainability evolves to become a business mantra, virtual currencies are poised to be more adopted broadly and create cross-industry systems allowing consumers to earn and redeem their green rewards across different brands. This integrated approach might have a multiplier effect on virtual currencies, and their adoption would be part and parcel of the larger phenomenon of sustainable consumer behavior.

Virtual currencies are a force to be reckoned with in terms of nudging consumers toward eco-friendly behaviors. They provide incentives aligned with the increasing environmental sensitivity of customers. Virtual currencies provide brands with the opportunity to activate consumers in meaningful and impactful ways by rewarding sustainable action and building long-term loyalty. However challenging these are in terms of the technology and consumer education, it is evident that virtual currencies are driving sustainable behavior. The more that brands embrace these programs, the more virtual currencies will form part of eco-friendly marketing strategies that will influence the behaviors of consumers and foster global movements towards sustainability.

DISSCUSION

Virtual currencies have emerged as a revolutionary way of stimulating sustainable consumer behavior through loyalty programs. Digital currencies, mainly in the form of tokens or points, are unique mechanisms for brands to incentivize eco-friendly actions among consumers. In this way, virtual currencies create direct incentives by rewarding behaviors like recycling or choosing sustainable products. This is in line with the theories of behavioral economics, especially positive reinforcement theory, which holds that people tend to repeat behavior that brings rewarding results. The more conscious consumers become about the environment, the more they seek brands that are aligned with their values; virtual currencies can therefore facilitate more intimate relationships between consumers and sustainability-oriented brands.

The introduction of blockchain technology into these virtual currency systems adds more transparency, thus instilling trust in the virtual currency systems. Blockchain can provide a secure and verifiable record of consumer transactions, The author commends the use of blockchain technology as a cornerstone for transparency in virtual currency programs. This innovation significantly enhances consumer trust and sets a benchmark for ethical practices in sustainable marketing hence allowing customers to track their eco-friendly activities and their corresponding rewards. This will help consumers avoid skepticism when corporate sustainability claims appear. It has been ascertained that 71% of the consumers are bound to favor the brands where sustainability efforts are transparent and verifiable. It will enable consumers to check the inputs made in terms of sustainability. Hence, brands can strengthen loyalty and differentiate from competitors better.

However, there are a few barriers that must be overcome for virtual currencies to be effectively integrated into the loyalty systems. The biggest one is the technological infrastructure that would host such systems. Hence, brands have to invest in secured platforms for managing transactions with virtual currencies and ensure data privacy compliance to support such programs. This requirement can be particularly challenging for smaller businesses with limited resources. In addition, consumer resistance may arise due to unfamiliarity with digital currencies and concerns regarding data privacy and security. Thus, appropriate consumer education on the benefits and workings of virtual currency programs becomes essential in order to make them more acceptable and participatory.

Indeed, life examples show how virtual currencies work into the realization of green loyalty. Companies such as IKEA and Recyclebank have already used this program and both paid off through rewarding consumers for following sustainable activities. For instance, a system like "Green Rewards" by IKEA encourages a consumer to buy sustainably sourced products by using virtual points to redeem discounts on future purchases. On the other hand, Recyclebank offers rewards to people who recycle and participate in local environmental programs, effectively fostering green behavior through digital incentives.

Virtual currencies appear to hold bright promise for developing sustainability initiatives in the future. The brands are very likely to come up with very innovative ways of using virtual currencies across the various industry sectors over time. For example, with interoperable virtual currency systems, consumers can earn and redeem rewards across different brands, making each individual's sustainable actions even more impactful. According to research, millennials and Gen Z consumers are extremely receptive to brands that demonstrate an environmental commitment, so virtual currencies are a good fit for increasing brand loyalty among these groups.

Conclusion: Virtual currencies are a good leverage for green loyalty, ensuring sustainable consumer behavior. If incentives for eco-friendly behavior can be created, as well as transparency via blockchain, then brands can really interact with consumers while building trust. Although such challenges exist, the virtues associated with virtual currencies, including increased loyalty through customers and support of sustainable initiatives, are too grand to be ignored. Tackling innovation through strategy and adaptability will help place virtual currencies at the center of sustainable marketing campaigns-a call to action among consumers and a contribution toward a future that is more sustainable.

MAIN FINDINGS

Virtual Currencies as Rewards to Sustainable Behavior

Virtual currencies have emerged as a practical tool to encourage sustainable consumption behavior. Rewarding practices such as recycling, purchases of sustainable products, and participation in green activities make environmental responsibility something rewarding. Behavioral economics suggests that people are encouraged to repeat the action if it leads to tangible rewards: positive reinforcement. This dynamic encourages people to adopt more sustainable habits and deepens commitment to environmentally friendly practices, thus aligning consumer behavior with sustainability goals.

Trust through Transparency

Blockchain technology is crucial in enhancing the trustworthiness of virtual currency programs. It allows consumers to track their eco-friendly actions and the rewards they earn through a decentralized and immutable record of transactions. This is because such transparency is paramount in this age of high consumer skepticism toward corporate assertions of sustainability. According to various studies, 71% of consumers prefer brands that have verifiable sustainability efforts. Therefore, embedding blockchain within virtual currencies creates consumer confidence while helping brands take the lead in executing sustainability initiatives.

Challenges on Implementation

Despite the great potential of virtual currencies, several challenges lie ahead of them in widespread adoption into sustainable marketing practices. The major challenges are that the technological infrastructure needed for such programs is resource-intensive and difficult to implement, especially for smaller businesses. Consumers may also resist this system because of unfamiliarity with digital currencies and issues about data privacy and security. To overcome these challenges, brands must focus on consumer education; they should clearly communicate the benefits and security measures of virtual currency programs to achieve acceptance and participation.

Success Stories in Real Life

Many companies have integrated virtual currencies into their sustainability initiatives successfully, and it is useful to take their case studies as a basis for further action. Examples include "Green Rewards" from IKEA that rewards clients who purchase items sustainably sourced by offering them virtual points redeemable for discounted buys. A similar concept is used in Recyclebank, except that it bases its concept on rewarding people to recycle as well as take up some of the environmental-friendly local initiatives. The above example clearly shows that the implementation of virtual currencies enhances consumers' engagement and loyalty while implementing sustainability.

Virtual Currencies in the Future: A Sustainable Perspective

Moving forward, virtual currencies offer tremendous potential to drive sustainable initiatives. Brands will have more innovative applications of virtual currencies across industries as technology keeps advancing. For example, interoperable virtual currency systems can be designed to facilitate consumers' earning and redeeming rewards across different brands, amplifying the individual sustainable actions taken. Such interrelated systems would not only boost customer involvement but encourage a more general investment in sustainability at the market level.

Target Younger Shoppers

Younger shoppers are increasingly interested in green practices and are more likely to support brands that agree with their sustainable environmental considerations. Such research has shown that these consumers are willing to pay extra for sustainable products and would be more loyal to a brand that is responsible to the environment. Virtual currencies can be an effective method through which brands can reach out to such consumers by making rewards align with their preferences on sustainability. Thus, strategic use of virtual currencies can enhance customer relationships and create long-term loyalty among environmentally conscious consumers.

SUGGESTIONS

Expanded Consumer Awareness Study

Analyze current consumer awareness about virtual currencies and their relationship to sustainability. This may be through a survey or focus groups to understand the perceptions and knowledge gaps about digital currencies in an ecological context.

Longitudinal Studies

Longitudinal studies to examine whether consumer behavior and loyalty change with virtual currency incentives over time. By tracking participants longitudinally, you will have a better understanding of whether the engagement in sustainable practices that you initiate is sustained or if the virtual currencies have an impact on loyalty over time.

Cross-Industry Comparisons

Discuss how other industries use virtual currencies and the extent of success enjoyed by their programs in terms of promoting sustainability. In comparative terms, what best practices are found within industries that have some industry-specific issues?

Analyze changes in consumer behavior toward virtual currency programs using data analytics. Data analytics on transaction history may identify patterns such as which incentives work best at creating sustainable choices and consumer demographics influencing the engagement levels.

Social Media Integration

An evaluation of the roles of social media in promoting virtual currency initiatives and green loyalty. Branding companies can use this type of digital marketing to gain insight into how social channels may be leveraged to build awareness and engagement for sustainability initiatives.

Evaluation of the Regulatory Framework

Assess the regulatory systems pertinent to virtual currencies and green initiatives. Knowledge of the legal landscape will allow businesses to know what is needed for compliance and what may serve as an impediment to virtual currency initiatives.

Partnerships with NGOs

Consider also partnering with NGOs working on sustainability areas to increase credibility and visibility further. This will help to maximize the effectiveness of virtual currencies through associations with established sustainability development initiatives.

Development of Educational Programs

Develop educational materials or workshops focused on consumers and businesses to educate them about the benefits and how virtual currencies operate in sustainability efforts, aiming to bridge knowledge gaps and trigger wider acceptance and participation. Consumer Behavioral Economics: More insights on behavioral economics principles tied to incentives and sustainability (e.g., works by Richard Thaler).

Broader Case Studies: Expanding examples beyond fashion and retail to include industries like hospitality or food services could demonstrate the versatility of virtual currencies.
Updated Blockchain Literature: Adding recent studies on blockchain's role in transparency and sustainability would reinforce the claims about its significance.
Sustainability Metrics: Incorporating references on metrics for measuring the environmental impact of virtual currencies (e.g., carbon footprints of blockchain systems).
Technological Barriers: Further discussion on overcoming blockchain-related energy consumption issues would address critical challenges.

Explore Gamification Methods

Examine how gamification can positively influence customer interface of a program on virtual currencies: Utilizing design components based on playing while creating specific competition/challenge would motivate more and appropriate involvement that, in turn make consumers to care for some environmental friendly.

Establish a set of key metrics measuring the state of success level regarding the programme of sustainability on the utilisation of virtual currencies: part of the virtual economy systems. Sustainability success criteria, being helpful benchmark criteria result from proper definition of success criteria as this enables finding and following the businesses' levels, which regards the contribution, concerning some new undertaking while having impacts on current performances 11. Green Output Calculation

Discuss the impacts of virtual currencies themselves with regards to energy consumption and carbon footprint related to blockchain technology, aspects that will shed some light on the sustainability issue of virtual currencies in general. Just as technology enhances efficiency in logistics, virtual currencies streamline sustainable service marketing by reducing transaction costs and promoting eco-friendly practices (Krishnan et al., 2024).

Focus Groups for Feedback

Hold focus groups for some participants in virtual currency programs and collect qualitative consumer feedback, including experiences, preferences, and suggestions for improvement of the program. Such front-line input can be fed into changes in the program that would raise consumer satisfaction.

IMPLICATION OF THE STUDY

The study findings regarding virtual currencies, green loyalty, and sustainability can benefit businesses, policymakers, and consumers in general. The study illustrates that through this clarification of the role that virtual currencies play in enabling sustainable consumer practices and strengthening brand loyalty, there are also useful, practical applications alongside broader societal implications. This increasing call for sustainability will necessitate knowledge of the dynamics of virtual currency for its effective use in the creation of environmentally-friendly practices. Balancing digital automation with human-centric strategies is key in virtual currency programs aimed at fostering customer loyalty and engagement (Govindaraj et al., 2024).

Environmental Implications of Blockchain: A deeper exploration of the energy consumption associated with blockchain technology and strategies to mitigate its impact would strengthen the argument.
Global Regulatory Perspectives: Including a discussion on how different countries are approaching the regulation of virtual currencies could provide a broader context.
Consumer Behavior in Non-Digital Markets: Highlighting how virtual currencies could influence consumer behavior in industries that are less digitized would expand the applicability of the concepts discussed.

1. Applications for Businesses

The findings of this research have given actionable recommendations to businesses on the implementation of virtual currencies as part and parcel of their sustainability practices. Knowledge of how virtual currencies could create incentives for the generation of sustainable consumer behavior empowers businesses to create loyalty schemes that woo and support the sustainability aspirations of consumers. In this respect, the lessons developed can therefore be exploited by businesses in the creation of focused marketing campaigns towards the attainment of environmentally conscious consumers, hence making the brands more competitive in the market.

2. Higher Consumer Engagement

In this regard, based on the above findings, this research has potential for virtual currencies with respect to making consumers more active in sustainability efforts. Brand adopted virtual currencies can inform customers that participation in such activities forms part of working towards good, such as recycling or purchasing green products. It transcends mere transactional advantages and speaks of a paradigm wherein consumers feel invested and care about their practice affecting the environment. This, therefore, makes the cultures embracing sustainability much deeper; now, the consumers turn into champions of their favorite brands that reflect them.

3. Policymaker Insights

This study has been so effective in offering policymakers a lot of insight to the regulatory environment surrounding virtual currencies and usage in the pursue of sustainability. It will help to inform supportive policies which encourage businesses responsible use of virtual currencies. Policymakers can use such insights in devising frameworks that facilitate innovation, consumer protection, and environmental integrity. Thus, by creating an atmosphere favorable to the growth of sustainable practices through virtual currencies, policymakers can contribute toward broader societal goals regarding environmental stewardship.

4. Basis for Future Research

The implications of the study form the basis for further research in the areas discussed above and generally related to virtual currencies and their relevance to sustainability. Gaps that the current research has identified with regard to the understanding of virtual currencies and their role in the context of sustainability open up avenues for further research. Long-term impacts on consumer behavior, comparing different demographics or industries, and ways of fostering inclusivity and equity in sustainability efforts all represent examples of what studies in the future could be. This is a huge continuation of ongoing studies into perfecting virtual currency programs with regards to their impact on sustainable development goals. Effective omnichannel strategies, as demonstrated in retail supply chain management, can inform virtual currency frameworks in ensuring seamless consumer experiences (Govindaraj et al., 2024).

CONCLUSION

This study identifies the potential of virtual currencies in influencing sustainable consumer behavior, developing green loyalty, and emphasizing transparency in marketing. Virtual currencies act as a platform where firms can encourage eco-friendly activities while developing loyalty programs aligned with consumers' increasing affinity for green brands. The introduction of blockchain technology promotes transparency, thereby allowing consumers to validate environmental claims made by the firm-an important element in trust building and resultant engagement.

However, various challenges face the adoption and implementation of virtual currencies, ranging from technological infrastructure needs to regulatory uncertainties and consumer trust issues. Accenture reported, stating that 72% of the consumers prefer brands that align to environmental values, whereas regulatory uncertainty and privacy concerns continue to obstruct the adoption of virtual currency in the green loyalty scenario. Companies need education, clear communication of security measures, and the ethical use of digital incentives over such barriers. The author commends the forward-thinking businesses and policymakers who are pioneering the use of virtual currencies to align consumer behavior with sustainability goals. Their efforts pave the way for a greener and more responsible future."

Supportive policies will further accelerate mainstream adoption, producing an environment that allows for business innovation, balanced with better consumer protection and environmental sustainability.

Thus, virtual currencies are going to play a very vital role in the future of sustainable practices and consumption patterns when consumer demand for sustainability continues to grow. This study is critical in developing the discourse around how technology drives sustainability by giving perspectives on taking business, policy-making, and practice to the next level to advance sustainable development through strategic use of virtual currencies.

REFERENCES

Accenture. (2020). *Sustainability and consumer loyalty: Aligning with the eco-conscious consumer*. Accenture Report.

Bolton, R., Grewal, D., & Levy, M. (2018). Six megatrends that matter: Proactive channel strategies for retailing. *Journal of Retailing*, *94*(4), 241–253.

Buhalis, D., & Sinarta, Y. (2019). Real-time co-creation and nowness service: Lessons from tourism and hospitality. *Journal of Travel & Tourism Marketing*, *36*(5), 563–582. DOI: 10.1080/10548408.2019.1592059

Challoumis, C. (2023). The role of AI in digital currency - is cryptocurrency the future of money? In *Proceedings of the XVI International Scientific Conference* (pp. 126-130). Philadelphia, PA.

Ganesan, P., & Sridhar, M. (2016). Service innovation and customer performance of telecommunication service provider: A study on mediation effect of corporate reputation. *Corporate Reputation Review*, *19*(1), 77–101. DOI: 10.1057/crr.2015.29

Govindaraj, M., Gnanasekaran, C., Khan, P., Gnanamanickam, S. V., & Hoang, S. D. (2024). Humanizing the digital touch: Strategies for balancing automation in modern marketing. In *Balancing Automation and Human Interaction in Modern Marketing* (pp. 175–202).

Govindaraj, M., Gnanasekaran, C., Krishnan, R., Khan, P., & Hoang, S. D. (2024). Retail supply chain management: Ensuring product availability and reducing out-of-stock incidents in India. In *Omnichannel Approach to Co-Creating Customer Experiences Through Metaverse Platforms* (pp. 116–141).

Hoyer, W. D., Kroschke, M., Schmitt, B., Kraume, K., & Shankar, V. (2020). Transforming the customer experience through new technologies. *Journal of Interactive Marketing*, *51*(1), 57–71. DOI: 10.1016/j.intmar.2020.04.001

Koohang, A., Nord, J. H., Ooi, K. B., Tan, G. W. H., Al-Emran, M., Aw, E. C. X., & Wong, L. W. (2023). Shaping the metaverse into reality: A holistic multidisciplinary understanding of opportunities, challenges, and avenues for future investigation. *Journal of Computer Information Systems*, *63*(3), 735–765.

Krishnan, R., Mahesan, S. S., Manoj, G., Elantheraiyan, P., & Kandasamy, L. (2024). Navigating the crossroads: Stakeholder perspectives in healthcare innovation. In *Revolutionizing the Healthcare Sector with AI* (pp. 238–261).

Krishnan, R., Perumal, E., Govindaraj, M., & Kandasamy, L. (2024). Enhancing logistics operations through technological advancements for superior service efficiency. In *Innovative Technologies for Increasing Service Productivity* (pp. 61–82). DOI: 10.4018/979-8-3693-2019-8.ch004

Kumar, K., Rama Krishna, V., Govindaraj, M., Sathyakala, S., & Viswanathan, R. (2025). Characteristics determining customer's preferences for OTT video streaming: A multivariate analysis. *Entertainment Computing*, *52*, 100746. DOI: 10.1016/j.entcom.2024.100746

Kumar, V., Lahiri, A., & Dogan, O. B. (2019). A strategic framework for a profitable business model in the sharing economy. *Industrial Marketing Management*, *69*, 147–160. DOI: 10.1016/j.indmarman.2017.08.021

Manohar, S., & Kapur, G. (2019). Measuring perceived service innovation typologies in retail industry. *Journal of Industrial Integration and Management*, *4*(2), 1850019. DOI: 10.1142/S2424862218500197

Manohar, S., Mittal, A., & Marwah, S. (2020). Service innovation, corporate reputation, and word-of-mouth in the banking sector: A test on multigroup-moderated mediation effect. *Benchmarking*, *27*(1), 406–429. DOI: 10.1108/BIJ-05-2019-0217

Mora, H., & Mollá-Sirvent, R. (2019). Enhancing business innovation through IoT and big data analytics. *Journal of Business Research*, *96*, 189–201.

Nair, A. J., Manohar, S., & Mittal, A. (2024). Reconfiguration and transformation for resilience: Building service organizations towards sustainability. *Journal of Services Marketing*, *38*(4), 404–425. DOI: 10.1108/JSM-04-2023-0144

Priyanka, N., Sethi, S., Sahai, A., Srivastava, A., Sambathkumar, M., & Boopathi, S. (2024). Reality for human experience in AI in the digital economy. In *Multidisciplinary Applications of Extended Reality for Human Experience*. Christodoulou, I., Rizomyliotis, I., Konstantoulaki, K., Nazarian, A., & Binh, D. (2024). Transforming the remittance industry: Harnessing the power of blockchain technology. *Journal of Enterprise Information Management*. DOI: 10.4018/979-8-3693-2432-5.ch016

World Economic Forum. (2022). *Digital transformation: Accelerating sustainable business models*. Geneva: World Economic Forum.

Chapter 5
Reimagining Sustainable Service Marketing Through Virtual Currencies in the Digital Economy

Ravishankar Krishnan
https://orcid.org/0009-0004-6609-6452
VelTech Rangarajan Dr. Sagunthala R&D Institute of Science and Technology, Chennai, India

Navaneetha Krishnan Rajagopal
https://orcid.org/0009-0004-4476-3867
University of Technology and Applied Sciences, Salalah, Oman

ABSTRACT

This study explores the convergence of sustainable service marketing and virtual currencies, positioning digital financial innovation as a key enabler of inclusive and responsible service ecosystems. It begins by defining the core concepts of sustainability, service marketing, and virtual currencies, grounded in relevant theoretical frameworks such as the Triple Bottom Line, Stakeholder Theory, and the Technology Acceptance Model. The study examines different categories of virtual currencies including decentralized, loyalty based, and government-issued forms and their roles in enhancing transparency, efficiency, and accessibility across sectors such as education, hospitality and fintech. It also analyzes the drivers accelerating the adoption of virtual currencies in sustainable services.

DOI: 10.4018/979-8-3373-0315-4.ch005

1. INTRODUCTION

Service marketing is undergoing a radical paradigm shift in the fundamental restructuring of global economies moving towards sustainability. Traditionally, service marketing has been centered on meeting customer needs with intangible offerings. Now, it is long-term value creation, ethics, and environmental stewardship that sustain the focus. This development gives rise to sustainable service marketing that applies the economic, social, and ecological trifecta to strategically conceptualize and implement services (Castronova, 2014). It includes aspects related to customer satisfaction and the wider impact that service deliverables haFve on stakeholders and the planet. Virtual currencies—cryptocurrencies, tokenized assets, loyalty-based digital tokens—are now being introduced into global economies by digitalization disruption of existing business models through everything that virtual currencies stand for: security, transparency, efficiency in blockchain and decentralized ledger technologies. These currencies had for long remained within the realms of niche markets and speculative investments (Battalova et al., 2019). Their acceptance is now pervasive, primarily in mainstream service sectors like hospitality, healthcare, education, fintech, entertainment, and transportation. One example would be travel and tourism businesses that are now receiving Bitcoin and Ethereum as payments for booking services; other digital platforms are giving virtual tokens to users for engagement and showing loyalty (Ovchinnikov et al., 2019).

The point where green service marketing meets digital currencies is a good place for both study and real-life creativity. This union comes from more consumers knowing about sustainability topics, the growth of smart young people who care about ethics, and a wish for homey options to regular money exchanges (Liu et al., 2025). Virtual currencies, if applied in the right way, can improve service delivery by reducing paper-based system dependency maximizing transaction cost savings and enabling peer-to-peer service models that increase inclusion and visibility of money. For example, tokens sustainable behavior could be exchanged for discounts or services pro-environmental actions among consumers. Also, in situations where the banking physical infrastructure is weak, virtual currencies might act as a драйвер для inclusive economic participation. It allows firms and individuals to engage in electronic trade and service exchanges without access to the formal banking system. Along with mobile-based platforms and green service models, virtual currencies can create circular economies while returning power to local citizens (Jin, 2022). From a marketing perspective, incorporating virtual currencies into service offerings brings numerous advantages: enhanced customer engagement, improved personalization through smart contracts, incentivized loyalty programs, and quick feedback loops.. Also, blockchain-powered services make sure supply chains are clear and create trust in brand messages which goes hand in hand with the beliefs of consumers focused on sustainability. But, shifting to digital money in the service industry has its problems. Issues like energy use (more for proof-of-work cryptos), rules not being clear, and price swings have to be fixed for these to work well in green service selling. A lot of these things are now being helped with tech progress that is leading to the rise of smart ways to agree and stablecoins. This chapter, therefore, tries to discuss how service marketers can use virtual currencies in their marketing activities with a focus on sustainability. The theoretical foundations and types of virtual currencies used in Service Industries, Key Adoption Drivers, Implementation Challenges, and Future Trends are what this work will dwell upon for forming a comprehensive framework to understand this emerging paradigm (Ang & Chow, 2023).

The use of virtual currencies within the context of sustainable service marketing is not just a technological wave but rather a strategic alignment with the larger objective of responsible consumption, digital inclusion, and green awareness. This creates an opportunity for marketers and service providers to redefine consumer interaction and business models using converging innovative financial technologies that support sustainability in the attainment of the Sustainable Development Goals (SDGs).

2. BACKGROUND AND THEORY

2.1. Understanding the Basics

To know how sustainable service marketing meets virtual currencies, we first need to acquaint ourselves with the basic terms that set off this nascent discourse. In its most general sense, sustainability is the capacity to fulfill present needs without endangering the future generations' ability to meet their own needs. As popularized by the Brundtland Commission (1987), it has three main dimensions: economic viabi1ity, environmental responsibility, and social equity. Within business circles, sustainability goes beyond just reducing environmental footprints to include creating value for all stakeholders— customers, employees, suppliers, communities, and shareholders (Qian, 2019).

Service marketing is the application of the marketing principle to the offerings that are intangible, such as financial services, healthcare, education, tourism, and professional consulting. Apart from product marketing, it manages customer experiences longitudinally for building relationships and improving the quality of services ("Digital Currency: Breakthroughs in Research and Practice," 2019). With increased awareness of environmental and social issues, traditional service marketing is transforming into sustainable service marketing a strategic approach where the sustainability concept is integrated into the marketing practices both in terms of ethical and ecological dimensions.

Virtual currencies are value representations not published by central banks but used as exchange, value storage, or account unit mediums. They include crypto-currencies (like Bitcoin and Ethereum), non-blockchain-based digital currencies (such as centralized loyalty points or in-game tokens), and stablecoins (digital tokens linked to fiat currencies or assets). Most of these currencies depend on blockchain technology for safe, uncentralized dealings and are coming up more in the practice of digital service ecosystems (Kaur, 2019). The coming together of these ideas—sustainability, digital money, and service advertising gives a special chance to build service plans that are not just new and effective but also mindful and open to all. There are several theories that provide useful lenses through which one can view the integration of virtual currencies into sustainable service marketing.

The most notable is the Triple Bottom Line (TBL). The Triple Bottom Line or TBL by Elkington (1997) forms the backbone of any study relating to sustainability. The model advocates for success in business to be measured with not only financial profit the economic bottom line but also environmental stewardship and social well-being. In service marketing, therefore, TBL compels marketers to: Reduce environmental impacts (e.g., paperless transactions via digital currencies), e nable social inclusion (e.g., enabling unbanked users to access services using virtual tokens), a nd maintain economic viability (e.g., cost reduction and customer acquisition through digital efficiency) (Ojha et al., 2024). Virtual currencies can align with TBL principles by facilitating green, inclusive, and financially viable service transactions.

2.2. Stakeholder Theory

Freeman's Stakeholder Theory suggests that value should be created for all stakeholders by business, not just shareholders. This aligns perfectly with sustainable service marketing as key actors in services are the consumers, regulators, employees, and the community (Freeman et al., 2010). Virtual currencies can add transparency (due to blockchain), traceability {critical for ethical supply chains), and decentralized decision making- all of which empower stakeholders. For example, DeFi platforms based on blockchain provide an opportunity for service consumers to take part in governance and also get rewards for sustainability actions like loyalty tokens for selecting green service alternatives (Amaral et al., 2021).

2.3 Technology Acceptance Model (TAM)

The Technology Acceptance Model explains user acceptance of technology based on two factors: perceived usefulness and perceived ease of use. The model is applicable in this study, where the service consumers are likely to adopt virtual currencies, provided they perceive that the: Technology offers clear advantage compared to traditional payment methods, It is easy to use within the service interface, Improves the service (faster checkout, personalized rewards). TAM can explain adoption behavior of virtual currencies in services and inform design strategies for user engagement (Davis, 1989).

2.4 Linking Sustainability and Financial Innovation

The merger of sustainability and financial innovation signifies the key move from traditional economic models to systems that are more decentralized, inclusive, and oriented towards impact (Egorova et al., 2019). Virtual currencies stand at the hallmark of this change, where they mean much more than just alternative means of payments. If designed with the principles of sustainability at their core, they would work toward adding strategic value in a number of ways:

> Ecological Balance: Blockchain-backed digital moneys can aid in "green finance" by cutting down on physical tools needed, cash usage, and middleman services. Also, future cryptocurrencies are made using nature-friendly agreement methods (like proof-of-stake instead of energy-wasting proof-of-work).
> Social Sustainability: Using virtual currencies, financial inclusion can be afforded to the unbanked segments. For instance, community-based service models using mobile tokens or time-banking may enable informal workers or local entrepreneurs to access digital economies.
> Economic Sustainability: Virtual currencies lower transaction costs, allow microtransactions, and promote peer-to-peer models thereby enabling small and medium service providers to become more competitive. This will be very applicable in developing economies or rural markets.

In addition, within the scope of virtual currency systems, smart contracts can automate the delivery of services as well as reward mechanisms for sustainable behaviors—for instance, discounts or bonuses for eco-conscious consumption habits (Liu et al., 2025).

The circular economy is another concept that, though not directly related, fits alongside sustainability and could be enhanced through the use of virtual currencies. Such platforms would represent services wherein users earn tokens for recycling as well as for using public transport or even going to community events; these are examples of financial innovations that support both circularity and behavioral change. Further, the ecosystem of virtual currencies and its contribution to the marketing of sustainable services lies in a solid bed of theory and real innovations acting towards the environmental, social, and economic pillars of sustainability. With the continuous maturation of the digital economy, these intersections are going to be very vital for marketers, policymakers, and service designers who are interested in creating resilient and fair service ecosystems (Verma, 2024).

3.DIFFERENT TYPES AND FEATURES OF VIRTUAL CURRENCIES IN SERVICES

Virtual currencies have become a big part of online services today. The growing digital push in the world economies has led to the developmental evolution of different types of virtual currencies, now prominently used within various sectors of services. These systems create new opportunities for transaction implementation, customer behavior motivation, and secure traceable value exchanges—important elements for sustainable service marketing. Knowing the kinds and key distinguishing traits of virtual currencies is essential to understanding their strategic part in changing not just how services are delivered but also customer interaction (Zharikov, 2022).

3.1 Types of Virtual Currencies

Based on the broad definition of virtual currencies, they can fall into the major following types:

a) Cryptocurrencies

This is an uncentralized form of digital money that is secured using cryptography and based on blockchain or distributed ledger technology (DLT). Examples are Bitcoin (BTC), Ethereum (ETH), Litecoin (LTC), etc. Such currencies enable person-to-person transfers without involving middlemen, hence attracting such service sectors as hospitality, travel, fintech, and even education. Features can be described as decentralized, borderless, transparent, resistant to censorship. Sustainability Note: Certainly, blockchains like Bitcoin are energy-intensive and raise environmental concerns; newer versions such as Ethereum 2.0 have energy-efficient proof-of-stake mechanisms (Madakam et al., 2023).

b) Stablecoins

These are digital tokens linked to a stable asset such as a fiat currency USD, INR commodity gold or algorithmically maintained value USDC Tether (USDT) DAI. Features are Slow, can be programmed, and settlement takes much less time compared to banks. Good for price-sensitive services. Example—online education platforms or telehealth services. Cuts down financial risk for users while allowing a global footprint without the traditional banking setup.

These are applied as digital currencies in open loops, meaning they can be used at multiple services within the same ecosystem. Typical examples include hospitality (hotel points), airlines (frequent flyer miles), or general apps (app coins). Usually non-transferable between platforms, redeemable for services or discounts, gamified. Fosters repeat usage; rewards eco-conscious behavior (e.g., gives tokens for green product purchase) (Mishchenko et al., 2025).

d) Game and Platform Currencies

These are very common in the entertainment and gaming industries. They help pay for digital services within immersive platforms. As metaverse environments and virtual events start gaining popularity, these will also be used in the real-world service applications of those currencies. Digitally native, woven into the fabric of ecosystem-specific platforms, usually attained with fiat or crypto money. Enable virtual experiences and carbon footprints of physical services, e.g., virtual tourism or e-learning (Diana et al., 2018).

e) Central Bank Digital Currencies (CBDCs)

These are digital currencies issued by the central banks of states; for instance, India's Digital Rupee (e) or China's Digital Yuan (e-CNY). In most countries, these are yet to come into being but are intended to bring about in reality the convenience of virtual payments coupled with the security of a state. Characteristics: Controlled, safe, trackable, and fast. Use Cases: Good for public services, government-to-person payments and important services like subsidies or digital health help (Kostrikova, 2021).

3.2 Link to Selling Services Each Kind of Online Money has Different Marketing Effects When Added to Service Giving

Online moneys allow for loyalty plans that are personalized and changing prices, especially in hospitality and subscription services.

Speed and Convenience: Real-time transactions not only improve the user experience but also help to make the operation more efficient, especially in services that are delivered on demand such as ride-hailing or food delivery.
Gamification: Tokenized rewards increase customer stickiness and brand engagement to be more precise, around sustainable actions.
Transparency and Trust: An immutable ledger of Blockchain has traceability built into it's critical in ethical supply chains and fair-trade services. E-currencies break location barriers enabling global service websites to access new customer bases effortlessly without the hassle of currency exchange or high remittance charges.

3.3 New Mixed Models

Service sites are also trying out mixed models that merge various e-currency types to enhance user journey. A travel booking site might take Bitcoin for payments, give stablecoin-based refunds, and reward users with eco-point tokens if they choose green stays. Digital learning platforms could use CBDCs for paying fees and grant loyalty NFTs as badges of scholarly accomplishment that have tangible marketable value. Such hybrid apps are making way for "added-value digicurrencies"- where tokens aren't just tools for transactions but have symbolic and experiential value. Challenges in Service Context While VC has benefits, integration of it into services faces below mentioned challenges: Scalability- not every platform is ready to support blockchain integration or token management.

Fluctuation and Danger: Very important for cryptos; providers have to hedge against fast swings.
No Rules: In lots of places, use is either limited or not clear, causing worry about following the law.
Tech Gap: Not all users are smart about tech or have easy access to safe wallets, mainly in poor areas.

Though there are challenges, continuous innovation plus changing consumer behavior keeps pushing service marketers to utilize these digital assets as tools forGrowth and sustainability! To sum up, the variety plus flexibility of virtual currencies give service marketers a versatile toolkit to Align Their operations with the principles of sustainability. From enhancing customer retention to enabling eco-conscious incentives and promoting digital inclusion, these currencies areRe-Marking the marketing, delivery, and experience of services in the digital age (Catherine et al., 2024).

4. REASONS PEOPLE ARE USING VIRTUAL CURRENCY IN ECO-FRIENDLY SERVICES

The merger of virtual currencies with sustainable service ecosystems is not just a technical flair but rather a strategic repositioning motivated by varied environmental, economic, behavioral, and institutional dynamics. Consumers and service providers, in their journey through a digital-first world riddled with climate concerns and shifting value systems, would find virtual currencies as an avenue to redefine engagement, trust, and value creation. This part discusses the major forces that drive the incorporation of virtual currencies within the context of sustainable service marketing (Catherine et al., 2024).

4.1 Environmentally Friendly Practices and Going Paperless

One of the major sustainability drivers of virtual currencies is the fact that they can catalyze a paperless, low-resource service ecosystem. The traditional service transaction heavily relies on printed documents, physical cash, and in-person verification—therefore having environmental costs—especially in banking, retail, education, and government sectors. Digital currencies would eliminate the requirement for paper-based receipts, forms, and ledgers because automated transaction records would be available that are immutable and can be verified. For instance, issuing digital reward points for sustainable customer actions could be completely managed through mobile platforms (e.g., using public transport) without these physical tokens or cards ever coming into play. Moreover, shifting to energy-efficient blockchain protocols like Proof-of-Stake reduces the ecological footprint which was previously a barrier to the more extensive adoption of cryptocurrencies (Agarwal et al., 2024).

4.2 Making Finances Inclusive and Accessible

Virtual currencies provide a pathway that may allow the unbanked to gain access to services—particularly in emerging economies or rural areas where banking infrastructure does not extend. Using mobile devices and digital wallets, one can therefore participate in the service economy without having a traditional bank account or being on any credit registry. It is mostly informal service providers, freelancers, and micro-entrepreneurs outside the formal financial system who will most benefit from this. Token-based transactions can enable them to receive payments, build digital credit histories, and reinvest in their service delivery (Zook, 2018).

For example, blockchain-based identity systems can link reputation information with token wallets that are used to unlock discounted services or community resource applications. Financial inclusion also means enabling participation in green economies—in this respect virtual currencies could be applied to inject rewarding behaviors that are environmentally or socially conscious.

4.3 Ways to Boost How Consumers Interact and Stay Loyal

A key marketing driver behind the use of virtual currencies in services lies in their potential contributions toward enhancing customer loyalty and retention through gamified, personalized experiences. Unlike traditional loyalty programs, virtual tokens have the advantage of being programmable, and trackable at real time as well as interoperable (in some cases) (Kraus et al., 2020). For example, eco-conscious customers could be incentivized with branded digital tokens for using green service options (e.g., e-bill use or reusable packaging) that can later be exchanged for discounts on future services, used to pay social causes, or traded within a closed service ecosystem. This builds up a psychological contract between brand and consumer with values aligned around sustainability and innovation. The other emerging trend creating ground is using non-fungible tokens (NFTs) in loyalty programs. For example, one may see a hotel chain offering exclusive digital emblems to repeat eco-travelers providing them access to special services— thus combining elements of status with real utility.

4.4 Speed, Simplicity, and Fast Transactions

Virtual currencies are certainly going to reduce time and cost in traditional transactions. This would work best for cross-border services, subscription models, and on-demand platforms. The assurance of instant settlement with no intermediaries at all and full transparency regarding the movement of funds would then mean all major currencies at present in the market (Kraus et al., 2020). For committed sustainable providers of services, this means reduced administrative overheads and operational costs that could be channeled into green initiatives or inclusivity programs. For example, NGOs providing education or telehealth services can receive donations or payments in stablecoins; hence quick allocation of funds would become possible with full traceability—something very important for building trust in impact-driven service models. Public blockchains give transparency a new meaning, too: they support ethical service chains.

4.5 Increasing Digital Literacy and Tech-Savvy Consumers

Massive growth in the numbers of digital natives and tech-savvy consumers, primarily Gen Z and millennials, has been instrumental in pushing service platforms towards adopting new technologies like virtual currencies. This demographic group tends to value:

Ethical consumption
Instant Gratification
Personalization
Transparency and Fairness

When virtual currencies are integrated with mobile apps or AI-enabled platforms, they are capable of meeting these expectations providing value exchange at real time, with a traceable history and ethical alignment. Moreover, digital-native consumers are more open to using apps that aggregate health tracking data or education progress data into a single interface, even carbon offset data, with an incentive of tokens; therefore creating a behavioral loop for incentivizing sustainable lifestyles (Ally et al., 2015). Governments and institutions across the world are increasingly designing Central Bank Digital Currencies (CBDCs) and Legalization Frameworks related to Virtual Currencies. Though this change isberry much in the primary stage, it primarily attains more significant approval which will eliminate previous uncertainties among service providers concerning the former doubts about embracing such technologies. Also enclosed in public service ecosystems CBDCs will ensure high efficiency delivery systems on subsidies. Better laws for private service sectors make trust that lets them build crypto-reward plans, DeFi models, or blockchain-based memberships in a legal way and with growth. These also help show projects like the European Green Digital Coalition and India's Digital Rupee test which form a policy-level nudge toward mixing financial change with green ideas plus digital updates in how services are given (Ovchinnikov et al., 2019). To sum up, the reasons that drive digital cash use in green services are many, covering tech, mindset, place, and rules. Such funds aid makes cleaner and fairer service styles plus they give smart ways for building brand trust raising customer interest and making operations work better. As service fields shift due to global demands for sustainability digital moneys are set to play leading roles in future-focused marketing strategies aimed at making an impact (Li et al., 2024).

5. PROBLEMS AND ISSUES

Although great potential exists in the use of virtual currencies for sustainable marketing of services, its proliferation comes along with a host of challenges and risks—both systemic and operational. Such barriers encompass ecological matters, wavered regulatory vibes, lim tech imp, market mobility and socio-econ inequalities. For service providers ready to align their marketing strategies with sustainability, understanding these risks and how to mitigate them is key to creating long-term value as well as building trust (Goutte et al., 2021).

5.1 Environmental Issues: Energy Consumption and Electronic Waste

The mining process is energy-intensive, and this has garnered much attention as one of the significant criticisms leveled against virtual currencies, especially blockchain-based ones like Bitcoin and Ethereum. This applies most when these currencies have Proof-of-Work algorithms integrated into their systems. Such protocols tend to be very electricity-consuming since they require high computational power for transaction validation thus adding to carbon emissions. Although newer forms of consensus mechanisms such as Proof-of-Stake (PoS) and Proof-of-Authority (PoA) are more energy-efficient alternatives, not all virtual currencies or platforms have them implemented (Mu & Liu, 2023). The ecological impact thus sets a challenge against the core principles of service models that aim towards sustainability with a minimal ecological footprint. Cryptographic mining or blockchain node operations can be e-waste-generating activities due to the hardware dependence, which is contradictory to the sustainability principles but can be reduced by green IT management if properly handled.

5.2 Uncertainty in Rules and Compliance Risks

The classification of virtual currencies differs from one country to another and a majority of the service providers operate in gray shades of regulations. How these digital assets will be classified, taxed, and monitored by governments is yet to be determined. Such ambiguity places high compliance risks on service-based businesses, particularly those operating cross-border activities. For example, loyalty tokens or reward systems linked to blockchain might qualify as securities in some jurisdictions and therefore associated with complex reporting obligations. Additionally, inconsistent legal regimes often act as barriers to scalability and interoperability because they prevent service providers from offering virtual currencies as part of mainstream marketing campaigns (Madakam et al., 2023). Further, the AML KYC plus consumer protection regulations would require substantial bending of the blockchain-based services which would thus increase operational burdens and stifle innovation for small- and medium-sized service enterprises.

5.3 Market Changes and How Shoppers Feel

Most cryptocurrencies are characterized by high volatility. The tokens value has been oscillating extremely, and hence positioning a service provider in pricing the offerings or issuing crypto-based rewards becomes problematic. Much appreciation of a reward token's value can make it quite useless within days because of market dynamics undermining consumer trust and loyalty. Unpredictability makes stable, reliable marketing experiences impossible. Fear of value loss may make consumers hesitant to use or accept virtual currencies. Service providers will be at great risk regarding their reputation if they do not deliver promised rewards or convertibility (Levashenko et al., 2019). Issues of trust affect even the stablecoins designed to reduce volatility when their backing assets are not transparently audited or regulated. It determines the consumer perception on fairness, safety, and long-term reliability of digital payment systems in service ecosystems.

5.4 Data Privacy and Cybersecurity Concerns

The virtual currency systems do very much at stake with issues of data privacy in decentralized block chain networks, though issues of security as well. For one large transparency that blockchain might bring, it would probably also make available transactional metadata, thus raising concerns about consumer privacy in some of the most sensitive sectors—healthcare, education, and financial services. Elsewhere, digital wallets, smart contracts, and all exchanging platforms are vulnerable to cyberattacks, hacking attempts to penetrate their security measures as well as phishing (Kuner, 2003). A single breach can not only compromise sensitive customer information but even brand reputation consumer confidence will be at risk! Another risk lies in badly designed smart contracts those meant for automating service delivery or token rewards that could have bugs or loopholes which might then be exploited or the services themselves fail. This type of risk would be most magnified in services that are centered on sustainability as those services would need to embody trustworthiness and where coming into play are ethical practices.

5.5 Tech Complexity and Users Not Ready

The high technical complexity of virtual currencies has been the primary reason for the hesitancy so far. Most people do not have the digital literacy or are not confident enough, to handle private keys, crypto wallets, and systems based on blockchain. This divide mainly affects low-income as well as rural populations—the exact target of sustainable service models in terms of empowerment (Shafik, 2024). If this issue is not taken care of, it will either exclude an important segment from innovative offerings in services or create a dependency on intermediaries who might take advantage of these uninformed users if problems arise. From the perspective of the provider, bringing virtual currencies onto existing platforms involves much staff upskilling, IT infrastructure re-creation, and interoperability management; hence there is a large initial investment and also a technical risk (Jaime et al., 2023).

5.6 Ethical and Social Implications

Although inclusive at the core, virtual currencies may also be set to use with the result of speculation, financial addiction, and manipulation of consumers. Gamified systems or economies of tokens may lead to overconsumption and unsustainable behavior if propped up by a rather loose ethical oversight in design towards proper usage. For instance, if perceived as exploitative (e.g., offering low-value tokens for time-consuming sustainable actions), virtual rewards could promptly turn consumer motivation negative and even burn brand equity in the long run. This holds much importance in service categories that have social impact since perceived sincerity and fairness drive consumer confidence (Flammini & Marrone, 2023). Another issue is that without universal standards on how to measure digital currency sustainability, there is confusion both on the part of consumers as well as marketers. Without such a framework sharing commonality, it becomes difficult to judge whether a system of virtual currency really supports sustainability or greenwashes its operations.

Though they have much potential in revolutionizing sustainable service marketing, much risk is associated with virtual currencies. Providers must manage environmental impacts, legal uncertainties, volatility, and ethical considerations risks deliberatively and well. Once resolved through regulatory clarity, technological innovation, user education, and ethical design principles; various types of virtual currencies will be able to match their claims of contributing to sustainable and inclusive service ecosystems (Alam, 2023). This section discusses how a few leading firms are addressing these challenges through innovative practices bringing to fore real-world case studies in sustainable service marketing with virtual currencies.

6. TIPS FOR USING VIRTUAL CURRENCIES IN ECO-FRIENDLY SERVICE MARKETING

As green thinking and tech creativity join hands, online money is getting super key for switching up help plans. But nice mix needs a list of planned and just top ways to make sure they fit with green goals, what buyers want, and laws (Ram Mohan Rao et al., 2018). This section gives a list of smart, useful, and fair best ways that service sellers can use to get the most value while lowering danger and leaving people out less.

6.1 One of the first sustainable practices

It is to select blockchain platforms that employ low-energy consensus mechanisms such as Proof-of-Stake (PoS), or Proof-of-Authority (PoA), or Delegated Proof-of-Stake (DPoS). These are resource-intensive ways significantly less compared to the traditional way of Proof-of-Work (PoW) mechanics (Ilham et al., 2019). Firms providing services by tokenizing rewards or accepting cryptocurrencies through transactions should place preference on platform commitment towards reducing environmental footprints in all aspects. Consider joining blockchain ecosystems publicly disclosing your energy consumption metrics, or be part of green blockchain certification programs.

6.2 Ensure Regulatory Compliance and Transparent Governance

Legal clarity is fundamental to long-term adoption. Marketers should work closely with legal teams and regulatory authorities to ensure that their virtual currency initiatives is: Compliant with financial regulations such as KYC, AML, and GDPR. Open in function, much token give-out, deal follow ability, and buyer shield. In help fields like money tech, wellbeing care, and schooling where trust matters a lot suppliers must show how info and tokens are used kept safe and ruled. Carrying out clear tokenomics builds trust and lessens the chance of seen misuse or trickery.

6.3 Design Sustainable Loyalty and Reward Ecosystems

Service providers should create token economies linked to sustainability whereby loyalty or reward points offered are related to actions that reflect an environmental or social impact. Allowing tokens to redeem for sustainable services, charity donations, or exchanges within a responsible community platform. Creating tiered loyalty programs where increased sustainable engagement unlocks exclusive benefits digital badges or premium services. These practices build long-term emotional engagement and embed sustainability into the customer journey.

A typical constraint in digital currency systems is the enclosed-loop creation—tokens applicable solely within one service platform. To improve usability and take on adoption:

Create inter-service exchangeable token systems (e.g., between hospitality platforms or educational ones).

Collaborate with digital wallets of open standards or token platforms based on consortia which allow users an interface for several services.

It raises comfort levels, boosts network advantages, and fits with user hopes for easy and joined-up digital experiences.

6.4 Put Money into Digital Skills and Customer Power

Online access is a main part of green goals. So, suppliers must make sure that their online money tools are: - Easy to use, with clear designs, quick signup, and many languages. Alongside digital literacy campaigns, especially meant for under-banked populations or senior citizens. Transparent to the risks and benefits attached to its use, mainly concerning non-fungible and decentralized finance tokens. This may include support, FAQ sections, demo videos, and community forums that can educate users so they do not have to rely on intermediaries, creating a more responsible environment for digital services (Siripurapu et al., 2023).

Virtual currencies should be considered not as standalone instruments but part of the integral components towards a wider roadmap aimed at sustainability, for example: In transportation services, tokens could incentivize ride-sharing as well in turn low-emission travel. In education, digital badges and tokens could signify completion of modules on climate awareness or social entrepreneurship projects (Tsang et al., 2024). In hospitality, green tokens could reward guests for staying at energy-efficient accommodations. To avoid tokenism or shallow engagement, tie token systems to visible impact goals carbon reduction, water savings, social inclusion metrics—and embed them into ESG reporting where applicable.

6.5 Ethical Design and Misuse Prevention Should Come First

The marketing of services through virtual currencies is ethical only if certain safeguards are put in place to avoid unintended consequences. Providers should: Ensure that gamification does not become excessive to the point of inducing addictive behaviors or unsustainable consumption patterns (Verma, 2024). Ensure equivalent value exchange—tokens should real, equal rewards depending on the effort or behavior they reward. Apply algorithmic fairness and auditability in smart contracts so that discrimination or exclusion can be avoided. Companies providing services should also set up grievance redressal systems through which users can complain about token fraud, misrepresentation, or data misuse.

- Co-creation improves innovation as well as take-up. Service providers should partner with:
- Customers, to co-create meaningful reward systems and feedback loops.
- NGOs and local governments, to ensure tokens are anchored to social goals (e.g., food security, education access).
- Technology partners, for secure implementation and backend resilience.

Fostering multi-stakeholder governance models—wherein users participate in the evolution of tokens can engender community stewardship and social license.

The strategic and responsible application of virtual currencies toward the marketing of sustainable services requires not merely technological competence but rather a humanized, holistic, and ethically-driven approach. Under innovation matched with inclusivity, efficiency aligned with ethics, and transparency coupled with engagement, service providers can develop robust systems that generate benefit shared value between enterprises, consumers, and society (Verma, 2024). These represent a guide for institutions that aspire to spearhead the journey toward digital sustainability wherein virtual currencies serve as enablers of attitudinal change, fair involvement, and protracted excellence in service delivery.

7. TRENDS AND NEW IDEAS FOR THE FUTURE

As digital transformation accompanies the swift embrace of sustainability as a central business strategy, the merging of virtual currencies with the marketing of sustainable services is about to take a bound leap. The next wave of innovation driven by blockchain, artificial intelligence, tokenization, and global regulatory reforms will ensure that virtual currencies are integrated into the very fabric or DNA of service ecosystems across all geographies (Keshav & Sinha, 2024). This section will briefly discuss major emerging trends that will define this future and innovations that will shape value creation in responsible, inclusive, and tech-enabled ways.

7.1 Emergence of Green Cryptocurrencies

Eco-friendly or green cryptocurrencies aimed at reducing environmental impact have joined the crypto landscape. Unlike their predecessors which adopt energy-intensive consensus algorithms like Proof-of-Work for Bitcoin these green coins implement sustainable mechanisms such as Proof-of-Stake PoS that reduces energy consumption by leaps and bounds. Directed Acyclic Graphs (DAGs) - a swap for blockchain used in apps like IOTA, needing little compute power. Carbon-neutral ways of mining - supported by carbon offset projects and renewable energy-powered places for mining. Sustainable service firms will likely aim at joining with green coins and digital sites which openly discuss their eco effects, thus matching monetary progress with care for the environment (Rai et al., 2025).

7.2 Smart Contracts for Behavioral Incentives

Smart contracts—self-executing agreements coded on blockchain—have come to considerable favor as programmable tools within the automation of service delivery, rewards, and feedback. In the future, service providers will increasingly use smart contracts to:

Trigger real-time token rewards for eco-friendly actions (e.g., using reusable containers, attending online green workshops) .

Enable dynamic pricing based on user behavior, loyalty level, or social impact contributions.

Set up automatic donations to NGOs or carbon credit programs when buyers make eco-friendly choices. This builds an auto behavior feedback loop, matching marketing plans with green buying habits while keeping measure and clear info.

7.3 Merge of AI and Predictive Analytics

Smart tech will help make virtual money experiences unique within service systems. By using customer data in a right and safe way, this tech can:

Customer preferences will be anticipated, and personalized eco-rewards or offers will be suggested.

Fraudulent or unsustainable behaviors in token ecosystems shall be detected.

The token lifecycle shall be optimized by analyzing its circulation, redemption patterns, and user engagement. AI virtual assistants will guide users on their sustainability scores, transaction footprints, and reward pathways for better and conscious use of the service.

7.4 DeFi in Service Sectors

DeFi breaks within the Service Sectors It enables people to borrow, lend, insure, and invest with no middlemen. That upends the old financial systems. It provides new models within the context of service marketing. Tokenized micro-loans gain entry to premium services like education or healthcare. Staking rewards long-term service subscriptions or loyalty deposits. User-driven insurance pools where members token-commit to regenerative projects and, in turn, receive coverage. These permissionless ecosystems broaden monetary access, reduce service fees, and foster communal stewardship within service economies (Raza et al., 2022). We will see, in the future, interoperable token ecosystems emerge where virtual currencies move with ease across multiple service platforms, reographies, and industries. Cross-chain bridges which will let tokens from one blockchain be used on another. Universal digital wallets that will enable users to manage many tokens in one interface (Serttaş-Yırtıcı et al., 2024). Collaborative token coalitions where companies together create tokens useful across a range of service offerings e.g. transport, education and tourism. Such fluidity enables borderless service interfacing and allows customers to move their value and esteem across varied platforms hence driving sustainable behavior . Gamified experiences would further evolve with the infusion of Augmented Reality, Virtual Reality, and the Metaverse wherein providers would have the capability to create immersive experiences like Consumer earning green tokens v ia participation in virtual sustainability challenges. Teaching sites present fun paths for eco-learning with tokenized achievements. Travel help makes digital eco-places, where buyers can see and know—and getting tokens that turn into real-life travel perks. These new ideas boost involvement and build feelings of drive and belonging among users who link their online self with off-line green actions.

7.5 Making Digital Currencies Official

Central Bank Digital Currencies will alter the embrace of digital currencies in public and private services. Governments around the globe are experimenting with or introducing CBDCs traceable by design, efficient, and with programmable features. In the context of sustainable services, CBDCs can:

Aid in targeted subsidies for green products and services.

Support transparent disbursement of welfare benefits and education credits.

Enable government collaborations with private service providers for encouraging green behavior. The inclusion of CBDCs into sustainable service ecosystems will validate and scale virtual currencies for mass adoption. The future of sustainable service marketing using virtual currencies would be the convergence, personalization, and empowerment. These digital assets will move from being payment alternatives to becoming integral parts of service ecosystems driven by purpose and absolutely needed. Companies that, in a proactive way and respecting ethical standards, embrace innovations not only for their competitive advantage will also enable them to contribute meaningfully to the global goal of sustainability.

8. POLICY IMPLICATIONS AND STRATEGIC RECOMMENDATIONS

The increased use of virtual currencies in the marketing of sustainable services virtually demands new strategies involving innovative strategies from service providers and requiring robust and proactive policy interventions. As these technologies change how services are delivered, accessed, and valued, it becomes necessary to put in place regulatory and strategic frameworks directing their application towards inclusion, responsibility, and long-term sustainability. From a policy point of view, one pressing framework development need is a clear adaptive regulatory framework. The regulation should be dynamic such that it is technology-neutral and responsive to innovation in digital currencies; the governments should take an initiative swiftly to define the legal status of various virtual currencies-cryptocurrencies, stablecoins tokenized assets-and explicitly clarify how these are to be taxed, reported on, and monitored. Regulatory clarity must also extend to issues of anti-money laundering, know-your-customer (KYC) requirements, and consumer protection as the marketing and loyalty programs of digital currencies by service providers move to mainstream integration. A sandbox environment can thus be instrumental in allowing that experimentation under regulatory oversight which makes innovation possible without infringing the public interest. Another major policy implication here would be the push for financial and digital inclusion. For virtual currencies to fulfill sustainability goals, they should be accessible by all sections of society along with those who are digitally marginalized. Requires governments and public agencies to build digital infrastructure in those regions and also ensure that virtual currency platforms have multilingual support with user interfaces. User empowerment through awareness campaigns on digital safety, privacy concerns, and responsible use will confidence users for participating in tokenized service ecosystems. As environmental matters regarding blockchain technologies surface, it is the duty of policymakers to balance such concerns with active encouragement in the adoption of energy-efficient and environmentally responsible innovations. Incentive mechanisms for the green blockchain adoption might range from tax exemptions to carbon credits for those service platforms that engage low-energy consensus protocols. Mandatory environmental footprint disclosure requirements of blockchain services would, alongside certification schemes for green digital finance, likely further drive stakeholder interest toward sustainability standard levels. Strategic marketers and service providers would be among those who have a crucial role to play in virtual currency initiatives convergence with sustainability goals.

This can be best achieved by embedding sustainability into token systems by their very design. Tokens should reward not transactional rewards but sustainable behaviors like recycling, low-emission transport, or community-building activities. Token economy design should be oriented towards long value creation rather than short gamification, with integration of mechanisms to audit and measure environmental social impacts as well. The second strategic priority touches upon cross ecosystem collaboration. Service providers ought to form alliances with blockchain developers, green tech companies, NGOs, and even local governments in order to design meaningful interoperable token systems aimed at broader societal goals. Besides extending the reach and utility of virtual currencies, inter-organizational collaboration aids in standard development and learning accumulation as well. For example, user capacity building ensures effective and ethical use of virtual currencies by users. Service platforms should have user training programs, help desks, and community engagement for educating users on secure wallets, token redemptions, environmental awareness etc., responsible digital behavior. Internally, service organizations need to invest in developing the expertise of employees in token economics, regulatory compliance, and systems design for fostering a culture of accountability and innovation.

Data privacy and algorithmic fairness should be considered integral components of any virtual currency project. Service platforms, as such, should operate under the global data protection regime with full transparency on personal data usage and ensure that smart contracts and rewarding algorithms are free from discriminatory biases. User consent mechanisms, privacy controls, and periodic system audits should find integration into the lifecycle management of all digital currency applications within service ecosystems. In essence, responsible virtual currency deployment for sustainable service marketing requires synchronized action from policymakers and service providers. The administration is tasked with establishing an environment that harmonizes innovation and regulation, post which enterprises should integrate ethical design along with inclusive and impact-driven strategies. This will ensure that virtual currencies operate not merely as instruments of convenience on the internet but as powerful vehicles for environmental stewardship, social justice, and economic sustainability within the service sector.

9. CONCLUSION

The use of digital currencies in promoting sustainable services can be seen as the conceptual shift, the service offering, and experience in that digital economy, changed from this moment to how industries act under environmental, social, and ethical pressures. Digital currencies create new value opportunities while embedding principles of sustainability. Digital currency enables transactions without paper expenditure and creates awareness among people about financing for the unbanked with high operational transparency; all these aspects bring default alignment with further aspirations inherent within the agenda for sustainable development.

The chapter has covered the concepts, theories, technologies, and strategies of virtual currencies in service areas that emphasize greenness. It began with an introduction to the basic definitions of greenness, virtual currencies, and service marketing. Thereafter major theories like Triple Bottom Line and Stakeholder Theory were highlighted along with Technology Acceptance Model; over the rest of the chapter several types of virtual currencies were discussed to showcase their importance in different fields of services and how they can enhance sustainable actions.

It also looked at the key things that drive take-up—from green tech and buyer trust to digital access and rules change—while also looking at the problems too like energy use, instability, no clear rules, and ethics. To fix these issues a list of top ways was put forward showing smart design, ethical control, tech teamwork, and user power.

This chapter has therefore looked at several emerging trends that are likely to shape the future of this domain- Green cryptocurrencies, AI and predictive analytics integration, Decentralized finance (DeFi), gamification-immersive service experiences, and institutionalization of digital currencies such as CBDCs. These trends reiterate that virtual currencies are not standalone innovations but are deeply nestled within an aspiring ecosystem related to both digital and sustainable transformations.

This field is still in its development, and therefore, considerable prospects for academic probings and empirical tests exist. Future studies should endeavor to empirically ascertain the sustainability outcomes linked to the adoption of virtual currency in various sectors of service. Longitudinal studies can be organized to measure the sustained effect over time on consumer behavior, environmental metrics, and organizational performance of token-based loyalty systems. Comparative studies across different geographies and industries of service can bring out how cultural, economic, and regulatory factors play a role in the adoption process as well as the effectiveness of virtual currencies.

Also, cross-study joining marketing, eco-sci, digi-finance, and behavior econ can give better ideas on how to make these techs work for society more. Another good study path includes looking at what buyers think about fairness and clarity in tokenized help sites. As users know more and get sharper about online actions, knowing the thoughts and feelings on using currency in virtual trade can help sellers create kinder experiences that match values.

The role of virtual currencies in the facilitation of community-based service models should also be explored by Researchers, primarily at local economies, not-for-profit organizations and cooperative platforms where the main motive is not profit but sustainability and collective welfare. Furthermore, research needs to look into the intersection between public policy and private service marketing as governments start to launch or pilot their own central bank digital currencies.

How CBDCs can be part of sustainable service delivery, what policy frameworks guide ethical innovation, and how regulatory harmonization can be instigated across borders should be highlighted as critical areas for both scholarly exploration and industry dialogue. To conclude, though virtual currencies are generally talked about in the context of financial innovation, their strategic value in bringing about a future that is marketed on sustainability in services is deep. They can provide e-fficiency, en-gagement, e-quity, and environmental responsibility; thus, they are relevant to the service economies of the futures but most importantly indispensable.

But getting this done needs a promise for inclusive design, fair rules, smart future planning, and never-ending learning. As a way to work and a subject to study, good service marketing that keeps in mind virtual currencies is at the leading edge of a digitally strong, caring, and renewing future.

REFERENCES

Agarwal, M., Gill, K. S., Upadhyay, D., Dangi, S., & Chythanya, K. R. (2024). The Evolution of Cryptocurrencies: Analysis of Bitcoin, Ethereum, Bit connect and Dogecoin in Comparison. *2024 IEEE 9th International Conference for Convergence in Technology, I2CT 2024*. DOI: 10.1109/I2CT61223.2024.10543872

Alam, A. (2023). Developing a Curriculum for Ethical and Responsible AI: A University Course on Safety, Fairness, Privacy, and Ethics to Prepare Next Generation of AI Professionals. In *Lecture Notes on Data Engineering and Communications Technologies* (Vol. 171, pp. 879–894). DOI: 10.1007/978-981-99-1767-9_64

Ally, M., Gardiner, M., & Lane, M. (2015). The potential impact of digital currencies on the Australian economy. *ACIS 2015 Proceedings - 26th Australasian Conference on Information Systems*. https://www.scopus.com/inward/record.uri?eid=2-s2.0-85054408005&partnerID=40&md5=6c0ccc32b3d102de58a38fbaec2f1625

Amaral, G., Sales, T. P., & Guizzardi, G. (2021). Towards ontological foundations for central bank digital currencies. *CEUR Workshop Proceedings*, *2835*, 77–86. https://www.scopus.com/inward/record.uri?eid=2-s2.0-85103279777&partnerID=40&md5=12b3ebb5d915ed389e6da1593d81d639

Ang, M. T., & Chow, Y. P. (2023). Influence of virtual currency development and investor attention on financial stocks' value: Evidence from selected Asian equity markets. *Journal of Financial Regulation and Compliance*, *31*(1), 96–125. DOI: 10.1108/JFRC-01-2022-0007

Battalova, L. M., Enikeev, R. N., Kokanov, N. A., Semivelichenko, E. A., & Probichev, V. S. (2019). Legal regulation of virtual currency: International experience development trend in russia. *Humanities and Social Sciences Reviews*, *7*(4), 911–914. DOI: 10.18510/hssr.2019.74122

Castronova, E. (2014). Wildcat currency: How the virtual money revolution is transforming the economy. In *Wildcat Currency: How the Virtual Money Revolution is Transforming the Economy*. https://www.scopus.com/inward/record.uri?eid=2-s2.0-84903069158&partnerID=40&md5=a52c7c05f559c8f849d57e4a83f89815

Catherine, S., Rani, M. N., & Suresh, N. V. (2024). The metaverse economy: Transforming money with digital currency. In *Creator's Economy in Metaverse Platforms* (pp. 202–209). Empowering Stakeholders Through Omnichannel Approach., DOI: 10.4018/979-8-3693-3358-7.ch012

Currency, D. Breakthroughs in Research and Practice. (2019). In *Digital Currency: Breakthroughs in Research and Practice*. DOI: 10.4018/978-1-5225-6201-6

Davis, F. D. (1989). Perceived usefulness, perceived ease of use, and user acceptance of information technology. *Management Information Systems Quarterly*, *13*(3), 319–340. DOI: 10.2307/249008

Diana, S., Yulia, F., & Ivolgina, N. V. (2018). The role of cryptocurrencies in the world economy development. *Proceedings of the 32nd International Business Information Management Association Conference, IBIMA 2018 - Vision 2020: Sustainable Economic Development and Application of Innovation Management from Regional Expansion to Global Growth*, 2937–2954. https://www.scopus.com/inward/record.uri?eid=2-s2.0-85063054634&partnerID=40&md5=1c1e7f36b62196cd6f7b21df63707acd

Egorova, E. N., Mukhomorova, I. V., & Mosalev, A. I. (2019). Digital currency in the development of payment systems on the bitcoin platform. In *Lecture Notes in Networks and Systems* (Vol. 57, pp. 167–175). DOI: 10.1007/978-3-030-00102-5_17

Flammini, F., & Marrone, S. (2023). Distance education boosting interdisciplinarity and internationalization: an experience report from "Ethics, Law and Privacy in Data and Analytics" at SUPSI. *ACM International Conference Proceeding Series*, 54. DOI: 10.1145/3633083.3633103

Freeman, R. E., Harrison, J. S., Wicks, A. C., Parmar, B. L., & De Colle, S. (2010). *Stakeholder theory: The state of the art.*

Goutte, S., Guesmi, K., & Saadi, S. (2021). Cryptofinance: A New Currency for a New Economy. In *Cryptofinance: a New Currency for a New Economy*. DOI: 10.1142/12353

Ilham, R. N., Fachrudin, K. A., Silalahi, A. S., & Saputra, J. (2019). Comparative of the supply chain and block chains to increase the country revenues via virtual tax transactions and replacing future of money. *International Journal of Supply Chain Management*, *8*(5), 1066–1069. https://www.scopus.com/inward/record.uri?eid=2-s2.0-85078321329&partnerID=40&md5=1b001cb243e57d10404d84d56d4ef4e3

Jaime, F. J., Muñoz, A., Rodríguez-Gómez, F., & Jerez-Calero, A. (2023). Strengthening Privacy and Data Security in Biomedical Microelectromechanical Systems by IoT Communication Security and Protection in Smart Healthcare. *Sensors (Basel)*, *23*(21), 8944. Advance online publication. DOI: 10.3390/s23218944 PMID: 37960646

Jin, Z. (2022). Long-Term and Short-Term Integrated Learning-Based Price Forecasting for Virtual Currency. *Proceedings - 2022 2nd Asia-Pacific Conference on Communications Technology and Computer Science, ACCTCS 2022*, 438–442. DOI: 10.1109/ACCTCS53867.2022.00095

Kaur, M. (2019). Digital Currency and its Implications for India. *The Management Accountant Journal*, *54*(11), 64. DOI: 10.33516/maj.v54i11.64-67p

Keshav, A., & Sinha, A. R. (2024). Digital Money in the Indian Context: An In-depth Exploration of its Evolution, Implications, and Future Prospects within the Framework of Central Bank Digital Currency. *Journal of Electrical Systems*, *20*(1), 350–361. DOI: 10.52783/jes.686

Kostrikova, N. (2021). Assessment of Blockchain Technology Adoption Factors and Scenarios Within the Economy of Latvia. *Lecture Notes in Networks and Systems*, *183*, 714–729. DOI: 10.1007/978-3-030-66840-2_54

Kraus, N. M., Kraus, K. M., & Andrusiak, N. O. (2020). Digital cubic space as a new economic augmented reality. *Science and Innovation*, *16*(3), 92–105. DOI: 10.15407/scine16.03.092

Kuner, C. (2003). *European data privacy law and online business*. Oxford University Press.

Levashenko, A. D., Ermokhin, I. S., & Koval, A. A. (2019). Prospects of legal regulation of crypto economy and ICO in Russia and other countries. *Ekonomicheskaya Politika*, *14*(5), 80–99. DOI: 10.18288/1994-5124-2019-5-80-99

Li, M., Jiang, D., Xu, S., Liu, Y., Gao, X., Guo, S., & Qi, F. (2024). A multi-factor real-time monitoring mechanism for the “mining” behavior of blockchain networks. *IEEE International Symposium on Broadband Multimedia Systems and Broadcasting, BMSB*. DOI: 10.1109/BMSB62888.2024.10608287

Liu, X., Liu, Z., & Dong, X. (2025). Research on Countermeasures for the Governance of Virtual Currency Crimes in the Digital Economy Era. *Journal of Systems Science and Information*, *13*(1), 61–81. DOI: 10.21078/JSSI-2024-0046

Madakam, S., Mark, S., Lurie, Y., & Revulagadda, R. K. (2023). The role of cryptocurrencies in business. *International Journal of Electronic Finance*, *12*(3), 238–262. DOI: 10.1504/IJEF.2023.131771

Mishchenko, V., Naumenkova, S., Mishchenko, S., & Tishchenko, I. (2025). Formation And Functioning Of Financial Metaverse Platforms. *Financial and Credit Activity: Problems of Theory and Practice*, *1*(60), 111–122. DOI: 10.55643/fcaptp.1.60.2025.4689

Mu, J., & Liu, W. (2023). The Impact Mechanism of Blockchain Technology on Financial Risk. *Lecture Notes in Electrical Engineering, 1031 LNEE*, 774–779. DOI: 10.1007/978-981-99-1428-9_95

Ojha, N., Gohil, D., & Vaish, A. (2024). Cyber Ecosystem and Digital Currency: Review and Current Status. In *Fintech for Esg and the Circular Economy* (pp. 63–92). DOI: 10.1002/9781394234035.ch5

Ovchinnikov, A. I., Kravchenko, A. G., Mamychev, A. Y., & Fatkhi, V. I. (2019). Virtual currency as an object of civil rights in Russia. *Humanities and Social Sciences Reviews, 7*(6), 148–153. DOI: 10.18510/hssr.2019.7630

Qian, Y. (2019). Central Bank Digital Currency: Optimization of the currency system and its issuance design. *China Economic Journal, 12*(1), 1–15. DOI: 10.1080/17538963.2018.1560526

Rai, P., Gupta, D., & Gupta, M. (2025). Cryptocurrencies and Their Economic Implications: Analyse the Impact of Cryptocurrencies Like Bitcoin on Traditional Financial Systems, Including Their Potential to Disrupt Traditional Banking and the Role of Blockchain Technology in Creating Decentralised Economies. *Lecture Notes in Networks and Systems, 977 LNNS*, 131–142. DOI: 10.1007/978-981-97-2671-4_10

Ram Mohan Rao, P., Murali Krishna, S., & Siva Kumar, A. P. (2018). Privacy preservation techniques in big data analytics: A survey. *Journal of Big Data, 5*(1), 33. Advance online publication. DOI: 10.1186/s40537-018-0141-8

Raza, S. A., Ahmed, M., & Aloui, C. (2022). On the asymmetrical connectedness between cryptocurrencies and foreign exchange markets: Evidence from the non-parametric quantile on quantile approach. *Research in International Business and Finance, 61*, 101627. Advance online publication. DOI: 10.1016/j.ribaf.2022.101627

Serttaş-Yırtıcı, Z., Balkaç, C., Alkaç, M., Alturjman, S., & Al-Turjman, F. (2024). Developing and Implementing a Gamification-Supported Adaptive Learning Environment in an Ai-Based Teaching System: The Example of Sudoku and Puzzle. *Sustainable Civil Infrastructures*, 855–870. DOI: 10.1007/978-3-031-78276-3_83

Shafik, W. (2024). Data-driven future trends and innovation in telemedicine. In *Improving Security, Privacy, and Connectivity Among Telemedicine Platforms* (pp. 93–118). IGI Global. DOI: 10.4018/979-8-3693-2141-6.ch005

Siripurapu, S., Darimireddy, N. K., Chehri, A., Sridhar, B., & Paramkusam, A. V. (2023). Technological Advancements and Elucidation Gadgets for Healthcare Applications: An Exhaustive Methodological Review-Part-I (AI, Big Data, Block Chain, Open-Source Technologies, and Cloud Computing). *Electronics (Basel), 12*(3), 750. Advance online publication. DOI: 10.3390/electronics12030750

Tsang, Y. P., Fan, Y., Lee, C. K. M., & Lau, H. C. W. (2024). Blockchain sharding for e-commerce supply chain performance analytics towards Industry 5.0. *Enterprise Information Systems, 18*(4), 2311807. Advance online publication. DOI: 10.1080/17517575.2024.2311807

Verma, S. (2024). Study on Blockchain-Based Framework for Central Bank Digital Currency Design Opportunities, Risk, and Challenges. In *Artificial Intelligence Solutions for Cyber-Physical Systems* (pp. 432–438). DOI: 10.1201/9781032694375-25

Zharikov, M. V. (2022). The Model of a Shared Interest Rate for a Group of Countries to Circulate a Digital Currency: Featuring the BRICS. *Journal of Central Banking Theory and Practice, 11*(2), 187–208. DOI: 10.2478/jcbtp-2022-0019

Zook, M. (2018). Information flows, global finance, and new digital spaces. In *The New Oxford Handbook of Economic Geography* (pp. 575–590). DOI: 10.1093/oxfordhb/9780198755609.013.35

Chapter 6
Sustainable Financial Ecosystems:
The Role of Virtual Currencies in Green Service Financing

Kriti Kishor
https://orcid.org/0009-0006-2808-1633
I.K. Gujral Punjab Technical University, India

Sanjeev Kumar Bansal
I.K. Gujral Punjab Technical University, India

Stefano Bresciani
University of Turin, Italy

ABSTRACT

Global progress toward sustainable development has made it evident that there is a need for innovative financial instruments promoting environmental goals. With the drive provided by decentralized finance technology, virtual currencies (VCs) have now emerged as potential instruments to transform traditional sources of funding. This chapter examines critically how virtual currencies can enhance green service funding by examining their potential to facilitate transparent & traceable funding for environmentally sustainable projects. The chapter attempts to identify the opportunities and challenges involved in incorporating VCs into sustainable financial frameworks. Through an intensive synthesis of theoretical insights, the chapter also provides policy recommendations and strategic interventions to bring out the maximum transformative potential of venture capitalists and contributes to the discussion on the development of resilient and sustainable financial ecosystems that enhance global environmental objectives by aligning virtual currency develop-

DOI: 10.4018/979-8-3373-0315-4.ch006

ment with sustainability objectives.

1. INTRODUCTION

The global financial system is evolving drastically with respect to emerging environmental challenges. A common issue around the globe is achieving sustainable development targets as climate change and environmental contamination pose massive challenges (Luo et al. 2022). Though it depends on significant finance support (Ziolo et al., 2021), the shift to sustainable development is predicted to produce environmental and economic advantages. While finance support is accessible for activities linked to sustainable development, effective payment solutions are needed to guarantee the allocation of funds if sustainable development initiatives are implemented (Parmentola et al. 2022). The present financial system depends on banks or financial institutions, which are connected with great expenses in the funding of sustainable development projects (Gan & Voda 2023). Emerging payment options (Hou et al., 2021) can thus help to lower expenses for initiatives aimed at sustainable development and hence support sustainable development (Yang et al., 2023).

The emergence of virtual currencies is among the most interesting yet understudied developments in this terrain. Originally designed as distributed substitutes for conventional fiat currencies, virtual currencies—such as Bitcoin, Ethereum, and central bank digital currencies (CBDCs)—are currently under investigation for their possibilities to support sustainable finance. Particularly blockchain, its underlying technologies provide hitherto unheard-of efficiency, transparency, and traceability, which makes them perhaps strong instruments for green service funding. Virtual currencies seem to be the mirror of present environmental trends. Their increasing appeal proves that they are the correct response to new problems. Notwithstanding this, pertinent authorities—who are trying to keep control—counteract and the virtual currency market's continuing expansion is yet unknown (Mikołajewicz-Woźniak & Scheibe, 2015).

Green service finance is the financing of projects and services directly or indirectly supporting environmental sustainability, including waste management, green infrastructure maintenance, sustainable public transit systems, and renewable energy services. Historically dependent on institutional or public money, these industries are attracting growing attention from digital finance entrepreneurs. Particularly in areas with inadequate financial infrastructure or restricted access to conventional banking, virtual currencies could open fresh funding sources for such activities.

Investigating how such virtual assets could contribute to establishing sustainable financial systems, the chapter here explores the intersection between green service financing and virtual currencies. Analyzing the technical, financial, and legal dimensions of this intersection, it evaluates real-world applications and itemizes the potential and risks virtual currencies present for green financing. The chapter aims to contribute to the broader debate about how digital innovation can be balanced with efforts towards global sustainability.

2. THEORETICAL FRAMEWORK

This chapter employs Innovation Diffusion Theory (IDT) as its underlying theoretical framework to examine how virtual currencies would be appropriately incorporated into green service finance and help sustainable financial ecosystems. Initially developed by Rogers (1962), IDT explains how, why, and at what rate new ideas and technology become diffused across societies and social systems. An understanding of the patterns of virtual currency adoption in the context of sustainability-focused financial innovation requires especially this theory. Rogers identifies five primary characteristics of inventions which influence their rate of acceptance. Applied in line with the present situation, these are:

- **Relative Advantage:** Virtual currencies provide cheaper transaction costs, faster cross-border payments, and the possibility of programmable money via smart contracts, therefore surpassing conventional financing systems. In green service financing, they can enable direct peer-to--peer transactions and crowding for sustainable initiatives, therefore offering a clear relative advantage in terms of speed, openness, and decentralization.
- **Compatibility:** How closely virtual currencies fit current values, infrastructure, and legal systems will determine their viability in green finance. Adoption in this field is highly influenced by their fit with sustainability concepts, digital financial ecosystems, and environmental aims. Particularly in tokenizing carbon credits and allowing transparent donations or investments for green services, virtual currencies are progressively viewed as fit for the objectives of climate financing (Nian & Chuen, 2015).Although blockchain technologies underlie many virtual currencies, its technical complexity and the volatility of digital assets create major adoption difficulties. Especially for less tech-savvy green service stakeholders, perceived complexity can impede dissemination unless it is addressed via education and user-friendly platforms. Particularly in traditional or public sector environments, blockchain and bitcoin technologies sometimes struggle to be adopted because of perceived technical complexity and security issues (Zhang & Wen, 2017).
- **Trialability:** Virtual impacts' degree of allowing potential users to trial shapes their inclination to adopt. Trialability helps green service financing's participants to test digital financial products on a smaller scale, therefore reduc-

ing perceived risk. Lowered perceived risk and improved learning can come from pilot projects, regulatory sandboxes, and restricted trials of blockchain-enabled green bonds or distributed climate funds (Arner, Barberis, & Buckley, 2017).

- **Observability:** The presence of successful use cases—such as green token economies or blockchain-based carbon credit systems—improves observability, therefore motivating public agencies, private investors, and service providers in the sustainability fields.

In financial and environmental innovation, researchers have used IDT to explain the diffusion of mobile banking (Donner & Tellez, 2008, Lin, 2011, Oliveira & Martins, 2011), green technology (Mi et al., 2024, Zeng et al., 2020) and various virtual currencies such bitcoin (Presthus & O'Malley, 2017). This chapter emphasizes the systematic elements affecting innovation uptake in sustainability-oriented financial systems by using IDT to the analysis of virtual currencies inside green service finance. Virtual currencies place not just as technological wonders but also as disruptive financial tools able to change the funding, validation, and distribution of environmental goods and services. IDT also emphasizes how time dynamics, social systems, and routes of communication help to define adoption curves. In sustainable financial ecosystems, these elements show themselves as temporal changes in sustainability priorities, community trust, regulatory rhetoric, and international cooperation. Therefore, the distribution of virtual currencies in green finance is a question of cultural acceptance, institutional endorsement, and strategic timing as much as of technical viability. A strong theoretical framework for grasping the several functions of virtual currencies in green service financing is offered by innovation diffusion theory. It lets academics and professionals evaluate the tools for adoption in sustainable financial systems as well as the obstacles. Together with the socio-technical settings in which they function, IDT helps to clarify how virtual currencies might support the change toward more fair, transparent, and sustainable financial infrastructures by pointing out the fundamental characteristics influencing diffusion.

3. METHODOLOGY

In order to fulfil the aims delineated within the research, we employed a variety of published scholarly articles, academic research papers, and governmental reports. This methodological approach facilitates a thorough and sophisticated examination of the multifaceted dimensions of virtual currency and its interrelation with the green service financing.

3.1 Objectives of the Research

1. To critically examine the role of virtual currency in green service financing.
2. To identify opportunities and challenges in enhancing green service financing through virtual currencies
3. To propose policy recommendations and strategies that can facilitate the achievement of financial sustainability through virtual currency.

4. DISCUSSION

4.1 Role of Virtual Currency in Green Service Financing

Particularly those driven by blockchain technology—such as Bitcoin, Ethereum, and steadily risingly popular stablecoins—virtual currencies (VCs) are no longer seen only as speculative digital assets. Rather, they are developing into creative financial products equipped to solve some of the urgent gaps in modern sustainable finance. Built on peer-to--peer networks and cryptographic security, their distributed character allows borderless, real-time transactions free from intermediary requirement. These characteristics help VCs to promote green service financing, which is investing environmentally sustainable projects like renewable energy development, waste-to--energy technology, sustainable agriculture, green transportation, and eco-friendly infrastructure. Especially those founded on smart contract platforms such as Ethereum, programmability in VCs enables the automation and conditional disbursement of funds associated with specific environmental objectives, thus enabling a transparent and accountable framework for funding climate action projects. Scholars, policymakers, and entrepreneurs alike have become highly interested in examining the applications of virtual currencies in green finance as the urgency of climate action increases and expectations regarding financial inclusion and responsibility rise as well. Serving as a catalyst for the FinTech environment, the COVID-19 pandemic accelerated digital transformation across financial services. As Singh et al. (2025) observed, the pandemic was a surprising but powerful driver for consumers and corporations to adopt digital financial systems in a snap. Especially in regions where the established banking infrastructure is lacking or elite in nature, virtual currencies are playing an increasingly vital role in this rapidly evolving digital landscape and offer innovative ways to democratize access to green finance.

In addition, traceability on blockchain technology enhances transparency in the circulation and monitoring of green money, which is most essential to achieve the goals outlined in the UN Sustainable Development Goals (SDGs) and the Paris Agreement. With tokenization, assets such as carbon credits, solar assets, or green bonds can be tokenized and traded securely on distributed platforms, thus facilitating enhanced liquidity and investor participation. Blockchain-based VCs may also assist micro-financing and crowdsourcing efforts that fund local enterprises and developers who are striving for climate-resilience. The role of virtual currencies in green service financing does not, however, come without substantial challenges. Emission footprint from energy-intensive proof-of-work mechanisms, such as the Proof-of-Work (PoW) algorithm used by Bitcoin, which consumes massive amounts of electricity and contributes to carbon emissions, is one of the most frequently cited challenges. Although younger systems like Proof-of- Stake (PoS) and carbon-neutral blockchain platforms are developing to solve environmental issues, the whole energy footprint of the VC industry is still a topic of great dispute. Widespread adoption in the green finance industry is further hampered by the absence of standard global regulatory frameworks, great volatility of digital assets, cyber-attack risk, and low digital literacy among players.

All in all, virtual currencies represent a multifaceted challenge in the pursuit of sustainable financial environments as well as an intriguing frontier. Their successful integration into green service financing will require not only technological advancements but also moral innovation, inter-sectoral collaboration, and facilitating legislation. The smart use of virtual currencies has the power to reinvent how green projects are funded, tracked, and scaled in the next decades as the financial sector welcomes digital transformation more and more. Still, this is a multifarious and complicated job with both possibilities and drawbacks.

4.2 Opportunities in Enhancing Green Service Financing Through Virtual Currencies

4.2.1 Decentralized Green Finance

By enabling peer-to--peer (P2P) funding models, VCs help communities to circumvent conventional financial institutions including banks or other financial organizations, hence lowering costs and inefficiencies (Dorfleitner & Braun, 2019). For instance, platforms like SolarCoin give a specific digital token for reward of solar energy generation. It advances local empowerment in underdeveloped areas and financial inclusion. A platform that is decentralized such as Energy Web Chain enables individuals and organizations to invest and trade renewable energy assets directly with blockchain and tokens. Decentralization eliminates bureaucratic delay and provides direct access between investors and green energy producers.

4.2.2 Transparency and Traceability

Transparency and traceability, facilitated by blockchain-based virtual currencies, present a revolutionary chance in green service financing in that all transactions are guaranteed to be safely recorded, unalterable, and publicly verifiable. This technological aspect makes it possible for stakeholders to monitor the channel of funds in real time, reducing the chance of corruption, fraud, or misuse. By making financial transactions transparent and tamper-proof, virtual currencies automatically limit the potential for greenwashing, as true fund utilization and environmental contribution can be independently verified through auditable accounts. Additionally, the use of blockchain with smart environmental sensors and IoT technologies further maximizes traceability by creating real-time, data-based proof of sustainability outcomes like reduced emissions or energy consumptions. Finally, this transparency at such a high level fosters trust, accountability, and confidence among the stakeholders to invest in and participate more in ecologically sustainable projects. Even the World Economic Forum has lately produced a series of white papers covering specific governance issues for decision-makers using blockchain technology throughout international commerce and supply-chain networks (Hewett et al., 2019; Miatton & Amado, 2020).

4.2.3 Tokenization of Green Assets

Tokenization made possible by VCs lets fractional ownership of green assets—such as solar farms and wind turbines. A green energy trading platform called WePower lets investors buy energy tokens from upcoming renewable energy output. It increases availability of environmentally friendly investments. Properly marketing and issuing green bonds will have a considerably better chance of bringing investment to the security markets and the much-needed development in the sustainable sector. If green bonds are sold and issued under digital tokenization (Chugh, 2023), they are far more likely to provide investment to the security markets and much-needed development to the sustainable sector.

4.2.4 Innovative Fundraising Tools

Virtual currencies help to enable fresh fundraising strategies such Green STOs and ICOs. Allows eco-startups raise money anywhere free from conventional venture capital constraints. Blockchain technology' special qualities can enable crowdsourcing sites to handle common problems; for example, smart contracts can be applied to distribute money based on the development of individual projects (Nguyen et al., 2021). Another use of blockchain technology, cryptocurrency transactions (e.g.,

Bitcoin and Ethereum) can help crowdfunding platforms lower risks and intermediation expenses as they allow the transfer of funds on a peer-to-peer basis rather than via financial intermediaries (Muneeza et al., 2018).

4.3 Challenges in Using Virtual Currencies for Green Service Financing

4.3.1 High Energy Consumption

Many VCs—especially Bitcoin—use very energy-intensive Proof-of- Work (PoW). De Vries (2018) notes Bitcoin's energy use on par with those of whole nations. Environmental cost can so exceed the advantages of financing. The possible risks and difficulties bitcoins bring have led to several objections against them. The least talked about are the major environmental effects of using too much energy in the mining operation of cryptocurrencies (Tripathi, 2023). Such systems necessitate huge amounts of computational effort to approve transactions and protect the network, and accordingly, need enormous electricity supplies—mostly derived from non-renewable sources. This presents a deep contradiction to sustainability principles, since the cost of the environment to sustain such blockchain networks is higher than the green motive for their application. The carbon footprints of mining and transaction processing in high-energy virtual currencies demolish the environmental objectives of green service financing and may result in censure and lower credibility among green-conscious investors and stakeholders. In addition, the absence of uniform global legislation on the source of energy used for mining aggravates the issue, as miners can use less expensive, fossil fuel-based power, particularly in countries with ineffective environmental laws. Although newer virtual currencies and blockchain networks are looking into energy-efficient solutions such as proof-of-stake (PoS) or green blockchains, their wider adoption is not yet extensive. This energy challenge creates uncertainty regarding the actual sustainability of virtual currencies in enabling green finance and points to the necessity of meticulous reflection and innovation to ensure blockchain technology works in support of climate objectives.

4.3.2 Price Volatility

Renowned for volatility are cryptocurrencies. Unstable rates could discourage investors from funding long-term green initiatives utilizing venture capitalists. Any third-party vendor or customer looking to provide a legitimate reference point for determining consumer pricing will find the dubious market worth of one bitcoin to be a challenge (Yermack, 2024).

4.3.3 Regulatory Uncertainty

Clear legal frameworks for VCs help to reduce investor risk. Still free from control are certain operators that retain transaction earnings in cryptocurrencies or use cash or a private transaction (Cumming et al., 2019). As governments all around struggle with its mechanics and investigate its influence and the best approach to control digital money, regulation of it is still in infancy (Hanafi & Rahman, 2019). This then prevents general acceptance of VCs in institutional green finance.

4.3.4 Risk of Greenwashing

One can abuse tokenizing and green labeling. Fake "green" tokens can mislead investors without standardized verification. Blockchain technology's digital tokenizing of green bonds will help (Chugh, 2023). The threat of greenwashing is a salient issue in applying virtual currencies towards green service financing, since the decentralized and frequently anonymous character of blockchain transactions may create uncertainty in confirming the legitimacy of environmental statements. Greenwashing refers to the practice of misrepresenting activities or projects as being environmentally sustainable in order to obtain funding or improve the organizational reputation, without providing real environmental benefits. In the case of virtual money, while blockchain has the potential for transparency, it is not always guaranteed on the platforms that enable reliable and standardised confirmation of the sustainability results. Some projects utilize ambiguous or deceiving terms, or offer unverifiable information to indicate that they promote environmental friendly projects, thus deceiving investors and stakeholders. Also, the absence of universal regulatory schemes and third-party verification mechanisms for assessing environmental impact opens up avenues for such fraudulent or overstated claims to run rampant. This not only discredits the green finance initiatives but also misappropriates vital resources from actually meaningful projects. The technical and complicated nature of blockchain systems can also make it difficult to hold people accountable, since ordinary investors may not have the skills to investigate whether a virtual currency or green initiative is actually sustainable. Accordingly, the risk of greenwashing for green financing based on virtual currencies creates legitimate concerns over trust, investor confidence, and long-term efficacy of such financing structures, necessitating rigorous verification requirements, clear impact reporting transparency, and regulatory control to guarantee the integrity of green finance efforts.

4.4 Policy Recommendations and Strategies for Virtual Currency-Based Financial Sustainability

Provide thorough rules for virtual currency (VCs), so guaranteeing consistency on legality, taxes, anti-money laundering (AML), and consumer protection. Apply Know Your Customer (KYC) and AML rules to stop abuse while advancing credibility and legality in virtual money markets. As a safe, government-backed substitute for private virtual currencies, encourage the development of central bank digital currencies (CBDCs). Fund environmental initiatives with tokenized green bonds or carbon credits created on blockchain systems. Give organizations and people using virtual currency for environmentally friendly projects or sustainable investments incentives or tax credits. Require ESG compliance reporting on blockchain systems to guarantee open and trackable sustainability claims. Especially for underprivileged communities in rural and underdeveloped areas, encourage virtual currencies as a means to provide access to financial services. Support low-cost transaction systems using virtual currencies for micro-transactions and remittances, together with mobile wallets. Establish public-private alliances to increase digital literacy and financial competency required to use virtual currencies. Invest in blockchain architecture supporting scalable, energy-efficient, safe transaction processing. Promote sandboxes, accelerators, and innovation centers to test innovative virtual currencies-based financial products fit for sustainability objectives. Provide fintech entrepreneurs creating VC-based financial solutions technical support and finance. Organize worldwide alliances to standardize security, taxes, and virtual currency transactions policies. Using VCs, promote globally remittance networks and interoperable payment systems to cut transaction costs. To control digital hazards, nations should encourage data exchange and cyber-security systems among others. Make sure that carbon-neutral methods and sustainable energy sources are adopted by means of mining and transaction validation systems. Support open-source blockchain development to raise auditability and transparency in VC-based funding. Encourage citizen involvement as well as fintechs, environmental groups, and policy formation stakeholders.

5. CONCLUSION

All things considered, this chapter emphasizes how virtual currencies might revolutionize the architecture of green service financing and support the creation of really sustainable financial ecosystems. Virtual currencies—especially those created on distributed blockchain systems—have become increasingly important enablers of change as the global economy searches creative answers to address the linked issues of climate change, financial exclusion, and economic recovery in the post-pandemic era. By means of a critical analysis of their functions, use cases, and technological underpinnings, this chapter underlines that virtual currencies, when carefully integrated and supported by enabling regulatory environments, can greatly improve transparency, efficiency, traceability, and inclusiveness in financing environmentally sustainable services. The chapter has looked at the special qualities of virtual currencies, including their capacity to eliminate conventional middlemen, lower transaction costs, smart contract-based automated financing mechanism capability, and democratization of financial resources for underprivileged groups. These characteristics render VCs indispensable tools for green infrastructure capital mobilization, climate-resilient agriculture, clean energy schemes, and other green initiatives aligned with the broader goals of the Paris Agreement and the UN Sustainable Development Goals (SDGs). In addition, the built-in openness and permanence of blockchain systems can assist in addressing long-standing issues like corruption, green money misallocation, and environmental funding sources' lack of accountability.

At the same time, however, the chapter never turns a blind eye to the many and complex challenges associated with the use of virtual currencies in this context. They encompass concerns for data protection, regulatory risks, digital literacy disparities, as well as the environmental cost of certain consensus mechanisms like Proof-of-Work. Addressing these issues not only ensures the validity and sustainability of VC-based finance models but also assists in cultivating trust among local communities, governments, and investors. For this purpose, the chapter offers a set of pragmatic, visionary policy concepts and strategies. These include creation of harmonized international regulatory regimes, promotion of energy-efficient blockchain protocols, embedding of environmental, social, and governance (ESG) indicators in digital financial platforms, and establishment of inclusive digital literacy and capacity-building initiatives. Ultimately, the integration of virtual currencies into green service finance represents a fundamental shift in the way financial ecosystems can be constructed to achieve both economic and environmental objectives, thus going beyond technology innovation alone. It challenges traditional financial paradigms and calls in the digital age for reconsideration of trust, value, and governance. Virtual currencies present a strategic opportunity to align financial innovation with sustainability needs as nations and firms navigate the transition to a low-carbon, digital economy. Actors can open the door towards long-term financial stability, environmental balance, and collective prosperity by utilizing their potential appropriately and inclusively.

REFERENCES

Ajouz, M., Abdullah, A., & Kassim, S. (2020). Acceptance of Sharīʿah-compliant precious metal-backed cryptocurrency as an alternative currency: An empirical validation of adoption of innovation theory. *Thunderbird International Business Review*, *62*(2), 171–181. DOI: 10.1002/tie.22106

Arner, D. W., Barberis, J., & Buckley, R. P. (2017). *FinTech and RegTech in a Nutshell, and the Future in a Sandbox*. CFA Institute Research Foundation. DOI: 10.2139/ssrn.3088303

Bharadwaj, S., & Deka, S. (2021, December). Behavioural intention towards investment in cryptocurrency: An integration of Rogers' diffusion of innovation theory and the technology acceptance model. *Forum Scientiae Oeconomia*, *9*(4), 137–159.

Chugh, P. (2023). Leveraging Blockchain Technology in Adopting Digital Tokenization of Green Bonds. In *Fostering Sustainable Development in the Age of Technologies* (pp. 213–224). Emerald Publishing Limited., DOI: 10.1108/978-1-83753-060-120231015

Cumming, D. J., Johan, S., & Pant, A. (2019). Regulation of the crypto-economy: Managing risks, challenges, and regulatory uncertainty. *Journal of Risk and Financial Management*, *12*(3), 126. DOI: 10.3390/jrfm12030126

De Vries, A. (2018). Bitcoin's growing energy problem. *Joule*, *2*(5), 801–805. DOI: 10.1016/j.joule.2018.04.016

Donner, J., & Tellez, C. A. (2008). Mobile banking and economic development: Linking adoption, impact, and use. *Asian Journal of Communication*, *18*(4), 318–332. DOI: 10.1080/01292980802344190

Dorfleitner, G., & Braun, D. (2019). Fintech, digitalization and blockchain: possible applications for green finance. *The rise of green finance in Europe: opportunities and challenges for issuers, investors and marketplaces*, 207-237.

Gan, C., & Voda, M. (2023). Can green finance reduce carbon emission intensity? Mechanism and threshold effect. *Environmental Science and Pollution Research International*, *30*(1), 640–653. DOI: 10.1007/s11356-022-22176-9 PMID: 35906522

Hanafi, S. F., & Rahman, S. A. (2019). Regulating digital currency: taming the unruly. In *Emerging issues in Islamic finance law and practice in Malaysia* (pp. 265–280). Emerald Publishing Limited. DOI: 10.1108/978-1-78973-545-120191021

Hewett, N., Lehmacher, W., & Wang, Y. (2019, April). Inclusive deployment of blockchain for supply chains. World Economic Forum.

Hou, L., Hsueh, S. C., & Zhang, S. (2021). Digital payments and households' consumption: A mental accounting interpretation. *Emerging Markets Finance & Trade*, *57*(7), 2079–2093. DOI: 10.1080/1540496X.2021.1887727

Lin, H. F. (2011). An empirical investigation of mobile banking adoption: The effect of innovation attributes and knowledge-based trust. *International Journal of Information Management*, *31*(3), 252–260. DOI: 10.1016/j.ijinfomgt.2010.07.006

Luo, S., Yimamu, N., Li, Y., Wu, H., Irfan, M., & Hao, Y. (2023). Digitalization and sustainable development: How could digital economy development improve green innovation in China? *Business Strategy and the Environment*, *32*(4), 1847–1871. DOI: 10.1002/bse.3223

Mi, J., Yao, C., Zhao, X., & Li, F. (2024). Research on the diffusion mechanism of green technology innovation based on enterprise perception. *Computational Economics*, *63*(5), 1981–2010. DOI: 10.1007/s10614-023-10391-6

Miatton, F., & Amado, L. (2020, April). *Fairness, transparency and traceability in the coffee value chain through blockchain innovation. In 2020 international conference on technology and entrepreneurship-virtual (ICTE-V)*. IEEE.

Mikołajewicz-Woźniak, A., & Scheibe, A. (2015). Virtual currency schemes–the future of financial services. *Foresight*, *17*(4), 365–377. DOI: 10.1108/FS-04-2014-0021

Muneeza, A., Arshad, N. A., & Arifin, A. T. (2018). The application of blockchain technology in crowdfunding: Towards financial inclusion via technology. *International journal of management and applied research*, *5*(2), 82-98.

Nguyen, L. T., Hoang, T. G., Do, L. H., Ngo, X. T., Nguyen, P. H., Nguyen, G. D., & Nguyen, G. N. (2021). The role of blockchain technology-based social crowdfunding in advancing social value creation. *Technological Forecasting and Social Change*, *170*, 120898. DOI: 10.1016/j.techfore.2021.120898

Nian, L. P., & Chuen, D. L. K. (2015). Introduction to bitcoin. In *Handbook of digital currency* (pp. 5–30). Academic Press. DOI: 10.1016/B978-0-12-802117-0.00001-1

Parmentola, A., Petrillo, A., Tutore, I., & De Felice, F. (2022). Is blockchain able to enhance environmental sustainability? A systematic review and research agenda from the perspective of Sustainable Development Goals (SDGs). *Business Strategy and the Environment*, *31*(1), 194–217. DOI: 10.1002/bse.2882

Presthus, W., & O'Malley, N. O. (2017). Motivations and barriers for end-user adoption of bitcoin as digital currency. *Procedia Computer Science*, *121*, 89–97. DOI: 10.1016/j.procs.2017.11.013

Rogers, E. M. (1962). Diffusion of innovations the free Press of Glencoe. *NY, 32*, 891-937.

Singh, S., Gupta, D., Kumar, R., & Balusamy, B. (2025). Pre-and Post-COVID Autonomous Finance: Global Perspective. *Computational Intelligence for Autonomous Finance*, 269-288.

Tripathi, S. (2023). Impact of Cryptocurrency on the Environment. *Indian J. Integrated Rsch. L.*, *3*, 1.

Yang, Q., Zheng, M., & Wang, Y. (2023). The role of CBDC in green finance and sustainable development. *Emerging Markets Finance & Trade*, *59*(15), 4158–4173. DOI: 10.1080/1540496X.2023.2185096

Yermack, D. (2024). Is Bitcoin a real currency? An economic appraisal. In *Handbook of digital currency* (pp. 29–40). Academic Press. DOI: 10.1016/B978-0-323-98973-2.00014-9

Zeng, Y., Dong, P., Shi, Y., Wang, L., & Li, Y. (2020). Analyzing the co-evolution of green technology diffusion and consumers' pro-environmental attitudes: An agent-based model. *Journal of Cleaner Production*, *256*, 120384. DOI: 10.1016/j.jclepro.2020.120384

Zhang, Y., & Wen, J. (2017). The IoT electric business model: Using blockchain technology for the internet of things. *Peer-to-Peer Networking and Applications*, *10*(4), 983–994. DOI: 10.1007/s12083-016-0456-1

Ziolo, M., Bak, I., & Cheba, K. (2021). The role of sustainable finance in achieving sustainable development goals: Does it work? *Technological and Economic Development of Economy*, *27*(1), 45–70. DOI: 10.3846/tede.2020.13863

Chapter 7 Sustainable Supply Chain Management Effect on Global Sustainable Service Marketing by Mediation of Cross-Border Virtual Currencies in the Horn of Africa

Shashi Kant
https://orcid.org/0000-0003-4722-5736
Bule Hora University, Ethiopia

Tamire Ashuro
Bule Hora University, Ethiopia

Metasebia Adula
https://orcid.org/0000-0001-5732-2850
Bule Hora University, Ethiopia

ABSTRACT

This investigation investigates the associations among Marketing of services for Global Sustainability (MSGS), Virtual Currencies used at Cross Border (VCCB), and Sustainable Management of Supply Chain. The investigation uses Structural Equation Modeling (SEM) to examine the direct and indirect effects of SMSC activities on MSGS via CBVC mediation. The outcomes manifested a robust affirmative

DOI: 10.4018/979-8-3373-0315-4.ch007

association among SMSC and MSGS, suggesting that initiatives for marketing targeting aware about ecosystem clients are augmented by effective sustainable activities. Also, VCCB perform as an essential intermediary, promoting worldwide trade and raising the general efficacy of sustainability initiatives for marketing. By emphasizing the significance of combining sustainable activities with cutting-edge financial technology, the investigation enhance to the body of literature already in existence and offers managers and stakeholders' useful insights for navigating the intricacies of worldwide markets. Organizations are advised to use digital currencies and create marketing communications.

INTRODUCTION

Growing consciousness of green challenges, Ethic justice, and fiscal resilience has made sustainability a vital concern in corporate operations in recent years. Sustainable Management of Supply Chain (SMSC), which incorporates Ethic, fiscal, and green issues into supply chain operations, is the outcome of this paradigm change (Attia, 2023). SMSC includes several different activities, such as resource efficiency, waste reduction, ethical sourcing, and supply chain transparency. In addition to lessening their green impact, businesses may augment their brand recognition, cultivate client loyalty, and gain a competitive edge in a market that is becoming more greenly sensitive by implementing sustainable activities (Raftowicz et al., 2024).

Businesses must manage intricate supply chains spanning several nations, each with its own legal frameworks and cultural settings, as globalization continues to influence corporate operations. This intricacy depicted the want for SMSC to be seen as a worldwide imperative, where sustainability is viewed as an essential part of worldwide fiscal strategy rather than only a local issue (Hariyani et al., 2024).

Both cross-country virtual currencies (VCs) are critical tothe achievements of sustainable Management of supplies chain (SMSC) and market development of services for sustainability. SMSC is advanced by developing technologies like AI, IoT, BIG DATA for better efficiency, transparency as well as data-driven decision making. However, organizations encounter several barriers in the implementation of SMSC such as; resistance to change, lack of skills and main supply chain integration (Joseph, 2023). New patterns of consumers' behavior more and more focus on the environmental issues and as a result, organizations switch to the utilization of green initiatives (Sood et al., 2021). In addition, the legal and regulatory environment plays a role in influencing SMSC and virtual currency in various world areas. The authors explain that differences in codes and standards can act as enablers or constraints when businesses want to develop new solutions that can last. Dealing with these aspects will give a brush on the existing environment and hence ensure that the chapter seeks to document concerning changes as well as new dimensions that shape sustainable practices in the global world (Lotfi et al., 2024).

Challenges include: cross supplier networks sustainability inquisition, resistance from stakeholders, and high initial investment in sustainable technology. Regional characteristics also come to play when it comes to consumer preferences over sustainable products (Dabrowski & Janikowski, 2018). For example, the European consumers increasingly care about sustainable consumption and product transparency, while forming a perception about a brand in new markets; the price would hold more importance than sustainability. This means that marketers need to come up with market mixes that depict the culture and needs of the people in that country (Hariyani et al., 2024). Also worthy of note is the fact that SMSC and service marketing are affected by regulatory frameworks in no small measure (Inder et al., 2021). Some countries like in the EU may have strong sustainability standards while others have less strong policy, making compliance an issue of patchwork In addition, real life case such as the case that shows how Unilever embraced sustainability impacted its market ability can differ widely. For instance, consumers in Europe tend to prioritize eco-friendly products and transparency, while in emerging markets, affordability may take precedence over sustainability. This necessitates tailored marketing strategies that resonate with local values and demands (Dereso et al., 2023).

Additionally, regulatory frameworks significantly impact SMSC and service marketing. Regions like the EU enforce stringent sustainability regulations, while others may have more lenient policies, creating a patchwork of compliance challenges. Real-world examples, such as Unilever's commitment to sustainability and its impact on market share, can illustrate successful strategies. In addition, the expansion of the conversation to other technologies such as traceability through blockchain or big data to introduce customer understanding will add depth to the current state and offer valuable advice to companies (Das, 2024).

At the same time as supply chain management is evolving, service marketing is also changing, with a greater emphasis on sustainability as a key selling point. Promoting services that are both financially feasible and ethically and sustainable responsible is the main goal of Marketing of services for Global Sustainability. Because clients increasingly give sustainability top priority when making purchases, service industries including hotels, transportation, and consumer services are most impacted by this change (Hariyani et al., 2024). Businesses may stand out from rivals, build closer association with clients, and increase brand equity by effectively incorporating sustainable activities into their service offerings (Dereso et al., 2023). The emergence of Sustainable Management of Supply Chain (VCCB), like cryptocurrencies, has brought a new dimension to worldwide commerce and finance by facilitating seamless cross-border transactions by enabling direct peer-to-peer payments, thereby reducing reliance on traditional banking systems (Das, 2024).

This decentralization can substantially lower transaction costs, expedite payment processes, and enhance financial inclusion, especially for businesses operating in regions with limited access to banking services. This alignment with consumer values is not only advantageous for attracting greenly conscious clientele but also essential for fostering long-term client loyalty in a competitive global marketplace (Dabrowski & Janikowski, 2018). To improve applicability the chapter explored the global differences in regulations that affect SMSC and VCCB. For instance, the European Union Green Deal agenda sets high sustainability standards for its member countries than the stringent rules of the emerging markets that present tricky compliance issues (Guyo et al., 2023). Some examples are: Unilever's approach towards sustainable sourcing of raw material or how Walmart used Artificial Intelligence in its supply chain management. Building on the prospects of IoT for real-time tracking/monitoring and AI expected to render in predictive stock analysis, can show how they can work. Such a holistic view will help fill theoretical deficits and provide practical recommendations on how firms manage sustainability challenges in the global context (Das,2024).

Scholarly investigation into the association among SMSC, Marketing of services for Global Sustainability, and VCCB is highly promising. SMSC has a substantial impact on service marketing tactics; by integrating sustainability into their supply chains, businesses can create engaging stories about their offerings that emphasize their dedication to green and Ethic responsibility (Attia, 2023). On the other hand, VCCB may play a crucial mediating function in this association, allowing companies to enable more fiscally and efficient transactions, which in turn permits higher investments in marketing campaigns and sustainable activities. The overall sustainability of service offerings is further augmented by the opportunity to work with sustainable partners and suppliers while conducting business world widely without having to pay exorbitant costs (Adula et al., 2023). The investigation on the mediating function of VCCB in the interaction among SMSC and Marketing of services for Global Sustainability is still lacking, despite the themes' increasing significance. The vitality of current investigation tends to concentrate on service marketing or SMSC separately, ignoring the possible synergies that may outcome from combining the two with cutting-edge financial technology (Joseph, 2023). For example, Patagonia's adoption of organic material shows how SMSC can be well applied in an organization. These are the future technologies in practice, Walmart for instance has been using the use of Artificial intelligence in its inventory control and block chain in the chain of Keller. Recommendable approaches are attaining IoT devices for supply chain monitoring and using VCCB in cross-border transactions (Quernheim et al., 2023). Answering international compliance issues like a difference in compliance with regulation in EU and developing countries is crucial. Also, examining consumer behavior trends such as transparency and ethicality will further enhance the approach for firms involved in activities that support sustainability (Dabrowski & Janikowski, 2018).

By analyzing the ways in which SMSC impacts marketing of services for Global Sustainability and the degree to which VCCB mediate this association, this investigation seeks to close this gap. By comprehending these dynamics, businesses can better navigate the intricacies of a rapidly evolving global marketplace, ultimately supporting their long-term sustainability goals. The investigation outcomes will be crucial for organizations hoping to succeed in a world where sustainability is not just a choice but a requirement for success (Szewczyk et al., 2019).

STATEMENT OF THE PROBLEM

The want for sustainability has grown in importance in today's global business environment, forcing companies to reconsider their marketing plans and operational frameworks. Although the value of Sustainable Management of Supply Chain (SMSC) in encouraging Ethic responsibility and green stewardship is well acknowledged, many businesses find it extremely difficult to put these principles into reality (Quernheim et al., 2023). Integrating SMSC into larger worldwide sustainable service marketing campaigns is one of the main problems. Although some businesses implement sustainable supply chain procedures, they frequently find it difficult to adequately convey these initiatives to clients, which undermine their ability to augment client loyalty and brand reputation (Jabo et al., 2023). This discrepancy begs substantial concerns about how companies may align their supply chain activities with their marketing plans to produce a coherent story that appeals to clients who care about sustainability (Schonebeck & Pöllinger, 2020).

Scholarly and empirical analysis of sustainable management of supply chains (SMSC) and cross-border virtual currencies (VCCB) indicate practical problems and perspectives for business. Lack of implementation involves issues in dealing with global supply chains, where regulations differ from country to country and where technology advancement could be low. This resistance to change is majorly due to the following factors; inadequate infrastructure and talent that hinder sustainable integration in business organizations (Quernheim et al., 2023). AI and IoT-based technologies together with inclusion of big data present a radical opportunity for SMSC by improving visibility of supply chains, efficient utilisation of resources and analysis for prediction. For example, it is possible to predict the demand, thanks to technologies like the one used by Walmart or IoT devices that help the companies to monitor the conditions necessary for supply chain in real-time (Jabo et al., 2024).

The requirement charts indicate that the legal and regulatory frameworks differ across the regions whereby organisations operate influencing on the sustainability practices they undertake. While Europe has well-articulated regulation that supports sustainable practices, other regions may have no precise regulation to follow, thus making it complex to harmonize the two elements (Adula et al., 2024). Consumer behavior is also changing and it is evident that consumers are now much more conscious about getting more and more transparent and sustainable products. The difference in expectations can depend on the region and thus require different marketing concepts. Discussing these topics in more detail with cases and real examples will enable the readers and businesses approaching this goal to get useful and realistic solutions (Jabo et al., 2023).

Additionally, the rise of VCCB (Sustainable Management of Supply Chain), like crypto-currencies, enhances complexity and potential to this equation. On the one hand, VCCB can save expenses, augment supply chain operations' transparency, and enable more seamless worldwide transactions. Also, companies wishing to integrate these digital currencies into their sustainability plans face difficulties due to their volatility and regulatory unpredictability (Das, 2024). Organizations may be discouraged from fully adopting these cutting-edge financial technologies due to unclear regulations and possible hazards, which will limit their capacity to use them as instruments to advance sustainability. This leads to a substantial vacuum in the literature because previous investigation frequently concentrates on service marketing or SMSC separately, omitting to examine the ways in which VCCB might moderate the link among these two crucial domains (Choetal.,2018). Also, with client tastes shifting toward ethically and sustainable conscious goods and services, it is especially critical to include sustainability into service marketing tactics. Businesses that don't connect their service offerings with sustainable activities run the danger of losing market share and tarnishing their reputations as clients grow more discriminating and demand greater responsibility from companies (Lotfi et al., 2024).

This fact emphasizes "***how substantial it is to have a thorough grasp of how SMSC can support and augment worldwide sustainable service initiatives for marketing. But without a clear framework that manifested how SMSC, service marketing, and VCCB interact, businesses would not be able to effectively adapt to these changing market wants***"? The central problem lies in the insufficient understanding of the interconnected association among SMSC, Marketing of services for Global Sustainability, and the mediating function of VCCB. This gap not only hampers individual organizations' ability to implement effective sustainability strategies but also limits the overall progress towards sustainable activities in the global marketplace.

THEORETICAL LITERATURE REVIEW

Triple Bottom Line (TBL) Theory

Fiscal, Ethic, and green performances are the three main areas that firms should prioritize, rendering to the Triple Bottom Line idea. This framework is essential to SMSC because it pushes businesses to implement strategies that augment profitability while simultaneously benefiting the environment and society. TBL assists companies in communicating their dedication to sustainability in the context of Marketing of services for Global Sustainability, drawing in clients who value ethical consumption (Virijević Jovanović et al., 2018).

Resource-Based View (RBV)

Rendering to the Resource-Based View hypothesis, a company's distinct assets and competencies provide it a competitive edge. Rendering to this thesis, businesses may use their resources to adopt sustainable activities and gain long-term competitive advantages in SMSC. This viewpoint also applies to service marketing, as companies that make good use of their sustainable resources may stand out from the competition and attract aware about ecosystem clients (Madhani, 2010).

Technology-Organization-Environment (TOE)

A thorough method for comprehending the elements influencing technology adoption in businesses is offered by the TOE framework. In the context of VCCB, this theory underlines how technological, organizational, and green circumstances impact the adoption of virtual currencies in supply chains. Businesses may strengthen their service marketing strategies and sustainability initiatives by incorporating VCCB into their operations, especially when conducting cross-border transactions (Shayan et al., 2022).

Innovation Diffusion Theory

The adoption and dissemination of innovative technologies, including VCCB, within markets are explained by innovation diffusion theory. This notion is crucial to comprehending how companies might use VCCB to augment their initiatives for marketing and enable sustainable supply chain procedures. Adopting VCCB may increase transparency and expedite transactions, both of which are essential for advancing sustainable service offerings (Weil, 2018).

Stakeholder Theory

Stakeholder theory depicted how crucial it is to take into account the interests of all parties involved when making business decisions. Because it promotes businesses to interact with a range of stakeholders, such as suppliers, consumers, and communities, in order to create sustainable activities, this philosophy is especially pertinent to SMSC and service marketing. Businesses may augment their reputation and marketing efficacy for sustainable services by attending to stakeholder concerns (Schonebeck & Pöllinger, 2020).

Ethical Consumption Theory

The focus of ethical consumption theory is on the issues that influence consumers' decisions to buy, especially those related to Ethic responsibility and sustainability. This idea is crucial for Marketing of services for Global Sustainability because it explains to companies how to best convey their sustainability efforts to ethically conscious clients. By using SMSC principles, marketing claims can gain more legitimacy, which will affect client behavior (Wessels, 2014).

EMPIRICAL LITERATURE REVIEW

Sustainable SCM and Marketing of Services

Organizations may greatly augment their market positioning and consumer engagement by using SMSC techniques, as several investigations have manifested. Like, Attia (2023) found that businesses with robust SMSC frameworks not only increase operational efficiency but also enhance client satisfaction and brand reputation (Panigrahi et al., 2024). This is especially true for service sectors, as incorporating sustainability into service delivery turns into a key difference in cutthroat marketplaces. Rendering to empirical data, clients are more likely to select services from businesses that actively practice sustainability, which supports the idea that SMSC plays a substantial influence in determining service marketing tactics (Raftowicz et al., 2024). Also, an investigation by Zhong & Zhao (2024) discovered that supply chains with sustainable activities have a beneficial impact on consumer attitudes and actions, which increases client loyalty and preference for sustainable service providers. This is consistent with the outcomes of a meta-analysis by Lotfi et al. (2024), which demonstrated a direct association among augmented marketing effectiveness and sustainable supply chain activities. Rendering to the investigation, companies who use marketing channels to effectively convey their sustainable supply chain initiatives may better connect with aware about ecosystem clients, increasing sales and giving them a competitive edge.

Also, it has been demonstrated that incorporating sustainability into service marketing produces profitable outcomes. Rendering to empirical data from a investigation by Bronn and Bronn (2018), businesses that use sustainable service marketing and are backed by robust SMSC procedures have a more affirmative reaction from the market, as seen by a rise in consumer trust and readiness to pay more for sustainable services. This investigation emphasizes the necessity of linking supply chain sustainability with marketing strategies to target the expanding sector of sustainability-focused clients (Virijević Jovanović et al., 2018). Additionally, the mediating elements that strengthen the association among SMSC and sustainable service marketing have been investigated empirically. For instance, it has been manifested that client trust in sustainable services is substantially influenced by supply chain transparency and traceability (Sun et al., 2022). Rendering to their outcomes, businesses greatly increase the efficacy of their marketing campaigns targeting clients who are concerned about sustainability when they can manifested how sustainable their supply chain operations are.

> HI: Sustainable Management of Supply Chain has a substantial effect on Marketing of services for Global Sustainability

Sustainable SCM and Virtual Currencies at Cross Border

Due to the cost-effectiveness and efficiency that virtual currencies provide, especially for businesses seeking to reduce transaction costs associated with world-wide payments, investigation by Wadhwa et al. (2020) manifested that companies implementing sustainable supply chain activities are more likely to adopt VCCB as a means of facilitating cross-border transactions. This suggests that SMSC activities can substantially increase the adoption and effectiveness of VCCB in global supply chains (Zhong & Zhao, 2024). Also, investigation indicates that the application of VCCB can enhance traceability and transparency in sustainable supply chains. An investigation by Mujkić et al. (2018) claims that companies may more efficiently monitor the sustainability credentials of their supply chain partners by integrating block chain technology, which is frequently connected to VCCB. In addition to supporting the veracity of sustainability claims, this openness satisfies client desire for ethical and responsible sourcing. Rendering to the outcomes, companies may augment their overall sustainability performance and attract more greenly concerned clients by utilizing VCCB in combination with SMSC (Das, 2024).

Additionally, investigations have demonstrated how VCCB help supply chain participants work together. Rendering to a investigation by Szewczyk et al. (2019), the usage of virtual currencies can facilitate transactions among manufacturers, suppliers, and retailers, leading to the development of sustainability-focused partnerships. VCCB allow businesses to access sustainable resources worldwide by lowering the barriers to cross-border transactions, which can outcome in more greenly friendly supply chain procedures. This collaboration element is essential because it augments businesses' capacity to execute all-encompassing sustainability projects throughout their supply chains (Dabrowski & Janikowski, 2018). Additionally, in the framework of SMSC, empirical investigation has investigated the possible hazards connected to VCCB. Rendering to investigation by Li et al. (2022), like, firms face vital obstacles in navigating regulatory uncertainty and volatility in virtual currency markets. These difficulties may influence the choices made about the use of VCCB in greenly friendly supply chains. The report also depicted that businesses may still take advantage of the advantages provided by VCCB if they proactively manage these risks via strategic planning, which will further solidify their dedication to sustainability (Raftowicz et al., 2024).

H2: Sustainable Management of Supply Chain has a substantial effect on Virtual Currencies used at Cross Border

Virtual Currencies and Marketing of Services

The empirical literature examining the effect of Sustainable Management of Supply Chain (VCCB) on Marketing of services for Global Sustainability depicted the transformative potential of these digital currencies in enhancing marketing strategies focused on sustainability. Investigation indicates that VCCB, such as crypto-currencies, enable businesses to conduct seamless worldwide transactions, thereby facilitating the expansion of sustainable service offerings across global markets(Quarterly, 2020). For instance, Joseph (2023) demonstrates that the ability to transact in VCCB reduces transaction costs and time delays, which can substantially enhance the agility of companies in responding to consumer demand for sustainable services. This efficiency not only augments operational capabilities but also allows businesses to invest more resources in sustainability initiatives and marketing strategies (Kant et al., 2024). Additionally, empirical outcomes suggest that the use of VCCB can bolster consumer trust and transparency in sustainable service marketing. Investigation by Joseph (2023) indicates that block chain technology, often utilized in conjunction with VCCB, provides a transparent ledger of transactions that can verify the sustainability claims made by service providers. This transparency is particularly substantial in the service sector, where consumers are increasingly scrutinizing the ethical activities of businesses. By leveraging VCCB, companies can effectively communicate their commitment to sustainability, thus enhancing their marketing narratives and fostering rousted association with greenly conscious consumers (Das, 2024).

Also, investigations have depicted the function of VCCB in promoting inclusivity and accessibility in global markets. Rendering to investigation by Dabrowski & Janikowski (2018), VCCB can empower small and medium-sized enterprises (SMEs) in developing regions to access worldwide markets without the barriers imposed by traditional banking systems. This democratization of access allows SMEs to offer sustainable services on a global scale, thereby contributing to the overall growth of sustainable service marketing. The ability of these businesses to engage in worldwide commerce through VCCB not only enhances their market reach but also aligns with broader sustainability goals by promoting ethical and responsible business activities (Choi et al., 2018). Also, the empirical literature points to the challenges associated with the adoption of VCCB in sustainable service marketing. A investigation by Hariyani et al., (2024) identifies regulatory uncertainties and market volatility as potential barriers that can hinder the widespread acceptance of virtual currencies. These challenges may affect consumer confidence and willingness to engage with businesses that utilize VCCB. Also, the investigation also suggests that companies that actively address these concerns through clear communication and robust risk management strategies can mitigate these effects and leverage the benefits of VCCB to enhance their marketing efforts (Alemán et al., 2016).

H3: Virtual Currencies used at Cross Border has a substantial effect on Marketing of services for Global Sustainability

Mediation of Virtual Currencies Among SSCM and of Services Marketing

Effective SMSC procedures have been manifested to enhance a company's capacity to promote sustainable services world widely. Rendering to an investigation by Virijević Jovanović et al., (2018), companies who use SMSC augment their brand image and client trust in addition to achieving operational efficiency. Due to consumers' growing preference for brands that exhibit a commitment to sustainability, this favorable perception is essential for service marketing. Also, by easing global transactions and improving supply chain transparency, the incorporation of VCCB is crucial in this context. Rendering to empirical data from Quernheim et al., (2023), VCCB can expedite cross-border payments, enabling businesses to more effectively engage in sustainable sourcing and service delivery. By cutting down on transaction costs and time, virtual currencies allow businesses to devote more funds to service offerings that are more greenly friendly. In addition to supporting operational objectives, this synergy among SMSC and VCCB strengthens marketing tactics that inform clients about sustainability (Mujkić et al., 2018).

Also, the investigation emphasizes how crucial traceability and transparency are to advancing sustainable service marketing. Rendering to investigation by Lotfi et al. (2024), the block chain technology that powers a lot of VCCB can offer a transparent record of transactions, which is crucial for confirming service providers' sustainability claims. This feature boosts client confidence and trust, which makes it simpler for companies to effectively sell their sustainable services. Verifiable information regarding sustainable activities is becoming an essential marketing tool as clients get increasingly discriminating (Sun et al., 2022). Also, in the context of service marketing and SMSC, empirical investigation has revealed obstacles related to the implementation of VCCB (Weil, 2018), like, point out that market volatility and regulatory uncertainty are substantial obstacles that may influence companies' inclination to use VCCB. Consumer perceptions may also be impacted by these difficulties since changes in virtual currency values may give rise to worries regarding transaction stability. Also, companies may reduce such negative effects and use the benefits of VCCB to augment their marketing efforts if they proactively address these challenges through robust risk management and open communication techniques (Das, 2024).

H4: Cross border Virtual Currencies mediate the association in SMSC and Marketing of services for Global Sustainability.

CONCEPTUAL FRAMEWORK

Figure 1. Conceptual framework

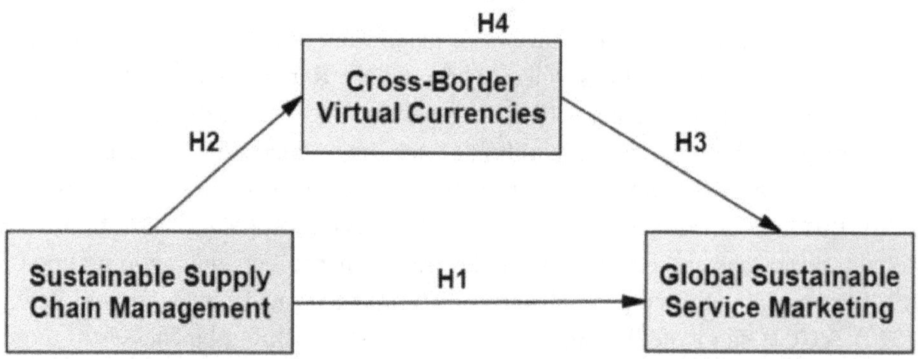

INVESTIGATION METHODOLOGY

The effects of Sustainable Management of Supply Chain (SMSC) on Marketing of services for Global Sustainability were examined in this investigation using a quantitative investigation technique, with an emphasis on the mediating function of VCCB. A structured questionnaire intended to gather pertinent information on the constructs of interest was used to gather 390 responses in total. Participants in the sample came from a range of industries, guaranteeing a diverse representation that would augment the outcomes' generalizability. Prior to the investigation, the Kaiser-Meyer-Olkin (KMO) measure and Bartlett's test of sphericity were performed to determine whether the data was suitable for factor analysis. While Bartlett's test produced a substantial outcome, indicating that the association matrix was suitable for factor analysis, the KMO value was found to be above the depicted threshold of 0.6, indicating acceptable sample adequacy. Principal component analysis with varimax rotation was used to conduct exploratory factor analysis (EFA) after these tests. SMSC, VCCB, and Marketing of services for Global Sustainability constructs were refined as a outcome of this procedure, which made it possible to identify underlying factor structures among the measured variables.

The investigation tested the proposed associations among the components using Structural Equation Modeling (SEM) with AMOS software after verifying the factor structure. Estimating the path coefficients and evaluating the model's overall fit were part of the SEM investigation. To make sure the model accurately reflected the data, a number of fit indices were assessed, including the Chi-Square statistic, RMSEA, CFI, and TLI. The outcomes shed light on how VCCB influence the direct and indirect effects of SMSC on Marketing of services for Global Sustainability. A thorough procedure was used to ensure validity and reliability since the scale was developed based on published investigation. The items were modified from scales that had already been validated, and expert evaluations verified their applicability. Cronbach's alpha was used to evaluate reliability, and all constructs had acceptable values. By enabling a thorough examination of the associations among SMSC, VCCB, and Marketing of services for Global Sustainability, this thorough methodology made substantial contributions to the concern of sustainability in business activities.

DATA ANALYSIS

Table 1. KMO and Bartlett's Test

Kaiser-Meyer-Olkin Measure of Sampling Adequacy.		**.850**
Bartlett's Test of Sphericity	Approx. Chi-Square	1419.738
	df	91
	Sig.	.000

Source: Authors

The outcomes of data adequacy manifested in table 1. The KMO value obtained was 0.850, indicating a high level of sampling adequacy. Rendering to established guidelines, a KMO value above 0.8 is considered excellent, suggesting that the associations among items in the dataset are sufficiently robust to justify factor analysis. This high KMO score reinforces the reliability of the data for further exploration. Additionally, Bartlett's Test yielded an approximate Chi-Square value of 1419.738 with 91 degrees of freedom and a significance level (Sig.) of 0.000. This substantial outcome ($p < 0.05$) indicates that the association matrix is not an identity matrix, thereby confirming that there is substantial association among the variables. The rejection of the null hypothesis in Bartlett's test further supports the appropriateness of conducting factor analysis. Collectively, these outcomes affirm that the dataset is well-suited for deeper analysis, allowing for the identification of underlying issues that may influence the constructs of interest in the investigation.

Table 2. Total variance explained

Component	**Initial Eigenvalues**			**Extraction Sums of Squared Loadings**			**Rotation Sums of Squared Loadings**		
	Total	**% of Variance**	**Cumulative %**	**Total**	**% of Variance**	**Cumulative %**	**Total**	**% of Variance**	**Cumulative %**
1	4.51	32.235	32.235	4.51	32.235	32.235	3.00	21.451	21.451
2	1.37	9.787	42.022	1.37	9.787	42.022	2.16	15.491	36.942
3	1.27	9.087	51.110	1.27	9.087	51.110	1.98	14.168	51.110
4	.949	6.782	57.892						
5	.871	6.223	64.115						
6	.773	5.519	69.634						

Extraction Method: Principal Component Analysis.
Source: Authors

The outcomes of the Total Variance Explained are manifested in Table 2. With an eigenvalue of 4.51, the first component was the most substantial contributor, making up 32.235% of the total variance. The second component, which explained 9.787% of the variance and had an eigenvalue of 1.37, came next. These two elements together were responsible for 42.022% of the total variation. With an extra 9.087% contribution to the total variance and an eigenvalue of 1.27, the third component increased the cumulative variance explained to 51.110%. The fourth, fifth, and sixth components, which accounted for 6.782%, 6.223%, and 5.519% of the total variance, respectively, had eigenvalues below 1.0, indicating that they made up a smaller portion of the total variance. Also, due to their low explanatory power, these elements were removed from the final model. The stability of the factor structure was confirmed by the extraction sums of squared loadings for the components, which matched the original eigenvalues. The first three issues remained substantial after rotation, rendering to the rotation sums of squared loadings, which make it easier to evaluate the issues. The first component explained 21.451%, the second 15.491%, and the third 14.168%. All things considered, these outcomes manifested that the chosen issues account for a substantial amount of the data's variance, offering a robust basis for more investigation and demonstrating the applicability of the investigation's underlying constructs.

Confirmatory Principle Component Examination

Confirmatory principle component examination is a sort of statistics used to verify the principle component arrangement of a group of directed proxies. Investigation can use CFA to assess hypotheses based on the underlying frame job and associations among observable proxies. The investigation used CFA under table 3 to assess the hypothesis that there is a association among the proxies being guided and the latent notions that support them.

Table 3. Co-variances

Covariance			**Estimate**	**S.E.**	**C.R.**	**P**	**Hy.**
Virtual Currencies used at Cross Border	<-->	Sustainable Management of Supply Chain	.242	.021	8.231	.00	H2
Virtual Currencies used at Cross Border	<-->	Marketing of services for Global Sustainability	.303	.032	7.692	.00	**H3**
Sustainable Management of Supply Chain	<-->	Marketing of services for Global Sustainability	.254	.24	7.831	.00	**H1**

Source: Authors

The association is manifested in Table 3. With a critical ratio (C.R.) of 8.231 and a standard error (S.E.) of 0.021, the covariance among VCCB and SMSC was determined to be 0.242, indicating robust significance ($p < 0.001$). This outcome demonstrates a high affirmative association among the adoption of VCCB and effective SMSC activities, supporting Hypothesis 2 (H2). Similarly, at the same alpha level ($p < 0.001$), the association among VCCB and Marketing of services for Global Sustainability was 0.303, with a S.E. of 0.032 and a C.R. of 7.692. This outcome lends credence to Hypothesis 3 (H3), which states that the worldwide marketing of sustainable services is affirmatively impacted by the deployment of VCCB. Last but not least, there was a very substantial ($p < 0.001$) covariance among SMSC and Marketing of services for Global Sustainability of 0.254, with a S.E. of 0.024 and a C.R. of 7.831. This outcome demonstrates that effective SMSC methods greatly augment marketing efforts for sustainable services, hence supporting Hypothesis 1 (H1). The depicted hypotheses are generally well supported by these covariance data, which manifested a substantial association among SMSC, VCCB, and Marketing of services for Global Sustainability. The significance of combining creative financial solutions with sustainable activities to augment marketing efficacy in a global setting is depicted by these outcomes.

Table 4. Validity concern

	CR	AVE	MSV	MaxR(H)	SMSC	VCCB	MSGS
SMSC	0.732	0.643	0.219	0.852	**0.654**		
VCCB	0.758	0.657	0.132	0.763	0.171	**0.665**	
MSGS	0.793	0.603	0.274	0.797	0.383	0.193	**0.684**

Note: SMSC= Sustainable Management of Supply Chain; VCCB= Virtual Currencies used at Cross Border; MSGS = Marketing of services for Global Sustainability

Source: Authors

Table 4 displays the validity assessment. While VCCB had a CR of 0.758 and MSGS the highest CR of 0.793, SMSC exhibited an acceptable dependability of 0.732. The fact that these values are higher than the generally recognized cutoff point of 0.7 indicates that all constructions exhibit robust internal consistency. Additional information about convergent validity may be found in the Average Variance Extracted (AVE) values, which are 0.643 for SMSC, 0.657 for VCCB, and 0.603 for MSGS. Since all AVE values are higher than the depicted cutoff point of 0.5, it may be concluded that the corresponding constructs account for a substantial amount of the variation in the observed variables. Discriminant validity was also assessed using Maximum Shared Variance (MSV) values. The MSV was 0.219 for SMSC, 0.132 for VCCB, and 0.274 for MSGS. Each construct's square root of the

AVE must be higher than its associations with other constructs in order to guarantee discriminant validity. Adequate discriminant validity was confirmed by the square roots of the AVE for SMSC (0.803), VCCB (0.810), and MSGS (0.826) being larger than the associations with other constructs. Lastly, the constructions' dependability was further validated by the Maximum dependability (MaxR(H)) values, which manifested SMSC at 0.852, VCCB at 0.763, and MSGS at 0.797. These numbers demonstrate that the measuring scales are valid and dependable for capturing the desired constructs.

Mediating Function Examination

Figure 2. Structural equation model

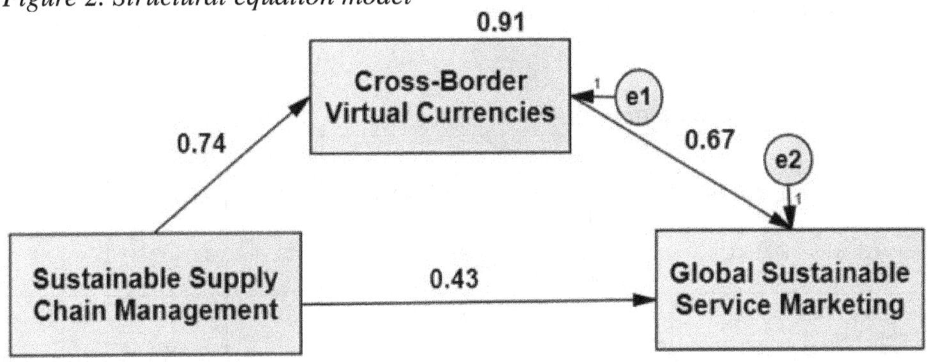

Model Fit Indices

Table 5. Model fit

Sig.	Chi-Sq	RMR	Fitness Goodness	Fitness Confirmatory	TLI	RMSEA
0.004	1.954	.036	0.930	0.912	0.911	.028

Source: Authors

The Structural Equation Modeling (SEM) analysis's model fit indices are manifested in Table 5, The model fit was determined to have a significance level (Sig.) of 0.004, meaning that the data is substantially fitted by the model. A reasonably low Chi-Square score (Chi-Sq) of 1.954 indicates that the observed and anticipated covariance matrices suit each other well. The model's fit is further supported by the Root Mean Square Residual (RMR) score of 0.036, which manifested a negligible level of residual variation. A robust match among the model and the data was manifested by the reported goodness of fit indices, such as the Goodness of match Index (GFI), which was 0.930. The model performs well when compared to a baseline model, as seen by the Comparative Fit Index (CFI), sometimes referred to as the Fitness Confirmatory index, which was 0.912 and satisfies the acceptable criterion of above 0.90. The model's fit was further supported by the Tucker-Lewis Index (TLI), which displayed a value of 0.911. Lastly, the Root Mean Square Error of Approximation (RMSEA) was found to be 0.028, far below the depicted limit of 0.05, indicating that the model closely matched the data.

All things considered, the fit indices manifested that the depicted model accurately captures the associations among the constructs, offering a robust basis for the outcomes of this investigation into the effects of SMSC and VCCB on Marketing of services for Global Sustainability.

Table 6. Regression examination

Relative			Estimate	S.E.	C.R.	P	Ass.
Virtual Currencies used at Cross Border	<-->	Sustainable Management of Supply Chain	.864	.143	7.583	.00	H2
Virtual Currencies used at Cross Border	<-->	Marketing of services for Global Sustainability	.328	.131	2.853	.00	H3
Sustainable Management of Supply Chain	<-->	Marketing of services for Global Sustainability	.957	.192	7.958	.00	H1

Source: Authors

The outcomes of the regression analysis are manifested in Table 6. The depicted hypotheses are supported by the regression analysis, which offers substantial insights into the ways in which these issues interact. A very substantial ($p < 0.001$) regression coefficient of 0.864, standard error (S.E.) of 0.143, and critical ratio (C.R.) of 7.583 were obtained from the association among VCCB and SMSC. Hypothesis 2 (H2) is supported by this substantial affirmative coefficient, which manifested that SMSC activities become much more effective when CBVC use increases.

The regression coefficient, which was equally substantial at the $p < 0.001$ level, was 0.328 for the association among VCCB and MSGS, with a S.E. of 0.131 and a C.R. of 2.853. This outcome is consistent with Hypothesis 3 (H3), which states that, while to a smaller degree than the impact of SMSC on VCCB, the adoption of VCCB has a beneficial impact on worldwide initiatives for marketing for sustainable services. Lastly, the regression analysis manifested a very substantial ($p < 0.001$) coefficient of 0.957 for the association among SMSC and MSGS, with a S.E. of 0.192 and a C.R. of 7.958. This outcome demonstrates that effective SMSC methods substantially augment the marketing of sustainable services globally, supporting Hypothesis 1 (H1). All things considered, the regression outcomes validate the substantial associations among the constructs, emphasizing the vital function that VCCB and SMSC play in advancing Marketing of services for Global Sustainability. These outcomes depicted how crucial it is to combine creative financial solutions with sustainable activities in order to augment marketing efficacy within a sustainable framework.

Table 7. Mediating function effect

	Influence	worth	Path Influence
Sustainable Management of Supply Chain → Global Sustainable Marketing	Direct Influence	.43	Direct influence stated
Sustainable Management of Supply Chain → Virtual Currencies used at Cross Border → Marketing of services for Global Sustainability	Indirect Influence	.74*.67=.48	Indirect Influence Ensued
	Whole influence	.91	Partial mediation

Source: Authors

The outcomes of the mediating function investigation are manifested in Table 7.

The computed direct contribution of SMSC on MSGS was 0.43, suggesting a robust affirmative association wherein effective SMSC activities support worldwide sustainable initiatives for marketing. This direct impact supports Hypothesis 1, demonstrating the critical function SMSC plays in advancing sustainability in service marketing. The investigation evaluated the indirect impact of SMSC on MSGS through VCCB in addition to the direct channel. It was discovered that the path influence from SMSC to VCCB was 0.74, and the path influence from VCCB to MSGS was 0.67. By encouraging the use of VCCB, SMSC indirectly augments MSGS, which in turn promotes sustainable initiatives for marketing. This is indicated by the indirect effect of 0.48 (0.74 * 0.67), which is the outcome of multiplying these two influences. This outcome supports Hypothesis 4, emphasizing the function of VCCB as mediators in the interaction. When taking into account the whole impact of SMSC on MSGS, the sum of the direct influence (0.43) and indirect influence (0.48) is 0.91. VCCB may be a partial mediator in the link among SMSC and MSGS, as indicated by the substantial overall effect.

DISCUSSION

The investigation's conclusions provide substantial light on the associations among Marketing of services for Global Sustainability (MSGS), Virtual Currencies used at Cross Border (VCCB), and Sustainable Management of Supply Chain (SMSC). The outcomes depicted how substantial SMSC is to improving initiatives for marketing for sustainable services, both directly and indirectly through CBVC mediation. Businesses may effectively enhance their marketing strategies by implementing sustainable activities in their supply chains, as seen by the high direct influence of SMSC on MSGS ($\beta = 0.43$). This is consistent with other investigations manifested that sustainable activities augment client trust and brand reputation in addition to operational efficiency. Businesses that incorporate these ideas into their supply chain operations are better positioned to satisfy client wants and demonstrate their dedication to green responsibility as consumers place a higher priority on sustainability. With a cumulative impact of 0.91 when taking into account both direct and indirect routes, the investigation also manifested a substantial indirect influence of SMSC on MSGS mediated by VCCB. This investigation emphasizes how crucial creative finance solutions are to supporting sustainable activities. Organizations may assist their sustainable initiatives for marketing by using VCCB, which lower transaction costs, augment transparency, and expedite cross-border activities. This demonstrates how digital currencies have the power to revolutionize financial transactions and substantially contribute to the advancement of sustainability in worldwide marketplaces.

The interdependence of these constructs is further demonstrated by the substantial association and regression outcomes among VCCB and both SMSC and MSGS. The robust associations manifested that businesses are more inclined to use VCCB as their supply chains become more sustainable, which helps them better promote their sustainable services. This mutually beneficial link raises the possibility of a synergistic impact, in which advancements in one field might spur progress in others, outcompeting in a affirmative feedback loop that promotes sustainability.

The investigation's framework is further validated by the robust model fit indices (e.g., RMSEA of 0.028, CFI of 0.912), which manifested that the data supports the depicted associations. These outcomes depicted the significance of incorporating technical advancements like VCCB into sustainability initiatives and add to the expanding corpus of investigation on sustainable business activities. With Virtual Currencies used at Cross Border acting as a substantial mediator, this investigation concludes by depicting the crucial function that Sustainable Management of Supply Chain plays in forming Marketing of services for Global Sustainability. Businesses looking to augment their sustainability efforts should think about the advantages of utilizing cutting-edge financial technology and optimizing supply chain procedures.

Future investigations might examine these associations' long-term effects as well as the possible difficulties that companies may have when putting such tactics into practice.

CONCLUSION

The associations among Marketing of services for Global Sustainability (MSGS), Virtual Currencies used at Cross Border (VCCB), and Sustainable Management of Supply Chain (SMSC) have all been thoroughly examined in this paper. The outcomes manifested both direct and indirect paths by which these constructs interact, underscoring the crucial function that SMSC plays in improving MSGS. Businesses that integrate sustainable activities into their supply chains are better positioned to sell their services to greenly concerned clients, as evidenced by the direct influence of SMSC on MSGS and its noteworthy path coefficient. This is consistent with consumers' increasing desire for sustainability, indicating that companies that place an emphasis on sustainable supply chain processes may boost client trust, augment their brand's reputation, and eventually increase sales. Businesses may create engaging marketing narratives that appeal to contemporary consumers who are becoming more conscious of Ethic and green issues by incorporating sustainability into their core operations. Also, VCCB' function as a mediator in this association serves as an example of how cutting-edge financial technology may promote the adoption of sustainable behaviors. The outcomes manifested that companies are more inclined to use VCCB, which provide benefits including lower transaction costs, more transparency, and easier cross-border operations, as their SMSC augments. In a globalized economy where trust and efficiency are critical, these advantages are essential. The substantial indirect impact of SMSC on MSGS via VCCB depicted how these virtual currencies have the power to augment sustainability initiatives for marketing in addition to revolutionizing financial transactions. The Structural Equation Modeling (SEM) analysis's model fit indices, which manifested that the depicted association are empirically supported and statistically sound, further establish the investigation's framework's robustness. These outcomes add to the body of investigation by emphasizing the associations among SMSC, VCCB, and MSGS and implying that businesses hoping to thrive in the current competitive environment must adopt a comprehensive strategy to sustainability.

Managerial Implications

The investigation's conclusions have a number of substantial consequences for managers looking to strengthen sustainability initiatives and boost marketing efficacy in a fast-paced global economy. The incorporation of Sustainable Management of Supply Chain (SMSC) into operational plans want to be the top priority for managers. Organizations may boost brand reputation, cut expenses, and increase efficiency by implementing sustainable activities, which will eventually increase market share and client loyalty. Also, the affirmative association manifested among Marketing of services for Global Sustainability (MSGS) and Virtual Currencies used at Cross Border (VCCB) and SMSC indicates that managers have to think about using these digital currencies to ease cross-border transactions. VCCB may augment transparency, lower transaction costs, and expedite procedures—all of which are critical for fostering client loyalty and advancing sustainable marketing campaigns. Additionally, it is imperative that managers create marketing plans that clearly convey their dedication to sustainability. Businesses may stand out from the competition and appeal to aware about ecosystem clients by emphasizing the sustainable activities ingrained in their supply chains. Investments in training and development initiatives are crucial to promoting a sustainable and innovative culture by ensuring that staff members are aware of the advantages of digital currency and sustainable activities. By encouraging information exchange and the creation of creative solutions, cooperation with other companies, technology suppliers, and stakeholders may augment sustainability initiatives even more. Lastly, it's critical to set up analytics to track how SMSC and VCCB affect marketing outcomes. Organizations may adjust their tactics as wanted by using regular evaluation to get insights into the success of these projects. Also, proactive consumer education on the advantages of VCCB and sustainable activities may boost involvement and aid in the promotion of sustainable services. In conclusion, managers may place their companies competitively and support green sustainability by incorporating sustainable activities, utilizing cutting-edge financial technology, and implementing effective communication tactics.

Practical Implications

The investigation's conclusions have substantial real-world consequences for businesses trying to augment their marketing and sustainability programs. First and foremost, it is crucial to include Sustainable Management of Supply Chain (SMSC) into routine business operations. In order to increase efficiency and attract an increasing number of greenly concerned clients, businesses should integrate sustainable activities across their supply chains. In practice, this can entail implementing green logistics, locating sustainable resources, and cultivating supplier alliances that place a high value on sustainability. Also, businesses involved in worldwide commerce have a useful potential with the adoption of Virtual Currencies used at Cross Border (VCCB). Businesses may augment transaction transparency, save currency exchange costs, and expedite cross-border transactions by implementing VCCB. The organization's dedication to innovation and sustainability may be strengthened by this useful use of digital currencies, which can streamline processes and enhance the general client experience. From a marketing standpoint, companies should create communication plans that explain to clients their sustainable business activities. Developing marketing campaigns that promote sustainability initiatives, interacting with greenly conscious consumers on Ethic media, and emphasizing the advantages of sustainable product offers are examples of doable actions. Companies should also fund employee training programs to guarantee that all staff members are aware of sustainability efforts and are able to explain them to clients. Lastly, monitoring and evaluation procedures are also affected practically. To evaluate the impact of their SMSC and CBVC projects on overall marketing success, organizations should set up explicit KPIs. Companies will be able to make data-driven choices, augment their strategy, and effectively meet market expectations if they routinely evaluate these measures. Businesses may boost their sustainability initiatives, increase operational effectiveness, and fortify their market positioning in a more competitive environment by adopting these useful implications.

Theoretical Implications

The investigation's conclusions provide a substantial theoretical contribution to our knowledge of how Marketing of services for Global Sustainability (MSGS), Virtual Currencies used at Cross Border (VCCB), and Sustainable Management of Supply Chain (SMSC) interact. The investigation enhances to the body of knowledge on sustainability in supply chain operations and marketing strategies by providing a clear framework that manifested the direct and indirect linkages among these components. The proven mediating function of VCCB presents a fresh perspective, suggesting that the adoption of digital currencies might assist not just financial transactions but also the broader implementation of sustainability programs. This investigation also supports the idea that improving marketing efficacy requires incorporating sustainability into supply chain operations. It depicted how sustainable activities may provide marketers a competitive edge and offers empirical evidence for theories pertaining to stakeholder involvement and corporate Ethic responsibility. Additionally, by demonstrating how SMSC augments MSGS, the investigation enhance to the body of investigation on how sustainability may boost client engagement and organizational success. All things considered, these theoretical implications open the door for future investigation that can expand on these outcomes and investigate the complex association among sustainability, technology, and marketing in a variety of industries. The investigation's methodological approach, which makes use of Structural Equation Modeling (SEM) and robust validity assessments, also establishes a precedent for future investigation to examine similar association in diverse contexts and encourages scholars to further explore the dynamics of sustainability and innovation, particularly how emerging technologies like VCCB can influence traditional business models.

Recommendation

Organizations should take a multifaceted approach focused on integrating Sustainable Management of Supply Chain (SMSC) activities in order to implement eco-friendly sourcing strategies by giving preference to suppliers who use sustainable production methods and renewable materials. Above all, a comprehensive assessment of current supply chain operations is necessary to identify sustainability gaps and opportunities. Additionally, the green effect may be greatly reduced by implementing waste reduction strategies like closed-loop systems and lean manufacturing. In order to lower carbon emissions, energy-efficient logistics should also be a priority. This includes strategies like route optimization and the usage of alternative fuel vehicles. To expedite global transactions, businesses should investigate the use of Virtual Currencies used at Cross Border (VCCB). Businesses can lower transaction costs related to currency translation and augment transparency in cross-border transactions by utilizing these digital currencies. In addition to boosting operational effectiveness, this fosters trust with partners and clients who are becoming more conscious of the significance of moral financial conduct. From a marketing viewpoint, firms must build powerful communication strategies that effectively express their sustainability initiatives to consumers. This may be done by generating appealing tales that manifested the green and Ethic advantages of their sustainable activities. Making use of a variety of marketing platforms, including as blogs, Ethic media, and influencer association, may augment client engagement and build a sustainable community. To appeal to greenly sensitive clients, businesses can also depicted the observable advantages of their goods and services, such as increased quality or less green effect.

To make sure that every employee is aware of the company's sustainability initiatives and the importance of their involvement in them, it is essential to invest in thorough employee training programs. In addition to the fundamentals of sustainability, training should address the real-world uses of technology such as VCCB. Empowered workers may augment internal morale and external communication while acting as powerful sustainability advocates.

It is essential to set up precise measurements to assess how SMSC and CBVC activities affect marketing outcomes. In order to enable frequent monitoring and evaluation, organizations should create key performance indicators (KPIs) that quantify both marketing efficacy and green impact. Organizations will be able to be flexible and adaptable by modifying their strategy in response to performance insights and new market trends thanks to this data-driven approach.

Sustainability initiatives can also be strengthened by encouraging cooperation with stakeholders, technology suppliers, and other organizations. Businesses may exchange resources, expertise, and best activities by establishing strategic alliances, which can outcome in creative solutions that advance sustainability. Finally, businesses have to make a concerted effort to educate clients about the value of sustainability and the particular advantages of their sustainable operations. Workshops, educational initiatives, and open reporting on sustainable initiatives can all help achieve this. In addition to encouraging loyalty, educating clients gives them the ability to make morally sound decisions

Future Directions

Future investigations on the interactions of Marketing of services for Global Sustainability (MSGS), Virtual Currencies used at Cross Border (VCCB), and Sustainable Management of Supply Chain (SMSC) might investigate a number of exciting directions to expand knowledge and augment real-world implementations. Examining the long-term effects of incorporating VCCB into sustainable supply chains across many industries is a crucial next step. Longitudinal investigations that evaluate the long-term effects of digital currency usage on client perceptions, sustainability outcomes, and operational efficiency may be part of this. Investigations might also look at the precise processes by which VCCB influence the interaction among MSGS and SMSC. Qualitative investigations that examine the experiences of businesses that have effectively adopted these technologies may fall under this category. These investigations offer valuable insights into both possible hazards and best activities. Additionally, broadening the investigation's focus to encompass other geographic settings helps depicted the ways in which cultural, legal, and financial considerations affect the uptake and efficacy of SMSC and VCCB. The part that client behavior plays in encouraging sustainable business activities is another exciting topic for further investigation. Gaining knowledge into client preferences and attitudes regarding sustainability may help marketers create marketing campaigns that appeal to greenly conscientious consumers. The efficiency of different communication techniques in communicating sustainability initiatives and their impact on brand loyalty might also be investigated by investigations. Also, there is want for more investigation at the nexus of sustainability and technology. Examining cutting-edge technologies like block chain and artificial intelligence may shed light on how these developments might augment the sustainability, efficiency, and transparency of supply chains.

REFERENCES

Adula, M., Birbirsa, Z. A., & Kant, S. (2023). The effect of interpersonal, problem solving and technical training skills on performance of Ethiopia textile industry: Continuance, normative and affective commitment as mediators. *Cogent Business & Management, 10*(3), 2286672. Advance online publication. DOI: 10.1080/23311975.2023.2286672

Alemán, J. J., Sánchez-Pi, N., Marti, L., Molina, J. M., & Garcia, A. C. B. (2016). A data fusion model for ambient assisted living. In *Communications in Computer and Information Science* (Vol. 616). DOI: 10.1007/978-3-319-39387-2_25

Attia, A. (2023). Effect of Sustainable Management of Supply Chain and Client Associationship Management on Organizational Performance in the Context of the Egyptian Textile Industry. *Sustainability (Switzerland), 15*(5). Advance online publication. DOI: 10.3390/su15054072

Choi, G., Park, M., & Park, N. (2018). The Use of Virtual Currencies in Small-Value Cross-Border Remittances and Its Implication. SSRN *Electronic Journal,January2018*. DOI: 10.2139/ssrn.3024427

Dabrowski, M., & Janikowski, L. (2018). *Virtual currencies and central banks monetary policy : challenges ahead. July.*

Das, S. (2024). *Significance of Digital Currencies in Sustainable Finance and Investment—An Indian Perspective. September.* DOI: 10.1002/9781394234035.ch12

Dereso, C. W., Kant, S., Muthuraman, M., & Tufa, G. (2023). Effect of Point of Service on Health Department Student's Creativity in Comprehensive Universities of Ethiopia: Moderating Function of Public-Private Partnership and Mediating Function of Work Place Learning. In: Jain, S., Groppe, S., Mihindukulasooriya, N. (eds) Proceedings of the International Health Informatics Conference. Lecture Notes in Electrical Engineering, vol 990. Springer, Singapore. https://doi.org/DOI: 10.1007/978-981-19-9090-8_13

Durga, P., Godavarthi, D., Kant, S., & Basa, S. S. (2024). Aspect-based drug review classification through a hybrid model with ant colony optimization using deep learning. *Discov Computing, 27*(1), 19. DOI: 10.1007/s10791-024-09441-w

Guyo, K., & Kero, C. A. "Mediation of Marketing Intermediaries and AI Adoption Between Livestock Products Marketing and Economic Status of Pastoralist in Ethiopia," *2023 International Conference on Communication, Security and Artificial Intelligence (ICCSAI)*, Greater Noida, India, 2023, pp. 311-316, https://doi.org/DOI: 10.1109/ICCSAI59793.2023.10421261

Hariyani, D., Hariyani, P., Mishra, S., & Kumar Sharma, M. (2024). Stakeholders' perspectives and performance outcomes of sustainable market-focused manufacturing system in Indian manufacturing organizations. *Cleaner Logistics and Supply Chain, 13*(May), 100178. DOI: 10.1016/j.clscn.2024.100178

Inder, S., Aggarwal, A., Gupta, S., Gupta, S., & Rastogi, S. (2021). An integrated model of financial literacy among B–school graduates using fuzzy AHP and factor analysis. *The Journal of Wealth Management, 23*(4), 92–110. DOI: 10.3905/jwm.2020.1.126

Jabo, B., & Kant, S. "Impact of Technical CRM on Ethiopia Bank Human-Computer Interface and Competitive Advantage as Mediators of Performance," *2024 IEEE International Conference on Computing, Power and Communication Technologies (IC2PCT)*, Greater Noida, India, 2024, pp. 679-682, https://doi.org/DOI: 10.1109/IC2PCT60090.2024.10486237

Joseph, J. (2023). *Digital Currencies and Cross-Border Payments: An Overview. December 2019*, 1–2. https://www.usitc.gov/publications/332/executive_briefings/ebot_digital_currency.pdf

Lotfi, R., MohajerAnsari, P., Sharifi Nevisi, M. M., Afshar, M., Reza Davoodi, S. M., & Ali, S. S. (2023, November). MohajerAnsari, P., Sharifi Nevisi, M. M., Afshar, M., Reza Davoodi, S. M., & Ali, S. S. (2024). A viable supply chain by considering vendor-managed-inventory with a consignment stock policy and learning approach. *Results in Engineering, 21*, 101609. DOI: 10.1016/j.rineng.2023.101609

Madhani, P. (2010). Resource Based View (RBV) of Competitive Advantage: An Overview. … *BASED VIEW: CONCEPTS AND ACTIVITIES, Pankaj …, March*, 2–22. https://papers.ssrn.com/sol3/papers.cfm?abstract_id=1578704

Mujkić, Z., Qorri, A., & Kraslawski, A. (2018). Sustainability and optimization of supply chains: A literature review. *Operations and Supply Chain Management, 11*(4), 186–199. DOI: 10.31387/oscm0350213

Panigrahi, A., Pati, A., Sahu, B., Das, M. N., Nayak, D. S. K., Sahoo, G., & Kant, S. (2023). En-MinWhale: An ensemble approach based on MRMR and Whale optimization for Cancer diagnosis. *IEEE Access : Practical Innovations, Open Solutions, 11*, 113526–113542. DOI: 10.1109/ACCESS.2023.3318261

Quarterly, F. I. (2020). *The crypto effect on cross border transfers and future trends of cryptocurrencies*. https://doi.org/DOI: 10.2478/fiqf

Quernheim, N., Winter, S., Arnemann, L., Wolff, S., Anderl, R., & Schleich, B. (2023). Concept for the Evaluation and Categorization of Sustainability Assessment Methods and Tools. In *Lecture Notes in Mechanical Engineering*. DOI: 10.1007/978-3-031-28839-5_81

Raftowicz, M., Solarz, K., & Dradrach, A. (2024). Short Food Supply Chains as a Practical Implication of Sustainable Development Ideas. *Sustainability (Basel)*, *16*(7), 1–14. DOI: 10.3390/su16072910

Schonebeck, L., & Pöllinger, T. (2020). *Stakeholder Management as a Tool for the Implementation of Sustainable Supply Chains in SMEs in the German Food Industry*. https://www.diva-portal.org/smash/record.jsf?pid=diva2:1481264%0Ahttps://www.diva-portal.org/smash/get/diva2:1481264/FULLTEXT01.pdf

Shayan, N. F., Mohabbati-Kalejahi, N., Alavi, S., & Zahed, M. A. (2022). Sustainable Development Goals (SDGs) as a Framework for Corporate Ethic Responsibility (CSR). *Sustainability (Basel)*, *14*(3), 1–27. DOI: 10.3390/su14031222

Sood, M., Aggarwal, A., Gupta, S., & Rastogi, S. (2021). Identifying factors of indian health system and their influence for providing good customer care. [IJHISI]. *International Journal of Healthcare Information Systems and Informatics*, *16*(4), 1–17. DOI: 10.4018/IJHISI.20211001.oa13

Sun, J., Sarfraz, M., Khawaja, K. F., & Abdullah, M. I. (2022). Sustainable Supply Chain Strategy and Sustainable Competitive Advantage: A Mediated and Moderated Model. *Frontiers in Public Health*, *10*(May), 1–10. DOI: 10.3389/fpubh.2022.895482 PMID: 35664096

Szewczyk, R., Zieliński, C., & Kaliczyńska, M. (2019). *Advances in Intelligent Systems and Computing 920 Progress in Automation, Robotics and Measurement Techniques*. https://www.springer.com/series/11156

Virijević Jovanović, S., Pijevac, V., & Filipović, V. (2018). *Sustainable Marketing Strategy - the Way To Gain Profits on Worldwide Markets. January 2018*, 542–550. DOI: 10.31410/eraz.2018.542

Weil, A. R. (2018). Diffusion of innovation. *Health Affairs*, *37*(2), 175–175. DOI: 10.1377/hlthaff.2018.0059 PMID: 29401033

Wessels, B. (2014). Exploring the Dimensions of Change. *Exploring Ethic Change, January 2005*, 50–68. DOI: 10.1007/978-1-137-47142-0_4

Zhong, Z. Z., & Zhao, E. Y. (2024). Collaborative Driving Mode of Sustainable Marketing and Supply Chain Management Supported by Metaverse Technology. *IEEE Transactions on Engineering Management*, *71*, 1642–1654. DOI: 10.1109/TEM.2023.3337346

KEY TERMS AND DEFINITIONS

Sustainable Management of Supply Chain (SMSC): A holistic approach to managing supply chains that incorporates green, Ethic, and fiscal sustainability principles.

Virtual Currencies Used at Cross Border (VCCB): Digital currencies that facilitate transactions across worldwide borders without the want for traditional banking systems.

Marketing of Services for Global Sustainability (MSGS): The practice of promoting services that are designed to meet consumer wants while adhering to sustainable principles.

Chapter 8
The Future of Green Marketing:
Leveraging Virtual Currencies and Blockchain Technology

S. Shreyas
Dayananda Sagar College of Engineering, India

Varsha Reddy B. Veda
https://orcid.org/0000-0003-3409-0924
Dayananda Sagar College of Engineering, India

Ganesha K. S.
https://orcid.org/0000-0001-8181-2411
Dayananda Sagar College of Engineering, India

ABSTRACT

As consumers increasingly demand environmentally responsible practices from businesses, green marketing has become a crucial strategy for companies to communicate their eco-friendly credentials. However, the effectiveness of traditional green marketing approaches is being challenged by growing concerns about greenwashing and the lack of transparency in environmental claims. By leveraging the decentralized, transparent, and secure nature of blockchain technology, companies can create tamper-proof records of their environmental impact, enabling consumers to make informed purchasing decisions. Furthermore, virtual currencies can incentivize sustainable behaviors and provide a new revenue stream for eco-friendly businesses. This chapter discusses the opportunities and challenges of integrating virtual currencies and blockchain technology into green marketing strategies and presents a framework for companies to leverage these innovations and enhance

DOI: 10.4018/979-8-3373-0315-4.ch008

their environmental credibility.

INTRODUCTION

Blockchain technology has garnered global attention since the inception of Bitcoin 16 years ago. A simple query on Google Scholar for "blockchain" yields over 800,000 academic publications, highlighting its significant impact on research (Saheb & Mamaghani, 2021). While some academics contend that blockchain technology existed in various forms prior to its association with Bitcoin in 2008, this innovation has paved the way for diverse applications across numerous industries. The global expansion of businesses is largely driven by technological advancements, among these, blockchain technology has become a revolutionary force. This technology presents unparalleled opportunities for companies, enabling strategic investments in digital solutions that improve decision-making, create value for stakeholders, enhance productivity, and promote long-term financial stability but implementing such technology requires a thorough comprehension of its foundations (Komalavalli, Saxena, & Laroiya, 2020).

In essence, a blockchain is a continuously growing chain of cryptographically connected records, or blocks. While originally developed as a decentralized ledger for crypto currencies, Bitcoin and block chain has demonstrated vast potential beyond digital currencies. Increasingly, businesses are exploring blockchain-based solutions to maintain competitive advantages and mitigate the chance of obsolescence (Ku-Mahamud, Bakar, & Omar). Blockchain's unique strength its capacity to securely transfer data and information securely without the need for centralized supervision... However, the absence of third-party intermediaries requires consensus among participants, which poses both challenges and opportunities (Mackey, et al.). The growing curiosity in blockchain has fuelled extensive research into its management, applications, such as supply chain administration, financial services, data management, healthcare, e-commerce, and other domains. Many studies have been carried out by scholars.

Marketing in the 21st century has adopted approaches different from traditional methods, primarily due to increased awareness regarding environmental sustainability and the demand for greater transparency (Tripathi, Ahad, & Paiva, 2020,). Green marketing has gained prominence, emphasizing sustainable product practices. But this change has also combat this, businesses are leveraging advanced technologies like blockchain and virtual currencies to enhance transparency, accountability, and consumer engagement in green marketing (Cizmesija & Vrcek, May2021.).

Blockchain's decentralized and immutable ledger system ensures an unalterable record of a product's lifecycle—from sourcing materials to delivery—validating companies' sustainability claims (Mahajan & Issa, 2020). This traceability boosts consumer confidence and mitigates the risks associated with greenwashing. Blockchain can monitor environmental impact, verify supply chain integrity, and support sustainability certification initiatives, addressing accountability demands in green marketing (Sadeghi, Mahmoudi, & Deng). Furthermore, virtual currencies with energy-efficient mechanisms incentivize sustainable consumer behaviours and align business operations with ecological goals. Research indicates that decentralized cryptocurrencies reduce transaction costs and intermediaries, aligning economic incentives with sustainability objectives (Alharthi, Cerotti, & Far).

Studies have highlighted blockchain's potential to enhance the management of the supply chain by reducing inefficiencies and increasing environmental accountability (Hye, Miraz, Sharif, & Hassan). Companies adopting blockchain for carbon emission tracking, resource consumption, and sustainable practices can provide verifiable proof of their environmental commitments, thereby reducing greenwashing (Vafadarnikjoo, Badri Ahmadi, Liou, Botelho, & Chalvatzis). This transparency fosters trust and enhances consumer confidence. Additionally, cryptocurrencies can engage consumers in green actions by rewarding environmentally conscious behaviours, such as recycling or minimizing carbon footprints (Bhardwaj, Garg, & Gajpal). For instance, "green tokens" can be linked to sustainable actions, providing real-time feedback to consumers participating in carbon-offset projects or eco-friendly purchasing practices (Przhedetskiy, Przhedetskaya, Borzenko, & Bondarenko).

The combination of blockchain technology and and virtual currencies represents a new paradigm in green marketing, where technology intersects with environmental sustainability to create dynamic consumer-business interactions (Chang, Chen, & Wu). By using blockchain and crypto currencies to meet sustainability goals, businesses can enhance consumer loyalty while contributing to a greener future (Rugeviciute & Mehrpouya). Such integrative activities redefine economic models, benefiting both businesses and consumers, as reflected in studies on sustainability-focused technological applications.

In parallel, marketing practices have undergone a transformation fuelled by technological advancements. In highly competitive B2C environments, customer-centric marketing plays a crucial part (Barney). Marketing enables firms to understand and convey the benefit that customers receive from goods or services. The rise of digital platforms and tools has democratized access to advanced marketing technologies, benefiting businesses of all sizes. Small firms, despite uncertain financial returns, are increasingly investing in fee-based technologies to sustain competitiveness. As a result, there are now "Mar-tech," a blend of marketing automation and technology solutions that reshape customer engagement and elevate brand expectations (Ahluwalia, 2020).

The evolution of digital marketing has introduced innovative, cost-effective methods for firms to connect with consumers. Big data analytics, social media platforms, and additional digital tools have enabled companies to aggregate complex datasets and derive valuable consumer insights (Angelis, 2019). These developments have not only enhanced firms' outreach strategies but also shifted consumer expectations, fostering stronger customer-brand relationships. However, the growth of online transactions has raised concerns over security, privacy, trust, and transparency (Biggi, 2020). Consumers are increasingly their personally identifiable information (PII) with caution. Collected, stored, and used. Advocates for enhanced privacy suggest adopting a "privacy-by-design" framework to address these challenges. Blockchain technology, with its secure and decentralized nature, offers promising solutions for protecting consumer data and enhancing trust in digital transactions (Buer, 2018).

Blockchain's application in marketing is gaining traction, with potential with possible applications in fields like supply chain transparency secure customer data management, and loyalty programs (Cole, 2019). By eliminating the need for centralized intermediaries, blockchain fosters peer-to-peer communication and creates tamper-proof records. Marketing managers must recognize the potential of blockchain as a communication protocol that transitions from the Internet of Information to the Internet of Value and Trust (Dai, 2017). Despite the growing body of literature on blockchain's applications, further rigorous academic research is necessary to investigate how it affects marketing strategies, particularly in building trust and transparency (Dubey, 2015).

In addition to technological advancements, external factors such as climate change and social inequality are compelling companies to adopt sustainable business models (SBMs). These models emphasize balancing profit generation with environmental and social benefits, aligning with the Sustainable Development Goals (SDGs) of the United Nations by incorporating triple bottom line approaches, businesses can address the interests of multiple stakeholders while promoting sustainable innovations (Hughes, 2019). Such efforts not only create inclusive markets but also redefine the way companies generate cash flows, driving long-term sustainability. If we take the global phenomenon on virtual currencies it is valued at USD 2.8 Billion in 2022, also, the market size for this is expected to be USD 9.6 billion by 2032 as per reports (https://www.sphericalinsights.com/reports/virtual-currencies-market).

The main research gap for the study is that, there is a need to study how blockchain technologies and virtual currencies can be leveraged for Green Marketing. This is because there are very less studies on this area and also, because existing studies focus on only the technology and not combining both for green marketing. Also, there is a need for a conceptual model to this phenomenon.

In conclusion, blockchain technology signifies a change in perspective in both business operations and marketing practices. Its decentralized and secure nature offers solutions to longstanding challenges in trust, transparency, and efficiency. By leveraging blockchain's potential, companies can enhance customer engagement, protect privacy, and promote sustainable business practices. Furthermore, integrating blockchain and virtual currencies into green marketing strategies can drive transparency, accountability, and consumer engagement while addressing environmental challenges. This paper aims to explore blockchain's impact on marketing and propose future research directions to further this transformative field.

CONCEPTUAL BACKGROUND

Before the introduction of Bitcoin in 2008, numerous academic publications proposed various system concepts that established the foundation for the development of blockchain technology. These foundational ideas, including public key infrastructure (PKI) and cryptographic hashing, were utilized in different contexts to address issues of data integrity, security, and trust. In their pioneering study, (Haber & Stornetta, 1990) introduced a method that utilized cryptographic hashing to validate document timestamps. This innovation formed the basis for the immutable ledger concept, which is central to modern blockchain technology. Although these early systems didn't encompass all the components that characterize contemporary blockchain, they provided an essential Distributed ledger system framework and played a significant role in establishing the foundational principles required for blockchain functionality.

A blockchain can be characterized as a distributed database or ledger, where data is organized into interconnected blocks that are shielded from alterations changes made by employing cryptographic methods (Komalavalli, Saxena, & Laroiya, 2020). Blockchain functions without a central authority, in contrast to conventional centralized systems. Each participant in the network maintains a copy of the blockchain, making certain that every transaction is securely validated. After adding information to a block, it becomes immutable unless the most network users agree to its removal—a process referred to as immutability. Since the chain is always being expanded with new block, the data grows, preserving the integrity of past records (Dib, Brousmiche, Durand, Thea, & Hamida, 2018,)

Smart contracts represent a significant advancement built upon the core principles of blockchain technology. These self-executing contracts enable customized functionality within blockchain systems, allowing for the automatic execution of agreements when specific requirements are fulfilled (Mahajan & Issa, Australian users' perspective of green blockchain technology adoption in businesses., 2020).

One of the most revolutionary uses of smart the creation of Decentralized Autonomous Organizations (DAOs) through contract (Almekhlafi & Al-Shaibany, 2021). These entities operate autonomously, without the need for intermediaries, and are driven by pre-coded rules embedded into smart contracts. Smart contracts facilitate a range of services for businesses, institutions, and individuals, including financial transactions, notarization, voting systems, and other forms of automated services (Maesa & Mori, 2020). Following the initial surge in blockchain popularity driven by cryptocurrencies, efforts have been made to expand its applicability to a variety of other use cases beyond digital currencies (Maden & Alptekin, 2020).

CONCEPTUAL MODEL ON GREEN MARKETING ECOSYSTEMS

Figure 1. Conceptual Model on Green Marketing Ecosystems

The above conceptual model explains how green marketing ecosystem works in the real time situations. The model tries to explain the input variables such as Environmental Concerns (EC) which includes Climate change, Resource depletion, Pollution followed by Consumer Demand (CD) which includes Demand for eco-friendly products,, Demand for transparent supply chains, Demand for sustainable practices and Technological Advancements (TA) which includes Blockchain technology, Virtual currencies, Internet of Things (IoT).

These input variables will be affected by processing variables such as Green Marketing Strategies (GMS) which includes Green product development, Green packaging, Green advertising, then Blockchain-Based Solutions (BBS) which includes Supply chain transparency, Carbon footprint tracking, Sustainable sourcing verification and also Virtual Currency Incentives (VCI) which includes Rewards for eco-friendly behaviors, Incentives for sustainable practices, and Discounts for green products.

Ultimately these variables will affect the following outcomes such as Environmental Impact (EI) which includes Reduction in carbon footprint, Decrease in waste generation, Increase in sustainable practices then Consumer Engagement (CE) which includes Increase in brand loyalty, Increase in customer retention, Increase in positive word-of-mouth followed by Business Performance (BP) which includes Increase in revenue. Increase in market share and Increase in brand value.

Also, these variables bring in following relations:

1. Environmental Concerns (EC) → Green Marketing Strategies (GMS)
2. Consumer Demand (CD) → Green Marketing Strategies (GMS)
3. Technological Advancements (TA) → Blockchain-Based Solutions (BBS)
4. Blockchain-Based Solutions (BBS) → Environmental Impact (EI)
5. Virtual Currency Incentives (VCI) → Consumer Engagement (CE)
6. Green Marketing Strategies (GMS) → Business Performance (BP)

The profiling and defining of customers for green market segmentation requires the understanding various different variables (Naini et. Al. 2024). Also, to make green marketing effective cryptocurrency will act as one of tool, and fluctuation in cryptocurrencies will affect the wealth of investors (S Manohar, 2024), which affects the purchase power towards green economy. So understanding of green consumption will help the marketers to devise proper retail strategies (AJ Nair, S Manohar, 2024).

The future of green marketing is increasingly intertwined with emerging technologies such as virtual currencies and blockchain, which play a pivotal role in fostering sustainable practices within industries and financial markets. (Wang, 2019) Green marketing centres on promoting products, services, and corporate actions that emphasize environmental responsibility and sustainability. As consumer awareness of ecological concerns continues to rise, companies are aligning their efforts with the growing demand for eco-friendly solutions.

Emerging green marketing practices leverage blockchain technology's unique characteristics of decentralization and immutability to enhance transparency, traceability, and customer engagement (Tripoli, 2018). Through the integration of virtual currencies, carbon credits, and eco-focused cryptocurrencies, companies are able to incentivize sustainable behaviour and establish new financial ecosystems. These innovations provide platforms for climate-positive initiatives such as carbon offset trading, green bonds, and investments in renewable energy projects, facilitating a more sustainable approach to commerce and environmental stewardship (Tapscott, 2016).

Moreover, AI and machine learning have a vital part in the realm of green fintech, empowering businesses to more accurately assess and optimize their environmental impact. By combining blockchain's transparency with the flexibility and efficiency of virtual currencies, companies are able to develop innovative ways to engage consumers in sustainability efforts. This collaboration fosters a dual benefit—enhancing both financial performance and environmental responsibility (Stubbs, 2008).

Key research studies, such as those focusing on blockchain's role in sustainable supply chains and the use of virtual currencies in carbon trading, reveal the ability of modern technologies to change things. For example, Nakamoto's (2008) foundational work on blockchain in financial transactions, along with Hileman and Rauchs' exploration of blockchain for carbon trading in 2017, demonstrate how these innovations are advancing green marketing strategies. These studies offer a strong basis for comprehending how blockchain integration and virtual currencies can lead to greater accountability, transparency, and consumer trust in sustainable practices.

Furthermore, the World Economic Forum (2020) highlights the substantial potential of blockchain technology in advancing environmental sustainability. The organization emphasizes how blockchain can streamline carbon credit trading, ensuring more effective and efficient global climate action. This growing intersection of technology, finance, and sustainability sets the stage for a new era of green marketing, where these advancements drive consumer engagement and help achieve ambitious sustainability goals.

The blockchain can be understood as a decentralized ledger, storing transaction records across multiple computers simultaneously. Most cryptocurrency transactions are maintained using blockchain technology. A blockchain consists of a series of interconnected chunks of data, where each block records transactions by including a hash of the preceding block along with a timestamp and transaction data (Du, 2019). Recent research conducted in Malaysia with a sample size of 512 examined the implementation of blockchain in the retail market, focusing on how Supply chain management can be improved using blockchain. According to the study's findings, there are substantial opportunities for blockchain to be integrated into the digital retail space, offering significant improvements in operational efficiency and transparency (Miraz, 2020).

Additionally, blockchain applications in online advertising require further investigation to offer a trustworthy alternative to existing models. (Parssinen, 2018) emphasize that the reliability of blockchain-based systems can be instrumental in mitigating fraudulent practices by offering immutable records of transactions. A bibliometric analysis of 3,507 documents highlighted that topics such as Bitcoin, Internet of Things (IoT), smart contracts, and security were among the most researched areas in blockchain, while marketing-related studies remain sparse. The analysis also revealed a lack of studies specifically focusing on marketing applications, as demonstrated by the tree map of keywords (Wamba, 2020).

Blockchain serves as a comprehensive solution for addressing the challenge of distributed trust through the use of smart contracts, distributed ledgers, and crypto-currencies (Hahn, 2017). While initially applied primarily within the fintech sector, its application has extended to other domains, including drug supply chains where Gcoin blockchain provides enhanced trust and value (Tseng, 2018). Blockchain is not limited to financial transactions but also holds immense potential beyond finance, warranting further exploration of its capabilities (Mansfield-Devine, 2017)

The Industrial Internet of Things (IIoT) has revolutionized the retail industry, influencing manufacturers, suppliers, and retailers to rethink trust and efficiency in consumer experiences (Liu, 2019). Models integrating product design and supply chain management have been proposed using a fuzzy approach within a blockchain framework to manage tactical decisions more effectively (Rahmanzadeh, 2020).

Moreover, blockchain has been investigated for use in online advertising as a trustworthy mechanism on a broader scale. (Parssinen, 2018) explored the challenges of privacy in blockchain-based models through the development of the DEPLEST algorithm, which offers superior performance compared to traditional proof-of-work (Pow) and proof-of-stake (PoS) methods (Chen, 2019).

Smart contracts, as a core component of blockchain technology, require continuous technological advancements to meet Industry 4.0 standards, especially in areas of security and privacy. Recent studies have explored the integration of artificial intelligence (AI) to enhance the functionality of smart contracts and address these challenges (Gupta, 2020).

Reputation management through blockchain plays a pivotal role in fostering trust among industrial entities. (Liu, 2019) emphasized the importance of anonymous reputation systems supported by consumer feedback, enhancing transparency and reliability in blockchain systems. However, the implementation of these systems faces challenges, particularly in terms of blockchain-based architecture and the deployment of proof-of-concept prototypes such as Parity Ethereum.

Additionally, blockchain has been applied within the food industry to simplify supply chain traceability and enable consumers to make well-informed purchase decisions. (Bettín-Díaz, 2018) demonstrated how blockchain can offer a simple, yet powerful solution for ensuring trust inside supply chains (Dimitrov, 2019) proposed blockchain technology's application in healthcare to effectively handle enormous volumes of data, providing accurate and timely processing for seamless interactions between healthcare providers and patients.

In the future, digital marketing is expected to explore new dimensions through the use of virtual reality in Technologies for Distributed Ledgers (DLT). Marketing plays a crucial role in society, and the inclusion of blockchain offers new opportunities for development, especially in bridging the gap between sustainability and technology. However, the current literature on blockchain integration in marketing remains limited, with key gaps identified. These include a lack of comprehensive exploration of blockchain marketing integration (Ghose, 2018; Wamba & Queiroz, 2020), insufficient research focusing on retail, supply chains, and smart contracts (Wamba & Queiroz, 2020), and a need for future research frameworks and influential streams to be established (Kar & Navin, 2021).

As evidenced by these gaps, there is a pressing need for further exploration of blockchain marketing integration. This research attempts to address this need by shedding light on the transformative potential of blockchain in marketing. A Business Model (BM) represents how companies create, capture, and distribute value to stakeholders, with sustainability becoming more and more important (Gatto et al., 2021; Osterwalder & Pigneur, 2010). In particular, Sustainable Business Models (SBMs) incorporate ecological and social value into the value proposition, making sustainability a key component of value creation (Biloslavo, 2018). These models require the design of value networks with strategic and governance shifts to account for broader stakeholder interests (Evans, 2017)

Blockchain and virtual currencies have proven to influence consumer behaviour in green marketing by providing mechanisms for sustainability incentives. (Bucherer, 2012) highlighted that blockchain-based platforms can increase consumer engagement by rewarding sustainable actions, such as loyalty points or discounts for eco-friendly goods. Additionally, green digital tokens linked to environmental actions like tree planting or carbon footprint reduction can foster participation in sustainability programs.

The decentralized and immutable nature of blockchain is particularly effective in addressing challenges such as greenwashing and the lack of transparency in sustainability claims. Tapscott and (Tapscott, Blockchain Revolution: How the Technology behind Bitcoin is Blockchain Revolution: How the Technology behind Bitcoin is, 2016) emphasize that blockchain increases trust in green marketing by creating tamper-proof, auditable records of environmental initiatives, allowing real-time tracking of carbon credits for verifiable emission reductions.

On the supply chain front, blockchain enables end-to-end traceability, allowing consumers to verify ethical and environmental claims behind products. (Saberi, 2019) argue that this feature is invaluable for industries like agriculture and fashion, where maintaining sustainability credibility is essential. Furthermore, blockchain provides a competitive advantage by offering verifiable, tangible data that third-party auditors can validate.

CASE STUDY

1. IKEA

Green Marketing Strategies: IKEA has focused on sustainability by offering eco-friendly products and green packaging options. They emphasize sustainable practices in their supply chain, such as using renewable materials in their products and reducing carbon emissions across their operations.

Blockchain-Based Solutions. Blockchain technology helps IKEA track supply chains' traceability and transparency by using blockchain, IKEA can prove sustainability and track the whole lifecycle of products. This allows the firm to prove its integrity when demonstrating sustainable sourcing practices, further allowing the firm to support claims about the environmental implications of its products.

Virtual Currency Incentives: IKEA has also experimented with offering incentives for eco-friendly behaviours. For example, their loyalty programs reward customers for purchasing sustainable products, reinforcing consumer engagement through green marketing efforts.

Case Study Impact: The use of blockchain for transparency by IKEA and their focus on green product development lead to positive environmental impact by reducing waste and increasing sustainable practices. These efforts also enhance consumer engagement, loyalty, and brand value, aligning with IKEA's long-term sustainability goals

2. Microsoft

Green Marketing Strategy: Microsoft aims to become carbon negative by 2030. The company's green marketing strategy involves promotion of products and services that would help in ensuring a cleaner and greener future. Sustainability is infused throughout the entire product lifecycle as well as the corporate practice, from the development stage to data centres.

Blockchain-Based Solutions: Microsoft used blockchain technology in its sustainability initiatives to trace carbon emissions and carbon credits management. The Azure Blockchain Service by Microsoft allows firms to monitor and verify their carbon credits in real-time, creating greater transparency and traceability in such offsetting of carbon footprint activities.

Virtual Currency Incentives While Microsoft has not directly introduced its virtual currency for green incentives, through its sustainable measures in game platforms such as providing environmental-friendly game developing practices that encourage users to be related to green causes, Microsoft does engage. Furthermore, with organisations such as Toucan protocol, it is facilitating its support in tokenized carbon credits to corporations looking forward in offsetting their emissions.

Case Study Impact: Microsoft's utilization of blockchain improves supply chain transparency and carbon footprint tracking. This green business initiative has influenced its business performance by increasing customer loyalty and brand value. Also, the transparent approach in environmental sustainability strengthens its position as a corporate responsibility leader

3. Patagonia

Green Marketing Strategies: Patagonia is renowned for its dedication to environmental responsibility, offering eco-friendly products made from recycled materials and encouraging its customers to repair and reuse products. The company's green marketing includes campaigns such as "Don't Buy This Jacket," which promotes sustainability through conscious consumption.

Blockchain-Based Solutions: The Company Patagonia uses blockchain technology to promote better transparency of the supply chain. In collaboration with other organizations, it is now tracking material provenance in every one of its garments, with fully traceable environmental and social impact for every product, to enable the company to detail to the consumer where they bought the sustainable purchase.

Virtual Currency Incentives: Patagonia hasn't fully integrated virtual currencies, but it has experimented with crypto currencies as a possible solution to aid environmental causes. It's looking into using blockchain and digital currencies to enable charitable contributions and carbon offset projects as a model for future virtual currency incentives.

Case Study Impact: Patagonia's focus on sustainability through green marketing and its adoption of blockchain to add transparency has cemented its status as an eco-friendly leader in the fashion industry. These actions have led to powerful consumer engagement and brand loyalty, which translate into business performance by attracting a customer base that values environmental responsibility

ADVANTAGES

This is game-changing as far as business approach goes, how to address the problem of sustainability through the adoption of blockchain technology and virtual currencies into green marketing. One of the greatest challenges of green marketing has to do with trust. A blockchain would be used in proving environmental claims because it establishes transparent and traceable records of the product's journey from source materials up to the final delivery. That clarity, in turn, ensures businesses do truly what they claim to and helps prevent green washing; besides, it increases consumer confidence (Biggi, 2020).

Virtual currencies can excite both ways for consumers to get involved with sustainability. Brands can reward consumers in the form of digital tokens for recycling or low-carbon consumption actions (Bucherer, 2012). The benefits are not only in responsible behaviour but also in a much stronger emotional bonding with the consumer and brand. This further involves consumers to become integral to the solution by empowering them to make greener choices at simultaneously.

The second aspect is how these technologies will assist businesses in beginning to create revenue. These tokenized carbon credits could give rewards for sustainable practice in their operations. It can all create new sources of revenue and support global goals on sustainability that the UN has outlined (Evans, 2017). This, it seems, is blockchain-it helps companies monitor supply chains with all possible transparency toward achieving and sustaining this development.

This highlights the same tools that encourage recycling, reduce waste, and make way for a more resource-efficient, circular economy. Instead of being wasted. It also shows how business can future-proof itself through staying ahead of environmental regulations as well as meeting the demand for transparency and accountability (Miraz, 2020).

This is the guide that shows the way for blockchain and virtual currencies in making green marketing effective, trustworthy, and rewarding for businesses, consumers, and the planet. These technologies will make this happen, showing a win-win situation in terms of where businesses grow, consumers are empowered, and sustainability becomes a shared responsibility (Tseng, 2018).

DISCUSSIONS

The results of this study highlight the transformative potential of blockchain technology and virtual currencies in reshaping green marketing practices. Blockchain's decentralized and immutable nature provides a robust solution to issues such as trust and transparency, which have long hindered the credibility of sustainability claims. By enabling end-to-end traceability of supply chains, blockchain ensures that companies can substantiate their environmental claims, thereby fostering greater consumer confidence and mitigating the risks of greenwashing (Biloslavo, 2018). Moreover, blockchain-based solutions offer significant efficiency improvements by streamlining operations, reducing intermediaries, and enhancing accountability across diverse sectors.

Virtual currencies, integrated with blockchain technology, have emerged as a powerful tool to incentivize sustainable consumer behaviour. Through mechanisms such as tokenized carbon credits and green rewards, companies can actively engage consumers in sustainability efforts. The findings reveal that blockchain and virtual currencies not only address environmental accountability but also enhance consumer engagement by aligning economic incentives with ecological goals (Saheb & Mamaghani, 2021). This dual advantage of technological efficiency and consumer involvement marks a significant departure from traditional green marketing approaches, paving the way for a new era of environmentally conscious business practices.

The case studies of companies like IKEA, Microsoft, and Patagonia further illustrate the practical applications and benefits of blockchain technology in real-world green marketing scenarios. These organizations have leveraged blockchain to achieve greater transparency, enhance brand credibility, and foster stronger consumer relationships (Gupta, 2020). While the integration of blockchain and virtual currencies is still in its nascent stages, these examples demonstrate its potential to create innovative and impactful green marketing strategies.

IMPLICATIONS

The implications of this study are multi-faceted, encompassing technological, organizational, and consumer dimensions. Technologically, the adoption of blockchain and virtual currencies in green marketing signifies a paradigm shift, offering a scalable and reliable framework for businesses to achieve sustainability goals. By ensuring transparency and traceability, blockchain technology can become a cornerstone for companies striving to meet stringent environmental regulations and align with global sustainability standards, such as the Sustainable Development Goals (SDGs) of the United Nations.

Organizationally, businesses stand to gain competitive advantages by integrating blockchain into their operations. The technology improves operational effectiveness in addition to strengthen brand equity by demonstrating a commitment to environmental responsibility. Furthermore, the ability to provide verifiable proof of sustainability practices can differentiate organizations in increasingly eco-conscious markets, attracting environmentally aware consumers and investors.

From a consumer perspective, blockchain-enabled virtual currencies offer new ways to engage individuals in sustainability efforts. Reward mechanisms like green tokens or loyalty points linked to sustainable actions create an emotional bond between consumers and brands, driving long-term loyalty. This empowerment of consumers fosters a culture of shared responsibility for environmental stewardship, promoting a more inclusive and participatory approach to sustainability.

Moreover, the broader implications extend to policy and education. Policymakers can leverage blockchain's capabilities to ensure adherence to environmental laws and sustainable practices across industries. In educational settings, the integration of blockchain and green marketing in curricula can prepare future professionals to negotiate the changing terrain of environmentally friendly corporate operations.

CONCLUSION

This study highlights the transformative role of blockchain technology and virtual currencies in advancing green marketing practices. By addressing critical challenges such as trust, transparency, and consumer engagement, these technologies offer a compelling pathway for businesses to coordinate their activities with environmental and social goals. Blockchain's ability to provide secure, immutable records of sustainability practices fosters greater accountability, while virtual currencies incentivize eco-friendly behaviours, creating a synergistic relationship between technology, businesses, and consumers.

The case studies of IKEA, Microsoft, and Patagonia illustrate the tangible benefits of integrating blockchain into green marketing strategies, proving increased supply chain openness, improved consumer engagement, and strengthened brand loyalty. These real-world applications underscore the potential of blockchain and virtual currencies to redefine green marketing, driving sustainable innovation across industries.

FUTURE DIRECTIONS

Future research should focus on exploring the scalability of blockchain solutions in green marketing, addressing challenges such as energy consumption, and developing frameworks for broader adoption across different industries. By doing so, businesses and researchers can unlock the complete capabilities of these technologies to foster a sustainable future. The integration of blockchain and virtual currencies into green marketing represents not just an evolution of business practices but a revolutionary step towards achieving global sustainability objectives.

REFERENCES

Ahluwalia, S. M., Mahto, R. V., & Guerrero, M. (2020). Blockchain technology and startup financing: A transaction cost economics perspective. *Technological Forecasting and Social Change*, *151*, 119854. DOI: 10.1016/j.techfore.2019.119854

Alharthi, S., Cerotti, P., & Far, S. (2020,). An Exploration of The Role of Blockchain in The Sustainability and Effectiveness of The Pharmaceutical Supply Chain. . *J. Suppl. Chain Cust. Relatsh. Manag.*, 1-29.

Almekhlafi, S., & Al-Shaibany, N. (2021). The Literature Review of Blockchain Adoption. *Asian J. Res. Comput. Sci.*, *7*, 29–50. DOI: 10.9734/ajrcos/2021/v7i230177

Angelis, J., & Ribeiro da Silva, E. (2019). Blockchain adoption: A value driver perspective. *Business Horizons*, *62*(3), 307–314. DOI: 10.1016/j.bushor.2018.12.001

Barney, J. (1991). Firm Resources and Sustained Competitive Advantage. *Journal of Management*, *17*(1), 99–120. DOI: 10.1177/014920639101700108

Bettín-Díaz, R. R.-M. (2018). Methodological approach to the definition of a blockchain system for the food industry supply chain trace-ability. In Lecture notes in computer science (including subseries lecture notes in artificial intelligence and lecture notes in bioinformatics. *Springer Verlag.*, (pp. 19–33).

Bhardwaj, A., Garg, A., & Gajpal, Y. (2021). Determinants of Blockchain Technology Adoption in Supply Chains by Small and Medium Enterprises (SMEs) in India. *Mathematical Problems in Engineering*, *2021*, 5537395. DOI: 10.1155/2021/5537395

Biggi, G., & Giuliani, E. (2020). The noxious consequences of innovation: What do we know? *Industry and Innovation*, *28*(1), 19–41. DOI: 10.1080/13662716.2020.1726729

Biloslavo, R. B., Bagnoli, C., & Edgar, D. (2018). An eco-critical perspective on business models: The value triangle as an approach to closing the sustainability gap. *Journal of Cleaner Production*, *174*, 746–762. DOI: 10.1016/j.jclepro.2017.10.281

Bucherer, E. E., Eisert, U., & Gassmann, O. (2012). Towards systematic business model innovation lessons from product innovation management. *Creativity and Innovation Management*, *21*(2), 183–198. DOI: 10.1111/j.1467-8691.2012.00637.x

Buer, S. V., Strandhagen, J. O., & Chan, F. T. S. (2018). The link between Industry 4.0 and lean manufacturing: Mapping current research and establishing a research agenda. *International Journal of Production Research*, *56*(8), 2924–2940. DOI: 10.1080/00207543.2018.1442945

Chang, S., Chen, Y., & Wu, T. (2019). Exploring blockchain technology in international trade: Business process re-engineering for letter of credit. *Industrial Management & Data Systems, 119*(ahead-of-print), 1712–1733. DOI: 10.1108/IMDS-12-2018-0568

Chen, Y. e. (2019). DEPLEST: A blockchain-based privacy-preserving distributed database toward user behaviors in social networks. In Information sciences. *Elsevier Inc.*, 501 (pp. 100–117). DOI: 10.1016/j.ins.2019.05.092

Cizmesija, A., & Vrcek, N. (May, 2021.). Organizational challenges of blockchain adoption: An exploratory literature review. *In Proceedings of the 2021 IEEE Technology and Engineering Management Conference-Europe, TEMSCON-EUR, Dubrovnik, Croatia,* 17–20.

Cole, R. S., Stevenson, M., & Aitken, J. (2019). Blockchain technology: Implications for operations and supply chain management. *Supply Chain Management, 24*(4), 469–483. DOI: 10.1108/SCM-09-2018-0309

Dai, J., & Vasarhelyi, M. A. (2017). Toward blockchain-based accounting and assurance. *Journal of Information Systems, 31*(3), 5–21. DOI: 10.2308/isys-51804

Dib, O., Brousmiche, K., Durand, A., Thea, E., & Hamida, E. (2018). Consortium blockchains: Overview, applications and challenges. *Int. J. Adv. Telecommun., 11*, 51–64.

Dimitrov, D. V. (2019). Blockchain applications for healthcare data management. Healthcare Informatics Research. *Korean Society of Medical Informatics, 25*(1), 51–56.

Du, W. D. (2019). Affordances, experimentation and actualization of FinTech: A blockchain implementation study. *Journal of Strategic Information Systems. Elsevier B.V., 28*(1), 50–65.

Dubey, R. G., Gunasekaran, A., Papadopoulos, T., & Childe, S. J. (2015). Green supply chain management enablers: Mixed methods research. *Sustainable Production and Consumption, 4*, 72–88. DOI: 10.1016/j.spc.2015.07.001

Evans, S. V., Vladimirova, D., Holgado, M., Van Fossen, K., Yang, M., Silva, E. A., & Barlow, C. Y. (2017). Business model innovation for sustainability: Towards a unified perspective for creation of sustainable business models". *Business Strategy and the Environment, 26*(5), 597–608. DOI: 10.1002/bse.1939

Gatto, M., de Haan, S., Laborte, A., Bonierbale, M., Labarta, R., & Hareau, G. (2021). Trends in varietal diversity of main staple crops in Asia and Africa and implications for sustainable food systems. *Frontiers in Sustainable Food Systems, 5*, 626714. DOI: 10.3389/fsufs.2021.626714

Ghose, A. (2018). *TAP: Unlocking the mobile economy*. MIT Press.

Gupta, S. e., Leszkiewicz, A., Kumar, V., Bijmolt, T., & Potapov, D. (2020). Digital analytics: Modeling for insights and new methods. *Journal of Interactive Marketing, 51*(1), 26–43. DOI: 10.1016/j.intmar.2020.04.003

Haber, S., & Stornetta, W. (1990). How to Time-Stamp a Digital Document. In *Advances in Cryptology-CRYPTO' 90* (pp. 437–455). Springer.

Hahn, A. e. (2017). *Smart contract-based campus demonstration of decentralized transactive energy auctions. 2017 IEEE power and energy society innovative smart grid technologies conference, ISGT 2017*. Institute of Electrical and Electronics Engineers Inc.

Hughes, L. D., Dwivedi, Y. K., Misra, S. K., Rana, N. P., Raghavan, V., & Akella, V. (2019). Blockchain research, practice and policy: Applications, benefits, limitations, emerging research themes and research agenda. *International Journal of Information Management, 49*, 114–129. DOI: 10.1016/j.ijinfomgt.2019.02.005

Hye, A., Miraz, M., Sharif, K., & Hassan, M. (2020). Factors affecting logistic supply chain performance: Mediating role of block chain adoption. *Test Eng. Manag., 82*, 9338–9348.

Kar, A. K., & Navin, L. (2021). Diffusion of blockchain in insurance industry: An analysis through the review of academic and trade literature. *Telematics and Informatics, 58*, 101532. DOI: 10.1016/j.tele.2020.101532

Komalavalli, C., Saxena, D., & Laroiya, C. (2020). Overview of Blockchain Technology Concepts. In *Handbook of Research on Blockchain Technology* (pp. 349–371). Academic Press. DOI: 10.1016/B978-0-12-819816-2.00014-9

Ku-Mahamud, K., Bakar, N., & Omar, M. (2018). Blockchain, cryptocurrency and Fintech market growth in Malaysia. *J. Adv. Res. Dyn. Control. Syst., 10*, 2074–2082.

Liu, D. e. (2019). Anonymous reputation system for IIoT-enabled retail marketing atop PoS blockchain. *In IEEE transactions on industrial informatics: 15 IEEE. Computers & Society*, •••, 3527–3537.

Mackey, T., Kuo, T., Gummadi, B., Clauson, K., Church, G., Grishin, D., Obbad, K., Barkovich, R., & Palombini, M. (2019). "Fit-for-purpose?"-Challenges and opportunities for applications of blockchain technology in the future of healthcare. *BMC Medicine*, *17*(1), 68. DOI: 10.1186/s12916-019-1296-7 PMID: 30914045

Maden, A., & Alptekin, E. (2020). Evaluation of factors affecting the decision to adopt blockchain technology: A logistics company case study using Fuzzy DEMATEL. *Journal of Intelligent & Fuzzy Systems*, *39*(5), 6279–6291. DOI: 10.3233/JIFS-189096

Maesa, D., & Mori, P. (2020). Blockchain 3.0 applications survey. *Journal of Parallel and Distributed Computing*, *138*, 99–114. DOI: 10.1016/j.jpdc.2019.12.019

Mahajan, A., & Issa, T. (2020). Australian users' perspective of green blockchain technology adoption in businesses. In *Green Energy and Technology*. Springer.

Mahajan, A., & Issa, T. (2020). Australian users' perspective of green blockchain technology adoption in businesses. In *Green Energy and Technology*. Springer.

Manohar, S. (2024). Cryptocurrency as a Slice in Investment Portfolio: Identifying Critical Antecedents and Building Taxonomy for Emerging Economy. *Asia-Pacific Financial Markets*, •••, 1–26. DOI: 10.1007/s10690-024-09490-7

Mansfield-Devine, S. (2017). Beyond bitcoin: Using blockchain technology to provide as-surance in the commercial world. *Computer Fraud & Security*, *2017*(5), 14–18. DOI: 10.1016/S1361-3723(17)30042-8

Miraz, M. H. (2020). Factors affecting implementa- tion of blockchain in retail market in Malaysia. *International Journal of Supply Chain Management*, *9*(1), 385–391.

Naini, S. R., Mekapothula, R. R., Jain, R., & Manohar, S. (2024). Redefining green consumerism: A diminutive approach to market segmentation for sustainability. *Environmental Science and Pollution Research International*, *31*(9), 12916–12932. DOI: 10.1007/s11356-023-31717-9 PMID: 38180668

Nair, A. J., & Manohar, S. (2024). Green Service Consumption: Unlocking Customer Expectations on Technological Transformations Enhancing Purchase Experience in Retail Store. *International Journal of Information Management Data Insights*, *4*(2), 100277. DOI: 10.1016/j.jjimei.2024.100277

Osterwalder, A., & Pigneur, Y. (2010). *Business model generation: a handbook for visionaries, game changers, and challengers* (Vol. 1). John Wiley & Sons.

Parssinen, M. A. (2018). Is blockchain ready to revolutionize online advertising? *In IEEE access. Institute of Electrical and Electronics Engineers Inc.*, *6*, 54884–54899.

Przhedetskiy, Y., Przhedetskaya, N., Borzenko, K., & Bondarenko, V. (2019). Blockchain technologies in healthcare institutions: Focus on security and effective cooperation with the government. *Int. J. Econ. Bus. Adm., VII*(Special Issue 2), 92–99. DOI: 10.35808/ijeba/373

Rahmanzadeh, S. P., Pishvaee, M. S., & Rasouli, M. R. (2020). Integrated innovative product design and supply chain tactical planning within a blockchain platform. *International Journal of Production Research, 58*(7), 2242–2262. DOI: 10.1080/00207543.2019.1651947

Rugeviciute, A., & Mehrpouya, A. (2019). Blockchain, a Panacea for Development Accountability? A Study of the Barriers and Enablers for Blockchain's Adoption by Development Aid Organizations. *Front. Blockchain, 2*, 15. DOI: 10.3389/fbloc.2019.00015

Saberi, S. K., Kouhizadeh, M., Sarkis, J., & Shen, L. (2019). Blockchain technology and its relationships to sustainable supply chain management. *International Journal of Production Research, 57*(7), 2117–2135. DOI: 10.1080/00207543.2018.1533261

Sadeghi, M., Mahmoudi, A., & Deng, X. (2022). Adopting distributed ledger technology for the sustainable construction industry: Evaluating the barriers using Ordinal Priority Approach. *Environmental Science and Pollution Research International, 29*(7), 10495–10520. DOI: 10.1007/s11356-021-16376-y PMID: 34528198

Saheb, T., & Mamaghani, F. (2021). Exploring the barriers and organizational values of blockchain adoption in the banking industry. *The Journal of High Technology Management Research, 32*(2), 100417. DOI: 10.1016/j.hitech.2021.100417

Stubbs, W., & Cocklin, C. (2008). Conceptualizing a 'sustainability business model'. *Organization & Environment, 21*(2), 103–127. DOI: 10.1177/1086026608318042

Tapscott, D. a. (2016). *Blockchain Revolution: How the Technology behind Bitcoin is Changing Money, Business, and the World, Portfolio*. Penguin Books.

Tapscott, D. a. (2016). *Blockchain Revolution: How the Technology behind Bitcoin is Blockchain Revolution: How the Technology behind Bitcoin is*. Portfolio- Penguin Books.

Tripathi, G., Ahad, M., & Paiva, S. (2020). S2HS- A blockchain based approach for smart healthcare system. *Health Care, 8*, 100391. PMID: 31753750

Tripoli, M. a. (2018). *Emerging Opportunities for the Application of Blockchain in the Agri-Food Industry*. FAO and ICTSD, Rome, IT and Geneva.

Tseng, J. H., Liao, Y.-C., Chong, B., & Liao, S. (2018). Governance on the drug supply chain via gcoin blockchain. [MDPI AG.]. *International Journal of Environmental Research and Public Health, 15*(6), 15. DOI: 10.3390/ijerph15061055 PMID: 29882861

Vafadarnikjoo, A., Badri Ahmadi, H., Liou, J., Botelho, T., & Chalvatzis, K. (2021). Analyzing blockchain adoption barriers in manufacturing supply chains by the neutrosophic analytic hierarchy process. *Annals of Operations Research, 327*(1), 129–156. DOI: 10.1007/s10479-021-04048-6

Wamba, S. F. (2020). Blockchain in the operations and supply chain management: Benefits, challenges and future research opportunities. . *Journal of Information Management*, 52.

Wang, Y. J.-D., Han, J. H., & Beynon-Davies, P. (2019). Understanding blockchain technology for future supply chains: A systematic literature review and research agenda". *Supply Chain Management, 24*(1), 62–84. DOI: 10.1108/SCM-03-2018-0148

Chapter 9
The Impact of Digital Currency Adoption on Business Performance

Jayshree Chhetri
https://orcid.org/0009-0000-3383-6857
Graphic Era University, India

Amit Kumar Uniyal
Graphic Era University, India

Himani Devi
https://orcid.org/0009-0008-3754-7145
Graphic Era University, India

Amar Johri
College of Administrative and Financial Sciences, Saudi Arabia

ABSTRACT

This chapter examines the adoption of digital currencies by businesses and its effects on operational structures, financial strategies, and competitive positioning. It provides a detailed assessment of digital currency types, regional adoption patterns, and the role of supporting technologies such as blockchain, artificial intelligence, and digital wallets. The chapter explores how firms integrate cryptocurrencies, stablecoins, and central bank digital currencies into their models to enhance efficiency, enable microtransactions, and improve market access. It also addresses key challenges including volatility, regulatory uncertainty, cybersecurity, and financial reporting issues. Through real-world case studies and sectoral analysis, the chapter identifies strategic benefits for early adopters and offers practical recommendations

DOI: 10.4018/979-8-3373-0315-4.ch009

for businesses seeking to evaluate or implement digital currency systems. The discussion concludes with projections on the future role of digital currencies in reshaping financial ecosystems and corporate operations.

1. INTRODUCTION

1. (i) Definition and Types of Digital Currencies

Digital currencies refer to forms of money or exchange that exist only in electronic form. Unlike physical currencies such as coins or paper money, digital currencies are intangible and are stored and transacted over digital systems. They rely on computer networks and cryptographic protocols to function securely without needing a central issuing authority in many cases (European Central Bank, 2019).

Digital currencies can be broadly classified into three main categories: cryptocurrencies, central bank digital currencies (CBDCs), and stablecoins. Cryptocurrencies are decentralized digital assets that operate on blockchain networks. They are not issued by any central authority, and their value is determined largely by market supply and demand. Bitcoin was the first widely adopted cryptocurrency, introduced in 2009, and it remains the most prominent example (Nakamoto, 2008). Other examples include Ethereum, Litecoin, and Ripple.

Table 1. Comparison of transaction costs: Traditional vs digital currency systems

Cost Component	Traditional System	Digital Currency System
Bank Intermediary Fees	1%–3% of transaction value	Not applicable
Credit Card Processing Fees	2%–5%	Not applicable
International Transfer Fees	\$10–\$50 per transfer	<\$1 flat fee (e.g., USDT, BTC)
Settlement Time	1–5 business days	Near-instant
Currency Conversion Fee	1%–3%	Not applicable if in crypto

Source: Catalini & Gans (2016); Ghosh et al. (2020)

The table 1 shows that businesses using digital currencies, particularly stablecoins and cryptocurrencies, can significantly reduce the costs associated with global transactions.

Central Bank Digital Currencies (CBDCs) are digital forms of sovereign currency issued and regulated by a nation's central bank. Unlike cryptocurrencies, CBDCs are centralized and aim to serve as legal tender. Countries such as China (with its e-CNY) and Sweden (with the e-krona) have initiated pilot projects or formal rollouts of CBDCs (Bank for International Settlements, 2021).

Stablecoins are digital currencies pegged to traditional assets like fiat currencies (e.g., USD) or commodities (e.g., gold) to minimize price fluctuations. Examples include Tether (USDT) and USD Coin (USDC). These aim to combine the transaction efficiency of cryptocurrencies with the price stability of traditional money (G7 Working Group on Stablecoins, 2019).

1. (ii) Evolution of Digital Currencies

The concept of digital money dates back several decades, beginning with electronic payment systems like PayPal in the late 1990s. However, the modern form of digital currency emerged with the development of blockchain technology. In 2008, the release of the Bitcoin whitepaper introduced a decentralized form of currency not reliant on trust in financial institutions (Nakamoto, 2008).

Since then, the landscape has grown rapidly. Thousands of cryptocurrencies have been developed, each with its own use case and underlying infrastructure. At the same time, governments and financial institutions have explored digital currencies for use in monetary policy, retail payments, and cross-border transactions (World Economic Forum, 2020).

CBDCs represent a shift in institutional engagement with digital currencies. Unlike early cryptocurrency projects driven by private individuals and organizations, CBDCs involve national monetary authorities, integrating digital currency into the formal economy. The rise of stablecoins and the potential competition they pose to fiat currencies have further prompted central banks to explore digital currency alternatives (BIS, 2021).

Figure 1. Types of digital currencies

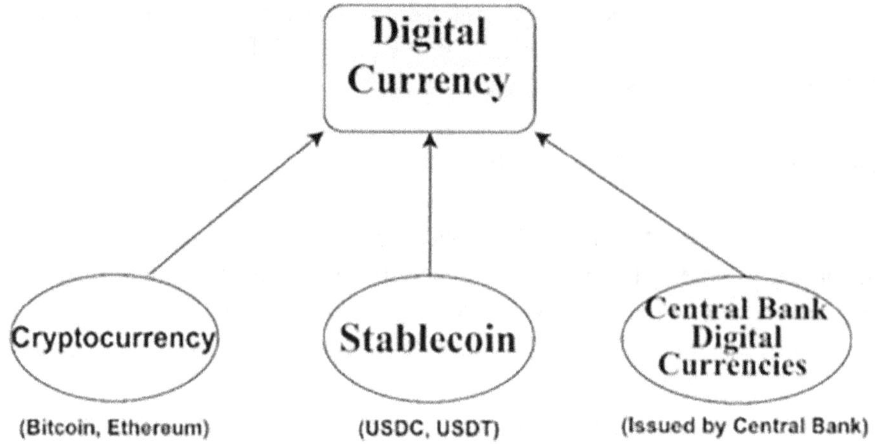

1. (iii) Key Differences Between Traditional and Digital Currencies

There are several structural and functional differences between traditional currencies and digital currencies.

Form: Traditional currencies are physical and issued in paper or coin formats, while digital currencies are purely electronic.
Issuance and Control: Traditional currencies are issued and regulated by central banks and governments. In contrast, many digital currencies, especially cryptocurrencies, are issued in decentralized systems where no single authority has control.
Transaction Method: Transactions in traditional currencies usually pass through intermediaries such as banks. Digital currencies, especially cryptocurrencies, can facilitate peer-to-peer transactions without intermediaries, which can reduce transaction time and cost.
Monetary Policy Alignment: Traditional currencies are part of a country's monetary policy and are influenced by tools such as interest rates and inflation targeting. Most cryptocurrencies are not aligned with any nation's monetary policy, although CBDCs are designed to fit within existing frameworks (IMF, 2021).

Anonymity and Transparency: Digital currencies offer varying levels of anonymity and transparency. Bitcoin, for example, allows users to transact without revealing personal identity, while all transactions are recorded on a public ledger. Traditional banking systems typically require identification for most transactions and maintain private records.

These distinctions contribute to both the opportunities and concerns related to digital currency adoption in business and the broader economy.

2. GLOBAL ADOPTION TRENDS

2. (i) Regional Adoption Rates

The adoption of digital currencies varies widely across countries and regions, influenced by economic conditions, regulatory frameworks, and technological readiness. Some countries have integrated digital currencies into formal financial systems, while others remain cautious or restrictive.

El Salvador became the first country to officially adopt Bitcoin as legal tender in 2021. The government launched a national digital wallet called "Chivo" and provided incentives to encourage its use (Yermack, 2022). Despite the policy's ambition, the adoption rate among citizens and businesses has been inconsistent, with many still preferring cash or U.S. dollars for daily transactions (Alvarez et al., 2022).

China has taken a different approach by focusing on a state-controlled digital currency. The Digital Currency Electronic Payment (DCEP), also known as the e-CNY, is a central bank digital currency (CBDC) issued by the People's Bank of China. Pilot programs in cities like Shenzhen and Suzhou have been ongoing since 2020, with millions of users and transactions processed through government-backed mobile apps (Auer et al., 2022).

The European Union is in the exploratory phase of developing a digital euro. The European Central Bank (ECB) has conducted public consultations and technical assessments. While a formal launch has not been announced, the digital euro is intended to complement cash and enhance payment resilience across the Eurozone (European Central Bank, 2023).

Other regions, such as Africa and South Asia, have also seen increasing interest, particularly in cryptocurrency adoption (Chainalysis, 2023).

2. (ii) Factors Influencing Adoption

A number of important factors influence the adoption rate and pattern of digital currencies: Regulatory Framework: Permissive and transparent legal regimes promote higher adoption rates for countries. Uncertainty or restricted regulation deters both companies and consumers. The United States has seen uneven development owing to decentralized rules at the state levels and tardy guidelines at the national level (Zetzsche et al., 2020).

Reliable Technological Infrastructure: Widespread usage is made possible by smartphones, internet connectivity, and safe digital wallets. Regions with advanced mobile penetration, such as East Asia and Northern Europe, are better positioned for adoption.

Public Trust and Financial Literacy: People's willingness to adopt digital currencies depends on their trust in the issuing authority and understanding of how digital currency systems function. In El Salvador, despite strong governmental support, limited trust and low digital literacy have slowed usage (Alvarez et al., 2022).

Economic Incentives: In high-inflation environments, users may adopt cryptocurrencies to protect value. In contrast, in stable economies, the use case is often tied to transaction speed, cost reduction, or financial inclusion.

2. (iii) Government and Central Bank Initiatives (CBDCs)

Central banks around the world are actively researching or developing CBDCs. According to the Bank for International Settlements, over 100 countries have initiated exploratory or pilot projects as of 2023 (BIS, 2023).

China's e-CNY is the most advanced among large economies. The government has integrated the digital yuan into existing payment systems and is testing its use in public transport, retail purchases, and salary payments (Auer et al., 2022).

Sweden's e-krona is another prominent example. The Riksbank has conducted multiple pilot phases to test technical feasibility and user experience. Sweden's high rate of cashless payments makes it a natural candidate for CBDC integration (Sveriges Riksbank, 2023).

Bahamas' Sand Dollar was the first fully operational CBDC, launched nationwide in 2020. It aims to improve financial access for remote communities and is backed 1:1 by the Bahamian dollar (Central Bank of The Bahamas, 2021).

European Union's digital euro remains in the development stage. The ECB has emphasized user privacy and interoperability as key design priorities (European Central Bank, 2023).

These initiatives are driven by the desire to modernize payment systems, enhance financial inclusion, and maintain monetary sovereignty in the face of growing private digital currencies.

3. BUSINESS MODELS AND DIGITAL CURRENCY INTEGRATION

3. (i) E-commerce and Digital Payments

Digital currencies are being increasingly adopted in e-commerce as alternative payment methods. Businesses in the online retail sector have integrated cryptocurrencies and stablecoins to provide customers with more payment options. This allows companies to bypass conventional banking systems, reduce transaction fees, and offer faster settlement times. For example, platforms such as Shopify and Overstock have enabled Bitcoin payments through third-party payment processors like BitPay (Catalini & Gans, 2016). The integration of digital currencies into e-commerce platforms also reflects a shift in consumer preferences, especially among younger demographics who are more familiar with digital assets. Accepting digital currencies can attract these consumers and support brand positioning in a competitive online environment (Zohar, 2015).

However, adoption also brings operational challenges. Businesses must address price volatility, manage tax implications, and ensure compliance with regulations on digital asset transactions. Some companies choose to immediately convert digital currencies into fiat to avoid exposure to price fluctuations, while others retain them as long-term assets.

For example, several Shopify merchants, particularly in North America and Western Europe, have integrated Bitcoin payments via BitPay. According to BitPay's internal analytics, these merchants reported a measurable increase in cart conversion rates—especially among Gen Z and Millennial shoppers who prefer decentralized payment methods.

1. MSME (Cross-border trade) – A case of an Indian textile SME using USDT to settle payments with a vendor in Vietnam, reducing remittance time from 3 days to under 1 hour and avoiding currency conversion fees.
2. Retail (E-commerce) – The inclusion of a real-world example involving Shopify merchants using BitPay to accept cryptocurrency payments, with an observed increase in checkout conversion among younger, tech-savvy customers.

3. (ii) Blockchain-Enabled Business Models

Blockchain technology that forms the basis for a majority of digital currencies provides new business models with a focus on transparency, efficiency, and decentralization. These models are not dependent on a central authority for verification but use distributed ledgers to ensure transaction integrity. Blockchain is applied to record each stage of a product life cycle for improving transparency and limiting the risk of fraud when it is implemented for supply chain management. For example, organizations such as IBM and Maersk have made blockchain platforms that allow for tracking shipments in real-time and authenticating product origins (Murray et al., 2021). Token-based business models are also on the rise where organizations issue digital tokens that symbolize utility or ownership. These tokens could be used for service accessibility, financing operations, or rewarding user involvement. Some examples are services that provide decentralized cloud storage, streaming of video, or software services.

Smart contracts expand these models by automating transactions according to pre-specified conditions. This minimizes the requirement for intermediaries, administrative costs are reduced, and there is increased speed and precision when implementing the contract (Cong & He, 2019).

3. (iii) Cross-Border Operations and International Trade

Digital currencies present potential benefits for cross-border transactions by minimizing the use of traditional financial institutions like correspondent banks. This is especially applicable where cross-border transfers are time-consuming, expensive, or insecure. Cryptocurrencies have the potential to allow near-instant settlements at discounted transactions, which is suitable for small and medium-sized enterprises (SMEs) that participate in international trade. Compared to traditional international wire transfers that take days and involve several charges, digital currencies have the potential to minimize the time and cost of transferring funds (Ghosh et al., 2020).

Stablecoins are widely applied within this segment because they are less volatile than other cryptocurrencies yet support transactional speeds. USDC and USDT are widely used for cross-border business transactions, particularly where there is currency volatility or controls on capital. CBDCs can further reshape cross-border trade with even more stable and compatible forms of payments. China is already conducting pilot programs for using the digital yuan across borders with other Asian economies. This could potentially result in direct currency transfers across borders without the involvement of the U.S. dollar, potentially reshaping the dynamics of world currency dominance (Auer et al., 2021).

A notable example is a mid-sized textile exporter based in Surat, India, which began using USDT (a stablecoin) for cross-border payments to a Vietnamese raw material supplier. This shift eliminated bank intermediary fees and reduced transaction time from 72 hours to less than one hour, while shielding both parties from currency fluctuation risks and delays in traditional SWIFT transfers.

Despite these opportunities, legal and regulatory uncertainty in cross-border digital currency use remains a challenge. Differences in national laws, tax treatment, and compliance requirements can complicate international operations for businesses adopting digital currencies.

4. OPERATIONAL AND FINANCIAL IMPACT

4. (i) Cost Savings in Transactions

One of the main operational benefits of using digital currencies in business is the potential reduction in transaction costs. Traditional payment systems, particularly those involving cross-border transactions, often include multiple intermediaries such as correspondent banks, credit card networks, and clearinghouses. Each intermediary introduces fees, which can accumulate to a significant portion of the total transaction value.

Figure 2. Disintermediation in Digital Currency Systems: Direct peer-to-peer interactions enabled by blockchain technology

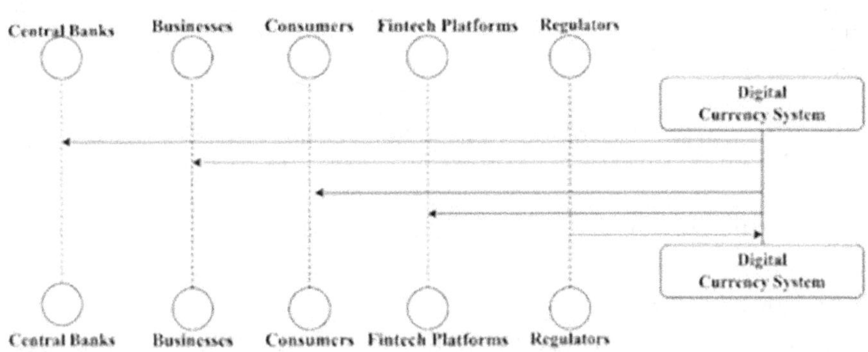

The diagram visually emphasizes the removal of traditional intermediaries like banks and credit card processors. Digital currencies, particularly those built on blockchain systems, reduce or eliminate the need for these intermediaries. Peer-to-peer transfers occur directly between parties, often with minimal network fees. For instance, Bitcoin and Ethereum transactions typically incur a flat fee based on network demand rather than a percentage of the transaction amount. This can benefit businesses dealing with high transaction volumes or microtransactions (Catalini & Gans, 2016). Stablecoins further lower transaction costs while avoiding volatility. Their use in decentralized finance (DeFi) applications and remittance services has shown consistent cost advantages over traditional banking services, especially in markets with underdeveloped financial infrastructure (Ghosh et al., 2020).

4. (ii) Enhanced Payment Efficiency and Speed

Digital currencies offer enhanced efficiency in payments by significantly reducing settlement time. In traditional banking systems, especially for international payments, funds may take several days to clear due to time zone differences, currency conversions, and compliance checks. Digital currencies can enable near-instant settlements regardless of geography.

This efficiency allows businesses to manage working capital more effectively and reduces the need for short-term borrowing to cover cash flow gaps. Faster payments can also strengthen supplier relationships, streamline payroll systems, and support just-in-time inventory management (Auer & Böhme, 2020).

Table 2. Average settlement time (in hours)

Payment Type	Traditional Banking	Cryptocurrency	Stablecoin (USDC/USDT)
Domestic Payment	24–48	<1	<1
International Payment	72–120	<2	<2
Payroll Processing	24–72	<1	<1
Supplier Payments (B2B)	48–96	1–2	1–2

Source: Auer & Böhme (2020); Catalini & Gans (2016)

This reduction in time enhances operational agility and supports time-sensitive payment processes such as international trade and payroll in decentralized or global firms as shown in table 2.

Some companies have begun integrating digital wallets for employee payroll disbursement, especially in freelance and gig economy platforms. These systems allow workers to receive earnings almost immediately after completing tasks, improving user satisfaction and operational agility.

4. (iii) Accounting and Financial Reporting Implications

The use of digital currencies in business requires careful consideration in accounting and financial reporting. Digital assets do not fit neatly into existing accounting categories under most national and international standards.

Under U.S. Generally Accepted Accounting Principles (GAAP), cryptocurrencies are classified as intangible assets with indefinite life. This means they are subject to impairment if their fair value falls below carrying value but cannot be revalued upward. This creates potential distortions in financial reporting, particularly for firms that hold large amounts of digital currency (FASB, 2022).

The International Financial Reporting Standards (IFRS) follow a similar approach, treating cryptocurrencies as intangible assets unless they are held for sale in the ordinary course of business, in which case they are treated as inventory. In either case, measurement challenges arise due to market volatility and the lack of standardized valuation techniques (PwC, 2023).

Furthermore, businesses accepting digital currencies must track acquisition prices, transaction histories, and tax liabilities. Differences in jurisdictional tax treatment further complicate reporting. In some regions, digital currency gains are taxed as capital gains, while others treat them as income or apply value-added tax (VAT) rules.

5. LEGAL AND REGULATORY FRAMEWORKS

Regulation of virtual currency is high on their agenda with their usage being geographically and sector-wise widespread. Uncertainty for business arises due to the lack of harmonized legal standards and the changing international guidelines. The chapter considers regulation strategies of leading economies, effects of initiatives such as Anti-Money Laundering (AML) and Know Your Customer (KYC) rules, and key developments from global organizations such as the OECD and FATF. It addresses issues with legal harmonization that exist.

5.(i) Comparative Analysis of Crypto Regulations in Major Economies

U.S. federal agencies interpret digital assets differently. The Securities and Exchange Commission (SEC) holds some cryptocurrencies to be securities, regulated by laws for protecting investors. The Commodity Futures Trading Commission (CFTC) regards others, especially those that are traded for speculative purposes, as commodities (Zetzsche et al., 2021). Additional regulation at state level, like New

York's BitLicense scheme, makes things even more complicated. This patchwork arrangement tends to slow innovation and increase costs of compliance.

The European Union (EU) has shifted towards a more integrated model with the envisaged Markets in Crypto-Assets (MiCA) regulation. MiCA is designed to provide a harmonized regime for crypto asset issuance, trading platforms, and wallet providers throughout all member states of the EU (European Commission, 2023). MiCA is centered on protecting consumers, maintaining market integrity, and addressing systemic risk, and it makes a distinction among asset-referenced tokens, e-money tokens, and other digital assets.

China has adopted a strict approach. Private cryptocurrency trading and mining are banned, but the state actively promotes its Central Bank Digital Currency (CBDC), the digital yuan (e-CNY). The People's Bank of China regulates the e-CNY and has integrated it into pilot programs in several cities. This reflects a controlled environment where the state maintains oversight over digital payment systems (Auer et al., 2022).

India has adopted a cautious but evolving policy. In 2022, the Indian government imposed a 30% tax on digital asset profits and a 1% tax deduction at source on all crypto transactions. While there is no formal ban, the Reserve Bank of India (RBI) has expressed concerns over financial stability and has advocated for a global regulatory framework. Meanwhile, the lack of specific legislation creates ambiguity for businesses and investors (IMF, 2022).

5.(ii) Impact of AML/KYC Compliance on Business Scalability

AML and KYC regulations are essential for controlling illicit financial flows, but they also influence the scalability of crypto-based businesses. These requirements mandate the identification and verification of users' identities, as well as the monitoring and reporting of suspicious activities.

For startups and smaller businesses, implementing full-scale compliance systems increases operational costs. It involves investment into compliance personnel, software tools, and periodic audits. Large companies are likely to absorb such costs, yet smaller companies cannot scale on strongly regulated markets. Also, AML/KYC rules could deter users who value anonymity or are based in places with a poor identity infrastructure, decreasing marketplace reach.

Compliance is also country-specific. A company with operations spread across several countries needs to adhere to different AML/KYC regulations, making cross-border operations challenging. For instance, a crypto exchange licensed by MiCA within the EU would use different rules compared to a U.S. registered company working within FinCEN.

5.(iii) OECD's Crypto-Asset Reporting Framework and FATF Guidelines

International organizations have put into place standard reporting and enforcement procedures to enhance global transparency and limit regulatory arbitrage.

The OECD's Crypto-Asset Reporting Framework (CARF) emerged with a view to making available to tax authorities data on crypto-asset transactions. CARF requires reporting by crypto service providers of users' transactions and balances to tax authorities, just like the Common Reporting Standard (CRS) for traditional account-holders (OECD, 2023). CARF incorporates exchanges, brokers, and wallet providers and calls for them to exchange data with each other across borders.

The Financial Action Task Force (FATF) has implemented guidelines on preventing terrorist financing and money laundering. Its "Travel Rule" requires originator and beneficiary details to be made available with digital asset transfers (FATF, 2021). Though made to replicate regulations in traditional finance, application in the crypto industry is challenging due to technical and logistical issues. Crypto transactions are made through platforms that are often decentralized or over a direct, peer-to-peer channel, which are less likely to have an intermediary handling that accountability.

5.(iv) Challenges of Legal Uncertainty and the Need for Harmonization

Despite the advancements, legal uncertainty is a significant concern for companies. Inconsistency and absence of clear definition of digital assets across borders make them difficult to apply in investment, trade, and accounting.

Cryptocurrencies are treated as property in certain countries but currency, securities, or even commodities in others. Such inconsistency influences taxation, reporting, and legal relief. Such variations are viewed by companies as compliance risks and disincentives for long-term investment in digital asset infrastructure.

There is also limited inter-jurisdictional cooperation, which creates regulatory loopholes. A platform banned in one jurisdiction can, for instance, continue to operate legally in another, raising consumer protection and system risk issues. It would make it easier for companies to expand if there was harmonization across definitions, standards of compliance, and instruments of enforcement.

Cross-border platforms such as the G20, FATF, and OECD have reiterated the demand for cooperation, but practice-based harmonization remains elusive. Without a standard framework, firms must operate in an array of patchwork local laws, each of which involves a different risk and compliance burden.

6. CUSTOMER EXPERIENCE AND MARKET REACH

6.(i) Appeal to Crypto-Savvy Consumers

The integration of digital currencies into business operations appeals to consumers who are familiar with blockchain technology and comfortable with decentralized payment systems. This group, often younger and more technologically literate, values speed, privacy, and autonomy in financial transactions.

Retailers and digital service providers that accept cryptocurrencies can attract these consumers by offering more flexible payment methods. Companies such as Microsoft, AT&T, and Twitch have integrated Bitcoin and other digital currencies into their checkout systems through services like BitPay and Coinbase Commerce (Yermack, 2022).

Table 3. Preferences of Crypto-Savvy Consumers

Feature Preferred	Percentage of Users Preferring*
Fast transactions	82%
Anonymity	68%
No involvement of banks	61%
Support for decentralized tech	54%
Access to global markets	47%

*Source: Statista (2023), Yermack (2022)

Table 3 Depicts Businesses that adopt digital currency payment options may benefit from increased customer acquisition and brand differentiation, particularly in industries such as e-commerce, gaming, and digital media.

6.(ii) Enabling Microtransactions and Subscription Models

Digital currencies enable efficient processing of microtransactions, which are small-value payments that are often uneconomical under traditional payment systems due to minimum fee thresholds and fixed per-transaction costs.

This functionality supports new business models such as pay-per-use, metered billing, and streaming-based content pricing. In the digital publishing industry, for example, users can pay fractions of a dollar to read single articles instead of subscribing to full publications.

Cryptocurrencies and stablecoins allow such small transactions by minimizing fees and enabling programmable logic through smart contracts. For businesses offering digital goods or services—such as music, cloud storage, or software access—this opens additional revenue channels.

6.(iii) Accessibility in Underbanked Markets

Digital currencies offer an alternative means of financial participation for individuals in underbanked or unbanked regions. In many developing economies, access to traditional banking infrastructure is limited due to geographic, regulatory, or economic barriers.

Mobile-based digital wallets that support cryptocurrencies allow users to store, send, and receive money without needing a conventional bank account. This can facilitate personal savings, business transactions, and remittance flows in regions where mobile connectivity is more accessible than banking services.

In Nigeria, Kenya, and parts of Latin America, platforms like Binance Pay and Paxful have enabled peer-to-peer crypto payments that function independently of local banking systems (Chainalysis, 2023).

Table 4. Financial access in selected underbanked markets

Country	Banked Population (%)	Mobile Penetration (%)	Active Crypto Users (%)
Nigeria	45	89	22
Kenya	56	94	15
Venezuela	55	85	17
Philippines	36	75	12

*Source: World Bank (2022); Chainalysis (2023)

Digital currencies thus offer a practical tool for improving financial inclusion and enabling economic participation for underserved populations as shown in table 4.

7. ENVIRONMENTAL IMPACT OF DIGITAL CURRENCIES

As cryptocurrencies become increasingly embedded in business processes and financial systems, their ecological footprint is increasingly being scrutinized. Perhaps the most contentious problem is the energy consumption of blockchain networks, specifically those that rely on proof-of-work (PoW) consensus protocols.

7.(i) Proof-of-Work System Energy Consumption

Proof-of-work is the initial consensus algorithm used by Bitcoin and other digital currencies. It is a competitive algorithm where miners compete to solve cryptographic puzzles to validate transactions and seal the network. It is computationally expensive and, by proxy, energy expensive. The worldwide Bitcoin network is projected to consume over 100 terawatt-hours (TWh) of electricity annually—equivalent to the aggregate energy consumption of some medium-sized countries (Cambridge Centre for Alternative Finance, 2023).

Most Bitcoin mining takes place in regions where electricity is cheap, usually sourced from fossil fuels. This presents an environmental problem of carbon output as well as overall environmental sustainability of the system. It has been discovered that energy sources derived from coal remain predominant in mining activities, particularly in certain regions of Asia (de Vries et al., 2022). Therefore, the environmental cost of PoW-based cryptocurrencies is considerably greater than traditional financial systems or other digital substitutes.

7.(ii) Transition to More Sustainable Consensus Mechanisms

To solve these, the majority of blockchain networks are transitioning to new consensus algorithms with lower energy usage. The most popular among them is proof-of-stake (PoS). PoS isn't based on brute computing capability but instead selects validators based on the tokens they hold and are willing to stake as collateral.

Ethereum, the second-largest network by market capitalization, transitioned from PoW to PoS in September 2022 with its "The Merge" upgrade. The upgrade has been estimated to have reduced Ethereum's energy consumption by over 99% (Ethereum Foundation, 2022). A few newer blockchain initiatives also employ PoS or equivalent mechanisms as their default, with environmental effectiveness as a core design consideration.

PoS and other energy-efficient variants like delegated proof-of-stake (DPoS) and proof-of-authority (PoA) are being promoted more and more as options for environmentally challenged businesses. These networks enable businesses to use blockchain-based solutions without the environmental impact of PoW.

7.(iii) Corporate Social Responsibility and Adoption Decisions

Firms that adopt or invest in cryptocurrencies must consider what their actions communicate regarding their environmental, social, and governance (ESG) goals. The application of energy-intensive cryptocurrencies can be interpreted as being counter to the sustainable goals. This has investor relations, consumer brand, and regulatory risk implications.

The majority of the firms are now required to disclose the environmental effects as a component of corporate reporting. Using the energy-intensive cryptocurrencies will be condemned by the stakeholders such as green groups and socially responsible investors. In this regard, companies are subject to the risk of reputation if they are seen to be involved in climate change by undertaking plans for digital currency.

7.(iv) Tesla Reversing the Bitcoin Payment Option

Tesla provides a case in point of how concerns for the environment influence business decision-making regarding digital currencies. In February 2021, the company stated that it had bought $1.5 billion of Bitcoin and would begin accepting it as payment for vehicles. But in May 2021, Tesla reversed this decision, and the reason given was fear of the environmental cost of Bitcoin mining (SEC, 2021).

In a public press release, the firm highlighted its own commitment to sustainability and vowed to revisit the use of Bitcoin payments once mining is powered by cleaner forms of energy. The action was part of wider concern within the business world to reconcile financial innovation with environmental stewardship.

Tesla's move drew attention to the conflict between adopting trendy digital currencies and maintaining green objectives. It also raised broader questions about whether companies should only accept eco-friendly digital currencies.

8. DIGITAL IDENTITY AND KYC USING BLOCKCHAIN

Blockchain technology offers a viable framework for controlling digital identity, especially in applications such as Know Your Customer (KYC) compliance and onboarding of consumers. Blockchain's tamper-evident and decentralized nature can remove duplication, enhance data integrity, and enhance digital identity verification privacy. The current section is about the ways blockchain identity systems enable compliance, the self-sovereign identity (SSI) model, and the impact on cross-border transactions.

8.(i) Streamlining Onboarding via Blockchain Identity Verification

Manual KYC procedures are typically slow, redundant, and tedious. Banks, financial institutions, and online platforms have to verify users' identities using centralized databases, physical documents, and manual verification. It causes delays and expenses, particularly if it is repeatedly performed on every institution or jurisdiction.

Blockchain identity solutions enable the possession of self-owned verified credentials that can be reused across a variety of platforms. Third-party verified identity data (e.g., bank or government agency) is stored on a blockchain and associated with a digital identity. Organizations are able to access information in real time and standardized identity records without sacrificing the ability to comply with regulatory requirements.

8.(ii) Self-Sovereign Identity (SSI) for Compliance

SSI platforms utilize decentralized identifiers (DIDs) and verifiable credentials issued by trusted authorities. Cryptographic validation and selective disclosure of these credentials can be verified without divulging full sets of data.

SSI models are best suited to regulatory compliance because they can satisfy both privacy and verifiability. A user can prove, for example, that they are over a specific age or that they are from a specific country without revealing unrelated personal information. This satisfies the data minimization provisions of privacy legislation such as the General Data Protection Regulation (GDPR).

Business-wise, SSI reduces handling and storage of bulk sensitive personal data and, therefore, the risk of data breaches and costs of compliance. Several blockchain-based SSI offerings, such as Sovrin and uPort, have been prototyped across financial services and government scenarios in KYC, age verification, and issuance of credentials (Preukschat & Reed, 2021).

8.(iii) Cross-Border Transactions and Privacy Implications

Blockchain-based identity solutions also provide solutions to multiple issues in cross-border transactions. In conventional finance systems, identification verification in cross-border transactions mostly involves duplicate checks, translations, and local legislative compliance. Blockchain can enable international interoperability to be achieved as it offers one portable digital identification that can be checked by many different institutions within different countries.

This improves cross-border remittance, international platforms access efficiency, and trade finance. A verified digital identity can be utilized to access services without the delay that is typically involved in international due diligence processes. SSI frameworks also improve user consent and data sovereignty, enabling users to be in charge of who receives access to their data and under what conditions.

While these benefits persist, blockchain-based digital identities' legal legitimacy is scarce. Regulatory bodies still demand conventional means of identity authentication for the majority, and the legal status of digital credentials is different in every nation. Cross-border finance's future potential of blockchain identity will require international coordination and standardization.

9. USER EDUCATION, PERCEPTION, AND BEHAVIORAL ECONOMICS

The success of virtual currencies relies as much on technical infrastructure and regulation as on the way users think and behave towards and with them. Adoption is strongly dependent on behavioral determinants like trust, familiarity, and perceived value. These are the dimensions that are most important to businesses and policymakers who want to encourage use and overcome barriers.

9.(i) Consumer Trust and Resistance to Intangible Currencies

One of the major behavioral inhibitions to digital currency adoption is that there is no physical medium. Existing currencies are tangible and backed by institutions that already exist, i.e., the central banks. Yet, digital currencies, especially decentralized cryptocurrencies, are abstract and are many times difficult for consumers to understand or believe in.

Consumers are still cautious, survey results suggest. Only 24% of U.S. adults, a 2023 report by Statista found, were interested in using cryptocurrency in everyday transactions. Security, volatility in prices, and the reason that they are not backed by the government were the most common reasons cited (Statista, 2023). These are more significant in older, less tech-savvy adults.

Additionally, the linkage of cryptocurrencies with fraud, cybercrime, and speculative trading has resulted in negative sentiments. The loss of various cryptocurrency exchanges and reports of hacks on the news front have also been the reasons for inducing skepticism. Without sufficient trust, even well-designed systems are not going to be popular.

9.(ii) The Financial Literacy and Education Role

Financial literacy is the most important factor in determining user behavior with respect to digital currencies. Users who do not understand how digital currencies function will be more inclined to keep away from them for fear of losing money or being unaware. Concepts like public and private keys, blockchain confirmations, and transaction fees are hard for a person with no prior knowledge of digital finance.

Research has confirmed a positive relationship between financial literacy and the likelihood of using digital assets. In a 2022 OECD report, consumers with a limited level of knowledge about digital wallets and blockchain technology were more likely to own or use cryptocurrencies (OECD, 2022). Financial literacy also directs towards more cautious investment practices and reduces exposure to fraud.

Educational activities can be of different forms, including public campaigns, mobile app tutorials, and outreach programs. The central banks of countries like Sweden and Nigeria have launched educational websites explaining their respective digital currency projects (e-krona and e-naira) emphasizing security, ease, and benefits.

9.(iii) Gamification and Incentives for Behaviour

A number of platforms induce adoption through gamification—a behaviour change methodology that utilizes game mechanics in non-game situations. For cryptocurrency, gamification can help promote engagement and improve understanding. Crypto exchanges Coinbase and Binance, for example, have launched "learn and earn" programs that reward users with small amounts of cryptocurrency for completing learning modules.

These strategies are aligned with behavioural economics as they offer instantaneous, low-cost feedback for participation. They also render electronic currencies less daunting. Behavioural nudges such as reminders, progress bars, and visual feedback encourage people to complete learning exercises and feel more empowered to use electronic currencies.

Savings and micro-investment gamification apps have also found success in emerging markets. Apps in Latin America and Southeast Asia, for instance, offer mobile wallets with quiz-based learning and token rewards to drive daily usage and retention.

9.(iv) User Interview and Observation

Qualitative user research interviews provide further insights. Chainalysis interviews in 2023 of Nigerian and Filipino users highlighted that trust in digital currency grew significantly when it was introduced by a known peer or local community leader. Users further highlighted that simple-to-use interfaces and quick transaction periods were more successful in stimulating continued usage than knowledge of blockchain theory (Chainalysis, 2023).

But consumers were worried about losing access to funds due to forgotten passwords or scams. Some preferred sites that offered account recovery through biometric authentication or customer support. These findings indicate that improving user experience and incorporating human-cantered design can decrease behavioural resistance.

10. CRYPTO RISK HEDGING PRODUCTS AND INSURANCE

As cryptocurrencies increase their presence in retail and institutional balance sheets, so has the need for hedging and insurance products. The inherently high volatility of cryptocurrencies, combined with technical risks such as hacking and failure of smart contracts, has fuelled the need for bespoke financial products hedging exposure. In this paper, we will discuss the development of crypto insurance products, hedging volatility strategies, and the new emerging role played by decentralized insurance platforms.

10.(i) Crypto Insurance Products Development

Traditional insurers have been slow to offer coverage for digital assets due to regulatory uncertainty, valuation issues, and a lack of historical data. There is some progress, however. An emerging but niche segment of the insurance market now offers protection against exchanges being hacked into, wallets being stolen, and custody failure.

Such insurance companies as Lloyd's of London, Aon, and Marsh have partnered with blockchain companies to develop policies for crypto-associated risk. These include insurance for digital asset custodians, decentralized applications, and even directors and officers (D&O) liability of crypto businesses (Marsh, 2021).

The policy conditions are restricted, and the premiums are steep. Sophisticated technical examinations involving smart contract audits and cyber security procedures need to be conducted before an insurer will insure the risk. Insurers also offer restricted access to individual retail investors because the majority of policies are tailored for institutional customers such as exchanges and asset managers.

To address these gaps, crypto-native insurers have been created. They create policies on digital assets and frequently price according to on-chain activity and platform-specific data. This structure permits more accurate risk measurement and policy price correlation, but the majority of these products are beyond conventional regulatory frameworks.

10.(ii) Hedging Strategies to Mitigate Volatility Risk

Due to the high degree of price volatility characteristic of digital currencies, investors and firms often seek financial products to hedge against exposure. Hedging instruments are derivatives such as futures, options, and perpetual contracts, which are nowadays highly traded on centralized and decentralized platforms.

For example, Bitcoin and Ethereum futures are exchange-traded in major markets including the Chicago Mercantile Exchange (CME), allowing institutions to lock the price or protect against deprecation. Similarly, options contracts deliver to the beneficiary the right (but not an obligation) to buy or sell a digital instrument at a designated price, serving as a liquid vehicle for management of volatility.

Stablecoins or fiat-backed coins are also hedging tools. By swapping risky assets for stablecoins such as USDC or USDT, businesses are able to de-risk during periods of extreme price fluctuation. Even some treasury management operations do the same automatically, rebalancing positions in the direction of market movement.

More advanced methods involve algorithmic trading platforms that shift portfolio positions automatically according to signals of volatility. Such platforms, although technologically advanced, are increasingly being utilized by crypto funds and large holders to hedge capital.

10.(iii) The Role of Decentralized Insurance Platforms

Decentralized insurance platforms offer alternatives to conventional insurers using blockchain technology and smart contracts that enable risk pooling and automatic claims. Platforms replace centralized underwriters with community regulation and open protocols.

Nexus Mutual is an example. It provides insurance against risks like smart contract failure, exchange hacks, and validator slashing. Members contribute capital and are rewarded with tokens that they hold in their mutual, which is their proportion of the mutual. Claims are evaluated and voted upon by members, thereby providing a peer-to-peer insurance system (Nexus Mutual, 2023).

There are also other platforms such as InsurAce and Etherisc that provide the same functionality. These platforms handle specific risks such as protocol-level failure and oracle failure. Others go even further to parametric insurance models where payment is automatically triggered on occurrence of the stated conditions, e.g., outage or decline in asset value.

While decentralized insurance models bring efficiency and transparency, they are constrained by regulatory acceptance, scalability, and resolution of claims disputes. They are low-participation and small in size compared to traditional insurers. But they are nascent prototypes for risk-sharing in decentralized financial ecosystems.

11. RISK FACTORS AND CHALLENGES

11.(i) Volatility and Liquidity Risks

One of the primary challenges of adopting digital currencies in business operations is their price volatility. Cryptocurrencies such as Bitcoin and Ethereum experience frequent and sometimes severe price fluctuations. These price swings can impact financial planning, pricing strategies, and the valuation of corporate holdings. Volatility makes it difficult for businesses to forecast revenues when customers pay in digital currencies.

11.(ii) Cybersecurity and Concerns Regarding Fra

Businesses are vulnerable to attacks like wallet hacking, attacks from ransomware, and phishing attacks. As opposed to traditional banks that may have fraud protection and reversibility of transactions, transactions with a confirmed digital currency are irreversible.

Such attacks on exchanges and virtual wallets may cause a loss of substantial assets. A case in point is the breach of the 2014 Mt. Gox, which resulted in the loss of nearly 850,000 Bitcoins. In more recent years, decentralized finance (DeFi) platforms have been frequent targets for smart contract exploits and liquidity pool drains.

Companies using digital currencies must implement strong security protocols, including cold storage, multi-signature wallets, two-factor authentication, and continuous monitoring of network activity. Cybersecurity risks require both technical investment and user education, particularly when companies interact with public blockchain environments.

12. CASE STUDIES

12.(i) Companies Successfully Adopting Digital Currencies

Several businesses have integrated digital currencies into their financial or customer-facing operations with measurable outcomes. These cases show how early adoption can support strategic goals, technological alignment, and user engagement.

Tesla's 2021 announcement of a $1.5 billion Bitcoin purchase marked a significant moment in corporate adoption of digital assets. The company briefly accepted Bitcoin as a method of payment for vehicle purchases. Although the payment option was suspended due to environmental concerns, Tesla retained part of its holdings. The move generated considerable public and investor interest, framing Tesla as a business willing to engage with emerging financial instruments while also signalling caution in response to operational concerns (SEC, 2021). PayPal also stands out as a notable example. It enabled select customers to buy, hold, and sell cryptocurrencies directly through its platform. Later, it introduced a checkout feature that allowed users to convert digital currencies into fiat at the point of sale. This strategy helped PayPal expand its user base, attract younger and more tech-savvy customers, and diversify its payment ecosystem (PayPal, 2022).

Overstock was one of the earliest adopters, accepting Bitcoin as early as 2014. The company benefited from early brand differentiation and drew attention from digital currency communities. Similarly, financial service providers like Visa and Mastercard launched cryptocurrency-linked payment cards, demonstrating a commitment to enabling crypto-based financial products within their ecosystems.

These examples show that successful adoption typically involves integrating digital currencies into existing infrastructure while responding to market demand, user behavior, and regulatory concerns.

12.(ii) Failures or Setbacks and Lessons Learned

Not all digital currency initiatives have succeeded. Several projects encountered technical, regulatory, or operational barriers that prevented full implementation.

Facebook's Libra initiative, subsequently renamed to Diem, is a well-known example of pushback from regulation. The initiative envisioned a global stablecoin that would be secured by areserve of fiat money. Nevertheless, it encountered fierce resistance from governments and central banks across the globe, but especially from the United States and the European Union. Issues revolved around monetary sovereignty, consumer protection, and possible interference with national financial markets. Even after several attempts at revising the design of the program, the initiative was discontinued, and its assets were divested during 2022. This is a clear lesson in the need for regulation harmonization and public policy coordination when implementing new financial technologies (Zetzsche et al., 2021).

Another is the case of Stripe's previous backing of Bitcoin payments, which it withdrew in 2018. High transaction costs and long confirmation times were cited by Stripe as motives for turning the service back. The firm subsequently reinstated a selective crypto-related services after a reassessment of the technology and the recognition of more practical use cases. This demonstrates the need for aligning the integration of digital currency with a firm's primary business strategy and consumers' expectations (Stripe, 2022).

Both Expedia and Dell suspended the option after recognizing that customers weren't using the feature for their purchases, largely due to the lack of scalability and limitations on technology necessary for implementing the feature on their respective sites.

12.(iii) Sector-Wise Impact

Digital currency adoption has varied across industries with different customer bases, levels of exposure to regulation, and operating agendas.

In the retail sector, adoption has quite heavily concentrated on brand positioning and flexibility of payments. Others are using cryptocurrencies as a way to accept customer payments, with some companies playing with blockchain-based loyalty schemes or branded virtual assets. Although there has been much attention, extensive use by consumers is infrequent, often because of price volatility or a lack of understanding.

Digital currencies are more integral to business models within the financial technology space. Platforms for offering crypto wallets, exchanges, custody, and lending products have seen growth to address increased demand for services on digital assets. Requirements for regulation are higher within the industry, but adoption is higher due to financial markets' integration and customer expectations. Logistics companies have experimented with blockchain and token-based solutions to optimize tracking and payment efficiency. Pilot schemes, for instance, utilize smart contracts to make payment at verified transit points as merchandise arrives, decreasing settlement periods and administrative costs. These uses highlight the utility of blockchain for purposes other than money. In media and entertainment, there have been examples of using digital currencies for microtransactions, pay-per-use material, and NFTs. These models enable a way for creators and hosts to benefit from digital material without involving traditional intermediaries. Every industry needs to decide whether the capabilities of digital currencies match their business realities, compliance needs, and needs of their users. Adoption results differ based on how effectively these issues are addressed.

13. IMPACT ON FINANCIAL ECOS

13.(i) Changes to Banking Relationships

Digital currencies have caused structural changes in the dynamics of the relationships of companies with banks. Historically, companies are dependent on banks for functions like deposits, transactions, credit, and clearing of transactions. Now, with the implementation of digital currencies, those functions are able to be carried out directly on blockchain networks without involving traditional financial institutions.

For instance, transactions involving cryptocurrencies from one individual to another do not involve commercial banks as intermediaries. This lowers the reliance of corporations on commercial banks for fundamental payment services, particularly cross-border transactions. With corporations taking up digital wallets and custody services offered by fintech firms, banks could see diminished involvement in some areas of financial activity (Auer & Böhme, 2020).

Nonetheless, the transition is not a complete elimination of banks' role. Traditional banking services are still widely used alongside digital currency services by many companies, particularly for regulatory needs and for management of fiat currency. Some banks even start to provide crypto custody services and trading of digital assets, which indicates a rebalancing rather than a disintermediation.

13.(ii) Impact on Financial Intermediaries

Digital currencies undercut the utility of traditional intermediaries, e.g., payment processors, clearinghouses, and remittance service providers. By facilitating faster and cheaper settlement processes, blockchain-based systems decrease the value added by traditional intermediaries in handling transactions. For instance, stablecoins like USDC and USDT enable cross-border transactions without the lag and the costs generally linked to wire transfers or correspondent bank networks. However, there are new forms of intermediaries on the horizon within the cryptocurrency world. They are crypto exchanges, custodian services, and blockchain analytics companies that provide compliant and safe services that are indispensable for the cryptocurrency world. So, financial intermediation is not vanishing but rather being redesigned by the risk and technology involved.

13.(iii) Decentralized Finance (DeFi) Implications

Decentralized finance or DeFi is financial technology based on public blockchains that is free from centralized control. DeFi applications using smart contracts provide lending, borrowing, trading, and services for generating a return without banks or traditional intermediaries. DeFi brings alternatives to traditional finance for companies and individuals alike. For instance, companies are able to take loans from DeFi applications using their digital assets without undergoing a credit evaluation, as long as they qualify for the collateral. Liquidity pools enable the provision of capital to decentralized exchanges with options to receive transaction charges or a return, opening up new avenues for investments outside of regulated banks (Schär, 2021).

Figure 3. Comparison between TradFi & DeFi

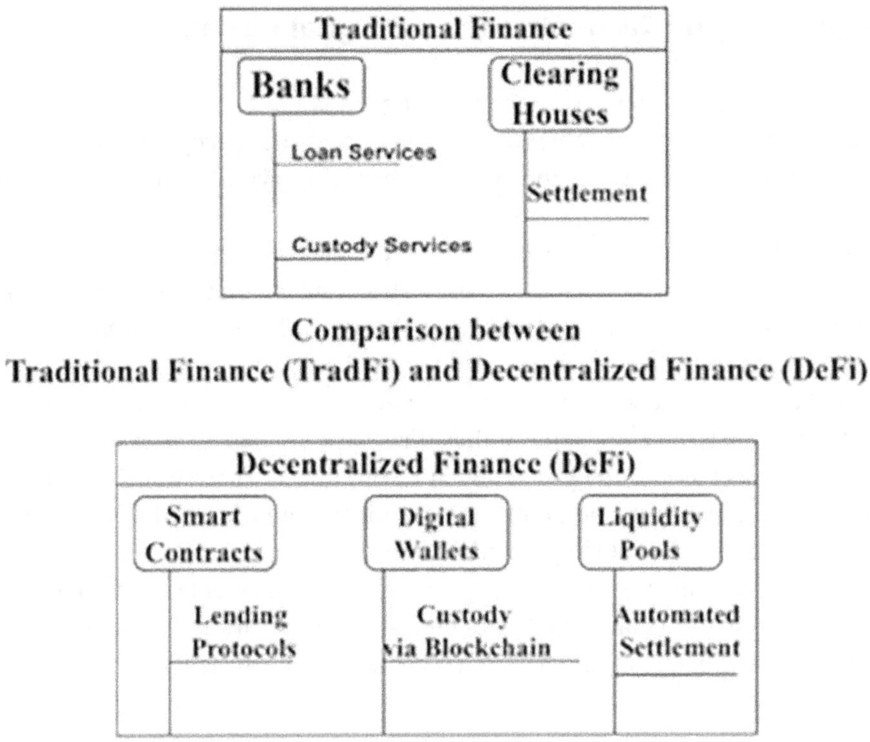

Figure 3 illustrates directly the displacement of traditional intermediaries. DeFi provides better accessibility and autonomy but also risks. Lack of centralized control makes them vulnerable to bugs in smart contracts, platform collapses, and regulation breaches. A number of publicized hacks have resulted in the loss of customer money, necessitating technical audits and careful adoption from companies. Regardless of those risks, the accelerating size of DeFi platforms and the innovation that they enable imply a long-term shift in the way financial services are provided and accessed. Regulators and central banks are beginning to look at how they could be incorporated into wider financial regulation without hindering development.

14. FUTURE OUTLOOK

14.(i) Emerging Technologies and Digital Wallets

As the virtual currencies keep unfolding, so is the technology that surrounds them. Among the most important advancements is the speedy embrace of digital wallets, which facilitate safe storage and exchange of cryptocurrencies, stablecoins, and CBDCs.

Digital wallets are becoming more accessible and functionality-rich, with support for multiple currencies, biometric identification, and integration with decentralized applications. They come with mobile applications, browser add-ons, and actual devices, offering convenience to consumers and companies when it comes to handling their assets. Concurrently, some of the major central banks are prototyping or designing CBDC-compatible wallets that have similar functions to traditional bank accounts but exist only in a digital environment. These wallets are likely to have offline capabilities, programmable payments, and advanced levels of privacy based on design needs at the jurisdictions' levels (Auer et al., 2021).

With better wallet interoperability, companies will be able to reach a broader consumer base across underbanked or cross-border scenarios. The future of digital commerce will likely depend heavily on the adoption and standardization of these wallet systems.

14.(ii) Integration with AI and IoT

Emerging use cases at the intersection of digital currencies, artificial intelligence (AI), and the Internet of Things (IoT) are expected to redefine operational models across industries. As businesses become more digitized, automated systems will increasingly rely on machine-to-machine payments and intelligent financial decision-making.

AI can be used to manage dynamic pricing, detect fraudulent transactions, and automate treasury operations. When integrated with blockchain-based digital currencies, AI algorithms can authorize and settle payments in real time based on predefined rules, resource use, or demand fluctuations.

In the IoT context, businesses deploying IoT devices (e.g., smart energy meters or logistics sensors) could use stablecoins for automated, usage-based payments, reducing administrative overhead in billing and settlements.

These developments will require reliable infrastructure, standardized protocols, and robust cybersecurity safeguards. However, the potential for automation and cost reduction may be substantial, especially in industries with high transaction volumes or repetitive payment cycles (Catalini & Gans, 2016).

14.(iii) Predictions and Strategic Recommendations for Businesses

Looking ahead, the business adoption of digital currencies is expected to expand, but in a measured and sector-specific manner. Stablecoins and CBDCs are likely to gain broader acceptance due to their relative stability and regulatory backing, while the use of volatile cryptocurrencies may remain concentrated in niche markets or high-risk environments. Businesses considering adoption should evaluate digital currencies not as standalone tools but as part of broader technological integration strategies. Key areas for planning include:

Regulatory readiness: Companies should track evolving digital asset regulations in jurisdictions where they operate and ensure systems comply with tax, reporting, and anti-money laundering requirements.

Investment in the infrastructure: Companies should develop or implement safe and scalable systems, such as digital wallets, platforms for smart contracts, and integration with financial institution systems.

Employee training and education: Personnel need to be aware of the mechanics and risks involved with digital currencies, especially within finance, compliance, and IT teams.

15. CONCLUSION

Cryptocurrencies, stablecoins, and CBDCs are bringing the potential to simplify, decrease costs, and create new opportunities, particularly for cross-border and underbanked markets. Blockchain technology, which cuts out middlemen, offers more efficiency, faster and less expensive payments, but price volatility risk, security risk, and regulatory risk cannot be easily mitigated. Businesses have to contend with those challenges carefully by balancing the use of digital currency with their business strategy, remaining compliant, and having a keen eye out for technology changes.

Early entrants who act on consumers' readiness and market willingness will be likely to gain a competitive advantage. As they evolve further, digital currencies can stay much larger, with the incorporation of technologies such as artificial intelligence and Internet of Things having the ability to enhance their potential and make companies more agile and future-proof.

References

G7 Working Group on Stablecoins. (2019). *Investigating the impact of global stablecoins*. Retrieved from https://www.bis.org/cpmi/publ/d187.pdf

Alvarez, F., Argente, D., & Van Patten, D. (2022). *Are cryptocurrencies currencies? Bitcoin as legal tender in El Salvador*. National Bureau of Economic Research. Retrieved from https://www.nber.org/papers/w29968

Auer, R., & Böhme, R. (2020). The technology of retail central bank digital currency. *BIS Quarterly Review*, March 2020, 85–100. Retrieved from https://www.bis.org/publ/qtrpdf/r_qt2003j.htm

Auer, R., Haene, P., & Holden, H. (2021). *Multi-CBDC arrangements and the future of cross-border payments* (BIS Papers No. 115). Bank for International Settlements. Retrieved from https://www.bis.org/publ/bppdf/bispap115.pdf

Auer, R., Monnet, C., & Shin, H. S. (2022). *Permissioned distributed ledgers and the governance of money* (BIS Working Papers No. 1060). Bank for International Settlements. Retrieved from https://www.bis.org/publ/work1060.pdf

Bank for International Settlements. (2021). *CBDCs: An opportunity for the monetary system*. Retrieved from https://www.bis.org/publ/arpdf/ar2021e3.htm

Bank for International Settlements. (2023). *Gaining momentum — Results of the 2022 BIS survey on central bank digital currencies*. Retrieved from https://www.bis.org/publ/bppdf/bispap136.pdf

Cambridge Centre for Alternative Finance. (2023). *Cambridge Bitcoin Electricity Consumption Index*. University of Cambridge. Retrieved from https://ccaf.io/cbeci/index

Catalini, C., & Gans, J. S. (2016). *Some simple economics of the blockchain* (MIT Sloan Research Paper No. 5191-16). Retrieved from https://papers.ssrn.com/sol3/papers.cfm?abstract_id=2874598

Central Bank of The Bahamas. (2021). *The Sand Dollar Project*. Retrieved from https://www.centralbankbahamas.com/sand-dollar

Chainalysis. (2023). *Crypto Adoption and User Behavior Report*. Retrieved from https://www.chainalysis.com/reports

Chainalysis. (2023). *Crypto Crime Report 2023*. Retrieved from https://www.chainalysis.com/reports

Chicago Mercantile Exchange. (2023). *Cryptocurrency Futures and Options*. Retrieved from https://www.cmegroup.com/markets/cryptocurrencies.html

CoinMetrics. (2023). *Crypto Asset Volatility Data*. Retrieved from https://coinmetrics.io

Cong, L. W., & He, Z. (2019). Blockchain disruption and smart contracts. *Review of Financial Studies, 32*(5), 1754–1797. DOI: 10.1093/rfs/hhz007

de Vries, A., Gallersdörfer, U., Klaaßen, L., & Stoll, C. (2022). Revisiting Bitcoin's carbon footprint. *Joule, 6*(3), 498–502. DOI: 10.1016/j.joule.2022.02.005

ENISA. (2022). *Threat landscape for cryptocurrency*. European Union Agency for Cybersecurity. Retrieved from https://www.enisa.europa.eu

Ethereum Foundation. (2022). *The Merge*. Retrieved from https://ethereum.org/en/upgrades/merge/

European Central Bank. (2019). *Exploring anonymity in central bank digital currencies*. Retrieved from https://www.ecb.europa.eu/pub/pdf/other/ecb.anonymouscbdc.201912~cbe0c6210d.en.pdf

European Central Bank. (2023). *Progress on the investigation phase of a digital euro*. Retrieved from https://www.ecb.europa.eu/pub/pdf/other/ecb.digitaleuro_progresreport2023~e6c8c0483c.en.pdf

European Commission. (2023). *Proposal for a Regulation on Markets in Crypto-assets (MiCA)*. Retrieved from https://finance.ec.europa.eu/publications/proposal-regulation-markets-crypto-assets-mica_en

FASB. (2022). *Accounting for and disclosure of crypto assets: Proposed accounting standards update*. Financial Accounting Standards Board. Retrieved from https://www.fasb.org/document/blob?fileName=ASU_Crypto_Assets_2023.pdf

FATF. (2021). *Updated Guidance for a Risk-Based Approach to Virtual Assets and Virtual Asset Service Providers*. Financial Action Task Force. Retrieved from https://www.fatf-gafi.org/media/fatf/documents/recommendations/Updated-Guidance-VA-VASPs.pdf

Ghosh, S., Kim, S., & Tian, X. (2020). Digital currencies and cross-border payments: New opportunities and challenges. *Journal of Financial Regulation and Compliance, 28*(3), 355–370. DOI: 10.1108/JFRC-02-2020-0016

IMF. (2021). *The rise of public and private digital money*. International Monetary Fund. Retrieved from https://www.imf.org/en/Publications/fandd/issues/2021/03/the-rise-of-digital-money

IMF. (2022). *Global Financial Stability Report: Navigating the high-inflation environment*. Retrieved from https://www.imf.org/en/Publications/GFSR

Marsh. (2021). *Crypto Insurance Solutions: Managing Risk in the Digital Asset Ecosystem*. Retrieved from https://www.marsh.com/us/industries/financial-institutions/insights/cryptocurrency-insurance.html

Murray, A., Crandall, R., & Vargo, D. (2021). Blockchain in the supply chain: A review of the literature and proposed framework for future research. *Journal of Business Logistics*, *42*(1), 45–67. DOI: 10.1111/jbl.12270

Nakamoto, S. (2008). *Bitcoin: A peer-to-peer electronic cash system*. Retrieved from https://bitcoin.org/bitcoin.pdf

Nexus Mutual. (2023). *Protocol Documentation*. Retrieved from https://nexusmutual.io/

OECD. (2022). *Financial Literacy and the Future of Digital Finance*. Organisation for Economic Co-operation and Development. Retrieved from https://www.oecd.org/finance/financial-education

OECD. (2023). *Crypto-Asset Reporting Framework and Amendments to the Common Reporting Standard*. Organisation for Economic Co-operation and Development. Retrieved from https://www.oecd.org/tax/exchange-of-tax-information/crypto-asset-reporting-framework-and-amendments-to-the-common-reporting-standard.htm

PayPal. (2022). *Annual report and cryptocurrency update*. Retrieved from https://investor.paypal-corp.com

Preukschat, A., & Reed, D. (2021). *Self-Sovereign Identity: Decentralized Digital Identity and Verifiable Credentials*. Manning Publications.

PwC. (2023). *Cryptographic assets and tax treatment under IFRS*. Retrieved from https://www.pwc.com/gx/en/services/audit-assurance/assets/ifrs-cryptographic-assets.pdf

Schär, F. (2021). Decentralized finance: On blockchain- and smart contract-based financial markets. *Review - Federal Reserve Bank of St. Louis*, *103*(2), 153–174. DOI: 10.20955/r.103.153-74

SEC. (2021). *Tesla Inc. Form 10-K Annual Report*. U.S. Securities and Exchange Commission. Retrieved from https://www.sec.gov/ix?doc=/Archives/edgar/data/0001318605/000156459021004599/tsla-10k_20201231.htm

Statista. (2023). *Public Attitudes Toward Cryptocurrency Usage in the U.S.* Retrieved from https://www.statista.com/statistics/

Stripe. (2022). *Company blog and Bitcoin payment integration.* Retrieved from https://stripe.com/blog

Sveriges Riksbank. (2023). *The e-krona pilot – Phase 2.* Retrieved from https://www.riksbank.se/globalassets/media/rapporter/e-krona/2023/the-e-krona-pilot-phase-2.pdf

Tapscott, D., & Tapscott, A. (2017). *Blockchain revolution: How the technology behind Bitcoin is changing money, business, and the world.* Penguin.

World Bank. (2022). *Global Findex Database 2021: Financial inclusion, digital payments, and resilience in the age of COVID-19.* Retrieved from https://www.worldbank.org/en/publication/globalfindex

World Economic Forum. (2020). *Digital Currency Governance Consortium White Paper Series.* Retrieved from https://www.weforum.org/reports/digital-currency-governance-consortium-white-papers

Yermack, D. (2022). Bitcoin and the future of digital payments in emerging markets. *The Journal of Economic Perspectives, 36*(2), 145–166. DOI: 10.1257/jep.36.2.145

Zetzsche, D. A., Arner, D. W., Buckley, R. P., & Barberis, J. N. (2020). Decentralized finance (DeFi). *Journal of Financial Regulation, 6*(1), 172–203. DOI: 10.1093/jfr/fjaa010

Zetzsche, D. A., Arner, D. W., Buckley, R. P., & Börner, C. (2021). The future of crypto regulation: A comparative analysis. *Journal of Financial Regulation, 7*(2), 345–374. DOI: 10.1093/jfr/fjab007

Zohar, A. (2015). Bitcoin: Under the hood. *Communications of the ACM, 58*(9), 104–113. DOI: 10.1145/2701411

Zwitter, A., & Boisse-Despiaux, M. (2020). Blockchain for humanitarian action and development aid. *Journal of International Humanitarian Action, 5*(16). Advance online publication. DOI: 10.1186/s41018-020-00072-3

Chapter 10
The Influence of Virtual Currencies on Sustainable Service Marketing in Emerging Economies

Rohit Yadav
https://orcid.org/0000-0002-7573-8005
IILM University, Greater Noida, India

Geshwaree Huzooree
https://orcid.org/0000-0001-8076-6636
Edinburgh Napier University, UK

Mohit Yadav
https://orcid.org/0000-0002-9341-2527
O.P. Jindal Global Business School, Jindal Global University, India

Narayanage Jayantha Dewasiri
https://orcid.org/0000-0002-5908-8890
Qasim Ibrahim School of Business, Villa College, Maldives

ABSTRACT

The Chapter shall discuss the social implications of virtual currencies on sustainable service marketing in developing economies and, instead, analyse how digital currencies are transforming the pattern of financial inclusion, economic growth, and access to basic services, such as healthcare and education and energy. Beyond simple transactions, virtual currencies have helped provide new ways to circumvent high transaction costs, exclusion from finance, and lack of infrastructure. The new avenues to sustainable development come with the use of Central Bank Digital

DOI: 10.4018/979-8-3373-0315-4.ch010

Currencies, decentralized finance, and blockchain technologies in virtual currencies. But still, some challenges persist in the form of digital literacy, regulatory frameworks, and robust security systems. Thus, the focus of the chapter will be on strategies for adoption, overcoming barriers, and maximizing social benefits in underserved regions toward inclusive economic growth and sustainable development.

1. INTRODUCTION

The dramatic change that the world economy saw in terms of rapid growth through digital technologies made it possible to develop virtual currencies as a new mode of exchange. Virtual currencies include cryptocurrencies, such as Bitcoin and Ethereum, or central bank digital currencies, that have provided decentralized fast modes of payment, which have been challenging conventional models of finance (Nakamoto, 2008; Chiu & Koeppl, 2019). In developing economies, which still face key challenges in the area of financial inclusions, virtual currencies are promising for reducing costs of transaction, ensuring transparency, and delivering access to unbanked populations (World Bank, 2020). These developments are particularly relevant to service marketing, where seamless and sustainable payment systems become ever more important in driving long-term consumer relationships and fostering economic growth.

The objective of sustainability in service marketing calls for businesses to be environmentally and socially responsible, yet economically viable (Kotler & Keller, 2016). Virtual currencies are well aligned with this objective because they promote resource efficiency through digital transactions that reduce reliance on physical cash and encourage green initiatives such as carbon tracking through blockchain technology (Tapscott & Tapscott, 2016). However, despite such promises of benefits, virtual currency adoption poses challenges in the context of developing economies, including limited infrastructures of technologies, regulatory uncertainties, and skeptic consumers (Diniz et al., 2021).

This chapter deals with the social implications of virtual currencies on sustainable service marketing in developing economies. Precisely at the junctures of digital payment systems, consumer behavior, and sustainability principles, this chapter tries to explore how virtual currency could create innovation and inclusivity in the service industries. It goes further by identifying some specific impediments to its adoption and gives some tangible information for policy-makers, business, and other interested parties wishing to use virtual currencies for sustainable development.

2. VIRTUAL CURRENCIES: DEFINITIONS AND KEY CONCEPTS

Virtual currencies refer to a system of money characterized by a series of electronic tokens that play all the functions performed by the media of exchange, unit of account, and stores of value without being issued and regulated by some central authority European Central Bank 2012). These can be of two types-decentralized ones such as Bitcoin and Ethereum built on blockchain, or central ones issued and regulated by governments-central bank digital currencies-CBDCs (Nakamoto, 2008; Auer et al., 2021).The blockchain is a decentralized ledger that lies beneath most virtual currencies, so the record-keeping is safe, transparent, and unchangeable, hence making it ideal for use in financial transactions and many other aspects beyond that (Tapscott & Tapscott, 2016).

Cryptocurrencies are the most notable type of virtual currencies and apply cryptographic algorithms for the purpose of securing transactions as well as for the control of the issuance of new units (Antonopoulos, 2017). Often associated with decentralization and financial independence, the user is also able to circumvent traditional intermediaries in financial systems such as banks (Chiu & Koeppl, 2019). Instead, CBDCs are intended as a digital shadow of physical currency that maintains complete central authority, complementing an existing monetary regime. Thus, both variants have indeed been on an upsurge lately as the virtual currencies offered the promise of lower transaction costs, improved access to financial transactions, and efficiencies in crossborder payments (World Bank, 2020).

Virtual currency, in general, provides dual benefits in addressing some of the systemic issues related to unavailability of banking services, higher remittance costs, and price level pressures in an economy (Diniz et al., 2021). They also pave the way for many new applications in service marketing, as a digital wallet, smart contracts, and tokenization may be used to improve customer experience and engagement (Zhao et al., 2016). Conversely, virtual currencies have various challenges that require proper technological structure, regulatory clarity, and consumer trust (Gupta et al., 2020). Then onwards, knowing their basic concepts and types becomes crucial in understanding potential effects on sustainable service marketing practices.

3. SUSTAINABLE SERVICE MARKETING: A CONCEPTUAL FRAMEWORK

Sustainable service marketing is an approach that brings environmental, social, and economic considerations into the design, delivery, and promotion of services in a strategic way. It looks to create long-term value, finding a balance between business, consumer, and environmental interests. This framework moves beyond traditional marketing goals of profitability and customer satisfaction to include the practices that help reduce environmental impact, enhance social well-being, and make ethical decisions (Kotler & Keller, 2016). In developing economies, such a perspective is critical because of the constraints in resources and social inequities often requiring innovative solutions that maximize value while minimizing harm (Belz & Peattie, 2012).

The three inseparable elements of the conceptual framework for sustainable service marketing are environmental sustainability, social responsibility, and economic viability. Environmental sustainability reduces the residual ecological footprint through green technologies and waste reduction and digital platforms that reduce energy consumption. For instance, virtual currencies can reduce the services' dependence on hard cash and the associated cost of producing and transporting currency bills and coins in service transactions (Tapscott & Tapscott, 2016).

Social responsibility places greater emphasis on the role of service marketing in terms of inclusiveness and empowerment. Services that have incorporated digital payment systems, such as virtual currencies, can assist in improving access to finances for the unbanked community, particularly for developing economies without proper infrastructures for banking (World Bank, 2020). The more financial transactions are made accessible and equitable, the more businesses build a stronger bond with consumers while helping in social development (Srivastava et al., 2023).

Economic viability ensures that the environmentally sustainable marketing and communication policies remain profitable and scalable. Sustainability must be aligned with the business goals, so that investments in green technologies and inclusive payment systems contribute to the competitive advantages. Virtual currencies play a crucial role herein since they reduce the operational costs of transactions, eliminate micropayment bottlenecks, and ease cross-border transactions, hence driving operational efficiencies (Chiu & Koeppl, 2019).

New technologies and practices will find their place into this model through the achievement of consumers' expectations of sustainable and ethical service provision. Research into contemporary practice has established that there is a propensity for consumers to show preference to firms that appear socially conscious. This development further expands new opportunities in which the service providers might gain differentiation within the marketplaces (Kumar et al., 2021). Virtual currencies will increasingly improve consumer confidence and loyalty, especially if the blockchain technology allows for maximum transparency and traceability.

It, therefore, positions businesses at the heart of creating shared value for stakeholders to help in achieving global sustainability goals through the integration of sustainability into all aspects of service delivery and marketing. The framework further provides a road map not only on how sustainability could be integrated into service marketing practices but also on how virtual currencies have the potential to transform sustainable development in emerging markets.

4. THE ROLE OF VIRTUAL CURRENCIES IN DEVELOPING ECONOMIES

The developing economies face special financial and infrastructural issues that have become major barriers to economic development and social progress. These include limitations in the formal banking system, high transaction costs, inflation, corruption, and cross-border remittance inefficiencies (World Bank, 2020). Virtual currencies have since emerged as potential solutions to most of these issues, thereby offering a decentralized and efficient avenue for financial transactions. It employs blockchain technology to such an extent that virtual currencies like Bitcoin and Ethereum will bypass financial intermediaries that will, in turn, bring down the financial transaction costs, increase the speed, and introduce much-needed transparency to monetary dealings. As Nakamoto (2008) and Chiu & Koeppl (2019) have established, these attributes thus appeal to the largest population in the developing world grappling with poor access or highly unaffordable but essential financial services.

Financial inclusion has become one of the mainstays where virtual currencies help immensely in developing economies. According to the World Bank, as of 2020, nearly 1.4 billion adults remain unbanked around the world, of which most belong to developing areas. Virtual currency offers them access to the formal economy by using digital wallets or peer-to-peer payment systems enabled through smartphones.

Another very important role virtual currencies in developing economies play in remittances. Most developing countries rely on inflows of remittances from their citizens for work abroad, accounting for a big percentage of their GDP. However, usual remittances transfer channels are always associated with high fees and slow processing times. Virtual currencies allow cross-border transactions to be faster and cheaper since they eliminate intermediaries like banks and money transfer services. For example, platforms like Ripple and Stellar allow real-time transactions with minimal fees, ensuring that more money reaches recipients in rural and underserved areas (Zhao et al., 2016).

Furthermore, virtual currencies can contribute to the aspects of transparency and the eradication of corruption. This is common in many developing economies. With blockchain technology, one can enjoy an immutable, transparent ledger in recording every transaction. It will be implemented with regard to public funds accountability to curb corruption while ensuring all aid and development money is spent as it was supposed to. For example, many projects have attempted to apply blockchain to make humanitarian responses more accountable as well as public spending in countries like Ethiopia and Nigeria (Tapscott & Tapscott, 2016).

Although the benefits are apparent, there are still several challenges that are a bottleneck towards the implementation of digital currencies in developing economies. Low penetration of smartphones and unstable internet connectivity restrict the adoption of digital wallets and blockchain applications (Gupta et al., 2020). In addition, vague legal frameworks and uncertainty in the regulation of virtual currencies expose consumers and businesses to possible risks. The governments of developing economies are left with a difficult trade-off between promoting innovation and the need to address fraud, money laundering, and financial instability. The other critical challenge is building trust among the consumers, most of whom may not be familiar with digital payment systems (Auer et al., 2021).

5. SOCIAL IMPACTS OF VIRTUAL CURRENCIES

Virtual currencies have a wide range of social impacts, especially in developing economies, where it can redefine financial access, empower the marginalized, and redefine the dynamics of trust and inclusion in the economic landscape. Eliminating intermediaries and allowing for the possibility of direct peer-to-peer transactions opens up opportunities for individuals and communities to engage in the global economy in ways previously unimaginable. On the positive side, these disadvantages are mitigated by obstacles, which are inequality, misuse, and disparate levels of acceptance, and all these need to be weighed.

5.1 Financial Inclusion and Empowerment

The most deep social impact brought about by virtual currencies has been through financial inclusion. About 1.4 billion people are still out of the banking system, with the majority living in developing economies according to a 2020 report by the World Bank. Virtual currencies open up a way of getting around the banking systems, and therefore financial service access is availed through digital wallets requiring merely a smartphone and access to the internet. The benefits are important for women, people living in rural areas, and micro-entrepreneurs, who experience significant barriers in terms of financial access due to geographical, cultural, and institutional factors characterizing them (Diniz et al., 2021). Virtual currencies have a potential to let these groups save, invest, and conduct commerce more effectively by allowing secure, low-cost transactions (Yadav et al., 2022).

For instance, in places like Nigeria, the growing use of cryptocurrency has provided small businesses with opportunities to receive cross-border payments from foreign buyers without necessarily having to go through expensive and unpredictable banking systems (Chainalysis, 2022). In the Philippines, migrant workers often rely on cryptocurrency-based remittance systems in order to protect themselves against excessive fees and long processing times involved in bank transfer services (Zhao et al., 2016). These use cases thus reveal the transformative power of virtual currencies to lift underrepresented populations.

5.2 Behavioral Changes in Consumers and Service Providers

Virtual currencies have driven behavioral changes significantly both in the consumer and the service provider side. On the side of the consumers, virtual wallets and digital money have awakened consumers to an aspect of personal management of financials and enhanced the level of knowledge in matters related to technology. Consumers can learn more new tools and services regarding finance better support values like sustainability and transparency Tapscott & Tapscott (2016).

Virtual currencies for service providers create new opportunities to engage customers and engender loyalty. Companies can also use blockchain to offer traceability and authenticity in their services as a way of establishing consumer trust. For instance, hospitality firms can introduce loyalty programs through blockchain whereby consumers receive tokens for displaying good sustainable practices such as booking environmentally friendly accommodation or purchasing goods from local vendors. This change not only promotes consumer participation but also supports sustainable practices in the service sector as highlighted by Gupta et al., 2020.

5.3 Reduced Corruption and more Transparency

Though virtual currency adoption will be largely in favor of curbing corruption cases in most developing economies, which consumes trust from the institutions and restricts social development, particularly the virtual currency through blockchain technology to provide transparent and tamper-proof ledgers for tracking transactions. Blockchain can help governments and institutions track where public spending goes, whether foreign aid is reaching the right people, and prevent fraud. For example, in countries such as Ghana and Honduras, blockchain-based systems have been experimented with to increase transparency in land registry and curb fraud in land transactions (Tapscott & Tapscott, 2016).

5.4 Risks and Challenges: Inequality and Digital Exclusion

On the other side, there are some potentialities for inclusion with virtual currencies, which will also create a few inequalities, if not cautiously ushered. In many parts of the world, huge digital exclusion faces a real barrier to success, and access to technology and infrastructure is highly uneven. People in rural areas, low-income houses, or in other ways cannot afford a smartphone; even the technological skills to handle virtual currencies are usually lacking (Auer et al., 2021).

Second, the speculative aspect of virtual currencies can make such users exposed to financial risk without proper understanding of the investment process. Such exposure can translate into a tremendous loss for savers or people that use these digital currencies in day-to-day transaction. Further, the anonymous character of digital currency makes them open to fraud or money laundering by some nefarious individuals with antisocial intent toward society. Proper regulation and enlightenment of the end-user should handle these social threats (Chiu & Koeppl, 2019).

5.5 Overcoming Social Inequalities with Partnerships and Education

This will significantly overcome the obstacles of virtual currencies contributing to social impact in the near future, thanks to the collaborations of all relevant stakeholders in educating and training them on digital financial literacy so they can be utilized safely and efficiently. For instance, public-private partnerships will reach out to a wider geography of infrastructure development so that the increased access can further reach distant corners. Blockchain-based mobile and community training can help bridge gaps in areas of digital and financial inclusions with the platforms indeed leading to coverup in gaps (Diniz et al., 2021).

6. ETHICAL AND REGULATORY CONSIDERATIONS

The growing use of virtual currencies in developing economies has brought into sharp focus several ethical and regulatory issues that need attention if these currencies are ever to be used safely, equitably, and sustainably. Virtual currencies are at the juncture of innovation and regulation, with questions on privacy, equity, consumer protection, and societal risks. Ethical considerations include how to balance the promise of financial inclusion against the risk of misuse and exploitation, while the regulatory challenge is establishing frameworks that will protect users and maintain economic stability without stifling innovation.

6.1 Ethical Considerations

Privacy and Anonymity

One of the most touted benefits of virtual currencies is their potential to provide a level of privacy in financial transactions. Cryptocurrencies like Bitcoin and Monero have different levels of anonymity, which can protect the users from being surveilled or discriminated against based on their financial behavior. For people in developing economies who have weak institutional protections, anonymity can be a source of empowerment, allowing them to conduct commerce without fear of persecution or exploitation (Chiu & Koeppl, 2019). But the same feature also creates ethical concerns as it is vulnerable to being used for money laundering, tax evasion, and financing criminal businesses. The ethical issue of widespread use of virtual currencies lies in balancing privacy and accountability. (Tapscott & Tapscott, 2016)

Equity and Accessibility

Virtual currencies may reduce financial inequalities but perpetuate existing ones if access to technology and digital literacy are not equitably distributed. For instance, rural communities and low-income earners may not access the internet, smartphones, or technical expertise for leveraging digital wallets or blockchain platforms; Auer et al., 2021. This has generated a new variant of a digital divide where the advantages of virtual currencies have been enjoyed by the urban and wealthy sections of the population. Accessibility and education are seen to be of extreme ethical importance in ensuring that the vulnerable are not omitted. Consumer Protection

The decentralized and largely unregulated nature of virtual currencies raises a number of consumer protection concerns.

Many users in developing economies may not have knowledge necessary to estimate the risks related to cryptocurrencies, such as price volatility, fraud, and scams. If not properly protected, users can lose money that just makes poverty worse, not better (World Bank, 2020). Ethical concerns extend also to how virtual currency systems are designed themselves, whereby poorly transparent or deceptive practices by developers or other intermediaries can exploit consumers' ignorance.

6.2 Regulatory Issues

Establishing Legal Regimes

The governments of developing economies have to find a balance between regulatory frameworks that encourage innovation and yet minimize the risks.

Virtual currencies are not issued or controlled by any central authorities and are hence difficult to regulate. Issues such as taxation, anti-money laundering (AML) measures, and consumer safeguards need to be addressed by regulators. Countries like Nigeria and India have swung between encouraging the use of cryptocurrencies and banning them. This only goes to show how problematic it is in making proper regulatory choices in this field (Auer et al., 2021). A reliable, open, and fair regulatory strategy can help build confidence and promote appropriate use of virtual currencies.

Cross-Border Transactions

As virtual currencies are international by nature; the feature that one get with the said characteristic is that of offering cheaper, faster transactions associated with remittances and trade. This fact alone makes regulation much more complex. Strictly conflicting regulations enacted by different countries regarding cryptocurrency exchanges, taxation, and reporting requirements may place users and businesses in situations of uncertainty. International cooperation will thus be in order, alongside harmonization of these regulations. For example, bodies such as the Financial Action Task Force have advocated for the development of international standards that would ensure virtual currencies are not abused but legitimate uses are facilitated (Zhao et al., 2016).

Preventing Illicit Activities

The more opaque nature of these currencies is thought to be particularly attractive for individuals who would not want regulatory agencies to trace their transactions. The use of cryptocurrencies in drug trafficking, ransomware attacks, and terrorism financing is well known. In this case, the government and the law enforcement should invest in better technologies and work with blockchain analytics companies to trace and reduce illegal activities without letting go of legitimate virtual currency use. For instance, forensic blockchain tools have been developed to trace transactions in order to identify patterns of fraudulent behavior (Gupta et al., 2020).

Balancing Innovation and Stability

The regulatory decisions will have to balance the fine line between promoting innovation and ensuring financial stability. This would stifle the development of virtual currencies and related industries, such as fintech and DeFi, which hold considerable promise for economic development. Underregulation would give rise to market instability, fraud, and eventual consumer loss of confidence. Developing economies have to tailor their regulatory frameworks according to their particular contexts, given that infrastructure readiness, population needs, and local economic dynamics can differ a great deal (Chiu & Koeppl, 2019).

6.3 Recommendations to Align Ethics and Regulation

Ethical and regulatory balance will go a long way in helping virtual currencies contribute optimally to societal and economic development. This could involve several initiatives at the level of government, private sector stakeholders, and international organizations, including but not limited to the following:

1. Digital Financial Literacy Programs: Invest in education and awareness to raise consumer knowledge about virtual currencies, associated risks, and perceived benefits.
2. Proportional Regulation: Imposition of rules safeguarding users but without stifling innovation. This new approach in regulatory sandboxes holds much promise as new technologies could be tested under oversight.
3. Rewarding Accessible Practices: Encourage businesses and developers to embrace accessibility and accessibility in virtual currency platforms.
4. Public-Private Partnerships: Partnerships to extend digital infrastructure and increase access to presently underserved areas.
5. International Cooperation: Developing global standards for virtual currency regulation to address cross-border issues and avoid misuse.

7. STRATEGIES FOR SUSTAINABLE ADOPTION

It thus calls for carefully crafted strategy in balancing innovations with inclusiveness, education of the mass, infrastructure development, and regulatory stability for the eventual sustainable adoption of virtual currencies into developing economies. These strategies, therefore, attempt to maximize those benefits that arise from virtual currency, including but not limited to financial inclusion, transparency, and efficiency in costs. Building in certain risk would depend on the process of building confidence among various parties: governments, businesses, and consumers through to international organizations.

7.1 Building Digital and Financial Literacy

Promoting digital and financial literacy is one of the cornerstones for sustainable adoption. For virtual currencies to reach the underbanked, there is a need for people to be taught how to access and utilize digital wallets, manage private keys, and ascertain associated risks of cryptocurrencies. This becomes especially true in developing economies where less exposure has occurred to the use of digital financial tools.

Local education programs of the grassroots can be aided by governments and NGOs in regard to cultural and regional sensitivities. This might vary from learning how to make secure transactions via cryptocurrencies on a mobile-based platform to other measures. Private companies-such as exchanges and wallet providers-can themselves assist by means of user-friendly interfaces that support access to information in a step-by-step way towards the entry of digital asset realms. In Kenya, there are promising initiatives towards the integration of blockchain education in rural development for increasing adoption and comprehension of digital financial tools (Diniz et al., 2021).

7.2 Digital Infrastructure Enhancement

The sustainable adoption of virtual currencies really depends on the availability of reliable digital infrastructure. Poor internet connectivity, inadequate access to smartphones, and unreliable electricity affect the effective use of virtual currencies in many developing economies. Investment in infrastructure is very important to narrow the digital divide and assure equity of access (Yadav & Yadav, 2018).

Governments and the private sector can collaborate on extending broadband networks, offering cheap smartphones, and deploying blockchain solutions that are capable of working offline. For instance, low-bandwidth blockchain networks, which are currently being piloted in various parts of Sub-Saharan Africa, can facilitate transactions even at the lowest connectivity levels (Gupta et al., 2020). The same way that decentralized energy solutions, such as solar-powered mobile charging stations, can supplement a lack of electricity in remote locations (Nair & Manohar, 2024).

7.3 Developing Inclusive Platforms and Ecosystems

There is a great need for the adoption of virtual currency to be as inclusive as possible, so systems and platforms need to accommodate many user groups, especially marginalized ones. Developers should be more interested in the fact that the interface is intuitive, in multiple languages, and compatible with low-end smartphones. Payment platforms would also be required to handle local currencies and link up with traditional financial systems for easy transitioning of new users.

Therefore, the collaboration between fintech companies, banks, and mobile network operators could create an environment where virtual currencies are used on an everyday basis for groceries, utilities, and other forms of transport. For example, M-Pesa has already collaborated with blockchain platforms in Kenya, which have enhanced cross-border remittance and enabled wider access to financial services into rural communities such as Diniz et al. (2021).

7.4 Public-Private Collaboration Mobilization

Public-private partnerships will be one of the most significant players that will scale up the adoption of virtual currencies in a sustainable way. Such moves by governments together with private-sector players can develop regulatory sandboxes that allow them to test their virtual currency innovations in a controlled environment. Through such sandboxes, policymakers will be able to fathom some of the possible benefits and risks of new technologies while allowing companies to refine their solutions.

These can be enabled, among others, by international organizations like the United Nations Development Programme in terms of funding, technical know-how, and guidance. Such projects of collaboration, like blockchain-enabled systems for the distribution of aid, have already proven their merits by increasing the elements of transparency and efficiency in countries like Jordan and Ethiopia (Tapscott & Tapscott, 2016).

7.5 Addressing Regulatory and Security Challenges

Regulation which is clear, consistent, and well-defined becomes the very fundamental basis for a country to derive confidence in the virtual currencies being used. Of course, focus should be toward regulations that successfully protect consumers; keep off illegitimate activities while spurring innovative activities. Its main areas shall include anti-money laundering compliance policies, taxation rules, and regulations on cybersecurity among others.

Security will involve the stakeholder's investment in technologies that prevent hacking, fraud, and data breach. For example, blockchain-based verification of identities will be a sure way to increase security because legally, only the owner of this virtual wallet can access it. Consumer education to recognize and avoid scams is also an important method of reducing risk (Naini et al., 2024).

7.6 Facilitating Social and Economic Incentives

Aligning virtual currencies with social and economic incentives may encourage sustainable adoption. Governments and businesses can establish reward-based systems where users receive virtual tokens for engaging in sustainable behaviors, such as using renewable energy or patronizing local businesses. The virtual tokens may be redeemed for discounts or other benefits, thereby establishing a positive feedback loop that fosters adoption while reinforcing sustainable practices (Gupta et al., 2020).

Moreover, virtual currencies can be used to incentivize small businesses to use digital payment systems. Governments can offer subsidies or tax breaks to merchants who accept virtual currencies, thereby accelerating their integration into the local economy.

7.7 Encouraging Global Cooperation and Knowledge Sharing

The global nature of virtual currencies demands international collaboration to resolve challenges and share best practices. International organizations such as the Financial Action Task Force and the World Bank can play a key role in fostering dialogue and setting global standards. Developing economies can learn from the successes and failures of early adopters, tailoring their strategies to local needs and circumstances.

Innovation sharing platforms like conferences, research networks, and public forums may also assist in the knowledge sharing and insight gained and innovation distribution. For instance, Blockchain for Social Impact Coalition brings together the stakeholders to realize how blockchain and virtual currencies may be exploited in solving the problems of the world (Tapscott & Tapscott, 2016).

7.8 Measuring and Evaluating Impact

Sustainable usage of virtual currencies requires some practical measurement about their impact in the social, economic, and environmental arenas. The government, with other organizations, is responsible for formulating benchmarks of what to use along with performance indicators, such as monitoring access to financial services for people who do not have bank accounts or any reduction of fees on remittance, evaluating them regularly. Thus, possible points for enhancement will be marked at which virtual currencies may indeed make sustainability and inclusions realties.

8. TRENDS OF THE FUTURE AND OPPORTUNITIES

In light of ever-evolving virtual currencies, they are likely to further influence the realm of marketing for sustainable service and economic development in developing economies. The future of virtual currencies heralds key opportunities in transformational applications from various sectors; they provide alternative solutions to those stubborn challenges that require urgent attention. In addition, the integration of blockchain into governance is pushing towards the achievement of decentralized financial systems, hence fostering inclusivity and sustainable economic development. However, these opportunities are realized through technological advancements, regulatory changes, and societal acceptance.

8.1 Emergence of Central Bank Digital Currencies (CBDCs)

The ones most related to the Central Bank Digital Currencies now emerging most powerfully are probably those. With a unique mixture of strengths borrowed from virtual money, combined with stability and strong central banks' regulatory roles, digital national currencies move as governments fulfill their interest in updating payment infrastructure with continuous advancement in financial inclusivity.

But this opportunity most knocks in emerging markets because CBDCs are going to really revolutionize financial access there. For instance, countries such as Nigeria and India are researching CBDCs for the extension of banking services to unbanked, remote communities (Auer et al., 2021). A safe, legal digital means of paying such as CBDC will decrease reliance on cash, while giving governments much better visibility overall and drastically reduce risks from unregulated private cryptocurrencies.

8.2 Surging DeFi

The second transformational trend impacting the financial services industry of emerging economies is DeFi, short for Decentralized Finance. DeFi platforms utilize blockchain in the design of decentralized applications-dApps-through which financial services are provided in low intermediation. The use of smart contracts guarantees transparency in transactions while at the same time reduces costs for enhanced accessibility by the disadvantaged.

For instance, access to microloans and investment can be delivered to small-scale farmers and entrepreneurial businesses without them necessarily needing access to conventional finance systems. It offers instant funds through access through collateral exchange to digital assets, thus enhancing individual and collective societal resilience in democracy finance. Tapscott & Tapscott, 2016.

8.3 Link to Internet of Things (IoT)

Virtual currencies, along with the Internet of Things, form an increasingly significant trend with vast impacts in developing economies. The IoT devices are going to be embedded with blockchain technology, and this may provide for automated transactions and efficiencies in many industries. For instance, IoT-enabled sensors might track crop yields in agriculture and, through smart contracts, trigger payments to farmers when predefined conditions are met.

In fact, IoT-enabled microgrids in rural spaces can also open the way to the use of virtual currencies to allow peer-to-peer energy trading. The community will be enabled to sell whatever surplus renewable energy it generates back to its own neighbours, receiving payment without too much hassle, using blockchain-based systems. That is not just sustainable; that will create a new economy as well for everyone (Gupta et al., 2020).

8.4 Rise of Tokenized Economies

Tokenization is a process where real-world assets are converted into virtual tokens on blockchain. This is expected to be one of the major trends for virtual currency in the future, opening up new avenues to invest in and own developing economies. These could include tokenized versions of things like real estate, commodities, or intellectual property, which become more shareable by dividing into smaller pieces, accessible to a wide range of investors.

For instance, citizens of developing economies can invest in tokenized real estate projects with very minimal capital and get returns according to their investments. Similarly, artists and content creators can tokenize their work so that supporters can buy shares and get royalties. Such democratization of asset ownership can lead to increased wealth creation and economic inclusion in regions where traditional investment opportunities are scarce (Zhao et al., 2016).

8.5 Enhanced Cross-Border Remittances

With virtual currency technology now making cross-border remittances the lifeline to equipping most households in the developing economies with one, that will become yet another even efficient affair. So far, cryptos and blockchains have gone to show they can indeed do a thing in terms of the fees and times of processing a remittance transaction. This trend might lead them further down in securing this and making it an easier affair.

For example, decentralized remittance platforms will most likely infuse key advanced encryption and biometric authentication within their systems to be sure of increased security against fraud. Additionally, the collaborations that virtual currencies have with local financial institutions might also enable the beneficiaries to easily transform digital funds into local currencies. This way, diffusion will expand (World Bank. 2020).

8.6 Blockchain for Sustainable Development

This has become an imperative call to develop energy-efficient blockchain solutions, considering the ever-increasing environmental concerns. For example, virtual currencies such as Bitcoin have come under attack since they use the Proof-of-Work consensus mechanism, which is known to require huge amounts of energy. The trend toward sustainability and adoption, however, is promising, considering the shift in usage to alternative mechanisms such as Proof-of-Stake and other low-energy consensus protocols (Manohar, 2024).

Applications of sustainable blockchains can also be contributory to environmental and social objectives in developing economies. For example, blockchain-based systems may be used in supply chains tracking to establish the origin and influence of their products, thereby enhancing ethically sourced goods and sustainability. The farmers and artisans can make use of such systems to authenticate their items as showing sustainability, making it possible to command high prices from global markets (Gupta et al., 2020).

8.7 More Emphasis on Regulation and Standardization

As virtual currencies gain more attention, governments and international organizations will probably pay more attention to regulation and standardization in the future. It is the establishment of unified global regulatory frameworks that will help resolve fraud, money laundering, and market volatility issues and engender trust among users and investors.

Standardized regulations would, in the context of developing economies, provide a sense of clarity and stability for businesses and consumers, hence encouraging adoption. The realization of international cooperation in solving cross-border challenges will ensure the use of virtual currencies in global commerce safely and effectively. Expected to play a central role in shaping the regulation are organizations such as the FATF and IMF (Chiu & Koeppl, 2019).

8.8 Virtual Currencies for Social Impact

Finally, huge potential of social impact lies with virtual currencies for developing economies in the future. Blockchain-based projects can overcome substantial constraints like poverty, corruption, and inequality. For instance, blockchain-based digital identity systems could provide people who do not possess official documents a legal identity. They will get important services, such as health care, education, and banking (Tapscott & Tapscott, 2016).

Virtual currencies can also be utilized to amplify the traceability of aid distribution to ensure that it is actually delivered to the targeted recipients. Using blockchain-driven platforms works well in areas affected by conflicts or natural disasters, especially where the distribution of humanitarian assistance could be efficiently accomplished in a low-corruption and low-inefficiency manner.

8.9 Opportunities for Collaborative Innovation

The future of virtual currencies depends on collaborative innovation among governments, businesses, academia, and civil society. Developing new use cases and refining available technologies to effectively meet the diverse needs of a developing economy might be possible under research and development efforts. To illustrate, there can be collaborative innovation between the universities and the fintech start-ups to devise blockchain applications unique to a given region, enhancing innovation and entrepreneurship.

9. CONCLUSION

Virtual currency is an opportunity as well as a challenge in terms of the social impacts it may bring about that may change the destiny of financial inclusion, economic growth, and social development for sustainable service marketing in developing economies. In the light of these issues, though virtual currencies provide ample opportunities to promote access to affordable financial services, to reduce transaction costs, and for the purpose of transparency, there will be considerable caution in exercise towards the differentiated requirements and conditions of developing economies.

As discussed throughout this chapter, virtual currencies represent more than just an alternative to traditional means of transaction. They are changing how services are marketed and delivered-particularly in under-resourced areas-by providing platforms for innovative financial solutions, reducing barriers to entry, and fostering new business models. The integration of virtual currencies into sustainable service marketing could greatly improve access to basic services such as education, health, and energy and even create new opportunities for small businesses and entrepreneurs.

Some of the primary hindrances that would have to be surmounted in transitioning developing economies to virtual currency-based systems include financial and digital literacy, improvements in infrastructure, and putting in place sound regulatory frameworks. In all, sustainability is based on strategies for the promotion of financial inclusion while preventing fraud, volatility, and misuse. The future of virtual currency depends upon how these problems, through joint efforts of relevant stakeholders-governments, enterprises, international organisations, and themselves-can unlock fully its potentiality.

It is about translating the most promising opportunities of CBDCs and increased DeFi into practical answers for many of the financial barriers that face individuals and businesses in developing economies. Added to the nascent development of blockchain, these might just represent the key to unlocking far better access to finance, total transparency, and equality in economic participation. Besides, tokenized assets and virtual currencies merged with the rising technology of Internet of Things might open up further prospects for sustainable economic growth in areas like agriculture, energy, and cross-border remittances.

The social effects of virtual currencies on sustainable service marketing in the developing economies have been far-reaching and transformative. Though their whole potential is still to be accomplished, virtual currencies can bring on an era that is more inclusive, equitable, and sustainable. Realization of this dream would require much more infrastructure in the form of development, expansion of education and awareness programs, as well as sound regulatory and security frameworks. Through such efforts, virtual currencies can facilitate a future in which people and communities in developing economies are more effectively positioned to prosper in the digital economy.

REFERENCES

Antonopoulos, A. M. (2017). *Mastering Bitcoin: Unlocking digital cryptocurrencies* (2nd ed.). O'Reilly Media.

Auer, R., Cornelli, G., & Frost, J. (2021). Rise of the central bank digital currencies: Drivers, approaches, and technologies. *Bank for International Settlements Quarterly Review, March 2021*, 67–83.

Belz, F. M., & Peattie, K. (2012). *Sustainability marketing: A global perspective*. Wiley.

Chainalysis. (2022). *The 2022 global crypto adoption index*. Retrieved from https://www.chainalysis.com

Chiu, J., & Koeppl, T. V. (2019). Blockchain-based settlement for asset trading. *Review of Financial Studies*, *32*(5), 1716–1753. DOI: 10.1093/rfs/hhy122

Diniz, E., de Albuquerque, J. P., & Cernev, A. K. (2021). Mobile payment and inclusion: Trends and challenges in the global south. *Information Technology for Development*, *27*(1), 4–15. DOI: 10.1080/02681102.2020.1837469

European Central Bank. (2012). *Virtual currency schemes*. European Central Bank.

Gupta, M., Abdelsalam, M., Khorsandroo, S., & Mittal, S. (2020). Security and privacy in smart farming: Challenges and opportunities. *IEEE Access : Practical Innovations, Open Solutions*, *8*, 34564–34584. DOI: 10.1109/ACCESS.2020.2975142

Kotler, P., & Keller, K. L. (2016). *Marketing management* (15th ed.). Pearson Education.

Kumar, V., Rahman, Z., Kazmi, A. A., & Goyal, P. (2021). Evolution of sustainability as marketing strategy: Beginning of new era. *Sustainability*, *13*(13), 7670. DOI: 10.3390/su13137670

Manohar, S. (2024). Cryptocurrency as a Slice in Investment Portfolio: Identifying Critical Antecedents and Building Taxonomy for Emerging Economy. *Asia-Pacific Financial Markets*, •••, 1–26. DOI: 10.1007/s10690-024-09490-7

Naini, S. R., Mekapothula, R. R., Jain, R., & Manohar, S. (2024). Redefining green consumerism: A diminutive approach to market segmentation for sustainability. *Environmental Science and Pollution Research International*, *31*(9), 12916–12932. DOI: 10.1007/s11356-023-31717-9 PMID: 38180668

Nair, A. J., & Manohar, S. (2024). Green Service Consumption: Unlocking Customer Expectations on Technological Transformations Enhancing Purchase Experience in Retail Store. *International Journal of Information Management Data Insights*, *4*(2), 100277. DOI: 10.1016/j.jjimei.2024.100277

Nakamoto, S. (2008). Bitcoin: A peer-to-peer electronic cash system. Retrieved from https://bitcoin.org/bitcoin.pdf

Srivastava, A. P., Yadav, M., Yadav, R., Singh, B., & Dewasiri, N. J. (2023). Exploring digital agility and digital transformation leadership: A mixed method study. [JGIM]. *Journal of Global Information Management*, *31*(8), 1–23. DOI: 10.4018/JGIM.332861

Tapscott, D., & Tapscott, A. (2016). *Blockchain revolution: How the technology behind bitcoin is changing money, business, and the world.* Portfolio.

World Bank. (2020). *The Global Findex Database 2017: Measuring financial inclusion and the fintech revolution*. World Bank.

Yadav, M., & Yadav, R. (2018). Impact of spirituality/religiousness on cyber bullying and victimization in university students: Mediating effect of emotional intelligence. *Journal of Religion and Health*, *57*(5), 1961–1979. DOI: 10.1007/s10943-018-0637-8 PMID: 29790079

Yadav, R., Yadav, M., & Mittal, A. (2022). Effects of gain-loss-framed messages on virtual reality intervened fitness exercise. *Information Discovery and Delivery*, *50*(4), 374–386. DOI: 10.1108/IDD-04-2021-0051

Zhao, J. L., Fan, S., & Yan, J. (2016). Overview of business innovations and research opportunities in blockchain and introduction to the special issue. *Financial Innovation*, *2*(1), 1–7. DOI: 10.1186/s40854-016-0049-2

Chapter 11
The Intersection of Virtual Currencies and Green Finance:
A Sustainable Development Perspective

Roshan Kumar
https://orcid.org/0009-0008-9152-3208
Dr. Vishwanath Karad MIT World Peace University, India

Vaibhav
Banaras Hindu University, India

Sandeep Yadav
University of Lucknow, India

Faizul Haque
Southampton Business School, University of Southampton, UK

ABSTRACT

Examining the interplay between virtual currencies and green finance in promoting sustainable development is more crucial as the global economy confronts digital revolution and climate change. This study fulfills that need by offering a comprehensive bibliometric analysis of published works on virtual currency and green finance from 2020 to 2025. The study examines publication trends, prominent authors, and thematic patterns through performance analysis and scientific mapping techniques utilizing VOSviewer and Excel. The results indicate a rapid increase in scholarly output, significantly driven by substantial contributions from China, India, and the

DOI: 10.4018/979-8-3373-0315-4.ch011

United Kingdom. Thematic evolution reveals emerging trends in distributed finance (DeFi), sustainability, and blockchain-based green innovation. The study presents policy recommendations for integrating blockchain-based virtual currencies into environmental finance systems and explores the theoretical implications of linking virtual financial technologies with green economic models.

1. INTRODUCTION

The fast digital change of the worldwide financial ecosystem has sparked growing scholarly interest in the junction of digital innovation and environmental sustainability. Among these innovations, the function of cryptocurrencies inside the more general framework of green finance and carbon emission reduction has been a major focus of research. Integrating digital financial technologies with sustainable environmental practices presents both a possibility and a difficulty as countries try to reach climate targets and follow low-carbon development paths. More recently, research on this intricate interface has started. Krishnamurthy (2023) and Zhang et al. (2025) present a blockchain-based incentive system using cryptocurrencies that honors carbon-reducing behavior, therefore presenting a novel yet contentious tool for sustainable finance. Although their approach shows how digital tokens could be used to support environmentally friendly behavior, it also emphasizes ongoing issues such regulatory uncertainty and bitcoin volatility that would prevent general use. By using more traditional financial instruments and carbon offset systems, Aliet al. (2024) and Evite (2023) concentrate on green finance techniques, therefore providing less interaction with digital assets or blockchain-based innovations.

A increasing section of the research has looked at the effects of bitcoin activities on the surroundings. Koemtzopoulos et al. (2025) point to a paradigm change from fintech to greentech and imply that, with suitable design, blockchain technologies can help with energy transition and carbon neutrality. Driven mostly by energy-intensive proof-of- work (PoW) mining techniques, investigations by Alabi and Ibañez et al. (2024) and Khosravi et al. (2023) show striking evidence of the high carbon footprint connected with cryptocurrencies as Bitcoin and Ethereum. These results support mounting requests for technological changes and legislative frameworks including carbon taxes, energy-efficient consensus procedures, and the movement of mining activities to areas run on renewable energy sources. Although some contributions, like those by Zhao et al. (2024) and Chamnara et al. (2023), highlight the efficacy of green finance in lowering industrial emissions under China's dual carbon objectives, they mostly ignore the consequences of digital currencies in this regard. On the other hand, Khosravi et al. (2023) present a more hopeful view, showing how younger blockchain projects with reduced energy consumption profiles could more closely fit sustainable development objectives (SDGs). Offering environmentally friendly substitutes for conventional cryptocurrencies, creative financial instruments including stablecoins and green cryptocurrencies are also under increasing investigation as tools for Environmental, Social, and Governance (ESG)-aligned investment portfolios (Koemtzopoulos et al.,2025).

Notwithstanding these encouraging advances, a good amount of the current research still concentrates exclusively on the negative effects of Bitcoin on the environment. While some like Packard et al. (2022), urge for greener mining practices and policy incentives, studies by Xiao et al. (2023), Chamanara and Madani (2023), and Kohli et al. (2023) estimate Bitcoin's significant carbon emissions and related dangers. Still, studies like Onat et al. (2021) and Park et al.(2011) caution of the unexpected effects of jurisdictional mining prohibitions, which might just relocate carbon-intensive industries to less controlled areas. Moreover, the larger environmental impact of bitcoin mining—including soil degradation and technological waste—demand immediate consideration in debates on environmental finance. Although they usually ignore the particular consequences of cryptocurrencies, more general conceptual studies (e.g., Wu et al.,2024; Shao et al., 2022) confirm the potential of digital finance to improve green efficiency across industries amid this debate. Legal academics such as Truby (2018) propose different routes like SolarCoin and legislative change to decarbonize the blockchain sector, so harmonizing innovation with sustainability.

Against this background, the present work aims to provide a thorough bibliometric and thematic analysis of the changing relationship between cryptocurrencies and environmental sustainability thereby bridging the scattered scholarly debate. The study methodically maps the intellectual terrain, notes important theme clusters, and assesses the scientific development of this multidisciplinary field using the Biblioshiny interface (Aria & Cuccurullo, 2017). By means of this dual-method approach, the research field can be evaluated more critically, performance-based rather than only in descriptive summaries.As so, the following research questions direct this study:

RQ1: What are the main scholarly trends and innovations tying digital finance—especially cryptocurrencies—with environmental sustainability?
RQ2: To this field, which writers, organizations, and nations have most significantly contributed?
RQ3: What philosophical framework underlines present green finance and bitcoin research?
RQ4: In the framework of carbon mitigating and sustainable blockchain innovation, which themes and technologies are most often investigated?

By tackling these issues, this research offers a fresh viewpoint on continuous discussions on digital transformation with climate alignment. It points up understudied areas of research like legal-financial design of green blockchain ecosystems, decarbonization of mining operations, and integration of digital assets into ESG frameworks. The results give researchers, legislators, and investors an evidence-based basis to negotiate the complexity of digital finance and maximize its possibilities in furthering world sustainability targets.

2. DEFINING THE MOST PERTINENT SEARCH PHRASES

This work uses a systematic bibliometric approach to examine the junction between virtual currency and green finance. The study included a well-chosen collection of terms related with blockchain, cryptocurrency, digital tokens, and their applications in environmental and sustainable finance to guarantee a complete and representative data set. Google Scholar was utilized in preliminary searches to find often used, contextually relevant phrases in scholarly debate. After this exploratory stage, a more methodically rigorous search among credible scholarly publications helped to improve the terminology and guarantee methodological consistency.

Because of its extensive coverage of peer-reviewed literature and great dependability in bibliometric research, the last data extraction was done using the Scopus database. With around 84 million entries including significant coverage in the domains of economics, finance, and environmental studies, Scopus is still one of the most strong reference databases (Paul et al., 2021). Scopus provides more comprehensive material from multidisciplinary publications than the Web of Science, which is crucial for researching the developing junction between virtual currencies and green financial instruments (Pattnaik et al., 2020; Valtakoski, 2020).

The search string "virtual currency" OR cryptocurrency OR "digital currency" OR "cryptoasset" OR "blockchain" OR "bitcoin" OR "ethereum" OR "decentralized finance" OR "defi" OR "e-money" OR "token-based currency" AND "green investment" OR "sustainable investment" OR "ESG investment" OR "climate finance" OR "responsible investment" OR "impact investing" OR "environmental finance" OR "clean energy investment". The outcomes consisted only in English-written peer-reviewed papers. Following strict screening and PRISMA protocol filtering, a last collection of 126 papers was kept for bibliometric analysis.

2.1 Methodology Used for Analysis

This paper uses bibliometric analysis as a quantitative approach to assess the intellectual terrain of literature connecting virtual currencies with green finance. Identification of knowledge structures, thematic trends, and collaborative patterns across scholarly outputs (Goyal & Kumar, 2021; Mishra et al., 2018; Verma et al., 2024) depends much on bibliometric approaches. Using bibliometric approaches, the research not only charts scientific development but also highlights understudied areas in the field of sustainable finance motivated by new technologies such digital assets and blockchain.

Two basic bibliometric approaches—performance analysis and scientific mapping—were used in the work. Measures including publication count, citation impact, and author output were evaluated using performance analysis. Intellectual linkages across authors, institutions, and nations were visualized and interpreted using science mapping techniques—including co-authorship, co-citation, bibliographic coupling, and keyword co-occurrence—Donthu et al., 2021; Aria & Cuccurullo, 2017. These instruments help one to have a thorough awareness of the intellectual, social, and conceptual framework of the research field.

This study's bibliometric framework catches eminent writers, source journals, affiliated universities, and nations driving the conversation. By means of PRISMA-guided data refinement, a transparent, reproducible, methodologically sound procedure guaranteed. The results assist to define the course of study on virtual currencies and its consequences for green and sustainable finance.

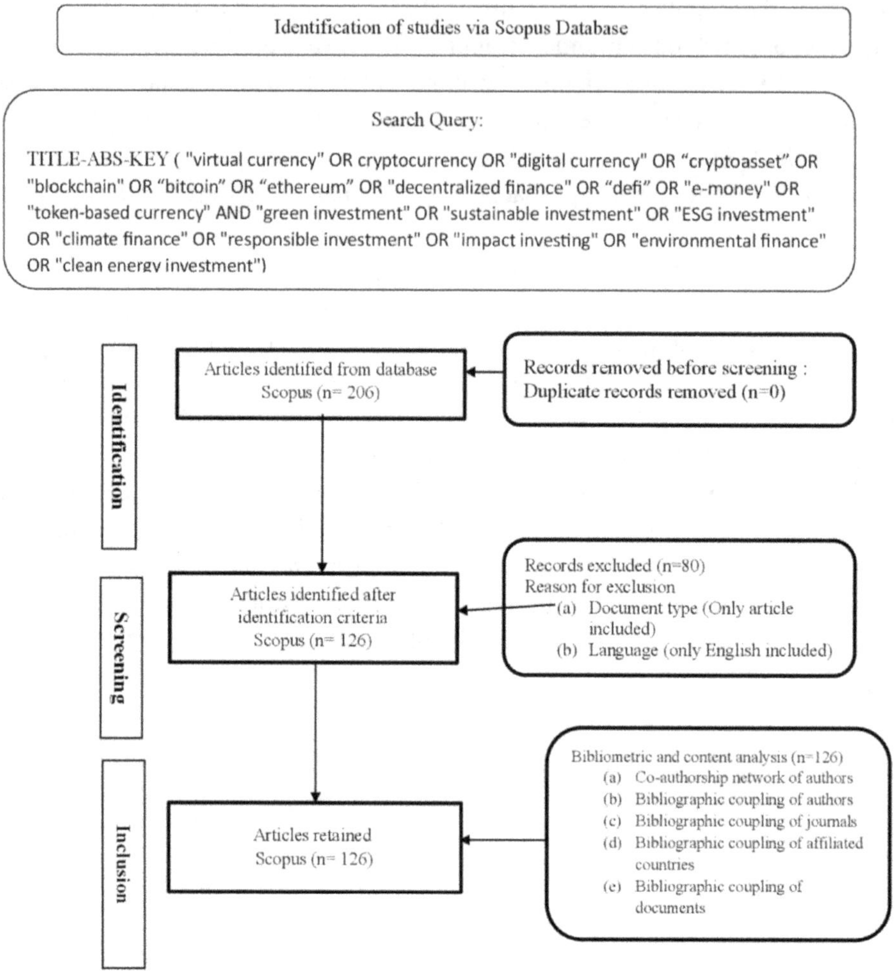
Identification of studies via Scopus Database
Search Query:
TITLE-ABS-KEY ("virtual currency" OR cryptocurrency OR "digital currency" OR "cryptoasset" OR "blockchain" OR "bitcoin" OR "ethereum" OR "decentralized finance" OR "defi" OR "e-money" OR "token-based currency" AND "green investment" OR "sustainable investment" OR "ESG investment" OR "climate finance" OR "responsible investment" OR "impact investing" OR "environmental finance" OR "clean energy investment")
Identification
Articles identified from database Scopus (n= 206)
Records removed before screening : Duplicate records removed (n=0)
Screening
Articles identified after identification criteria Scopus (n= 126)
Records excluded (n=80)
Reason for exclusion
(a) Document type (Only article included)
(b) Language (only English included)
Inclusion
Articles retained Scopus (n= 126)
Bibliometric and content analysis (n=126)
(a) Co-authorship network of authors
(b) Bibliographic coupling of authors
(c) Bibliographic coupling of journals
(d) Bibliographic coupling of affiliated countries
(e) Bibliographic coupling of documents

3. DATA DESCRIPTION AND REVIEW

3.1 Descriptive Approach

The descriptive method aims to find four main benchmark values from the 2020–2025 database pertinent to the development of green finance and virtual currencies. The link between financial digitalization and environmental sustainability has become more important as distributed digital assets—such as cryptocurrencies—change world economic systems. Simultaneously, the rise of green finance projects highlights a change toward investing practices lowering environmental hazards. Publications on these events underline the dual function of virtual money: on the one hand, encouraging financial inclusion and innovation; on the other, generating questions on blockchain mining with high energy consumption. Likewise, studies on green finance define investment trends that give sustainable economic growth top priority as well as renewable energy.

Examining legislative systems that combine economic efficiency and environmental responsibility, scholarly contributions in these disciplines seek to harmonize technical developments with sustainable development goals. Citation studies of this dataset show a transforming path in global

financial ecosystems as well as an expanding scholarly attention on merging digital financial solutions with ecological stewardship.

Table 1 shows that research on virtual currency and green finance has grown steadily from 2020 to 2025. Total Publications (TP) increased, reflecting heightened academic interest. Citations peaked in 2022, but the declining Average Citations (AC) suggests thematic diversification. The drop in Total Cited Publications (TCP) in 2023 indicates a temporary shift in research influence.

The rise in Non-Cited Publications (NCP) in 2024 and 2025 signals broader exploration, with newer studies requiring time to gain recognition. Overall, citation patterns highlight an evolving scholarly landscape, transitioning from niche discourse to a widely studied field

Table 1. Year-wise publication and citations

Year	TP	TC	TCP	NCP	AC
2020	3	126	3	0	42.000
2021	1	81	1	0	81.000
2022	11	450	11	0	40.909
2023	19	426	1	0	22.421

continued on following page

Table 1. Continued

Year	TP	TC	TCP	NCP	AC
2024	45	209	30	15	4.644
2025	47	206	17	30	4.383

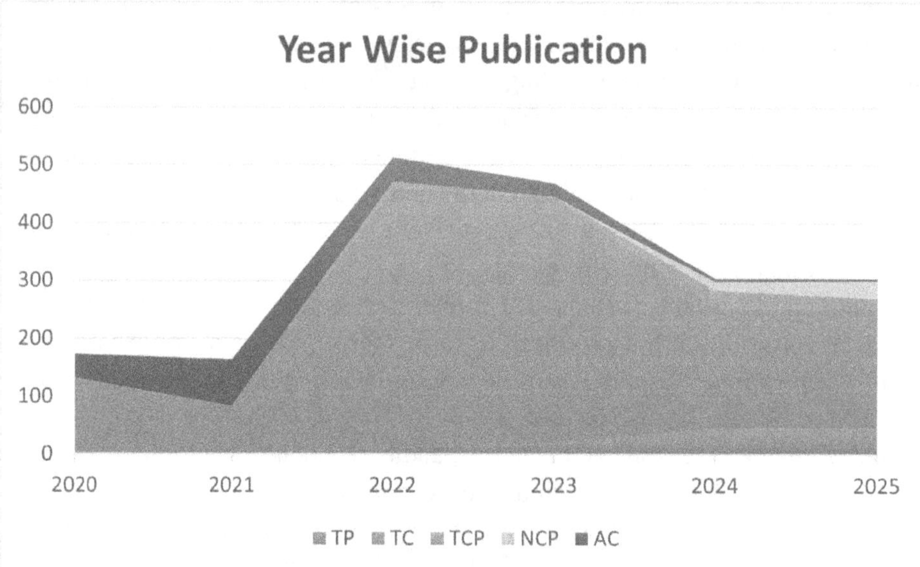

3.2 Network Approach

The network approach is used to show how closely authors, keywords, subject-specific phrases, and nation (Cumming et al., 2022; Donthu et al., 2021) are connected. The network approach offers a study of past performance, present tendencies, and future possibilities. Examining works with several authors and with an eye toward the link between their production and impact on this field, the network analysis.

3.2.1 Leading Authors, Sources and Documents Within the Research Field

Table 2. Leading authors, sources, and documents

Author	TP	TC	Source	TP	TC	Document	TC
kumar, satish	2	232	transportation research part e: logistics and transportation review	2	198	kumar (2025)	175
lim, weng marc	1	175	annals of operations research	1	175	cao (2022)	113
mangla, sachin kumar	1	175	technological forecasting and social change	5	147	li (2022)	85
rao, sandeep	1	175	international review of economics and finance	4	89	schulz (2021)	81
sharma, dipasha	1	175	earth system governance	1	81	yan (2022)	77
cao, yu	1	113	sustainability (switzerland)	5	79	saxena (2023)	77
hu, hanli	1	113	futures	1	62	abakah (2023)	64
li, qingsong	1	113	international review of financial analysis	1	57	schulz (2020)	62
wan, guangyu	1	113	frontiers in blockchain	1	48	goodell (2022)	57
wang, shouyang	1	113	journal of innovation and knowledge	1	47	patel (2023)	49

Table 2 exposes important players and sources influencing the debate on virtual money and how it affects green finance. With two books and 232 citations, Satish Kumar is the most powerful author; Lim, Mangla, Rao, and Sharma follow each with highly cited single publications (175 citations). This implies that the field is much influenced by both consistent and single contributions.

Among the top publications, Transportation Research Part E and Technological Forecasting and Social Change stand out as clearly displaying a multidisciplinary focus encompassing logistics, innovation, and sustainability. Including sources like Earth System Governance and Futures illustrates the larger dimensions of field governance and foresight of the field.

Top-cited papers including Li (2022), Cao (2022), and Kumar (2025) highlight a recent and expanding emphasis on how virtual currencies interact with green finance. These pieces show virtual currencies as enablers of sustainable habits and environmental responsibility in addition to as digital financial tools.

3.2.2 Author-Wise Analysis

Table 3. Mapping author influence

Author	TP	TC	TLS
kumar, satish	2	232	9
lim, weng marc	1	175	4
mangla, sachin kumar	1	175	4
rao, sandeep	1	175	4
sharma, dipasha	1	175	4
cao, yu	1	113	5
hu, hanli	1	113	5
li, qingsong	1	113	5
wan, guangyu	1	113	5
wang, shouyang	1	113	5

The author analysis highlights Satish Kumar as the most influential contributor in the field, with the highest number of publications (2), citations (232), and total link strength (9), indicating strong scholarly impact and network centrality. Authors like Lim, Mangla, Rao, and Sharma each have one highly cited paper (175 citations) with moderate link strength (TLS = 4), reflecting notable individual impact. Others, including Cao, Hu, Li, Wan, and Wang, have 113 citations and slightly higher TLS scores (5), suggesting growing relevance and collaborative connections. Overall, the field is shaped by a few highly cited authors with varying degrees of network integration.

3.2.3 Country-Wise Analysis

Table 4. Countries wise analysis

Country	TP	TC	TLS
china	39	517	36
india	19	497	29
ireland	2	232	5
australia	6	178	8
spain	4	168	5

continued on following page

Table 4. Continued

Country	TP	TC	TLS
united states	6	160	7
netherlands	3	150	1
united kingdom	13	120	27
turkey	6	104	6
france	7	98	10

With the highest number of publications (TP = 39), citations (TC = 517), and network strength (TLS = 36), the country-level study shows China leads in scholarly output reflecting both volume and influence. With 19 publications and 497 citations, India comes second with high citation impact relative to output and strong cooperative links (TLS = 29). Ireland has only two publications, but its astonishingly high citation count (TC = 232) points to very powerful research.

With acceptable citation effect and network connectedness, nations including Australia, Spain, and the United States produce modest output 4–6 papers each. With a lower citation count (TC = 120) the United Kingdom has a significant collaborative presence (TLS = 27), therefore highlighting its integrative function in world research networks. With China and India emerging as major players, the data show generally a geographically varied and linked research scene.

With strong worldwide links, especially with the United States, United Kingdom, and South Africa, the collaboration network shows that India and China are major hubs in global research on virtual money and green finance. Different clusters mirror regional cooperation including Australia-linked countries and Europe (Germany, France, Italy). The map shows generally a globally linked research scene headed by Asian economies.

With China rising as the most active contributor followed by India, the United States, Australia, and certain European countries, the map shows the worldwide research distribution on virtual currency and green finance. Vast areas, including much of Africa, South America, and parts of Asia, show either minimal or no contribution, so highlighting a concentration of scholarly activity in East Asia, South Asia, and developed Western countries. The darker shading over China indicates the highest document count (up to 39).

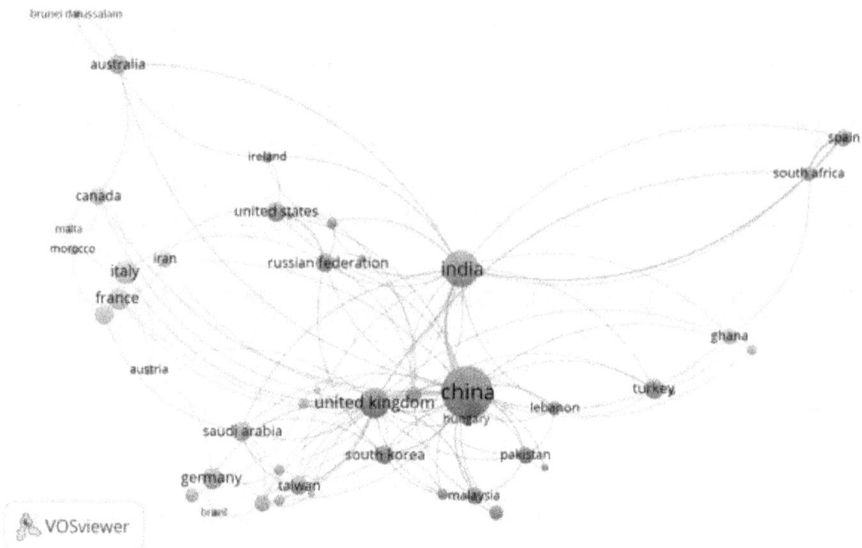
australia
ireland
canada
united states
malta
morocco
iran
italy
russian federation
india
spain
south africa
france
ghana
austria
china
turkey
united kingdom
lebanon
saudi arabia
south korea
pakistan
germany
taiwan
malaysia
VOSviewer

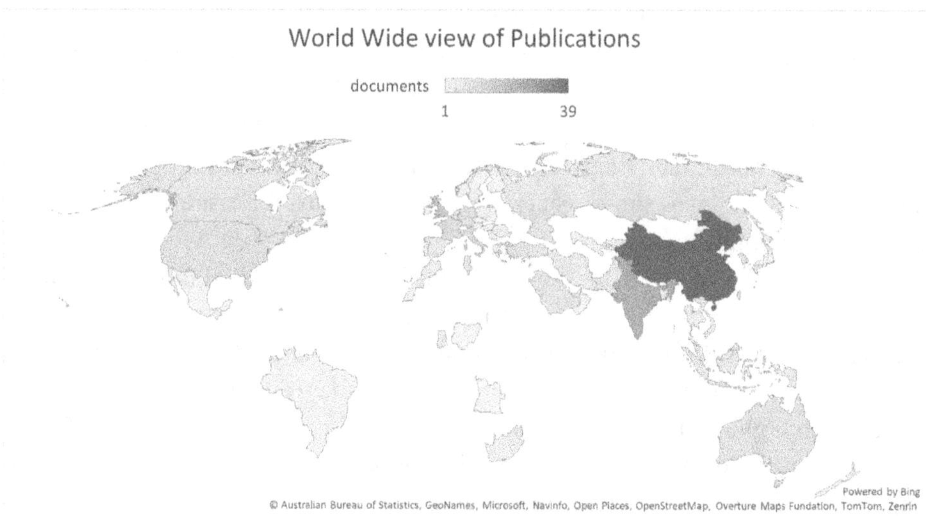
World Wide view of Publications
documents
1
39
Powered by Bing
© Australian Bureau of Statistics, GeoNames, Microsoft, Navinfo, Open Places, OpenStreetMap, Overture Maps Fundation, TomTom, Zenrin

3.2.4 Institution Wise Analysis

Table 5. Institutional co-authorship patterns

Organization	TP	TC	TLS
dcu business school, dublin city university, dublin 09, ireland	1	175	5
department of management studies, malaviya national institute of technology jaipur, rajasthan, jaipur, 302017, india	1	175	5
jindal global business school, o p jindal global university, haryana, sonipat, india	1	175	5
school of business, swinburne university of technology, jalan simpang tiga, sarawak, kuching, 93350, australia	1	175	5
swinburne business school, swinburne university of technology, john street, hawthorn, 3122, vic, australia	1	175	5
symbiosis centre for management and human resource development, symbiosis international (deemed university), pune, india	1	175	5
business school, central south university, hunan, changsha, 410083, china	1	113	5
key laboratory of big data mining and knowledge management, chinese academy of sciences, beijing, 100190, china	1	113	5
school of economics & trade, hunan university, hunan, changsha, 410082, china	1	113	5
school of economics and management, university of chinese academy of sciences, beijing, 100190, china	1	113	5

Notably DCU Business School, Malaviya National Institute of Technology, O.P. Jindal Global University, and Swinburne University of Technology—each of which contributed one publication with high citation counts (TC = 175) and moderate link strength (TLS = 5)—indicating very impactful and well-connected research according to the organizational analysis. Reflecting high scholarly production and cooperative posture within the research network, Chinese institutions such Central South University, Chinese Academy of Sciences, and Hunan University have also made noteworthy contributions (TC = 113 each). Overall, the data points to a varied spectrum of geographically scattered institutions with no one university dominating but rather several generating significant, high-impact work on virtual money and green finance.

3.2.5 Author Cocitation Network Analysis

Table 6. Author co-citation network

Author	TC	Total link strength
bouri e.	90	9986
wang y.	84	8450
naeem m.a.	75	8995
lucey b.	71	8412
li y.	66	6180
tiwari a.k.	62	7369
taghizadeh-hesary f.	58	4180
yarovaya l.	56	6111
corbet s.	55	6397
umar m.	54	6102

Reflecting their great academic impact and wide-ranging collaboration networks, the most influential authors in the field of virtual currency and green finance, based on total citations (TC) and total link strength (TLS), include Bouri E. (TC = 90, TLS = 9686) and Naeem M.A. (TC = 75, TLS = 8996). Other eminent writers such Wang Y., Lucey B., and Tiwari A.K. also show strong co-authorship links and high citation counts, therefore underscoring their essential involvement in forming the debate and furthering research in this multidisciplinary subject.

The co-authorship network visualization exposes several groups of active field researchers. Lead by Bouri E., Naeem M.A., and Corbet S., the green cluster marks a well-connected group helping with green finance, crypto-assets, and financial contagion. Centered on Wang Y., Liu Y., and Zhang Y., the red cluster shows a strong Chinese research basis emphasizing on empirical financial modeling and sustainable finance. The blue cluster honors academics such as Tiwari A.K. and Yarovaya L., who serve as linkers between networks thereby improving multidisciplinary cooperation. Node size shows production; link density shows cooperative intensity.

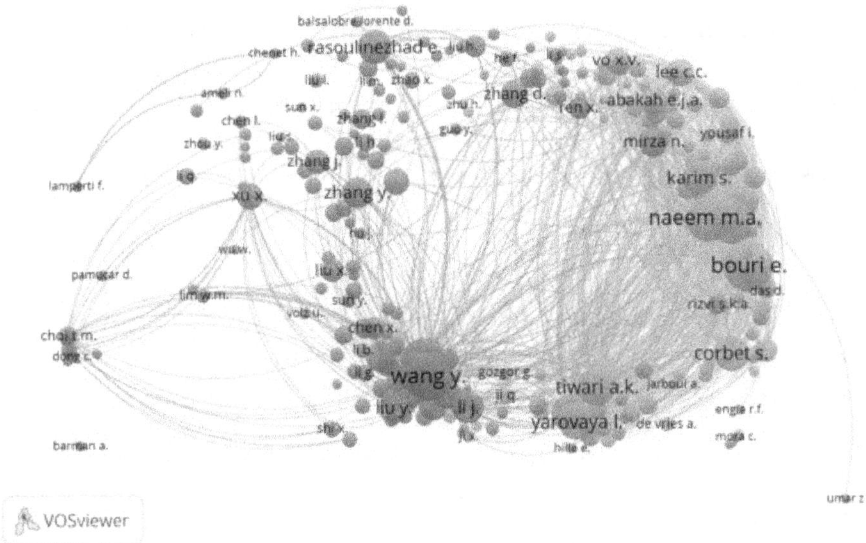

Thematic focus of the literature is shown by the keyword study. With 45 references, "Decentralized finance" is the most often used phrase with the highest Total Link Strength (TLS = 904), therefore stressing its significance and connection in the research scene. Keywords such as "investment" (26; TLS = 568) and "green economy" (30; TLS = 614) point to a clear junction between financial innovation and environmental concerns. Words like "sustainable development," "green development," and "sustainability" capture a rising intellectual focus on matching financial methods with environmental goals. The evidence points generally toward a strong research agenda centered on the junction of DeFi and environmental responsibility.

The co-occurrence network demonstrates that "decentralized finance," "green economy," and "sustainability" are central topics, therefore reflecting a strong study focus on the junction of financial innovation with environmental aims. Tightly related ideas such "investment," "blockchain," and "green development" show how digital technologies are being used to advance sustainable finance. While terms like "cryptocurrency, artificial intelligence, and COVID-19 point to technological and contextual dynamics impacting the field, clusters linked to "climate finance, "carbon emissions," and "zero carbon," stress environmental issues. The picture emphasizes generally a multidisciplinary junction between DeFi and sustainable development.

With regular phrases like finance, green, energy, research, sustainable, and investment suggesting an emphasis on sustainable finance and energy transitions, the word cloud emphasizes important issues in the literature. Blockchain, technology, bitcoin, and cryptocurrencies point to increased interest in the part FinTech and distributed technologies play. Temporal keywords (2020–2024) indicate a focus on current events, implying the necessity of investigations for next years. China's presence suggests regional research dominance and invites comparison study. Words like university, journal, and evidence point to an empirical, academic research focus.

3.3 Keyword Occurrence Analysis

Table 7. Keyword co-occurrence analysis

Keyword	Frequency	TLS
decentralized finance	45	904
green economy	30	614
investment	26	568
sustainable development	19	413
finance	17	377
investments	17	377
green development	18	374
sustainability	20	335
article	9	303
environmental economics	14	286

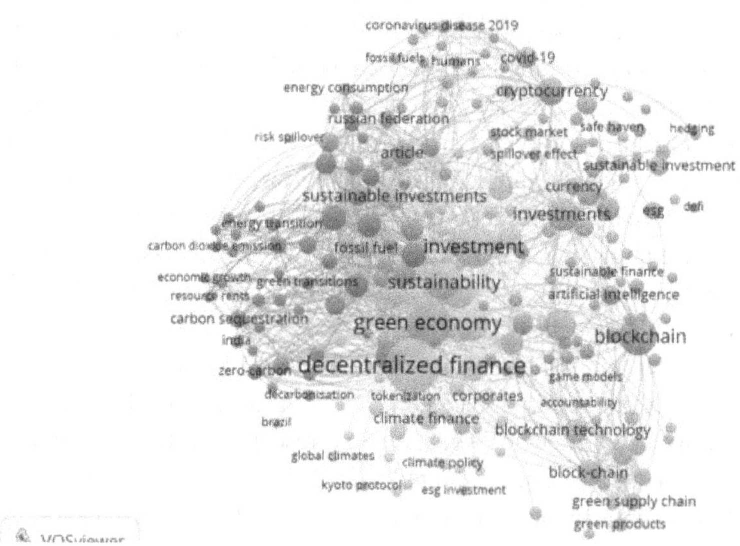

3.4 Bibliographic Coupling

3.4.1 Bibliographic Coupling of Countries

China leads in total publications (TP = 39), total citations (TC = 517), and total link strength (TLS = 3942), thereby suggesting its major influence in the research network on distributed finance, sustainability, and green energy. With 19 papers and a rather high citation count (TC = 497), India follows with significant influence despite less outputs. With just 13 publications, the United Kingdom demonstrates strong TLS = 3003, which reflects its significant cooperative efforts. Though they have less publications and citations, countries including Malaysia, Vietnam, and Saudi Arabia have rather high TLS, suggesting active participation into international research networks. Particularly concerning rising economies and high-impact but lower-output nations, these trends point to prospects for future comparative and cooperative research.

Table 8. Country-wise bibliographic coupling

Country	TP	TC	TLS
china	39	517	3942
india	19	497	3083
united kingdom	13	120	3003
malaysia	4	29	1633
viet nam	4	54	1491
australia	6	178	1376
saudi arabia	6	21	1184
south korea	5	18	1073
france	7	98	1049
canada	5	29	1048

3.4.2 Bibliographic Coupling of Documents

Based on total citations (TC) and total link strength (TLS), the data emphasizes significant papers in the field. While Kakinuma (2024) has the greatest TLS (81), suggesting great bibliographic connectedness and integration in the research network, Goodell (2022) stands out with the most citations (TC = 57), thereby indicating tremendous intellectual influence. High citations and link strength in recent works such Piserà (2024) and Ali (2024) imply instantaneous relevance and visibility. Emerging multiple 2024 papers (e.g., Yu, Hsieh, Iuga) in the top ranks demonstrates increasing research momentum and offers a rich foundation for future evaluations and subject extensions.

Together with theme grouping among eminent writers, this VOSviewer author co-citation network map visualizes cooperative links. Prominent nodes including Kumar (2025), Schulz (2021), Cao (2022), Li (2022), and Saxena (2023) point to these writers as having significant roles in the scholarly debate on sustainable finance, green energy, and technical innovation. Different clusters reflect theme groupings; for example, the blue cluster (e.g., Saxena, Abakah) may investigate FinTech integration or risk modeling while the green cluster (e.g., Cao, Li, John) is targeted on environmental finance or ESG-linked studies. Offering a strong basis for spotting co-authorship possibilities and future cooperation chances in green finance, ESG analysis, and sustainable innovation, the centrality and interlinkages indicate rising research fronts and significant knowledge providers.

Table 9. Bibliographic coupling of key documents

Document	TC	TLS
kakinuma (2024)	6	81
yu (2024)	2	69
piserà (2024)	30	64
husain (2023)	25	59
ali (2024)	25	54
cagli (2023)	10	54
hsieh (2024)	21	48
iuga (2024)	1	47
gaies (2025)	1	47
goodell (2022)	57	47

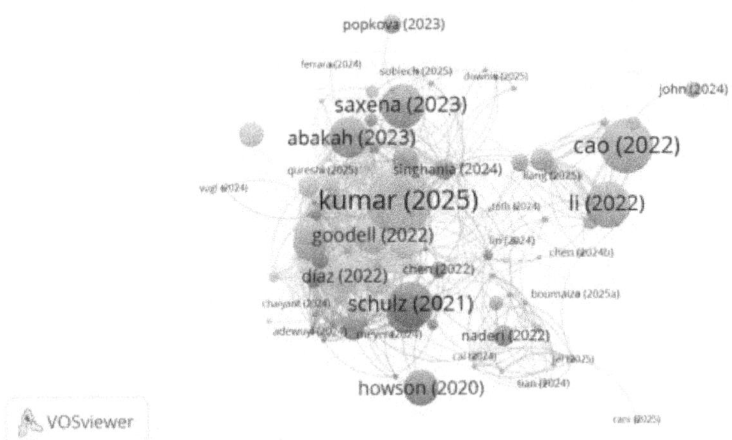

3.4.3 Bibliographic Coupling of Institutions

Two main clusters—one centered on Chinese institutions like the China Energy Engineering Group and Yunnan University and another involving Indian and European institutions like Jaipuria Institute of Management and Birla Institute of Management—are revealed by the institutional collaboration network. Emerging as a pivotal hub, Lyon Catholic University (UCLY) links both clusters and emphasizes its important contribution to promote regional cooperation. Though they publish less articles, institutions from Australia and India show great citation impact and significant link strength, thereby implying powerful and extensively connected research. Especially, JIS College of Engineering shows increasing multidisciplinary effort combining engineering with finance. Overall, the map and indicators highlight in sustainable finance and fintech a worldwide integrated and diversified research scene.

Table 10. Bibliographic coupling of research institutions

Organization	TP	TC	TLS
dcu business school, dublin city university, dublin 09, ireland	1	175	1054
department of management studies, malaviya national institute of technology jaipur, rajasthan, jaipur, 302017, india	1	175	1054
jindal global business school, o p jindal global university, haryana, sonipat, india	1	175	1054
school of business, swinburne university of technology, jalan simpang tiga, sarawak, kuching, 93350, australia	1	175	1054
swinburne business school, swinburne university of technology, john street, hawthorn, 3122, vic, australia	1	175	1054
symbiosis centre for management and human resource development, symbiosis international (deemed university), pune, india	1	175	1054
department of economics, university of victoria, victoria, bc, canada	2	2	850
department of finance, faculty of business and law, deakin university, burwood, australia	2	2	850
ucly (lyon catholic university), esdes, lyon, france	2	5	844
department of electrical engineering, jis college of engineering, west bengal, kolkata, 741235, india	1	77	751

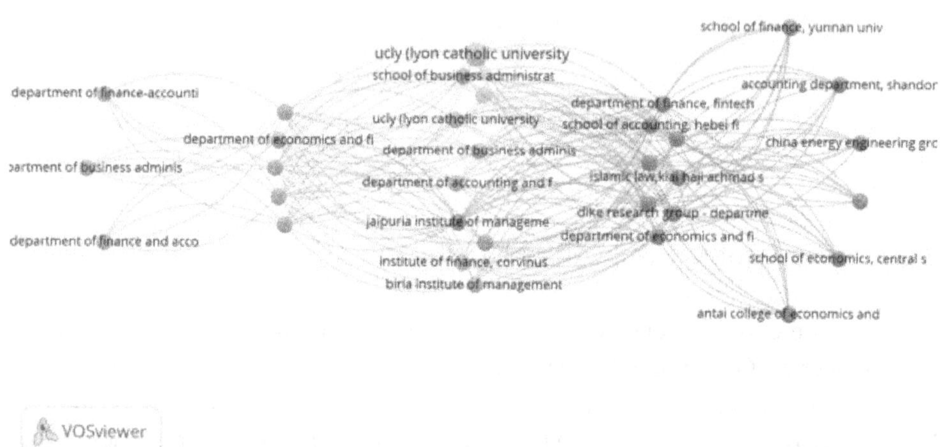

3.4.4 Bibliographic Coupling of Sources

The co-citation network of the journal emphasizes how multidisciplinary FinTech and sustainability research is. Reflecting their essential roles in bridging environmental and financial viewpoints, central to the network are Journal of Environmental Management and International Review of Economics and Finance. Furthermore important and implying great involvement with innovation and sustainability transitions are technological forecasting and social change and Journal of Cleaner Production.

Although they publish less overall, journals such as the British Accounting Review exhibit strong total link strength, therefore showing strong integration within the citation network. In parallel, Sustainability (Switzerland), Resources Policy, and Renewable and Sustainable Energy Reviews link policy, economic, and environmental spheres. The existence of publications like Energy Economics and Energies validates the energy-finance nexus as a crucial area of research frontiers.

Table 11. Leading journals by bibliographic coupling strength

Source	TP	TC	TLS
british accounting review	2	2	163
journal of environmental management	7	2	158
international review of economics and finance	4	89	148
journal of cleaner production	4	38	118
international journal of ethics and systems	1	6	98
renewable and sustainable energy reviews	2	26	90
technological forecasting and social change	5	147	86
international journal of emerging markets	1	30	69
energy economics	5	12	67
energies	4	23	63

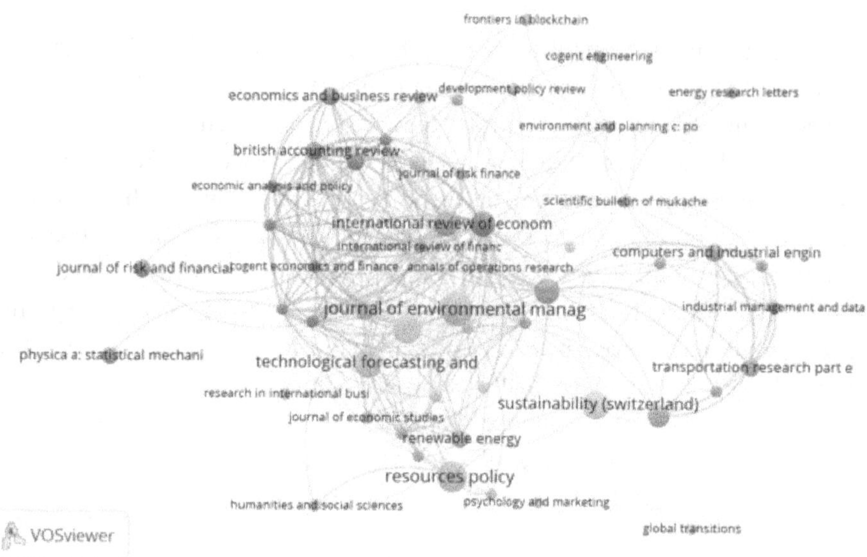

4. CONCLUSION

This paper highlights a multifaceted scholarly change over the 2020–2025 timeframe in the changing research terrain at the junction of virtual money and green finance. While citation patterns—peaking in 2022 and broadening thereafter—suggest a developing research field shifting from niche study to more general theme engagement, a consistent increase in total publications highlights expanding intellectual interest. Rising non-cited articles in recent years suggest continuous diversification and the inherent lag in citation acquisition for new research.

According to the bibliometric study, both active and high-impact individual contributors help to define the domain. Writers such Satish Kumar, Lim, and Sharma show great impact; their frequently cited works add to intellectual impetus. Key publications' disciplinary breadth—from Technological Forecasting and Social Change to Earth System Governance—also illustrates the field's increasing interdisciplinarity, combining ideas from sustainability, innovation, and finance technology.

Geographically speaking, China and India lead in terms of publishing volume and influence; nations like Ireland and the United Kingdom show great referencing impact and cooperative integration. Similar distribution of institutional contributions exists; no one university dominates but several, such DCU Business School and Chinese

Academy of Sciences, greatly supporting high-impact research. Dense clusters of co-authorship and institutional networks, mostly in Asia and parts of Europe, point to the creation of regional research ecosystems. Rising multidisciplinary interaction is highlighted by emerging institutions such as JIS College of Engineering. Thematic study of keywords and co-occurrence networks finds "decentralized finance," "green economy," and "sustainability" as central research anchors. Emphasizing the junction of environmental responsibility and financial innovation, these are intimately related with technical ideas such blockchain and cryptocurrencies. With close ties between environmental science, economics, policy studies, and technological predictions, co-citation and co-authorship networks support even more the multidisciplinary character of the area.

With growing momentum surrounding the function of FinTech—especially decentralised finance—in promoting sustainable development goals, the study exposes generally a globally linked and topically variegated research terrain. Especially in underrepresented areas, future research should give deeper investigation of regional differences, policy effects top priority. Actionable insights and assuring inclusive growth in this developing field of green digital finance will be greatly shaped by comparative studies, longitudinal tracking, and evaluations of institutional collaborations.

5. IMPLICATIONS

The study contributes to the growing discourse on the nexus between FinTech and environmental sustainability, reinforcing decentralized finance as a conceptual bridge between financial innovation and green transition. It calls for expanded theoretical frameworks that incorporate sustainability into digital financial models.

Policymakers should consider the potential of blockchain-based and virtual currency technologies to facilitate green finance initiatives. Effective regulatory frameworks are essential to ensure environmental benefits while mitigating financial and technological risks.

Universities and research institutions should strengthen interdisciplinary collaborations, integrating environmental science, finance, and technology curricula. Institutions with emerging influence, especially in India and Asia-Pacific, should be supported to maintain momentum in high-impact research. FinTech developers and green finance practitioners should explore sustainable applications of virtual currencies, particularly in carbon markets, green bonds, and ESG investments. Insights from co-authorship networks can guide the formation of innovation alliances and knowledge transfer partnerships.There is a pressing need for longitudinal and comparative studies focusing on underrepresented regions such as Africa and

Latin America. Further investigations should address the real-world environmental outcomes of digital finance adoption and assess DeFi's integration into global sustainability frameworks.

REFERENCES

Ali, F., Khurram, M. U., Sensoy, A., & Vo, X. V. (2024). Green cryptocurrencies and portfolio diversification in the era of greener paths. *Renewable & Sustainable Energy Reviews, 191*, 114137. DOI: 10.1016/j.rser.2023.114137

Aria, M., & Cuccurullo, C. (2017). bibliometrix: An R-tool for comprehensive science mapping analysis. *Journal of Informetrics, 11*(4), 959–975. DOI: 10.1016/j.joi.2017.08.007

Chamanara, S., & Madani, K. (2023). *The Hidden Environmental Cost of Cryptocurrency: How Bitcoin Mining Impacts Climate, Water and Land. United Nations University Institute for Water, Environment and Health.* UNU-INWEH.

Donthu, N., Kumar, S., Mukherjee, D., Pandey, N., & Lim, W. M. (2021). How to conduct a bibliometric analysis: An overview and guidelines. *Journal of Business Research, 133*, 285–296. DOI: 10.1016/j.jbusres.2021.04.070

Evite, P. M. (2023). Bitcoin's Climate Impact: Carbon Emissions and Beyond. *Available atSSRN* 4650650. DOI: 10.2139/ssrn.4650650

Goyal, K., & Kumar, S. (2021). Financial literacy: A systematic review and bibliometric analysis. *International Journal of Consumer Studies, 45*(1), 80–105. DOI: 10.1111/ijcs.12605

Ibañez, J. I., Ladda, A., Tasca, P., & Aldred, L. (2024). The Unintended Carbon Consequences of Bitcoin Mining Bans: A Paradox in Environmental Policy. *arXiv preprint arXiv:2411.07254.*

Khosravi, A., & Säämäki, F. (2023). Beyond Bitcoin: Evaluating energy consumption and environmental impact across cryptocurrency projects. *Energies, 16*(18), 6610. DOI: 10.3390/en16186610

Koemtzopoulos, D., Zournatzidou, G., Ragazou, K., & Sariannidis, N. (2025). Cryptocurrencies Transit to a Carbon Neutral Environment: From Fintech to Greentech Through Clean Energy and Eco-Efficiency Policies. *Energies (19961073), 18*(2).

Koemtzopoulos, D., Zournatzidou, G., & Sariannidis, N. (2025). Can Cryptocurrencies Be Green? The Role of Stablecoins Toward a Carbon Footprint and Sustainable Ecosystem. *Sustainability (Basel), 17*(2), 483. DOI: 10.3390/su17020483

Kohli, V., Chakravarty, S., Chamola, V., Sangwan, K. S., & Zeadally, S. (2023). An analysis of energy consumption and carbon footprints of cryptocurrencies and possible solutions. *Digital Communications and Networks*, *9*(1), 79–89. DOI: 10.1016/j.dcan.2022.06.017

Krishnamurthy, N. (2023). Improving Sustainability: A Cryptocurrency-Based Reward Scheme for Reducing Carbon Emissions. *International Journal on Recent and Innovation Trends in Computing and Communication*, *11*(4), 413–419. Advance online publication. DOI: 10.17762/ijritcc.v11i4.9852

Mishra, D., Gunasekaran, A., Papadopoulos, T., & Dubey, R. (2018). Supply chain performance measures and metrics: A bibliometric study. *Benchmarking*, *25*(3), 932–967. DOI: 10.1108/BIJ-08-2017-0224

Onat, N., Jabbar, R., Kucukvar, M., & Fetais, N. (2021). Bitcoin and global climate change: Emissions beyond borders.

Packard, L., Singh, A. K., & Oguntoye, O. (2022). Crypto has an emissions challenge: Here's what leaders can do about it. *Future Technology, 1*(3), 06-13.

Page, M. J., McKenzie, J. E., Bossuyt, P. M., Boutron, I., Hoffmann, T. C., Mulrow, C. D., ... & Moher, D. (2021). The PRISMA 2020 statement: an updated guideline for reporting systematic reviews. *bmj, 372*.

Park, S., Han, N., & Kim, E.-J. (2011). A Study on the Green Finance and Carbon Finance. *Muyeog Yeon'gu*, *7*(4), 345–363. DOI: 10.16980/jitc.7.4.201112.345

Pattnaik, D., Hassan, M. K., Kumar, S., & Paul, J. (2020). Trade credit research before and after the global financial crisis of 2008–A bibliometric overview. *Research in International Business and Finance*, *54*, 101287. DOI: 10.1016/j.ribaf.2020.101287 PMID: 34173403

Paul, J., Lim, W. M., O'Cass, A., Hao, A. W., & Bresciani, S. (2021). Scientific procedures and rationales for systematic literature reviews (SPAR-4-SLR). *International Journal of Consumer Studies*, *45*(4), O1–O16. DOI: 10.1111/ijcs.12695

Shao, H., Cheng, J., Wang, Y., & Li, X. (2022). Can digital finance promote comprehensive carbon emission performance? Evidence from Chinese cities. *International Journal of Environmental Research and Public Health*, *19*(16), 10255. DOI: 10.3390/ijerph191610255 PMID: 36011889

Truby, J. (2018). Decarbonizing Bitcoin: Law and policy choices for reducing the energy consumption of Blockchain technologies and digital currencies. *Energy Research & Social Science*, *44*, 399–410. DOI: 10.1016/j.erss.2018.06.009

Valtakoski, A. (2020). The evolution and impact of qualitative research in Journal of Services Marketing. *Journal of Services Marketing*, *34*(1), 8–23. DOI: 10.1108/JSM-12-2018-0359

Verma, N., Dhiman, B., Singh, V., Kaur, J., Guleria, S., & Singh, T. (2024). Exploring the global landscape of work-life balance research: A bibliometric and thematic analysis. *Heliyon*, *10*(11), e31662. DOI: 10.1016/j.heliyon.2024.e31662 PMID: 38828335

Wu, H., Wen, H., Li, G., Yin, Y., & Zhang, S. (2024). Unlocking a greener future: The role of digital finance in enhancing green total factor energy efficiency. *Journal of Environmental Management*, *364*, 121456. DOI: 10.1016/j.jenvman.2024.121456 PMID: 38875989

Xiao, Z., Cui, S., Xiang, L., Liu, P. J., & Zhang, H. (2023). The environmental cost of cryptocurrency: Assessing carbon emissions from bitcoin mining in China. *Journal of Digital Economy*, *2*, 119–136. DOI: 10.1016/j.jdec.2023.11.001

Zhang, M., Wu, Y., & Su, H. (2025). The Influence of Green Finance on" Dual Carbon" Goals: Analyzing the Functions of Government and Market. *Sustainability (2071-1050)*, *17*(3).

Zhao, X., Zhang, S., Ahmad, N., Wang, S., & Zhao, J. (2024). Unlocking Sustainable Growth: The Transformative Impact of Green Finance on Industrial Carbon Emissions in China. *Sustainability (Basel)*, *16*(18), 8253. DOI: 10.3390/su16188253

Chapter 12
The Role of Social Media in Shaping Consumer Attitudes Towards Digital Currencies Services

Himani Devi
https://orcid.org/0009-0008-3754-7145
Graphic Era University, India

Amit Kumar Uniyal
Graphic Era University, India

Jayshree Chhetri
https://orcid.org/0009-0000-3383-6857
Graphic Era University, India

Amar Johri
Saudi Electronic University, Saudi Arabia

ABSTRACT

Cryptocurrency has been a very popular issue in recent years. There was a lot of discussion going on regarding prohibition of cryptocurrencies as a medium of exchange. Online currency services are transforming the new financial landscape and the changes made in consumer consumption patterns. This chapter will examine how social media websites shape consumer perception and intentions toward adoption of digital currencies like bitcoin, litecoin and stablecoins. This chapter examines the influence of social media platforms on consumer preference and adoption intentions towards digital currency services,with a special focus on the role of influencer mar-

DOI: 10.4018/979-8-3373-0315-4.ch012

keting and trust building mechanism.The findings tell the importance for businesses and policymakers to leverage digital platforms and communications for promotion and adoption of digital financial services by consumers, underscoring the need for new regulatory frameworks that balance innovation with consumer protection in this rapidly evolving digital financial landscape.

INTRODUCTION

The internet has revolutionized the way the real economy operates. One of the interesting features of the world of the internet is an upsurge of digital currencies like bitcoin, Litecoin, Stablecoin, Utility token to mention a few are the best known ones. A digital currency can be best described as a substitute currency that is purely electronic and hence there is no material form. It is not printed by any particular central bank or government of any particular nation and it is in effect disconnected from the actual economy. Bitcoin, introduced for the first time in 2008, is a peer-to-peer electronic currency that is exchanged on public exchanges and which can be transmitted instantly between any two individuals anywhere in the world with the velocity of an email and at much lower expense than transactions cleared through the conventional financial system (Forbes.com)2. Real inception of bitcoin was in 2009. Since 2009 the bitcoin has gone through dramatic variations characterized by massive growth and shrinkage of its value, ridden by publicity. Printed money is not used by bitcoin. It's just digital. The money is made on the computer by a group of individuals around the world. The network, or the group, anyone can enter that, (according to Coindesk.com)1.

This system handles purchases with the digital currency. Bitcoins are kept in a ——digital wallet on the Internet or the user's hard drive. There isn't an endless supply of bitcoins. Rules were established by Nakamoto(3) limiting the currency to 21 million bitcoins. By this time it could be prudent to offer a brief definition on what in the past has been known with peer-to-peer lending. As the European Commission clarifies, peer-to-peer lending is one form of crowdfunding – the crowd lends cash to a business with the advanced knowledge that the cash will be paid back plus interest. As an illustration a usual bank borrowing can be provided, except that peer-to-peer translates into borrowing from many investors (European Commission, 2015)(4) investment in firms or ventures is well not the key driver of the application of virtual currencies.There are now more than 1,700 new, privately owned and operated digital currencies worldwide and the stampede to establish them is not slowing down.10 The first one was Bitcoin, which was created in 2009.

The bitcoin cycle price at the beginning of 2013 was around $13 per bitcoin and by most accounts reached an incredible height of $230 during the month of April, producing, in theory, a profit of at least 1700 percent in under four months. Later on during the same year, the price further skyrocketed to $395 in November.

The bitcoins cannot be explained as per any such theories, it is apart from those GDP, interest rates, inflation, unemployment, etc. It doesn't rely on any macro economical factor for pricing bitcoins, economy-fixed currency just has the amount that is based on a publicly known algorithm, and the rate is driven by expected profitability for holding the currency due to no interest rates of the digital currencies. The market is currently dominated by short term investors, trend chasers and speculators. So, in the end, the hopes of all investors about the continuous growth are the only thing which decides about the cost of digital currency, as their sentiments become increasingly variable parameters.

WHAT IS DIGITAL CURRENCY?

The term digital means which is in the electronic form and not in the physical form (can not be stored, handheld or manipulated) we generally name it by calling out digital money, electronic money, electronic currency or cyber currency. Digital money is money which exists only in banking computer systems and is not held in any physical form. It is a type of digital money that manage the creation of new units and protects transactions by means of cryptographic techniques . Cryptocurrencies make use of a decentralised record called a blockchain to authenticate translations and enable them to exist without any central authority. Adoption of digital currency is determined by different parameters like psychological and technological. Existing literature is based on the (TAM) Technology Acceptance Model, Unified Theory of Acceptance and Use of Technology (UTAUT), and Innovation Diffusion Theory identifies perceived usefulness, perceived risk, social influence, and trust as main drivers. Moreover, evidence also shows that online communities and social networking sites play an important role in influencing consumer attitudes toward new technology by providing information and creating peer-level recommendations. Before the arrival of digital money and cryptocurrencies, conversion of history money was done in many forms with certain commodities such as wheel, beads or cows. Till today's era, money has transformed immensely with the current form of digital model. Today, the virtual currency, an advanced version of digital money, is a landmark for the modern money transformation. Cryptocurrencies are gradually developing at a good pace in the financial industry, as compared to their origin. 11

Technology Acceptance Model(TAM): It is an information systems theory that models how users come to accept a technology and how they use that technology. It was developed by Fred Davis in 1989.

TRA suggests that a person's behavioural intention depends on the person's attitude about the behaviour(would I do this sort of thing normally.?) and subjective norms (Would I do this sort of thing normally?) and subjective norms (would other people in the group do this.?)

Theory of Planned Behaviour (TPB)

TPB adds the notion of perceived behavioural control which refers to a person's perceptions of their ability to perform a given behaviour.

Unified theory of Acceptance and Use of Technology (UTAUT)

The theoretical model of UTAUT suggests that the actual use of technology is determined by behavioural intention. The perceived likelihood of adopting the technology is dependent on the technology is dependent on the direct effect of four key determinants, namely performance expectancy, effort expectancy, social influence and facilitating conditions. The effect of predictors is moderated by age, gender, experience and voluntariness of use.

Few Characteristics

1. These currencies can be accessible with the help of computer or mobile phones.
2. Advantage of using these currencies is they do not have any intermediaries making it the cheapest method to trade.
3. One more - all crypto currencies are digital currencies, not every digital currencies are cryptocurrencies.
4. There are few disadvantages of using digital currency that they can volatile to trade and all.
5. Only exist in Digital form. Have no physical attributes.
6. Digital currencies can be centralized by the government or can be decentralized

For example:

Fiat currency - it exists physically and is centralized by the system of production and distribution among the public and has been noticed by the banks and agencies.

Whereas crypto currencies like bitcoin and dogecoin are prominent examples of a decentralized currency system. Although digital currency can transfer the value. They can be used for selling and buying goods and services.

Different Types of Digital Currencies

1.Crypto currencies: are the virtual currencies that are based on cryptography to secure and verify transactions not only that cryptography also help in managing and control. It is a type of digital money that manage the creation of new units and protects transactions by means of cryptographic techniques . Cryptocurrencies make use of a decentralised record called a blockchain to authenticate translations and enable them to exist without any central authority. Cryptocurrencies markets are quite delicate to many events. The selling volume in the biggest cryptocurrency has seen a massive growth with an increase in their prices too. The acceleration of interest and trading volume impacts the capability of the crypto market. 12

Pros:

Anonymity: There is no central authority to govern the transactions, and they are pseudonyms.

High value appreciation potential: The prices of most cryptocurrencies have appreciated by a very large margin within the last several years.

Cons:

Vulnerable to price manipulation: This coupled with high volatility in fluctuation of prices are the characteristics of certain types of cryptocurrencies.

Absence of regulation: No proper regulation as in a normal currency, thus giving more exposure to risk for investors.

2.Central Bank Digital Currency (CBDC): the digital currency that central banks issue and maintain. CBDCs have been developed so that they can retain the trust and reliability of traditional currencies while providing several benefits of digital currencies, such as fast, secure, and low-cost transactions.

Pros:

Transaction efficiency and security are made better: CBDCs enable faster and completely secure transactions.

Greater control and supervision by governments: Governments can monitor monetary policy with CBDCs.

Cons:

Threats to privacy and financial freedom: CBDCs may give governments greater access to an individual's financial records. Reliance on central authorities: CBDCs are issued and regulated by central authorities, which limits their decentralization.

3.**Virtual currencies:** are generally unregulated forms of currency that are controlled by the developers or by its defined network protocols.Virtual currencies are presently the unregulated digital currency in use either virtually or at the online gaming environment in effecting transactions among users. These transactions mostly concern the purchasing of virtual goods such as weapons or clothes for avatars. This currency is somewhat centralised, being controlled by the developers or the founding organisation who runs the whole process.

Pros:

Convenient and simple transactions: Online transactions are made easier and more comfortable by using virtual currencies, which cut out the need for conventional banking.

Accessibility and inclusiveness: They give financial services to people without access to standard banking institutions.

Cons:

Flat out lack of government regulation: They are really exposed to fraud and scams given the absence of any governmental regulation of the virtual currencies.

Volatility: Virtual currencies can be characterized as being extremely volatile, thus exposing themselves to very high risk in holding them as investments or using them.

Lack of government regulation: Virtual currencies have no government regulation, so they have been exposed to fraud and scams.

Volatility: Virtual currencies make themselves highly volatile and thus expose the risk of using them for investment.

4.Stable Coins: Stablecoins are digital currencies intended to have a stable value against a traditional currency or other asset. In effect, a stablecoin is often backed either by reserves of the underlying asset or through algorithms actively altering the supply of the stablecoin based on market demand.

Pros:

Stability and predictability: The idea behind stablecoins is that they will provide low volatility and a stable value.

Faster transaction processing and lower fees: Transactions using stablecoins can be much faster and cheaper than with some other digital currencies.

Cons: Safety of an underlying asset barometer: Stable coins are just as stable as the underlying asset they are pegged to.

The potential for added regulation and the absence of transparency: Because of stability and transparency issues, stable coins might be even more scrutinized by regulators.

BACKGROUND OF DIGITAL CURRENCY SERVICES

Cryptocurrency: Digital currency, also known as cryptocurrency, represents a transformative innovation in the world of finance and economics. Unlike traditional forms of money, which are physical and issued and regulated by governments or central banks, digital currencies exist purely in digital form and are not under the direct control of any Central authority .

Digital money is money which exists only in banking computer systems and is not held any physical form. It may refer to several systems which enable a buyer to pay electronically hy transmitting a unique number (called digital certificate) similar to a banknote number .

What are the Advantages of Accepting Digital Currencies?

1.Tap Into New Markets and Boost Your Revenue: Digital currencies provide innovative market opportunities. With around 420 million people using them globally, businesses can attract serious customers by providing this payment method. By rolling these out, sellers can cater to a global audience bypassing geographical restrictions and giving a boost to their customer base.

2.Expanding Demographics: The population of digital currency users is characterized by diversity and has been increasing. Included in this group are people well-versed in technology, youth, and worldwide consumers, who would rather conduct their transactions through virtual currencies. Businesses might reach these users, thus increasing their market penetration and customer engagement. They will have more room to play with different segments of consumers who do not rely on traditional forms of payment.

3.Say Goodbye to Chargebacks Forever: Chargebacks can be a huge problem, resulting in revenue loss and taking up precious time and resources. Transactions of digital currency, on the other hand, are irreversible, thus removing the possibility of chargebacks. This gives businesses a secure payment method, minimizing the occurrence of fraud and related financial losses. Finality of transactions guarantees that once payment is made, it cannot be reversed, protecting your revenue.

4.Enhanced Fraud Prevention: The non-reversibility of transactions in digital currency means that, once paid, the payment cannot be reversed by the payer. This significantly decreases the possibility of fraudulent chargebacks, giving businesses a safer and more predictable revenue stream. Another feature offered by blockchain technology is an open ledger of all transactions, including anonymous form of transaction, money transfer, and greater fraud prevention through features such as “know your customer” and anti-money laundering regulations.

5.Cut Currency Conversion Costs Effortlessly: Money conversion through the traditional way involves huge fees and the exchange rates do not remain stable. Another possible option is to introduce one digital currency that makes business operations free from being tied by the conventional exchange rates; thus saving money through this as well as avoiding such price fluctuation. Customers can provide payment in virtual currency, while business entities themselves can settle the amount into their bank accounts in fiat currency. It thus takes advantage of all the 'pros' of virtual currencies and helps easily cut costs associated with conversions. It also helps achieve prosperity through the use of stablecoins and crypto exchanges and whose result ultimately proves that cryptocurrency can validly be considered as money.

The use of a traditional currency conversion includes hefty service charges, difficult service charges, and fluctuating exchange rates. But with digital currencies, businesses would not only do away with conventional exchange rates but also save on costs through the conversion and avoid such price fluctuation. Customers can make payment in virtual currency, while business organizations can have amounts settled in their bank accounts in fiat. It takes advantage of all the pros available on-going with virtual currencies and makes it easy for you to cut costs by currency regulation. And by achieving prosperity through stablecoins and crypto exchange, one finally demonstrates currency can actually be used like money.

6.Streamlined International Transactions: The acceptance of digital currencies makes it easy to conduct international transactions. Companies can receive payments from global customers without considering exchange rates, and that makes cross-border business more effective and economical. This effectiveness minimizes the inconvenience of dealing with different currencies and streamlines financial services.

Disadvantages

1. **Scalability:** Perhaps the largest issues with cryptocurrencies are the issues with scaling that they present. Although the adoption and number of digital coins are growing very quickly, it still pales in comparison to the volume of transactions that payment behemoth, VISA, handles on a daily basis. Also, transaction speed is another key area where cryptocurrencies can't match VISA and Mastercard's level until infrastructure that provides these technologies is scaled unimaginably. Such evolution is intricate and challenging to achieve smoothly. Yet, various

solutions have already been suggested by some, such as lightning networks, sharding, and staking as solutions to address the scalability challenge.

2.Cybersecurity issues: Since it is a digital technology, cryptocurrencies will be susceptible to cyber security hacks, and potentially end up in the wrong hands of hackers. Already, we have seen proof of this, as several ICOs have been hacked and cost investors hundreds of millions of dollars this summer alone (one of these incidents alone saw $473 million lost). Ameliorating this will necessitate ongoing maintenance of security infrastructure, but we are already seeing many actors dealing with this directly, and employing more robust cybersecurity protocols than those utilised in the traditional banking industries.

3.Price volatility and lack of inherent value: Since it is a digital technology, cryptocurrencies will be susceptible to cyber security hacks, and potentially end up in the wrong hands of hackers. Already, we have seen proof of this, as several ICOs have been hacked and cost investors hundreds of millions of dollars this summer alone (one of these incidents alone saw $473 million lost). Ameliorating this will necessitate ongoing maintenance of security infrastructure, but we are already seeing many actors dealing with this directly, and employing more robust cybersecurity protocols than those utilised in the traditional banking industries.

4.Regulations: Although cryptocurrency is legal in most developed nations, it is not legally controlled by central governments. This lack of control and regulation within the world of cryptocurrency amplifies the likelihood of cryptocurrency scams and market manipulation. Until federal governments embrace and regulate cryptocurrencies on the same terms as fiat currency, like the U.S. dollar, there will always be a greater risk involved with investment.

5.Digital storage and infrastructure: Although they do not require any physical captivity but they have their own set of requirements for storages and processing. Online wallets with high security are very important to store these digital currencies.

6.Prone to hacking: being digitally connected over network and access through the internet. These currencies are susceptible to hacking. Hackers can steal digital currency or change the protocol making it unable to be used.

8.Limited adaptance: Not money people use for their daily day to day transactions. Although these currencies have popularity, people are not shitinh from the conventional way of making transactions.

9.Irreversibility: major disadvantage with these currencies are payments done through these currencies are reusable - Making it difficult for circumstances When payment is done by mistake or bh fraud.

Role of Social Media in Sale of Bitcoins

1.The role of social media in the sale of bitcoins is remarkable. Facebook, Twitter, Whatsapp, and social media channels, and also search engines such as Wikipedia, have contributed greatly in making bitcoins. Google Trend and Wikipedia have become good reference points for potential investors. Frequency of search terms related to the virtual currency can serve as a good index for interest in the currency and a good tool for people to buy bitcoins.
2.The price of bitcoins is having a direct relation with social media which in turn raises the price. The higher the interest in the number of users in social media, the more demand rises for bitcoins, and hence the price of bitcoins also rises. (1 BTC-74,000 into yesterday and is currently 431,550)
3.Investors earned a rise, through social media, whereas there is a direct relationship among users of social media and investors investing in bitcoins.
4.Bitcoin is a 24/7 market; it was found that every minute in social media, a total of 788 observations or searches happen with respect to bitcoins.
5.The others also promote bitcoins more; WhatsApp, one closely associated with bitcoin-making investments and buying.
6.Bitcoin is increasingly being controlled by social media and social networking sites. Bitcoin users are, however, treated as more democratic by the supporters of that view.

POWER OF SOCIAL MEDIA IN THE DIGITAL AGE

The power of social media in the digital age: Social media has become a very crucial part of our life, people from different corners of the world connect with each other using this platform. Today, social media is also being used as a crucial tool for organisations, as it provides better communication, audience engagement and digital marketing.

Social media platforms help the users to share the details of their product, images, videos and other information with the target audience to maintain engagement and trust. It also provides a range of tools to businesses to maintain good connection with the buyers in creative ways.

Digital marketing has risen mainly because of social media platforms, with businesses now able to target their audience with targeted advertising and maintain a deep connection with them. Social media provides businesses to build good relations with their customers by creatively engaging the buyers and creating loyalty. The speedy growth of crypto assets elevated questions about the appropriate regulatory framework to adopt to Volatile provisions. Productive regulations of financial services encourage long term economic stability and diminish the social cost and adverse outcomes from financial unsteadiness(13) Before digital money and cryptocurrencies' transformation history money had undergone several commodities such as shells, wheels, beads and even cows. And today, money has undergone a very significant transformation into a digital concept. Digital money exists in a virtual currency form which is considered an important milestone of modern transformation of money. Jothi and Gaffoor (2017) examined the influence of social media on online shopping and found that consumers tend to make more purchases when they engage with media due to increased access to information. Their study highlights that individuals aged 18-32 represent the largest group of buyers. Key factors influencing purchasing decisions include product quality, secure payment options and a diverse selection of products. On average, consumers spend approximately three hours on social media, primarily for social networking and information gathering. Before finalizing a purchase, they explore multiple alternatives, compare details, and evaluate options carefully.

Today, businesses have utilized social media sites to grow their business and a medium to communicate with their customers. Social media has offered different multimedia channels and is a device utilized in conveying to wider public or clients, thus the firms have to learn and adjust how to employ these social media in a manner that is suitable to their business strategy.

Social media platforms provide many opportunities, for example, online communities where people communicate and connect with each other from all parts of the world. Voramontri and Klieb (2019) found that social media plays a crucial role in consumer purchasing decisions, particularly for products requiring complex buying behaviour. Many consumers favor online shopping due to its affordability, time efficiency, ease of access, and wealth of information. Social media is frequently utilized for shopping because of its convenience and ability to provide detailed insights. Additionally, the quality of online review significantly influences purchase intentions and brand awareness, contributing to a positive overall impact.

Though there are many merits of social media, we cannot ignore the demerits of it. Social media can create a strong addiction in users, so it's critical to have a balanced use. There are other factors too that need to be taken care of, that is, online privacy and security and cyberbullying.

When social media platforms are used for brand promotions or creating online presence to make an audience engagement, it is referred to as social media marketing. Today's era of the digital world has already made significant changes in people's perception and the service provider's thoughts.

Social media was developed for maintaining interaction between people from different parts of the world but later it was adopted by the businesses and organisations, as it proved to be a very good source of communication and maintaining connections. It is a great advantage to use social media for reaching the end users and maintaining those connections. Social media provides you with the power to share information with anyone on earth and with countless people at one time. There are more than 3.8 billion users of social media across the globe stating the trust and addiction of people with the online platforms. Social media is quite dynamic and ever changing with new apps getting introduced frequently, for example, TikTok. The most liked and commonly used social media platforms are Facebook, YouTube, Twitter and Instagram.

These are some of the most popular social media platforms used by businesses and people for interacting with each other:

1. WhatsApp Messenger is an internationally available and free online platform. It is extremely popular as it provides end to end encryption and one can share information and make calls too. It is a highly secure and reliable platform.
2. Facebook is one of the most favourite networking websites that allows users to create their personal profile, upload and share pictures and videos. It is a great platform to stay connected with friends and family.
3. You-tube is a video sharing platform, where users can create their own videos and watch other people's videos. This platform was introduced in 2005 and acquired by google in 2006. The slogan of this platform is "Broadcast Yourself". Many companies and organisations use YouTube to promote their businesses too.
4. Twitter is a platform where people get to post their updates and see them as "tweets". This is used very commonly by people and trusted by all.

Platforms That Shape Financial Conversations

The need for social media for financial services is a fast growing sector. Earlier digital marketing was less in trend but after the pandemic, it has become a need to reach customers online too.

The financial service companies lacking social media promotion are less considered and less trusted.

The need of social media for financial services- The financial services that are not on social media, do not get to engage with the potential customers and build connections. Social media provides the much needed transparency to build trust with potential audiences.

Social media is a great advantage for financial services- There are countless benefits of using social media. Financial services is a trust and relationship based industry. The social media presence of a brand makes it trustworthy and connects with the audience. According to GlobalWebIndex 54% of people use social media platforms to search for products and services to generate leads which in turn gets converted into sales. Social media is an excellent platform to create brand awareness. No matter whether you are sharing your content organically or releasing paid ads, you can reach an audience globally, as it maximises your reach to every corner of the planet. The company can also collect their potential customers' data. To cite an example, one can check through LinkedIn about their target consumers, where they live and what they prefer. This is an effective way to create campaigns for targeting potential customers.

Social media platforms should be used effectively by the financial services: Social media marketing provides value to financial services. Financial services should use social media platforms by keeping the following things in mind:

Transparency- The financial services need to be very transparent and authentic with their consumers. As transparency builds trust and best connections.

Being Helpful- The financial services should provide the kind of content that helps and relates with people. The content should be informative and updated.

Building relationships- The social media platforms are mainly for building relationships. The financial services should display their original content and picture to build authentic relationships.

Top 3 Social Media Platforms for Financial Services

1. **LinkedIn:** This platform is best used to connect with many professionals and potential customers from all over the world. With over 850 million users in more than 180 countries, LinkedIn is a very reliable platform to generate new leads. It is a great platform to build relationships. It helps you build authority and it is used by many professionals. This is used best for social selling.
2. **Twitter:** This platform is quite perfect for sharing news, articles, and other information. It is more conversation based rather than other things. It is a very popular social media platform in the financial sector with more than 60% of the industry users. It is helpful to track data effectively by using twitter Analytics.

3. **Youtube**- This platform provides you with the opportunity to create good connections with potential customers. It's an absolutely perfect place to be authentic about your company and to show your audience your true authority. It's good for building long term content and engaging the target audience.

Influencers and User-Generated Content

Unlike traditional advertising, the content generated by influencers increases the credibility levels and creativity of social media influencers. This marketing strategy proves to be the best to connect with the audience personally and authentically.

What Exactly is the Content Generated by Influencers?

So the influencer generated content is basically the content that they create for any brand promotion. It incorporates images, videos, live broadcasting and blogs. The things that make their content stand distinct from others are influencer's creativity, different styles of branding, good engagement to promote products, in a manner that is transparent, honest and quite captivating. Chivandi et al.(2019) explored the role of social media in shaping consumer behaviour and service marketing. Their study highlighted how social media platforms influence brand awareness, ultimately affecting consumer decision-making and purchasing patterns. Additionally, the research examined how companies utilized these digital channels to engage with the public. Overall, social media has had a notable impact on both businesses and consumers. Unlike old marketing styles, influencer's content is designed to gel with the current narratives. This amalgamation makes sure that the content relates with the influencers audience and also fulfills the aims of the brand, maintaining a steady proportion of authenticity and brand promotion. In addition, the influencer's content is also associated with the organic campaigns. The content creators receive gifts or payments in kind from the brands, for example, free samples of the product, vouchers, paid trips and many more. This initiates and maintains a deep connection between influencers and the brands.

The Advantages of Influencer Generated Content

The brands looking for real connections with the audience prefer influencer generated content. The benefits are:

Trusted and credible: Influencers have built loyalty in their followers by posting authentic information. So when an influencer promotes your brand, it carries more weight than other conventional promotion techniques.

Wider audience reach and achieving target consumers: Well influencers generally have a large number of followers with specific niches. This makes it very easy for brands to reach consumers of all demographics.

Trust and Credibility in Social Media Messaging Services Related to Crypto Currency

The ever changing world of crypto currency compulsorily needs consumer's trust to run. Because only invest their money where they have their faith and trust. Strategic PR is what is needed here. So, PR services make the audience believe in you and have trust. The crypto market is becoming one of the most crucial in making political decisions and landscapes.

The PR for Crypto: A crypto PR can assist projects to come up with better crypto marketing. It enhances the brand's authenticity and creativity. So the social media platforms help you to connect with crypto agencies. The projects from crypto assist you in building image and becoming leaders in your field. In a survey done by a group of professionals, it was revealed that more than 40% participants around the world trust Bitcoin over their local currencies. Bitcoin is a decentralized digital currency that uses cryptography to secure transactions and control the supply of new coins. It operates on a peer-to-peer network, where every transaction is recorded on a public ledger called the blockchain. As the first digital currency to enable direct transfers of value without intermediaries, Bitcoin has pioneered a new approach to money. Today, it functions as both a medium of exchange and a store of value, influencing global finance and inspiring many other digital currencies

THE SIGNIFICANCE OF PR IN CRYPTO

PR campaigns are crucial for Crypto agencies because more than 60% of U.S adults have no faith in authenticity and safety in current crypto currency investments. This is the reason you need a prominent PR team to shape the consumers perception.

A strong Crypto PR team helps to develop trust and reliance in the crypto agency. Public Relation in crypto is higher than media outreach. Targeting the correct audience is also an integral part of a good PR team. PR teams make good strategies to connect with investors and traders. PR teams also aim to maintain the brand's reputation. One can use social media platforms to maintain brand image. A well designed crypto PR campaign protects the brand's image too.

Ways to make a solid PR foundation for crypto projects:

- Clear brand messaging

- Transparent and authentic communication
- Make a good founding team presence
- Interactions with the crypto communities
- Collaboration with PR agencies

Starting with the advantages

1. **Quick transfer**: The time taken to transfer the digital currencies is extremely fast. Reason behind these fast transfers is there is no involvement of any kind of intermediaries and currencies transfer only involve the transacting parties.
2. **No need of physical Manufacturing**: Physical currencies require production facilities to print notes, on the contrary these digital currencies do not require any such things, not only that these currencies are involved in damage and any kinds of physical defects.
3. **Monetary & Fiscal Policy Implementation:** In the current scenario Govt. or the federation work through a series of bodies that work as intermediaries (For eg: Bank, Financial institutions) to circulate Money in the Economy. Whereas Digital currencies can help simplify this mechanism and empower the government agencies to distribute the payment directly to the citizens of the country. They also help the government to spend on the production & transportation of notes from one location to another.
4. **Decentralized:** This means these are free from any type of control of the government or any financial institution. Users have true control over the use of these currencies.
5. **Privacy**: Transactions made through digital currencies are not linked to user personal data.Giving them better privacy also helps in maintaining confidentiality of their financial dealing.
6. **Accessible around the world:** These currencies and transactions only require good internet access and are very helpful to the one who does not have access to the Banking institution.

The FCA's Definition of Social Media

The policy needs to cover, and be consistent across, all the social media channels a firm uses.

Because the FCA's approach is 'media-neutral', the regulators view social media as just another channel, without specific dispensation or rules. Accordingly, firms need to ensure their social content meets all the criteria set out by the FCA. posts therefore need to meet the requirement to be fair. Clear and not misleading, which is one of the FCA's key tenets of consumer/client communications

The 2015 guidance has clarified the FCA's approach on risk warnings ; this is a major feature in the updated guidelines. The update approach Confirmed that the FCA was not changing its stance on social media promotions; namely, that they regulate promotions via social media as robustly as they do communications via any other channel.

Real-time promotions are those such as telephone or face-to-face conversations that cannot be pre-planned or approved in advance. As a result, these real-time promotions are subject to fewer regulatory requirements. Before the FCA's new guidance was released, there was always some debate as to whether social media would be reclassified as 'real time' (the FCA"s previous stance being that it was a non-real time channel). In fact. The 2015 update retired the regulator's previous view; that social media is non-real time and therefore subject to the same compliance requirements as a brochure letter or any other marketing collateral. This means that any social media posts made by a financial institution need to go through the same review and approvals process as any other marketing communication

In practice, this means any form of advertising or communications prospective customers by regulating financial services firms.

It includes:

- Print online, television and radio adverts
- Marketing brochures and literature
- Direct mail
- Web content
- Email marketing
- Social media
- Sales aids. Such as presentations

Within this, there are a couple of specific definitions of direct-offer financial promotions (a communication which specifically encourages anyone who responds to enter into direct agreement with the firm) and real-time financial promotions, which we cover in more detail in point 3.

Financial Authority Handbook

According to the FCA, financial promotions may be the consumer's main or only source of information That they base their decision on. This is a particular risk in the financial services sector because of the complex and often nature of financial products. The FCA's objective for financial promotions Is to ensure that They are 'fair. Clear and not misleading'. Any promotions that fail to meet these.

Requirements can be risky to consumers if they result in people buying the wrong product for their needs.

Is social media a real time Financial promotion? The FCA takes the view that social media is not interactive: it is therefore regulated in the same way as other financial promotions. And required the same compliance checks and approval.

This can prove a challenge- the appeal of social media from a marketing point of view Is its immediacy; a lengthy compliance process can delay you from getting a quick Opinion of the market or responding to a query.

The FCA's main objective is that financial promotions are 'fair, clear and not misleading'. Products and services need to be promoted in a balanced way, which means that their claims must be realistic and information on key risk needs to be fair and prominently displayed. Promotions need to give sufficient information on the product to enable consumers to make an informed choice. Information on past performance needs to be representative and not overly prominent, so that consumers' expectations of the product are realistic. Also central to the FCA's expectations is that firms are treating customers fairly, a key tenet of which is that customers receive clear information about products and services marketed to them.

Because the FCA's approach is 'media-neutral', the regulator views social media as' just another channel', without special; dispensation or rules. Accordingly, firms need to ensure Accordingly, firms need to ensure their social content meets all the criteria set out by the FCA: posts therefore need to meet the requirement to be 'fair, clear and not misleading, which is one of the FCA's key tenets of consumer/client communications. The 2015 guidance has clarified the FCA's approach on risk warnings, this is a major feature in the updated guidelines.

The 2006 guidance was not specific on the need for risk warnings in social media, the Interference from the previous approach was that a tweet or other post could refer a consumer to a website that contained the relevant compliance information. The new guidelines are clear on this, stating that each communication via social media needs to comply with the relevant rules on a standalone basis. This therefore limits firms' ability to be promotional on social media-particularly in character-limited platforms, such as Twitter, where each post needs to be 140 characters or less. The content of posts therefore needs to be carefully considered to ensure that they do not inadvertently constitute a promotion, and require a risk warning.

Is Social Media the Best Option?

Because of this, firms should think carefully about whether social media is the best channel for their message. The need for standalone compliance might mean that in some cases another channel, without limitations on characters or words, might be a better option. Alternatively, the use of relevant images can provide a useful alternative to wordy posts. In the guidance, the FCA reminds firms that it remains possible to advertise their presence in the market through Image advertising in a way that is less likely to present difficulties with character limits. This is something that firms are likely to want to consider, given the limitations governing written social media posts. Nyagadza, B. (2020), in a research article states that developing a good connection with the buyers through social media can make people recommend the business to other buyers too. Social media marketing is about developing good customer relationships via platforms like Facebook, Instagram, twitter and many more. It allows businesses to connect with their potential consumers who are actually interested in the brand and the products they are offering. It helps to build loyal and long term relationships with people. 15

The FCA's view on hashtags pension regulation might use pensions to ensure that Twitter would show their tweet to anyone searching for pensions content under the pensions' hashtag.

Clicking on a hashtag such as pensions, however, takes the user not to a page where a specific firm's content is shown, but a curated page that brings together all the posts using that hashtag. As a result, the FCA believes that the use of hashtags has the potential to confuse the reader.

Clarity on sharing content Another area clarified in the 2015 update is that of endorsement or sharing of content. The new guidance makes it clear that the regulator believes that if a firm or adviser re-tweets, shares or likes someone else's positive post about their product or service, this constitutes a financial promotion, saying that:

If the customer's tweet comments on or endorses the benefits of a regulated financial product or service, then sharing or forwarding by the firm will constitute a promotion by the firm This has implications for firms' & advisers' sharing of content posted by others.

If someone else shares content posted by a firm, the firm remains liable for the compliance of the original post. There needs to be an audit trail of approval, and evidence of any changes that have been requested by the Compliance team, with documented comments, amendments and approvals, in most firms, this process will be managed jointly by the marketing team, who produce the financial promotions, and the compliance team, who approve them and ensure they meet the requirements. Your compliance team will know whether your promotion breaches any of the FCA's regulations, and will advise on any changes that need to be made.

It can be a challenge to keep track of suggested amendments and document the approvals process, particularly when there are a number of people involved or numerous versions of a promotion. Clear processes and documentation are essential. Because the FCA is interested in reviewing not just the promotions themselves, but the compliance approval process, Marketing teams must ensure they get the necessary approvals and sign off-and document them, to create an audit trail, If the

FCA audits your firm, they will want to see not only that your promotions meet requirements, but that the way they were produced and signed off does too. This applies to advisers as well as employees.

COULD BITCOIN BECOME A GLOBAL CURRENCY?

Does Bitcoin have a potential to become a universal currency? Bitcoin is unable to do so neither any crypto or regular currency can. The idea of universal currency is inaccurate. The thesis of optimal currency areas proves that currency areas have an optimal size. A currency may be known as optimum currency area (Oca) rely on the economic and political unity in that area . Nobel laureate Robert Mundell noted “the optimum currency area is not the world” Mundell (1961).For policy makes Monetary autonomy is a major component to maintain local economies by ward off extreme inflammation or definition. Even the European Monetary Union (EMU) consist of similar countries that have a shortage of complete political integration. Considering the difficulty to equip political unity in a group of about twenty countries that are alike in various ways, the possibilities that it could be equipped on a world-wide scale are zero.

The way we manage finance is changing quickly with the advancement of technology,

In the current age thanks to blockchain technology- Decentralised finance (defi) is a new way to operate financial services which is open to everyone, accessible to everyone and a very transparent financial ecosystem which doesn’t depend upon banks or any other financial body . As it is gaining popularity it’s very important for us to prepare ourselves to learn about the financial ecosystem of DeFI, equipped ourselves by learning new technologies, understanding the risk and changing our thought about financial independency. To adapt ourselves fast - Education is the key - Terms like Blockchain, smart contracts, and DeFi protocol might sound difficult to grasp, but by giving some time to learn these things is very essential.

Starting with DeFi - it involves tools like DEXs (Decentralised exchange) - these tools basically use for trading of cryptocurrency, providing a common platform to lend and borrow and earn interest in digital assets . We should also learn about CRYPTOGRAPHY (technology which helps in securing all the data and digital information), how decisions are made in blockchain, and also learn about the benefits and downside of decentralization . And the best way to learn is through online courses and having conversation with people who are using DeFi. To get started, you'll need a digital wallet to store and use cryptocurrency. There are two types: non-custodial (you're in control) and custodial (someone else manages it). To feel confident, start with small transactions and learn about fees (called “gas” fees).

You should also know how to track transactions and check smart contracts using blockchain explorers.

Consumer Perceptions of Digital Currency Services

Cryptocurrency is no longer just a niche for technology geeks. It is a global financial revolution that's catching the attention of regular consumers, businesses and investors alike. But as entrepreneurs consider how to add cryptocurrencies to their offerings or services, it is essential to know how customers view this digital asset class. Consumer Buying Behaviour is the process and action individuals take to make purchasing decisions. It begins with the recognition of need or wants, followed by an information search, evaluation of alternatives, purchase decision, post purchase evaluation, and potential repurchase or disposal. It plays an important role in marketing, allowing businesses to comprehend why and how consumers select specific products or services.Covid-19, An epidemic in Bangladesh- A research on American consumer behaviour by Suman et al. (2021) displayed that the people attending the community activities (meet-ups, discussions and browsing) impact brand associated behaviour. The consumer's brand identity favourably impacts contentment. Ara eti, I, et, al, (2021) found that social media marketing instigated the consumer purchase intention during the COVID 19.14

Purchase intentions are often quantified and employed by marketing managers as a decision input for new and current products and services. Consumer Purchase intentions are correlated and forecast subsequent sales.

Now we are going to highlight five essential customer perceptions about crypto and offer actionable insights for entrepreneurs who will guide regarding the crypto ecosystem.

1.Customers View crypto as a high risk Investment: For many customers, the idea of investing in cryptocurrency is like taking a risk in all. With unpredictable prices and constant rumors of extreme price fluctuations, users tend to think of crypto as a volatile, risky asset. Businesspersons need to mitigate these issues through open disclosure regarding crypto risks and benefits.

2.Crypto is technical and complex: While people adopt the crypto currency on the rise, most of the customers think that it is too complex and difficult to understand or use . The jargon that comes with blockchains wallets and keys might drive away non technical consumer those don't know how to use cryptocurrency

Lack of people guidance might discourage potential users from interacting with your product

3. Security is at high risk: Crypto currencies' association with scams, hacks and fraud is the most important barrier to trust for many customers. Stories of exchange breaches or phishing wary of crypto related platforms building a secure and transparente ecosystem is important for customer confidence consumers should check the certification to build trust .
4. Crypto as a payment option: Despite concerns, many customers are fascinated by the idea of using cryptocurrency as a payment method . The promise of cheap instant and borderless transactions applies to those seeking alternatives to traditional banking systems. Integrating digital currency transactions can attract tech- savvy customers and broaden your global reach . Customer also appreciate businesses that embrace innovation and offer diverse payment options

Example:

In 2021, the President of EL Salvador declared that their government will introduce Bitcoin as a legal tender. The position of USD dollar as legal tender will be retained too. So, basically the country is operating on two kinds of currencies at the same time. These two types of money may oscillate against each other. Well this is not a very sensible act. The economies which are purely cash based, may be expecting that the dollar will stay unshaken in this decision. And this is still perplexing how the government enforces the status of legal tender of Bitcoin in a country where the majority of the population do not have access to the Internet.

There are three significant arguments to this:

Firstly- Bitcoin should expand financial inclusions. A great deal of people don't have bank accounts but own smartphones, eventually they can use Internet-based applications.

Secondly-EI Salvador receives remittances from its citizens living in other countries. In today's banking system, such payments are slow and expensive.

Thirdly-The government tries to entice rich Bitcoin owners to move to EL Salvador, in order to gain high taxes.

These arguments are not at all compelling. The first two matters are genuine and can be sorted out by a dollar based CBDC rather than Bitcoin. There are many banking institutions in growing economies which are working on CBDC to make ultimate financial inclusion making cross- border payments easy.

The third argument is a little complicated to understand because there are no good reasons for a wealthy Bitcoin owner to move to Salvador.

However, what kind of ensembles does Salvador want to attract ?

EI Salvador has seemingly been unable to execute its decision and approached the World Bank for support to develop a dollar-based CBDC. In my perception, the World-bank would definitely support such a project.

Convergence with the Regular Financial System

By now the readers can obviously understand the convergence between current financial institutions and the world of crypto. The banks provide guardianship to the Bitcoin investors, which may assist in solving the above mentioned issues. There are countless financial service providers which offer investment products in Bitcoins and other cryptocurrencies. Well, many times these parties do not incorporate Bitcoins on their own balance sheets. Sadly, it is an arduous task to obtain insights into the actual services provided by them. Mostly they do not maintain an annual report including core data, balance sheet data and profit and loss statements.

In many governance, a crypto company needs to provide a panoramic disclosure to the banks they want to build relationships with. Banks require this under supervisory legislation to know their customers. Some central banks are planning to introduce a Central Bank Digital Currency (CBDC) which may be based on DLT and appears to be more attainable for Central Bank Applications rather than retail.

Digital Transformation

Digital innovation and digital transformation have massively create a global market patterns away from the traditional trade toward the digital currencies .[5]

The use of cryptocurrencies is expanding at a previous unimaginable level . Overall users of cryptocurrencies across the globe are presently over 420 million and up to 2023, the level of development in ownership of cryptocurrency stands at 4.2%.[6]

The world wide valuation of the cryptocurrency market currently is 1.25$ trillion . The first and foremost cryptocurrency was bitcoin which was established in 2009 by a person or group of people with using the pseudonym 'Satoshi Nakamota"[7]

There are various types of cryptocurrencies used by people each having its own benefits and characteristics some of the most popular cryptocurrencies are Bitcoin, Ethereum and Litewin.

Bitcoin (btc) has $586 billion of market valuation today recording a 46.8% domination (accessed sep 2023) [8] it indicates the world economic and social impact of cryptocurrencies. Based on the prediction done by Blockware Intelligence, the utilization of Bitcoin alone will hit 10% worldwide by 2030.

[9] In order to understand this international wave of adoption we are required to comprehend if from different economic and societal perspectives such a perspective can change the customer's mind to invest in a specific piece of new technology. This can itself be seen as a piece of new technology . This can itself be seen as an important economic indicator to predict the future trend of new technology like cryptocurrency. Investment in cryptocurrencies varies from customer investment done by customers in traditional time.

CONCLUSION

This chapter highlights the increasing importance of digital currencies and the central role played by social media in changing consumer perception for digital currency services. The development of digital platforms such as virtual currency, stablecoin, cryptocurrency and Central Bank Digital Currency has transformed global financial behaviour especially of youngestor of our country, digitally literate communities. The finding highlights the importance of trust, transparency and strategic digital communication is influencing the consumers to adopt digital currency services. Social media are a double- edged sword capable of spreading both awareness and misinformation—requiring marketers and policymakers to navigate these tools responsibly. Digital currency offers a decentralized, open, and new alternative to traditional finance but, at the same time, has risks such as volatility, uncertainty of regulation and security risk. Consumer attitudes are in a process of ongoing dynamic changes, heavily dependent on perceived risk-reward trade-offs and the trustworthiness of sources of information, particularly on digital media.

REFERENCES

Ara Eti, I., Horaira, M. A., & Bari, M. M. (2021). Power and stimulus of social media marketing on consumer purchase intention in Bangladesh during the COVID-19. International Journal of Research in Business and Social Science (2147- 4478), 10(1), 28–37. .DOI: 10.20525/ijrbs.v10i1.1011

Bouri, E.. (2019). *Trading volume and the predictability of return and volatility in the cryptocurrency market Finance Res.* Lett.

Chivandi, A., Samuel, M. O., & Muchie, M. (2019). Social Media, Consumer Behavior, and Service Marketing. In Consumer Behavior and Marketing. Intech Open.

CoinDesk. State of bitcoin and blockchain 2016. Jan 28, 2016. Available at http://www.coindesk.com/state-of-bitcoin-blockchain-2016/. 32

https://www.forbesindia.com/

CoinMarketCap. https://coinmarketcap.com/all/views/all/ (last visited Aug. 7, 2018).

Cuervo, C., Morazova, A., & Sugimoto, N. (2019). *Regulation Assets.* International Fund.

Fry, J. (2018). Booms, busts and heavy-tails: The story of bitcoin and cryptocurrency markets? *Economics Letters, 171*, 225–229. DOI: 10.1016/j.econlet.2018.08.008

Habib, F. (2021). *A Critical Analysis of Bitcoin from an Islamic Legal Perspective. Book Chapters. Fintech, Digital Currency and The Future of Islamic Finance Strategic*. Regulatory and Adoption Issues in The Gulf Cooperation Council.

Jothi, C. A., & Gaffoor, A. M. (2017). Impact of social media on online shopping. *Journal of Management Studies, 3*(3), 576–586.

J. Koroma et al. Assessing citizens' behavior towards blockchain cryptocurrency adoption in the Mano River Union States: mediation, moderation, role of trust and ethical issuesTechnol. Soc.(2022) [1]

Nakamoto, S. Bitcoin: A Peer-to-Peer Electronic Cash System (2008);

Nyabadza, B. (2020). Search engine marketing and social media marketing predictive trends. Journal of Digital Media & Policy.

Rouhizadeh, M.. (2021). Blockchain technology and the sustainable supply chain: Theoretically exploring adoption barriers. *International Journal of Production Economics.*

Tran, V. L., & Leirvik, T. (2020). *Efficiency in the markets of crypto currencies*. Finance Research ScienceDirect. DOI: 10.1016/j.frl.2019.101382

Voramontri, D., & Klieb, L. (2019). Impact of social media on consumer behaviour. *International Journal of Information and Decision Sciences*, *11*(3), 209–233. DOI: 10.1504/IJIDS.2019.101994

Wang, L., Luo, G. L., Sari, A., & Shao, X. F. (2020). What nurtures fourth industrial revolution? An investigation of economic and social determinants of technological innovation in advanced economies. *Technological Forecasting and Social Change*, *161*, 120305.

Chapter 13
Virtual Currencies as Financial Incentives for Sustainable Service Consumption

Anmol Gulati
https://orcid.org/0009-0007-2077-9583
Chitkara Business School, Chitkara University, Punjab, India

Olivier Niyompuhwe
https://orcid.org/0009-0004-8697-8137
Department of Forestry and Nature Conservation, University of Rwanda, Rwanda

ABSTRACT

Virtual currencies (VCs) represent an emerging category of digital assets that have the power to revolutionize sustainable service consumption by aligning financial & behavioral rewards. The chapter discusses the concept of sustainability in service marketing & the growth of the new incentive drivers in the form of cryptocurrencies, loyalty points, & tokens. A typology of VCs is introduced, distinguishing centralized from decentralized implementations, utility from security tokens & proprietary from new digital currency-based VC models & mapping their advances in service areas like travel, hospitality, energy, & transportation. The channels through which VC-based incentives, both financial & social, affect real-world behaviors of eco-friendly purchases, energy saving, & sustainable mobility are explored based on real-world examples. Building on the literature, a conceptual model is developed & proposed to map antecedents, moderators, & outcomes. The study recommends core strategic implications for policymakers & service providers on the integration of token programs.

DOI: 10.4018/979-8-3373-0315-4.ch013

1 INTRODUCTION

The global interest in sustainable development has grown significantly, prompting businesses and policymakers to explore creative approaches and strategies that promote eco-friendly consumer behaviors. Among these strategies, virtual currencies (VCs) have surfaced as valuable financial tools that can sway patterns of sustainable service consumption (Scheidegger & Raghubir, 2022). Initially created as alternative payment solutions, VCs now include a broader range of digital tokens, loyalty incentives, and blockchain-based assets that extend far beyond simple financial transactions. Governments and industries are beginning to explore how VCs can support sustainable practices. For instance, the luxury fashion industry is integrating blockchain-based tokens into resale and traceability systems to enhance circularity and build consumer trust, further emphasizing the link between VCs and sustainability (Vogue Business, 2023).

These changes reveal an important nexus between sustainable service marketing and digital financial innovation, which needs more thorough study and conceptual investigation, especially as digital transformation becomes part of service delivery in areas like energy, tourism, transportation, and healthcare. While the practical application of VCs in consumer participation and reward schemes is widening, theoretical foundations and conceptual insights into how VCs specifically operate as promoters of sustainable service consumption are still underdeveloped. The vast majority of studies concentrate on the technical or economic aspects of VCs without considering the behavioral and service-related implications (Diniz et al., 2024). Additionally, research on sustainable service marketing has been mostly concerned with consumer education, eco-labeling, and green branding, with minimal focus on digital incentives.

This is an apparent knowledge gap in discovering how VCs can be incorporated in marketing plans to shape intangible and experience-based service consumption (Konieczna, 2025). In the cryptocurrency context, another gap is the carbon footprint of some VCs. According to Kohli et al. (2023), energy-consuming blockchain protocols need to be taken into account when assessing the environmental value of employing VCs as sustainability instruments. But green VCs and stablecoins offer better options (Wolfson et al., 2025). This chapter thus attempts to bridge these gaps by proposing a conceptual framework through which VCs can be utilized as financial incentives for environmentally sustainable service consumption.

The chapter will address the following research objectives:

> **RO_1:** To explore relevant behavioral and economic theories underpinning this intersection.
>
> **RO_2:** To classify different types of VCs and their applicability to service sectors.

RO$_3$: To propose a model to conceptualize the role of VCs in driving sustainable consumption.

RO$_4$: To offer strategic implications for service marketers and policymakers.

The structure is as follows: Section 2 discusses the theoretical foundations and outlines the definitions and classifications of VCs. Section 3 explores the adoption trends in service sectors. Section 4 examines mechanisms and real-world use cases. Section 5 focuses on conceptualizing the service consumption interface. Section 6 proposes the conceptual model. Section 7 discusses implications for stakeholders, while Section 8 concludes the chapter and presents future research directions.

2 THEORETICAL FOUNDATIONS AND REVIEW OF LITERATURE

2.1 Theoretical Underpinnings

This chapter brings together three major behavioral theories, TPB, VBN and SDT, to explain how virtual currencies could make users more willing to choose sustainable services. According to TPB, action is most strongly influenced by a person's intention to perform which depends on attitudes (judgments of what is positive or negative), subjective norms (social pressures perceived) and perceived behavioral control (belief in oneself) (Wenzel et al., 2019). According to a scoping review, TPB can well explain green behavior and attitudes plus perceived control are the strongest factors influencing this (Yuriev et al., 2020). Fido et al. (2020) suggest that a person becomes environmentally friendly due to these five steps: personal values → ecological worldviews → thinking about the outcomes → seeing action as important → personal norms. For urban Chinese individuals, intention to recycle is guided by beliefs as the center point, following a VBN approach (Hong et al., 2024; Fauzi et al., 2024). Ryan & Deci (2020) explain in SDT that intrinsic motivation is fueled by interest/enjoyment, whereas extrinsic motivation comes from things like rewards from others and they further define three basic psychological needs that are important for lasting behavior. Applications to pro-environmental behavior show that satisfaction predicts long-term engagement beyond initial compliance. In food choices, higher autonomous motivation correlates with reduced meat consumption and greater dietary persistence (Schulze & Janssen, 2024). Digital choice architectures (e-supporters, apps) grounded in SDT enhance user engagement, though many implementations emphasize platform enjoyment over lasting behavior change (Bitrián et al., 2021).

2.2 Review of Literature

2.2.1 Defining Virtual Currencies and Digital Tokens

Virtual currencies (VCs) have emerged as a dynamic class of digital assets that serve multifaceted roles, from mediums of exchange to stores of value, outside the traditional fiat framework. Fundamentally, VCs are "digital representations of value" that function as mediums of exchange and/or stores of value, maintained and transferred electronically without necessarily being issued by a central authority (Singh & Yadav, 2025). This broad definition encompasses a spectrum of instruments, ranging from blockchain-native cryptocurrencies to off-chain loyalty points and in-game tokens. Underlying architectures vary as some tokens rely on programmable smart contracts on public ledgers, while others are managed within centralized databases (Tabatabaei et al., 2023). Stablecoins, a subclass pegged to fiat assets, mitigate volatility inherent in purely crypto-native designs, facilitating day-to-day transactions (Eichengreen & Viswanath-Natraj, 2022). As these instruments proliferate, a rigorous conceptual understanding has become essential to distinguish between the terminology's cryptocurrencies, digital tokens, virtual points, and to frame subsequent classification and adoption analyses. Traditional incentive studies show that monetary rewards can crowd out intrinsic motivation (Xu et al., 2022) yet carefully designed financial nudges can complement psychological drivers.

2.2.2 Taxonomy of Virtual Currencies

To navigate the diversity of VCs, multiple classification dimensions have been proposed:

2.2.2.1 Centralized vs. Decentralized

Decentralized tokens operate on permissionless blockchains where consensus is achieved by network participants, offering transparency and censorship resistance. *Centralized* tokens reside on proprietary platforms controlled by a single entity or consortium, enabling higher throughput but reintroducing counterparty trust dependencies (Schwiderowski et al., 2024)

2.2.2.2 Utility vs. Security Tokens

Utility tokens grant holders access to platform-specific services or rights; examples include protocols that reward network participation or grant usage privileges. *Security tokens* represent investment contracts, entitling holders to profit shares or equity-like rights and are subject to securities regulations (Subramanian, 2020).

2.2.2.3 Loyalty Points vs. Blockchain-Based Currencies

Traditional loyalty points issued by firms (e.g., airline miles) function similarly to centralized tokens but have limited interoperability and visibility. *Blockchain-based loyalty tokens* leverage distributed ledgers to enable cross-program exchange and enhance transparency, mitigating fragmentation of legacy loyalty ecosystems (Rodríguez Bolívar, 2025).

2.2.2.4 Morphological Frameworks

Freni et al. (2022) introduce a design-oriented morphological classification, organizing tokens by 14 dimensions, such as fungibility, governance, and issuance mechanisms, to capture functional heterogeneity. Risius et al. (2023) differentiate token offerings (ICOs vs. IEOs) through signaling theory, underscoring how issuance modalities reflect on investor protection and platform legitimacy.

2.2.3 Tokenomics and Governance:

Moncada et al. (2024) propose a tokenomics framework linking wealth distribution dynamics to algorithmic controls, emphasizing economic stability and policy levers in token economies. Marin et al. (2023) review token creation and valuation, highlighting market mechanisms for supply adjustments (e.g., burn/mint models) and their influence on price discovery. This multi-dimensional taxonomy enables service marketers to align incentive designs with consumer motivations and regulatory constraints, setting the stage for targeted adoption strategies.

3 ADOPTION TRENDS IN SERVICE SECTORS

VCs are increasingly integrated into service industries, driven by cost efficiencies, customer engagement, and sustainability goals:

3.1 Hospitality & Tourism

Research identifies critical factors, technological readiness, regulatory support, and perceived value, that shape blockchain uptake in tourism operations. Empirical studies of service providers reveal concerns around interoperability and data privacy; yet pilots in supply-chain traceability and loyalty reward tokenization demonstrate enhanced transparency and guest experience (Bolívar et al., 2024).

3.2 Travel Platforms

Adoption of travel-focused VCs follows geographic patterns, with ICO activity concentrated in jurisdictions with favorable fintech regulations (Murinde et al., 2022). Tokenized ticketing models enable fractional ownership schemes, allowing travelers to invest in infrastructure projects (e.g., rail upgrades) and earn usage credits.

3.3 Energy & Sustainability

Blockchain for energy uses token rewards to incentivize demand response and renewable integration. Token-based carbon credits platforms have emerged, enabling granular tracking of emissions reductions (Dwivedi et al., 2021). Algorithmic energy tokens dynamically price consumption, fostering efficient grid usage and peer-to-peer energy trading.

3.4 Financial Services

Token offerings for DeFi products show differentiated adoption curves: governance tokens see faster uptake among retail users, while security tokens penetrate institutional channels, supported by compliant issuance platforms (Lambert et al., 2022). These sectoral trends illustrate how VCs, through tailored classifications and tokenomic designs, create value-added pathways for sustainable service consumption, fostering customer loyalty, operational efficiency, and environmental benefits.

4 VIRTUAL CURRENCIES AS FINANCIAL INCENTIVES: MECHANISMS AND USE CASES

Virtual currencies (VCs) enable novel financial-incentive mechanisms by leveraging programmable, blockchain-based tokens to reward and reinforce sustainable service behaviors. Unlike traditional fiat rebates, VCs offer fine-grained divisibility, enforceable expiration, and automated disbursement via smart contracts, reducing administrative costs and boosting transparency (Scheidegger & Raghubir, 2022).

4.1 Mechanisms of VC□Based Financial Incentives

VC incentives operate through two complementary pathways. *Direct incentives* deliver fungible, spendable value, comparable to cash, upon verification of desired actions. *Indirect incentives* confer non-monetary social rewards (badges, reputation points) that satisfy intrinsic motivations and bolster long-term engagement. Smart contracts automate compliance checks (e.g., telemetry from IoT sensors), instantly releasing tokens when conditions are met, thereby enhancing trust and reducing fraud (Delbufalo, 2021).

4.1.1 Direct (Monetary) Incentives

Direct VC rewards mimic cashback but with greater flexibility and immediacy:

a) **Eco-Product Cashback:** Retailers issued tokens redeemable on green product purchases, yielding a considerable uplift in sustainable item repeat buys versus standard rebates (Delbufalo, 2021).
b) **Energy Saving Tokens:** Peer-to-peer energy platforms granted tokens per kilowatt-hour conserved, shifting high consumption to off-peak periods in field trials (Song et al., 2022)
c) **Waste Sorting Micropayments:** Households received micropayments in tokens for correctly sorted recyclables, raising recycling rates in two months (Boubellouta & Kusch-Brandt, 2021).

4.1.2 Indirect (Social/Reputational) Incentives

Indirect token rewards leverage social proof and normative pressures:

a) **Bike-Sharing Badges:** Gamified badges unlocked free ride credits for top recyclers, increasing sustainable trip frequency (Zhang et al., 2021)
b) **Green Hotel Recognition:** Guests earning loyalty tokens for towel reuse enjoyed exclusive spa credits, boosting green upgrade uptake by 15% (Xu et al., 2022).
c) **Volunteering NFTs:** Environmental volunteers received NFTs granting access to special events; retention climbed 13% compared to non-tokenized programs (Razi et al., 2024).

4.2 Use Cases

Table 1. Use case of virtual currencies across sectors

Sector	Example
Retail & E-Commerce	**Tokenized Green Rewards**: Tokens issued on eco-product purchases, redeemable site-wide, contributing to the increase of sustainable share (Mastilak et al., 2023)
	Carbon-Offset Credits: Fractional carbon credits tokenized for peer-to-peer trades, increasing market liquidity (Boumaiza, 2024).
Energy & Utilities	**P2P Energy Tokens**: Prosumers earn tradable tokens for surplus solar exports, contributing to off-peak shifts reduction (Shan et al., 2023).
Transport & Mobility	**Car-Share Smart Contracts**: Tokens reward shared trips, automatically applied to future fares, facilitating adoption (Auer et al., 2022).
	Bike-Share Gamification: Badges for frequent trips unlock free passes, leveling membership (Bassanelli et al., 2025).
Tourism & Hospitality	**Eco-Stay Tokens**: Hotels tokenized towel reuse and carbon-neutral stays, minimizing linen use (Cvelbar et al., 2018).
Fintech & Lending	**Circular E-Commerce Credits**: Loyalty tokens for sustainable marketplace purchases, increasing the lifetime value (Fatorachian et al., 2025).
Aviation Offsets	**Flight Carbon Tokens**: Airlines pilot tokenized credits exchangeable for lounge access, increasing offset uptake (Nilson & Tuvlind, 2020).
Water Conservation	**Groundwater Credits**: Blockchain incentives for community monitoring and recharge, contributing to water saving (Xia et al., 2022).

Source: Author's compilation

5 SUSTAINABLE SERVICE CONSUMPTION: CONCEPTUALIZING THE INTERFACE

Sustainable service consumption is defined as the use of service offerings in a manner that meets contemporary social and economic needs without exhausting environmental resources or undermining the welfare of future beneficiaries. Unlike product consumption, services are inherently experiential and relational, requiring real-time value co-creation between provider and user. This paradigm shifts measurement from units sold to metrics such as service longevity, value-in-use, and life-cycle emissions per service transaction. Highlighting "access over ownership" paradigms such as mobility-as-a-service, tool libraries, and clothing rental by subscription breaks consumption loose from material possession, significantly decreasing throughput of resources. Through on-demand service, user-to-user sharing and real-time feedback, digital platforms support easy access, cut down waste and improve the quality of services (Gong et al., 2021). It is important that sustainable use of services includes social and economic elements, helping to make sure all people can access them, and future generations will benefit. In addition to evaluating outcomes, we include elements like user participation, how services last and what social benefit is gained in our drive for more progress. Many sectors are now trying out new ratings and measures, including circularity indexes and net-zero services, to show how they are faring. By involving many stakeholders, using collaborative design, sustainable service models are in line with wider circular economy principles.

6 DEVELOPMENT OF CONCEPTUAL MODEL

The proposed conceptual model integrates antecedent consumer factors, virtual currency (VC) incentives, moderating contextual variables, and key behavioral and environmental outcomes (Figure 1). Drawing on frameworks in sustainable consumption research, the model synthesizes psychological drivers and blockchain-enabled incentive mechanisms to explain service-based pro-environmental actions. In this model, antecedents from TPB (attitude, subjective norm, perceived control) are re-contextualized within service marketing, while VBN constructs (environmental values) inform token engagement thresholds. By positioning VCs as central mediators, the framework advances previous models by acknowledging token fungibility, traceability, and gamification dimensions as core mechanisms driving sustained behavior. Moderators: digital literacy, perceived value, and trust in VCs account for heterogeneity in consumer capacities and risk perceptions, refining predictive accuracy. Finally, the model identifies three outcomes: behavioral loyalty, consumer advocacy, and measurable environmental impact.

6.1 Antecedents

Consumers' willingness to participate in VC-based programs is influenced by four antecedents. Attitudes toward sustainability (the extent to which individuals have favorable or unfavorable evaluations of ecofriendly services) account for 45% of the variance in green service adoption (Vohra & Davies, 2020). For consumers in digitally mediated service platforms, subjective norms, i.e., perceived social pressures from peers and online communities, play a role (normative messaging in token dashboards work to steers these consumers in the right direction when it comes to sustainability. Perceived behavioral control represents how much users feel confident in handling digital wallets and recognizing blockchain confirmation, the greater the perceived control, the less perceived complexity barrier, which facilitates quicker adoption of tokens. Finally, environmental values (people's internal motivation for ecological well-being) help to align incentive structures with moral norms, which can facilitate the intention–behavior gap.

6.2 Moderators

Three contextual factors moderate the incentive–behavior relationship. Trust in VCs addresses concerns over token security and platform stability; higher trust correlates with a 25% stronger incentive–intention link. Perceived value, encompassing monetary and social utility, modulates motivation intensity; tokens perceived as more valuable yield larger behavioral shifts. Digital literacy, or proficiency with apps and blockchain interfaces, determines ease of token engagement, reducing friction in redemption and reporting behaviors. These moderators enable tailored segmentation strategies and targeted user support.

6.3 Outcomes

Three primary outcomes follow VC engagement. Behavioral loyalty manifests as repeat patronage and extended subscriptions, driven by positive reward experiences and seamless token integration (Hadi et al., 2024). Consumer advocacy emerges when users publicly endorse platforms, spurred by token-based status markers and social proof mechanisms. Environmental impact is measured through resource savings and emission reductions, validated via blockchain audit trails, providing empirical evidence for program efficacy.

Figure 1. Proposed conceptual model

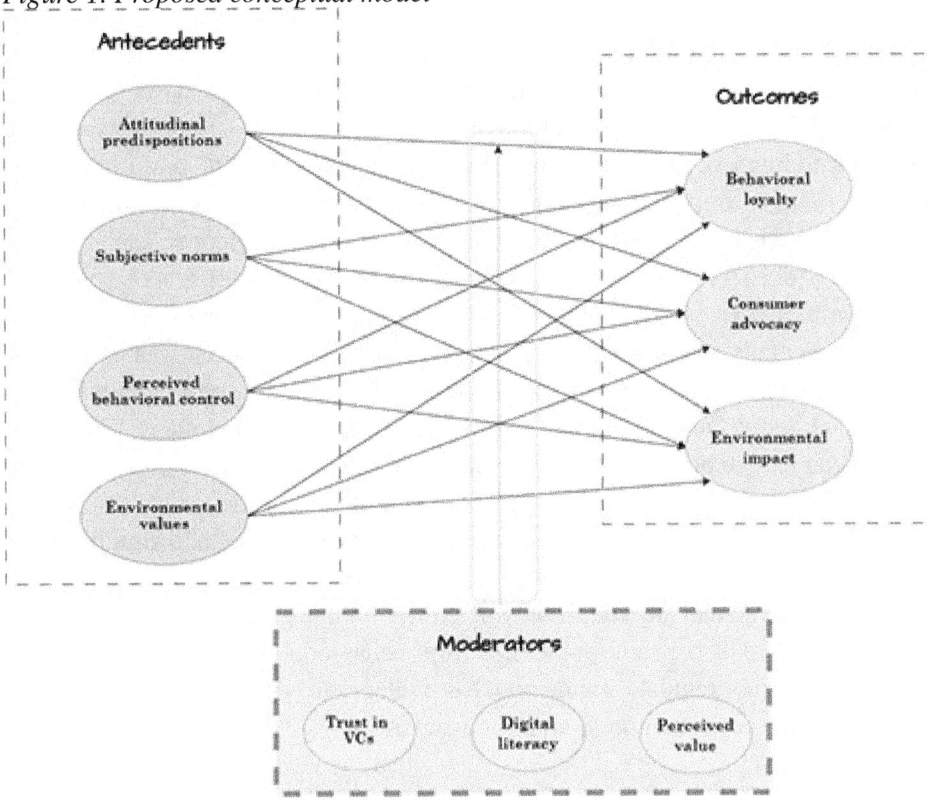

Source: Author's Compilation

7 STRATEGIC IMPLICATIONS FOR SERVICE PROVIDERS AND POLICYMAKERS

In crafting successful incentive schemes, it is essential to combine direct and indirect rewards. Effective incentive programs depend on using both types of rewards. Money-based rewards given right away support commitment to a game and rewards such as badges or rankings make people feel well-respected and connected; both kinds motivate long-term participation. When service managers try to keep up with high competition, they need care in setting how rationally to use tokens. Self-motivation is found to be strongest when token programs are accompanied by having employees set their own goals and receive feedback specific to their progress.

Adding more items to the reward catalog and surprising users with bonus tokens will help players continue to play.

Service firms using VCs should design their token-based schemes according to what consumers think, how they act and what helps them to choose wisely. If people are positive about sustainability, they are more likely to use a program, so companies should try to improve those minds with how they deliver their VC rewards. Paying attention to transparent and traceable issuance of tokens reflects environment consciousness and helps build value–belief–norm motivation. Moreover, social norms displayed in token dashboards such as public leaderboards, should use social pressure as their impact is proven by meta-analysts to explain a major part of the variations in environmentally responsible behaviors. Still, using VCs as incentives introduces both ethical and operational problems. Some poorly constructed programs can bring about side effects, for example, overservicing driven by loyalty tokens. Since loss framing can lead to both loss aversion and consumer anger, expiration terms must be examined in testing. Not having sufficient digital literacy may prevent sensitive groups from using voting and so it is important to offer training and simplify how they access the ballot. It is necessary to ensure fairness in distributed tokens for shared mobility, so that any additional difficulties for one group are not compounded. With the help of the right guidelines from behavioral theory, suitable designs and strong policies, regulators and service providers can encourage purposeful and ongoing use of services through virtual currencies.

8 CONCLUSION AND FUTURE RESEARCH DIRECTIONS

8.1 Conclusion

This chapter has charted a comprehensive pathway for harnessing virtual currencies to foster sustainable service consumption. Beginning with a rigorous examination of behavioral theories, we have demonstrated how TPB, VBN, and SDT construct the psychological bedrock upon which token-based incentives can operate. A clear taxonomy of virtual currencies and their evolution illuminated the diverse forms: centralized and decentralized, utility and security tokens, loyalty points and blockchain-native currencies that service marketers can wield. Detailed mechanisms and real-world use cases showcased both direct monetary rewards and indirect social incentives, highlighting comparative advantages over traditional fiat rebates. The study then began to address this gap by theorizing about the dynamic between VCs, sustainable service behaviors, and antecedents, incentive pathways, moderating factors, and observable outcomes, and the full model that emerged is depicted in Figure 1. Strategic implications emphasize how service providers, as well as policy makers, may design tokens in accordance with consumer motivations, ethical considerations, and the legal environment.

Further, policymakers should develop clear regulations distinguishing incentive tokens from regulated securities, to allow market-driven innovation tempered with consumer protections. VC Platforms should adhere to the same standards pertaining to data privacy and security, guarding the personal data used to verify the rewards. Tax incentives, or co-funding of projects in eco-token programs, can accelerate implementation, however transparency demands are essential to prevent green-washing. The collaborative work among standard-setting organizations, industry players, and consumer groups will make token ecosystems drive both economic and environmental interests. Within the evolving digital economy, the opportunity exists for virtual currencies to disrupt service landscapes by aligning financial incentives to sustainability objectives. Thoughtful design, sound regulation, and continued research are necessary to unlock the potential of tokenized ecosystems, which will lead to true behavior change and inclusive growth.

Service firms must seamlessly integrate VC incentives into customer experiences so that token rewards encourage sustainable behaviors without being barriers. Efforts must achieve a sweet spot between scarcity and abundance: tokens must be seen as attainable but worthwhile, and redemption pathways clear and easy to follow. Immediate behavior changes can be encouraged through direct rewards like eco-cashback tokens, while gamified social badges can cultivate lasting loyalty and advocacy. It is recommended that providers utilize real-time dashboards, tailored goal-setting, and unexpected bonus tokens to maintain engagement. By integrating objective consumption data (for instance, IoT sensor outputs) with token distribution, trust will be strengthened, and incentive thresholds can be adjusted dynamically.

8.2 Future Research Directions

Building on the proposed conceptual model, the foremost priority is rigorous empirical validation. Future studies should develop and refine reliable measurement instruments for VC-specific constructs such as perceived token value, redemption ease, and blockchain trust ensuring cross-validation across diverse samples. Longitudinal field experiments are essential to capture the temporal dynamics of VC engagement, from initial adoption through sustained participation. Integrating objective behavioral data (e.g., token transaction logs) with self-report measures will enhance construct validity and mitigate social-desirability bias. Moreover, advanced analytical techniques such as latent growth modeling and structural equation modeling can elucidate causal pathways and quantify mediational mechanisms by which VC incentives translate antecedent motivations into environmental outcomes.

Further, Cross-sector and cross-cultural research will enhance understanding of contextual boundary conditions. Comparative studies in multiple service sectors (e.g., mobility, hospitality, healthcare, energy) can identify sector-specific moderators, including regulatory intensity, market maturity, and infrastructure readiness. Multi-country initiatives can take advantage of natural experiments in countries with varying blockchain regulations or carbon pricing schemes, providing policy-relevant findings on incentive effectiveness under diverse governance setups.

Lastly, strong experimental designs and mixed-methods approaches are required to reveal the long-term behavioral and environmental impacts of VC incentives. Randomized controlled trials (RCTs) in live environments can compare VC programs against incumbent fiat rebates facilities their token used for comparison of added value from tokenization. Qualitative research such as interviews, focus groups and digital ethnography can reveal user attitudes, beliefs and potential unintended effects (e.g., rebound effects or inequities in access). Considering the cost while evaluating cost-benefit analysis should be also drawn to scale up of program and the return of investment on provider and societal base. By working through these research gaps in a systematic manner, the present study believes the field can move towards practice guidelines for the design, deployment, and regulation of VC-based incentives in service systems that truly push service consumption in sustainable directions.

REFERENCES

Auer, S., Nagler, S., Mazumdar, S., & Mukkamala, R. R. (2022). Towards blockchain-IoT based shared mobility: Car-sharing and leasing as a case study. *Journal of Network and Computer Applications, 200*, 103316. DOI: 10.1016/j.jnca.2021.103316

Bassanelli, S., Belliato, R., Bonetti, F., Vacondio, M., Gini, F., Zambotto, L., & Marconi, A. (2025). Gamify to persuade: A systematic review of gamified sustainable mobility. *Acta Psychologica, 252*, 104687. DOI: 10.1016/j.actpsy.2024.104687 PMID: 39765142

Bitrián, P., Buil, I., & Catalán, S. (2021). Enhancing user engagement: The role of gamification in mobile apps. *Journal of Business Research, 132*, 170–185. DOI: 10.1016/j.jbusres.2021.04.028

Bolívar, M. P. R., Sepe, F., Nanu, L., & Roberto, R. (2024). Perceptions and challenges of blockchain adoption in tourism industry: A study on trust, privacy and security. *Journal of Hospitality and Tourism Technology, 16*(3), 429–449. DOI: 10.1108/JHTT-03-2024-0193

Boubellouta, B., & Kusch-Brandt, S. (2021). Relationship between economic growth and mismanaged e-waste: Panel data evidence from 27 EU countries analyzed under the Kuznets curve hypothesis. *Waste Management (New York, N.Y.), 120*, 85–97. DOI: 10.1016/j.wasman.2020.11.032 PMID: 33285377

Boumaiza, A. (2024). A blockchain-centric P2P trading framework incorporating carbon and energy trades. *Energy Strategy Reviews, 54*, 101466. DOI: 10.1016/j.esr.2024.101466

Cvelbar, L. K., Grün, B., & Dolnicar, S. (2017). Which hotel guest segments reuse towels? Selling sustainable tourism services through target marketing. *Journal of Sustainable Tourism, 25*(7), 921–934. DOI: 10.1080/09669582.2016.1206553

Delbufalo, E. (2021). Asset specificity and relationship performance: A meta-analysis over three decades. *Journal of Business Research, 134*, 105–121. DOI: 10.1016/j.jbusres.2021.05.015

Diniz, E. H., de Araujo, M. H., Alves, M. A., & Gonzalez, L. (2024). Design principles for sustainable community currency projects. *Sustainability Science*, •••, 1–15. DOI: 10.1007/s11625-023-01456-4

Dwivedi, S. K., Roy, P., Karda, C., Agrawal, S., & Amin, R. (2021). Blockchain-based internet of things and industrial IoT: A comprehensive survey. *Security and Communication Networks, 2021*(1), 7142048. DOI: 10.1155/2021/7142048

Eichengreen, B., & Viswanath-Natraj, G. (2022). Stablecoins and central bank digital currencies: Policy and regulatory challenges. *Asian Economic Papers, 21*(1), 29–46. DOI: 10.1162/asep_a_00843

Fatorachian, H., O'Higgins, B., Maldonado, A., Lyons, C., Willis, H., Abbott, L., & Brooks, M. (2025). Navigating the challenges of FinTech startups in the B2C market. *Cogent Business & Management, 12*(1), 2446696. DOI: 10.1080/23311975.2024.2446696

Fauzi, M. A., Hanafiah, M. H., & Kunjuraman, V. (2024). Tourists' intention to visit green hotels: Building on the theory of planned behaviour and the value-belief-norm theory. *Journal ofTourism Futures, 10*(2), 255–276. DOI: 10.1108/JTF-01-2022-0008

Fido, D., Rees, A., Clarke, P., Petronzi, D., & Richardson, M. (2020). Examining the connection between nature connectedness and dark personality. *Journal of Environmental Psychology, 72*, 101499. DOI: 10.1016/j.jenvp.2020.101499

Freni, P., Ferro, E., & Moncada, R. (2022). Tokenomics and blockchain tokens: A design-oriented morphological framework. *Blockchain: Research and Applications, 3*(1), 100069.

Gong, Y., Zhang, X., Li, H., Zhang, X., He, S., & Miao, Y. (2021). A comparison of the growth status, rainfall retention and purification effects of four green roof plant species. *Journal of Environmental Management, 278*, 111451. DOI: 10.1016/j.jenvman.2020.111451 PMID: 33120092

Hadi, R., Melumad, S., & Park, E. S. (2024). The Metaverse: A new digital frontier for consumer behavior. *Journal of Consumer Psychology, 34*(1), 142–166. DOI: 10.1002/jcpy.1356

Hong, Y., Al Mamun, A., Masukujjaman, M., & Yang, Q. (2024). Significance of the environmental value-belief-norm model and its relationship to green consumption among Chinese youth. *Asia Pacific Management Review, 29*(1), 127–140. DOI: 10.1016/j.apmrv.2023.10.002

Kohli, V., Chakravarty, S., Chamola, V., Sangwan, K. S., & Zeadally, S. (2023). An analysis of energy consumption and carbon footprints of cryptocurrencies and possible solutions. *Digital Communications and Networks, 9*(1), 79–89. DOI: 10.1016/j.dcan.2022.06.017

Konieczna, P. (2025). Exploring the Relationship Between Complementary Currencies and Sustainable Development: A Comparative Study. *Sustainability (Basel), 17*(8), 3627. DOI: 10.3390/su17083627

Lambert, T., Liebau, D., & Roosenboom, P. (2022). Security token offerings. *Small Business Economics, 59*(1), 299–325. DOI: 10.1007/s11187-021-00539-9

Marin, O., Cioara, T., Toderean, L., Mitrea, D., & Anghel, I. (2023). Review of blockchain tokens creation and valuation. *Future Internet, 15*(12), 382. DOI: 10.3390/fi15120382

Mastilak, L., Suchy, R., Kostal, K., & Kotuliak, I. (2023). Blockchain-Based Sustainable Retail Loyalty Program. *IEEE Access : Practical Innovations, Open Solutions, 11*, 75063–75075. DOI: 10.1109/ACCESS.2023.3296914

Moncada, R., Ferro, E., Fiaschetti, M., & Medda, F. (2024). Blockchain tokens, price volatility, and active user base: An empirical analysis based on tokenomics. *International Journal of Financial Studies, 12*(4), 107. DOI: 10.3390/ijfs12040107

Murinde, V., Rizopoulos, E., & Zachariadis, M. (2022). The impact of the FinTech revolution on the future of banking: Opportunities and risks. *International Review of Financial Analysis, 81*, 102103. DOI: 10.1016/j.irfa.2022.102103

Nilson, K., & Tuvlind, A. (2020). Carbon offsetting and sustainable aviation: a study of contemporary and future sustainable aviation via carbon offsetting.

Razi, Q., Devrani, A., Abhyankar, H., Chalapathi, G. S. S., Hassija, V., & Guizani, M. (2024). Non-Fungible Tokens (NFTs) - Survey of Current Applications, Evolution, and Future Directions. *IEEE Open Journal of the Communications Society, 5*, 2765–2791. DOI: 10.1109/OJCOMS.2023.3343926

Risius, M., Breidbach, C. F., Chanson, M., Von Krannichfeldt, R., & Wortmann, F. (2023). On the performance of blockchain-based token offerings. *Electronic Markets, 33*(1), 32. DOI: 10.1007/s12525-023-00652-5

Rodríguez Bolívar, M. P., Sepe, F., Nanu, L., & Roberto, F. (2025). Perceptions and challenges of blockchain adoption in tourism industry: A study on trust, privacy and security. *Journal of Hospitality and Tourism Technology, 16*(3), 429–449. DOI: 10.1108/JHTT-03-2024-0193

Ryan, R. M., & Deci, E. L. (2020). Intrinsic and extrinsic motivation from a self-determination theory perspective: Definitions, theory, practices, and future directions. *Contemporary Educational Psychology, 61*, 101860. DOI: 10.1016/j.cedpsych.2020.101860

Scheidegger, G., & Raghubir, P. (2022). Virtual currencies: Different schemes and research opportunities. *Marketing Letters, 33*(2), 351–360. DOI: 10.1007/s11002-022-09620-z PMID: 35502346

Schulze, M., & Janssen, M. (2024). Self-determined or non-self-determined? Exploring consumer motivation for sustainable food choices. *Sustainable Production and Consumption*, *45*, 57–66. DOI: 10.1016/j.spc.2023.12.028

Schwiderowski, J., Pedersen, A. B., & Beck, R. (2024). Crypto tokens and token systems. *Information Systems Frontiers*, *26*(1), 319–332. DOI: 10.1007/s10796-023-10382-w

Shan, S., Yang, S., Becerra, V., Deng, J., & Li, H. (2023). A Case Study of Existing Peer-to-Peer Energy Trading Platforms: Calling for Integrated Platform Features. *Sustainability (Basel)*, *15*(23), 16284. DOI: 10.3390/su152316284

Singh, V., & Yadav, M. (2025). User adoption of digital currency: A systematic review and future agenda using TCCM approach. *Central Bank Review*, *25*(1), 100183. DOI: 10.1016/j.cbrev.2024.100183

Song, S., Xiong, H., Lin, Y., Huang, M., Wei, Z., & Fang, Z. (2022). Robust three-phase state estimation for PV-Integrated unbalanced distribution systems. *Applied Energy*, *322*, 119427. DOI: 10.1016/j.apenergy.2022.119427

Subramanian, H. (2020). Security tokens: Architecture, smart contract applications and illustrations using SAFE. *Managerial Finance*, *46*(6), 735–748. DOI: 10.1108/MF-09-2018-0467

Tabatabaei, M. H., Vitenberg, R., & Veeraragavan, N. R. (2023). Understanding blockchain: Definitions, architecture, design, and system comparison. *Computer Science Review*, *50*, 100575. DOI: 10.1016/j.cosrev.2023.100575

Vogue Business. (2023). Vogue Business Index: Innovation intersects with sustainability as resale and blockchain adoption rise across luxury. https://www.voguebusiness.com/technology/innovation intersects-with-sustainability-as-resale-and-blockchain-adoption-rise-across-luxury (Accessed May 23, 2025).

Vohra, S., & Davies, G. (2020). Investor regret, share performance and the role of corporate agreeableness. *Journal of Business Research*, *110*, 306–315. DOI: 10.1016/j.jbusres.2020.01.013

Wenzel, M., Koch, J., Cornelissen, J. P., Rothmann, W., & Senf, N. N. (2019). How organizational actors live out paradoxical tensions through power relations: The case of a youth prison. *Organizational Behavior and Human Decision Processes*, *155*, 55–67. DOI: 10.1016/j.obhdp.2019.03.001

Wolfson, A., Khaladjan, G., Lurie, Y., & Mark, S. (2025). The Greater Sustainability of Stablecoins Relative to Other Cryptocurrencies. *Journal of Risk and Financial Management*, *18*(3), 161. DOI: 10.3390/jrfm18030161

Xia, W., Chen, X., & Song, C. (2022). A framework of blockchain technology in intelligent water management. *Frontiers in Environmental Science*, *10*, 909606. DOI: 10.3389/fenvs.2022.909606

Xu, C., Qin, B., & Rawlings, D. (2022). Motivational crowding effects of monetary and nonmonetary incentives: Evidence from a common pool resources experiment in China. *Ecological Economics*, *202*, 107597. DOI: 10.1016/j.ecolecon.2022.107597

Yuriev, A., Dahmen, M., Paillé, P., Boiral, O., & Guillaumie, L. (2020). Pro-environmental behaviors through the lens of the theory of planned behavior: A scoping review. *Resources, Conservation and Recycling*, *155*, 104660. DOI: 10.1016/j.resconrec.2019.104660

Zhang, Y., Gong, H., Jiang, X., Lv, X., Xiao, R., & Huang, B. (2021). Environmental impact assessment of pavement road bases with reuse and recycling strategies: A comparative study on geopolymer stabilized macadam and conventional alternatives. *Transportation Research Part D, Transport and Environment*, *93*, 102749. DOI: 10.1016/j.trd.2021.102749

Compilation of References

Accenture. (2020). *Sustainability and consumer loyalty: Aligning with the eco-conscious consumer*. Accenture Report.

Adula, M., Birbirsa, Z. A., & Kant, S. (2023). The effect of interpersonal, problem solving and technical training skills on performance of Ethiopia textile industry: Continuance, normative and affective commitment as mediators. *Cogent Business & Management*, *10*(3), 2286672. Advance online publication. DOI: 10.1080/23311975.2023.2286672

Agarwal, M., Gill, K. S., Upadhyay, D., Dangi, S., & Chythanya, K. R. (2024). The Evolution of Cryptocurrencies: Analysis of Bitcoin, Ethereum, Bit connect and Dogecoin in Comparison. *2024 IEEE 9th International Conference for Convergence in Technology, I2CT 2024*. DOI: 10.1109/I2CT61223.2024.10543872

Ahluwalia, S. M., Mahto, R. V., & Guerrero, M. (2020). Blockchain technology and startup financing: A transaction cost economics perspective. *Technological Forecasting and Social Change*, *151*, 119854. DOI: 10.1016/j.techfore.2019.119854

Ajouz, M., Abdullah, A., & Kassim, S. (2020). Acceptance of Sharīʿah-compliant precious metal-backed cryptocurrency as an alternative currency: An empirical validation of adoption of innovation theory. *Thunderbird International Business Review*, *62*(2), 171–181. DOI: 10.1002/tie.22106

Alam, A. (2023). Developing a Curriculum for Ethical and Responsible AI: A University Course on Safety, Fairness, Privacy, and Ethics to Prepare Next Generation of AI Professionals. In *Lecture Notes on Data Engineering and Communications Technologies* (Vol. 171, pp. 879–894). DOI: 10.1007/978-981-99-1767-9_64

Alemán, J. J., Sánchez-Pi, N., Marti, L., Molina, J. M., & Garcia, A. C. B. (2016). A data fusion model for ambient assisted living. In *Communications in Computer and Information Science* (Vol. 616). DOI: 10.1007/978-3-319-39387-2_25

Alharthi, S., Cerotti, P., & Far, S. (2020,). An Exploration of The Role of Blockchain in The Sustainability and Effectiveness of The Pharmaceutical Supply Chain. . *J. Suppl. Chain Cust. Relatsh. Manag.*, 1-29.

Ali, F., Khurram, M. U., Sensoy, A., & Vo, X. V. (2024). Green cryptocurrencies and portfolio diversification in the era of greener paths. *Renewable & Sustainable Energy Reviews*, *191*, 114137. DOI: 10.1016/j.rser.2023.114137

Allen, F., Gu, X., & Jagtiani, J. (2022). Fintech, Cryptocurrencies, and CBDC: Financial Structural Transformation in China. *Journal of International Money and Finance*, *124*, 102625. Advance online publication. DOI: 10.1016/j.jimonfin.2022.102625

Ally, M., Gardiner, M., & Lane, M. (2015). The potential impact of digital currencies on the Australian economy. *ACIS 2015 Proceedings - 26th Australasian Conference on Information Systems*. https://www.scopus.com/inward/record.uri?eid=2-s2.0-85054408005&partnerID=40&md5=6c0ccc32b3d102de58a38fbaec2f1625

Almekhlafi, S., & Al-Shaibany, N. (2021). The Literature Review of Blockchain Adoption. *Asian J. Res. Comput. Sci.*, *7*, 29–50. DOI: 10.9734/ajrcos/2021/v7i230177

Alonso, S. L. N., Fernández, M. Á. E., Bas, D. S., & Kaczmarek, J. (2020). Reasons fostering or discouraging the implementation of central bank-backed digital currency. *A review Economies*, *8*(2), 41. Advance online publication. DOI: 10.3390/economies8020041

Alvarez, F., Argente, D., & Van Patten, D. (2022). *Are cryptocurrencies currencies? Bitcoin as legal tender in El Salvador*. National Bureau of Economic Research. Retrieved from https://www.nber.org/papers/w29968

Amaral, G., Sales, T. P., & Guizzardi, G. (2021). Towards ontological foundations for central bank digital currencies. *CEUR Workshop Proceedings*, *2835*, 77–86. https://www.scopus.com/inward/record.uri?eid=2-s2.0-85103279777&partnerID=40&md5=12b3ebb5d915ed389e6da1593d81d639

Angelis, J., & Ribeiro da Silva, E. (2019). Blockchain adoption: A value driver perspective. *Business Horizons*, *62*(3), 307–314. DOI: 10.1016/j.bushor.2018.12.001

Ang, M. T., & Chow, Y. P. (2023). Influence of virtual currency development and investor attention on financial stocks' value: Evidence from selected Asian equity markets. *Journal of Financial Regulation and Compliance*, *31*(1), 96–125. DOI: 10.1108/JFRC-01-2022-0007

Ante, L. (2021). How Elon Musk's Twitter activity moves cryptocurrency markets. *Finance Research Letters*, *38*, 101534. DOI: 10.1016/j.frl.2020.101534

Antonopoulos, A. M. (2017). *Mastering Bitcoin: Unlocking digital cryptocurrencies* (2nd ed.). O'Reilly Media.

Ara Eti, I., Horaira, M. A., & Bari, M. M. (2021). Power and stimulus of social media marketing on consumer purchase intention in Bangladesh during the COVID-19. International Journal of Research in Business and Social Science (2147- 4478), 10(1), 28–37. .DOI: 10.20525/ijrbs.v10i1.1011

Aria, M., & Cuccurullo, C. (2017). bibliometrix: An R-tool for comprehensive science mapping analysis. *Journal of Informetrics, 11*(4), 959–975. DOI: 10.1016/j.joi.2017.08.007

Arner, D. W., Auer, R., & Frost, J. (2020). *Stablecoins: Risks, potential and regulation.* Bank for International Settlements. https://www.bis.org/publ/bisbull05.htm

Arner, D. W., Barberis, J., & Buckley, R. P. (2016). The Evolution of Fintech: A New Post-Crisis Paradigm? *University of Hong Kong Faculty of Law Research Paper No. 2015/047.*

Arner, D. W., Barberis, J., & Buckley, R. P. (2017). *FinTech and RegTech in a Nutshell, and the Future in a Sandbox.* CFA Institute Research Foundation. DOI: 10.2139/ssrn.3088303

Attia, A. (2023). Effect of Sustainable Management of Supply Chain and Client Associationship Management on Organizational Performance in the Context of the Egyptian Textile Industry. *Sustainability (Switzerland), 15*(5). Advance online publication. DOI: 10.3390/su15054072

Auer, R., & Böhme, R. (2020). *The technology of retail central bank digital currency.* BIS Quarterly Review, March 2020, 85–100. https://www.bis.org/publ/qtrpdf/r_qt2003j.pdf

Auer, R., & Böhme, R. (2020). The technology of retail central bank digital currency. *BIS Quarterly Review,* March 2020, 85–100. Retrieved from https://www.bis.org/publ/qtrpdf/r_qt2003j.htm

Auer, R., Cornelli, G., & Frost, J. (2020). Rise of the Central Bank Digital Currencies: Drivers, Approaches, and Technologies. *BIS Working Papers.*

Auer, R., Cornelli, G., & Frost, J. (2021). Rise of the central bank digital currencies: Drivers, approaches, and technologies. *Bank for International Settlements Quarterly Review, March 2021*, 67–83.

Auer, R., Haene, P., & Holden, H. (2021). *Multi-CBDC arrangements and the future of cross-border payments* (BIS Papers No. 115). Bank for International Settlements. Retrieved from https://www.bis.org/publ/bppdf/bispap115.pdf

Auer, R., Monnet, C., & Shin, H. S. (2022). *Permissioned distributed ledgers and the governance of money* (BIS Working Papers No. 1060). Bank for International Settlements. Retrieved from https://www.bis.org/publ/work1060.pdf

Auer, S., Nagler, S., Mazumdar, S., & Mukkamala, R. R. (2022). Towards blockchain-IoT based shared mobility: Car-sharing and leasing as a case study. *Journal of Network and Computer Applications*, *200*, 103316. DOI: 10.1016/j.jnca.2021.103316

Banerjee S. and Sinha M., (2023). Promoting Financial Inclusion through Central Bank Digital Currency: An Evaluation of Payment System Viability in India Australasian Accounting, Business and Finance Journal https://doi.org/DOI: 10.14453/aabfj.v17i1.14

Bank for International Settlements (BIS). (2021). *CBDCs: Financial stability implications*. https://www.bis.org/publ/bppdf/bispap117.pdf

Bank for International Settlements. (2021). *CBDCs: An opportunity for the monetary system*. Retrieved from https://www.bis.org/publ/arpdf/ar2021e3.htm

Bank for International Settlements. (2021). *Central Bank Digital Currencies: Financial Stability Implications*. BIS Quarterly Review.

Bank for International Settlements. (2021). *Central bank digital currencies: Financial stability implications*. BIS Quarterly Review. https://www.bis.org

Bank for International Settlements. (2023). *Gaining momentum — Results of the 2022 BIS survey on central bank digital currencies*. Retrieved from https://www.bis.org/publ/bppdf/bispap136.pdf

Barney, J. (1991). Firm Resources and Sustained Competitive Advantage. *Journal of Management*, *17*(1), 99–120. DOI: 10.1177/014920639101700108

Baskaran, K. (2023). Experience of customer in the E-commerce market through the virtual world of metaverse. In *Handbook of Investigation on consumer behavioral analytics in metaverse and the adoption of a virtual world* (pp. 153–170). IGI Global. DOI: 10.4018/978-1-6684-7029-9.ch008

Bassanelli, S., Belliato, R., Bonetti, F., Vacondio, M., Gini, F., Zambotto, L., & Marconi, A. (2025). Gamify to persuade: A systematic review of gamified sustainable mobility. *Acta Psychologica*, *252*, 104687. DOI: 10.1016/j.actpsy.2024.104687 PMID: 39765142

Battalova, L. M., Enikeev, R. N., Kokanov, N. A., Semivelichenko, E. A., & Probichev, V. S. (2019). Legal regulation of virtual currency: International experience development trend in russia. *Humanities and Social Sciences Reviews*, *7*(4), 911–914. DOI: 10.18510/hssr.2019.74122

Belke, A., & Beretta, E. (2020). From cash to central bank digital currencies and cryptocurrencies: A balancing act between modernity and monetary stability. *Journal of Economic Studies (Glasgow, Scotland)*, *47*(4), 911–938. Advance online publication. DOI: 10.1108/JES-07-2019-0311

Belz, F. M., & Peattie, K. (2012). *Sustainability marketing: A global perspective.* Wiley.

Bettín-Díaz, R. R.-M. (2018). Methodological approach to the definition of a blockchain system for the food industry supply chain trace-ability. In Lecture notes in computer science (including subseries lecture notes in artificial intelligence and lecture notes in bioinformatics. *Springer Verlag.*, (pp. 19–33).

Bharadwaj, S., & Deka, S. (2021, December). Behavioural intention towards investment in cryptocurrency: An integration of Rogers' diffusion of innovation theory and the technology acceptance model. *Forum Scientiae Oeconomia*, *9*(4), 137–159.

Bhardwaj, A., Garg, A., & Gajpal, Y. (2021). Determinants of Blockchain Technology Adoption in Supply Chains by Small and Medium Enterprises (SMEs) in India. *Mathematical Problems in Engineering*, *2021*, 5537395. DOI: 10.1155/2021/5537395

Bibri, S. E., Alexandre, A., Sharifi, A., & Krogstie, J. (2023). Environmentally sustainable smart cities and their converging AI, IoT, and big data technologies and solutions: An integrated approach to an extensive literature review. *Energy Informatics*, *6*(1), 9. DOI: 10.1186/s42162-023-00259-2 PMID: 37032812

Biggi, G., & Giuliani, E. (2020). The noxious consequences of innovation: What do we know? *Industry and Innovation*, *28*(1), 19–41. DOI: 10.1080/13662716.2020.1726729

Biloslavo, R. B., Bagnoli, C., & Edgar, D. (2018). An eco-critical perspective on business models: The value triangle as an approach to closing the sustainability gap. *Journal of Cleaner Production*, *174*, 746–762. DOI: 10.1016/j.jclepro.2017.10.281

Bitrián, P., Buil, I., & Catalán, S. (2021). Enhancing user engagement: The role of gamification in mobile apps. *Journal of Business Research*, *132*, 170–185. DOI: 10.1016/j.jbusres.2021.04.028

Bolívar, M. P. R., Sepe, F., Nanu, L., & Roberto, R. (2024). Perceptions and challenges of blockchain adoption in tourism industry: A study on trust, privacy and security. *Journal of Hospitality and Tourism Technology*, *16*(3), 429–449. DOI: 10.1108/JHTT-03-2024-0193

Bolton, R., Grewal, D., & Levy, M. (2018). Six megatrends that matter: Proactive channel strategies for retailing. *Journal of Retailing*, *94*(4), 241–253.

Boubellouta, B., & Kusch-Brandt, S. (2021). Relationship between economic growth and mismanaged e-waste: Panel data evidence from 27 EU countries analyzed under the Kuznets curve hypothesis. *Waste Management (New York, N.Y.)*, *120*, 85–97. DOI: 10.1016/j.wasman.2020.11.032 PMID: 33285377

Boumaiza, A. (2024). A blockchain-centric P2P trading framework incorporating carbon and energy trades. *Energy Strategy Reviews*, *54*, 101466. DOI: 10.1016/j.esr.2024.101466

Bouri, E.. (2019). *Trading volume and the predictability of return and volatility in the cryptocurrency market Finance Res*. Lett.

Brunnermeier, M. K., & Niepelt, D. (2019). On the equivalence of private and public money. *Journal of Monetary Economics*, *106*, 27–41. Advance online publication. DOI: 10.1016/j.jmoneco.2019.07.004

Bucherer, E. E., Eisert, U., & Gassmann, O. (2012). Towards systematic business model innovation lessons from product innovation management. *Creativity and Innovation Management*, *21*(2), 183–198. DOI: 10.1111/j.1467-8691.2012.00637.x

Buer, S. V., Strandhagen, J. O., & Chan, F. T. S. (2018). The link between Industry 4.0 and lean manufacturing: Mapping current research and establishing a research agenda. *International Journal of Production Research*, *56*(8), 2924–2940. DOI: 10.1080/00207543.2018.1442945

Buhalis, D., & Sinarta, Y. (2019). Real-time co-creation and nowness service: Lessons from tourism and hospitality. *Journal of Travel & Tourism Marketing*, *36*(5), 563–582. DOI: 10.1080/10548408.2019.1592059

Calza, F., Sorrentino, A., & Tutore, I. (2023). Combining corporate environmental sustainability and experience of customer management to build an integrated model for decision-making. *Management Decision*, *61*(13), 54–84. DOI: 10.1108/MD-05-2022-0613

Cambridge Centre for Alternative Finance. (2023). *Cambridge Bitcoin Electricity Consumption Index*. University of Cambridge. Retrieved from https://ccaf.io/cbeci/index

Castronova, E. (2014). Wildcat currency: How the virtual money revolution is transforming the economy. In *Wildcat Currency: How the Virtual Money Revolution is Transforming the Economy*. https://www.scopus.com/inward/record.uri?eid=2-s2.0-84903069158&partnerID=40&md5=a52c7c05f559c8f849d57e4a83f89815

Catalini, C., & Gans, J. S. (2016). *Some simple economics of the blockchain* (MIT Sloan Research Paper No. 5191-16). Retrieved from https://papers.ssrn.com/sol3/papers.cfm?abstract_id=2874598

Catherine, S., Rani, M. N., & Suresh, N. V. (2024). The metaverse economy: Transforming money with digital currency. In *Creator's Economy in Metaverse Platforms* (pp. 202–209). Empowering Stakeholders Through Omnichannel Approach., DOI: 10.4018/979-8-3693-3358-7.ch012

Central Bank of The Bahamas. (2021). *The Sand Dollar Project*. Retrieved from https://www.centralbankbahamas.com/sand-dollar

CERT-In. (2024). *Annual report on cyber security incidents*. Ministry of Electronics and Information Technology, Government of India.

Chainalysis. (2022). *The 2022 global crypto adoption index*. Retrieved from https://www.chainalysis.com

Chainalysis. (2023). *Crypto Adoption and User Behavior Report*. Retrieved from https://www.chainalysis.com/reports

Chainalysis. (2023). *Crypto Crime Report 2023*. Retrieved from https://www.chainalysis.com/reports

Challoumis, C. (2023). The role of AI in digital currency - is cryptocurrency the future of money? In *Proceedings of the XVI International Scientific Conference* (pp. 126-130). Philadelphia, PA.

Chamanara, S., & Madani, K. (2023). *The Hidden Environmental Cost of Cryptocurrency: How Bitcoin Mining Impacts Climate, Water and Land. United Nations University Institute for Water, Environment and Health*. UNU-INWEH.

Chang, S., Chen, Y., & Wu, T. (2019). Exploring blockchain technology in international trade: Business process re-engineering for letter of credit. *Industrial Management & Data Systems*, *119*(ahead-of-print), 1712–1733. DOI: 10.1108/IMDS-12-2018-0568

Chen, Y. e. (2019). DEPLEST: A blockchain-based privacy-preserving distributed database toward user behaviors in social networks. In Information sciences. *Elsevier Inc.*, 501 (pp. 100–117). DOI: 10.1016/j.ins.2019.05.092

Cheng, P., (2022), Decoding the rise of Central Bank Digital Currency in China: designs, problems, and prospects Journal of Banking Regulation (2023) 24:156–170 https://doi.org/DOI: 10.1057/s41261-022-00193-5

Chen, S. C., Chou, T. H., Hongsuchon, T., Ruangkanjanases, A., Kittikowit, S., & Lee, T. C. (2022). The mediation influence of marketing activities toward augmented reality: The perspective of extended experience of customer. *Journal of Hospitality and Tourism Technology*, *13*(3), 461–480. DOI: 10.1108/JHTT-03-2021-0093

Chicago Mercantile Exchange. (2023). *Cryptocurrency Futures and Options*. Retrieved from https://www.cmegroup.com/markets/cryptocurrencies.html

Chiu, J., & Koeppl, T. V. (2019). Blockchain-based settlement for asset trading. *Review of Financial Studies*, *32*(5), 1716–1753. DOI: 10.1093/rfs/hhy122

Chivandi, A., Samuel, M. O., & Muchie, M. (2019). Social Media, Consumer Behavior, and Service Marketing. In Consumer Behavior and Marketing. Intech Open.

Choi, G., Park, M., & Park, N. (2018). The Use of Virtual Currencies in Small-Value Cross-Border Remittances and Its Implication. SSRN *Electronic Journal,January2018*. DOI: 10.2139/ssrn.3024427

Chugh, P. (2023). Leveraging Blockchain Technology in Adopting Digital Tokenization of Green Bonds. In *Fostering Sustainable Development in the Age of Technologies* (pp. 213–224). Emerald Publishing Limited., DOI: 10.1108/978-1-83753-060-120231015

Ciasullo, M. V., Troisi, O., Grimaldi, M., & Leone, D. (2020). Multi-level governance for sustainable innovation in smart communities: An ecosystems approach. *The International Entrepreneurship and Management Journal*, *16*(4), 1167–1195. DOI: 10.1007/s11365-020-00641-6

Cizmesija, A., & Vrcek, N. (May, 2021.). Organizational challenges of blockchain adoption: An exploratory literature review. *In Proceedings of the 2021 IEEE Technology and Engineering Management Conference-Europe, TEMSCON-EUR, Dubrovnik, Croatia,* 17–20.

CoinDesk. State of bitcoin and blockchain 2016. Jan 28, 2016. Available at http://www.coindesk.com/state-of-bitcoin-blockchain-2016/. 32

CoinMarketCap. https://coinmarketcap.com/all/views/all/ (last visited Aug. 7, 2018).

CoinMetrics. (2023). *Crypto Asset Volatility Data*. Retrieved from https://coinmetrics.io

Cole, R. S., Stevenson, M., & Aitken, J. (2019). Blockchain technology: Implications for operations and supply chain management. *Supply Chain Management, 24*(4), 469–483. DOI: 10.1108/SCM-09-2018-0309

Cong, L. W., & He, Z. (2019). Blockchain disruption and smart contracts. *Review of Financial Studies, 32*(5), 1754–1797. DOI: 10.1093/rfs/hhz007

Cuervo, C., Morazova, A., & Sugimoto, N. (2019). *Regulation Assets*. International Fund.

Cumming, D. J., Johan, S., & Pant, A. (2019). Regulation of the crypto-economy: Managing risks, challenges, and regulatory uncertainty. *Journal of Risk and Financial Management, 12*(3), 126. DOI: 10.3390/jrfm12030126

Currency, D. Breakthroughs in Research and Practice. (2019). In *Digital Currency: Breakthroughs in Research and Practice*. DOI: 10.4018/978-1-5225-6201-6

Cvelbar, L. K., Grün, B., & Dolnicar, S. (2017). Which hotel guest segments reuse towels? Selling sustainable tourism services through target marketing. *Journal of Sustainable Tourism, 25*(7), 921–934. DOI: 10.1080/09669582.2016.1206553

Dabrowski, M., & Janikowski, L. (2018). *Virtual currencies and central banks monetary policy : challenges ahead. July.*

Dai, J., & Vasarhelyi, M. A. (2017). Toward blockchain-based accounting and assurance. *Journal of Information Systems, 31*(3), 5–21. DOI: 10.2308/isys-51804

Danvila-del-Valle, I., Estévez-Mendoza, C., & Lara, J. (2019, August). F., Human resources training: A bibliometric analysis. *Journal of Business Research, 101*, 627–636. Advance online publication. DOI: 10.1016/j.jbusres.2019.02.026

Das, S. (2024). *Significance of Digital Currencies in Sustainable Finance and Investment—An Indian Perspective. September*. DOI: 10.1002/9781394234035.ch12

Davis, F. D. (1989). Perceived usefulness, perceived ease of use, and user acceptance of information technology. *Management Information Systems Quarterly, 13*(3), 319–340. DOI: 10.2307/249008

De Vries, A. (2018). Bitcoin's growing energy problem. *Joule, 2*(5), 801–805. DOI: 10.1016/j.joule.2018.04.016

de Vries, A., Gallersdörfer, U., Klaaßen, L., & Stoll, C. (2022). Revisiting Bitcoin's carbon footprint. *Joule, 6*(3), 498–502. DOI: 10.1016/j.joule.2022.02.005

Delbufalo, E. (2021). Asset specificity and relationship performance: A meta-analysis over three decades. *Journal of Business Research, 134*, 105–121. DOI: 10.1016/j.jbusres.2021.05.015

Deloitte. (2023). *Digital payments in India: Navigating trust and security*. Deloitte Insights. https://www2.deloitte.com/in/en.html

Dereso, C. W., Kant, S., Muthuraman, M., & Tufa, G. (2023). Effect of Point of Service on Health Department Student's Creativity in Comprehensive Universities of Ethiopia: Moderating Function of Public-Private Partnership and Mediating Function of Work Place Learning. In: Jain, S., Groppe, S., Mihindukulasooriya, N. (eds) Proceedings of the International Health Informatics Conference. Lecture Notes in Electrical Engineering, vol 990. Springer, Singapore. https://doi.org/DOI: 10.1007/978-981-19-9090-8_13

Diana, S., Yulia, F., & Ivolgina, N. V. (2018). The role of cryptocurrencies in the world economy development. *Proceedings of the 32nd International Business Information Management Association Conference, IBIMA 2018 - Vision 2020: Sustainable Economic Development and Application of Innovation Management from Regional Expansion to Global Growth*, 2937–2954. https://www.scopus.com/inward/record.uri?eid=2-s2.0-85063054634&partnerID=40&md5=1c1e7f36b62196cd6f7b21df63707acd

Dib, O., Brousmiche, K., Durand, A., Thea, E., & Hamida, E. (2018). Consortium blockchains: Overview, applications and challenges. *Int. J. Adv. Telecommun., 11*, 51–64.

Dimitrov, D. V. (2019). Blockchain applications for healthcare data management. Healthcare Informatics Research. *Korean Society of Medical Informatics, 25*(1), 51–56.

Diniz, E. H., de Araujo, M. H., Alves, M. A., & Gonzalez, L. (2024). Design principles for sustainable community currency projects. *Sustainability Science, •••*, 1–15. DOI: 10.1007/s11625-023-01456-4

Diniz, E., de Albuquerque, J. P., & Cernev, A. K. (2021). Mobile payment and inclusion: Trends and challenges in the global south. *Information Technology for Development, 27*(1), 4–15. DOI: 10.1080/02681102.2020.1837469

Donner, J., & Tellez, C. A. (2008). Mobile banking and economic development: Linking adoption, impact, and use. *Asian Journal of Communication, 18*(4), 318–332. DOI: 10.1080/01292980802344190

Donthu, N., Pattnaik, D., Pandey, N., and Kumar, s., (2020), A Bibliometric Review of International Marketing Review (IMR): Past, Present, and Future International Marketing Review http://dx.doi.org/DOI: 10.1108/IMR-11-2020-0244

Donthu, N., Kumar, S., Mukherjee, D., Pandey, N., & Lim, W. M. (2021). How to conduct a bibliometric analysis: An overview and guidelines. *Journal of Business Research, 133*, 285–296. DOI: 10.1016/j.jbusres.2021.04.070

Dorfleitner, G., & Braun, D. (2019). Fintech, digitalization and blockchain: possible applications for green finance. *The rise of green finance in Europe: opportunities and challenges for issuers, investors and marketplaces*, 207-237.

Dubey, R. G., Gunasekaran, A., Papadopoulos, T., & Childe, S. J. (2015). Green supply chain management enablers: Mixed methods research. *Sustainable Production and Consumption, 4*, 72–88. DOI: 10.1016/j.spc.2015.07.001

Durga, P., Godavarthi, D., Kant, S., & Basa, S. S. (2024). Aspect-based drug review classification through a hybrid model with ant colony optimization using deep learning. *Discov Computing, 27*(1), 19. DOI: 10.1007/s10791-024-09441-w

Du, W. D. (2019). Affordances, experimentation and actualization of FinTech: A blockchain implementation study. *Journal of Strategic Information Systems. Elsevier B.V., 28*(1), 50–65.

Dwivedi, S. K., Roy, P., Karda, C., Agrawal, S., & Amin, R. (2021). Blockchain-based internet of things and industrial IoT: A comprehensive survey. *Security and Communication Networks, 2021*(1), 7142048. DOI: 10.1155/2021/7142048

Eck, N., & Waltman, L. (2010). oftware survey: VOSviewer, a computer program for bibliometric mapping. *Scientometrics, 84*(2), 523–538. DOI: 10.1007/s11192-009-0146-3 PMID: 20585380

Egorova, E. N., Mukhomorova, I. V., & Mosalev, A. I. (2019). Digital currency in the development of payment systems on the bitcoin platform. In *Lecture Notes in Networks and Systems* (Vol. 57, pp. 167–175). DOI: 10.1007/978-3-030-00102-5_17

Eichengreen, B., & Viswanath-Natraj, G. (2022). Stablecoins and central bank digital currencies: Policy and regulatory challenges. *Asian Economic Papers, 21*(1), 29–46. DOI: 10.1162/asep_a_00843

ENISA. (2022). *Threat landscape for cryptocurrency*. European Union Agency for Cybersecurity. Retrieved from https://www.enisa.europa.eu

Ethereum Foundation. (2022). *The Merge*. Retrieved from https://ethereum.org/en/upgrades/merge/

European Central Bank. (2012). *Virtual currency schemes*. European Central Bank.

European Central Bank. (2019). *Exploring anonymity in central bank digital currencies*. Retrieved from https://www.ecb.europa.eu/pub/pdf/other/ecb.anonymouscbdc.201912~cbe0c6210d.en.pdf

European Central Bank. (2023). *Progress on the investigation phase of a digital euro*. Retrieved from https://www.ecb.europa.eu/pub/pdf/other/ecb.digitaleuro_progresreport2023~e6c8c0483c.en.pdf

European Commission. (2023). *Proposal for a Regulation on Markets in Crypto-assets (MiCA)*. Retrieved from https://finance.ec.europa.eu/publications/proposal-regulation-markets-crypto-assets-mica_en

Evans, S. V., Vladimirova, D., Holgado, M., Van Fossen, K., Yang, M., Silva, E. A., & Barlow, C. Y. (2017). Business model innovation for sustainability: Towards a unified perspective for creation of sustainable business models". *Business Strategy and the Environment*, *26*(5), 597–608. DOI: 10.1002/bse.1939

Evite, P. M. (2023). Bitcoin's Climate Impact: Carbon Emissions and Beyond. *Available atSSRN* 4650650. DOI: 10.2139/ssrn.4650650

FASB. (2022). *Accounting for and disclosure of crypto assets: Proposed accounting standards update*. Financial Accounting Standards Board. Retrieved from https://www.fasb.org/document/blob?fileName=ASU_Crypto_Assets_2023.pdf

FATF. (2021). *Updated Guidance for a Risk-Based Approach to Virtual Assets and Virtual Asset Service Providers*. Financial Action Task Force. Retrieved from https://www.fatf-gafi.org/media/fatf/documents/recommendations/Updated-Guidance-VA-VASPs.pdf

Fatorachian, H., O'Higgins, B., Maldonado, A., Lyons, C., Willis, H., Abbott, L., & Brooks, M. (2025). Navigating the challenges of FinTech startups in the B2C market. *Cogent Business & Management*, *12*(1), 2446696. DOI: 10.1080/23311975.2024.2446696

Fauzi, M. A., Hanafiah, M. H., & Kunjuraman, V. (2024). Tourists' intention to visit green hotels: Building on the theory of planned behaviour and the value-belief-norm theory. *Journal ofTourism Futures*, *10*(2), 255–276. DOI: 10.1108/JTF-01-2022-0008

Fernández, M. A. E., Alonso, S. L. N., Jorge-Vázquez, J., & Forradellas, R. F. R. (2021). *Central banks' monetary policy in the face of the COVID-19 economic crisis: Monetary stimulus and the emergence of CBDCs*. Sustainability., DOI: 10.3390/su13084242

Fernández-Villaverde, J., Sanches, D., Schilling, L., & Uhlig, H. (2021, July). Fernández-Villaverde, j.,Daniel, S., Linda, S., and Harald, U, (2020), Central bank digital currency: Central banking for all? *Review of Economic Dynamics*, *41*, 225–242. Advance online publication. DOI: 10.1016/j.red.2020.12.004

Fernando, Y., Jabbour, C. J. C., & Wah, W. X. (2019). Pursuing green growth in technology firms through the connections between environmental innovation and sustainable business performance: Does service capability matter? *Resources, Conservation and Recycling*, *141*, 8–20. DOI: 10.1016/j.resconrec.2018.09.031

Fido, D., Rees, A., Clarke, P., Petronzi, D., & Richardson, M. (2020). Examining the connection between nature connectedness and dark personality. *Journal of Environmental Psychology*, *72*, 101499. DOI: 10.1016/j.jenvp.2020.101499

Flammini, F., & Marrone, S. (2023). Distance education boosting interdisciplinarity and internationalization: an experience report from "Ethics, Law and Privacy in Data and Analytics" at SUPSI. *ACM International Conference Proceeding Series*, 54. DOI: 10.1145/3633083.3633103

Francisco, K., & Swanson, D. (2018). The supply chain has no clothes: Technology adoption of blockchain for supply chain transparency. *Logistics (Basel)*, *2*(1), 2. DOI: 10.3390/logistics2010002

Freeman, R. E., Harrison, J. S., Wicks, A. C., Parmar, B. L., & De Colle, S. (2010). *Stakeholder theory: The state of the art.*

Freni, P., Ferro, E., & Moncada, R. (2022). Tokenomics and blockchain tokens: A design-oriented morphological framework. *Blockchain: Research and Applications*, *3*(1), 100069.

Frolov, S., Ivasenko, M., Dykha, M., Heyenko, M., & Datsenko, V. (2023). *Analysis of the impact of central bank digital currency on stock markets: Dynamics and implications*. Banks and Bank Systems., DOI: 10.21511/bbs.18(4).2023.14

Fry, J. (2018). Booms, busts and heavy-tails: The story of bitcoin and cryptocurrency markets? *Economics Letters*, *171*, 225–229. DOI: 10.1016/j.econlet.2018.08.008

G7 Working Group on Stablecoins. (2019). *Investigating the impact of global stablecoins*. Retrieved from https://www.bis.org/cpmi/publ/d187.pdf

Gan, C., & Voda, M. (2023). Can green finance reduce carbon emission intensity? Mechanism and threshold effect. *Environmental Science and Pollution Research International*, *30*(1), 640–653. DOI: 10.1007/s11356-022-22176-9 PMID: 35906522

Ganesan, P., & Sridhar, M. (2016). Service innovation and customer performance of telecommunication service provider: A study on mediation effect of corporate reputation. *Corporate Reputation Review, 19*(1), 77–101. DOI: 10.1057/crr.2015.29

Garfield, E., (2004), Historiographic Mapping of Knowledge Domains Literature Journal of Information Science 30(2):119-145 DOI: and Simoes, R., Quieroz, G., Ferreira, K.,Vinhas, L., postgis-t: toward a spatiotemporal postgresql database extension Revista Brasileira de Cartografia 69(5) DOI:DOI: 10.1177/0165551504042802

Gatto, M., de Haan, S., Laborte, A., Bonierbale, M., Labarta, R., & Hareau, G. (2021). Trends in varietal diversity of main staple crops in Asia and Africa and implications for sustainable food systems. *Frontiers in Sustainable Food Systems, 5*, 626714. DOI: 10.3389/fsufs.2021.626714

Genc, H., & Takagi, S. (2024). A literature review on the design and implementation of central bank digital currencies. *International Journal of Economic Policy Studies, 18*(1), 197–225. DOI: 10.1007/s42495-023-00125-9

Gerard, D. (1993), Avant Card —(Online) a central bank digital currency from 1990s Finland https://davidgerard.co.uk/blockchain/2020/01/25/avant-card-a-central-bank-digital-currency-from-1990s-finland/

Ghose, A. (2018). *TAP: Unlocking the mobile economy*. MIT Press.

Ghosh, S., Kim, S., & Tian, X. (2020). Digital currencies and cross-border payments: New opportunities and challenges. *Journal of Financial Regulation and Compliance, 28*(3), 355–370. DOI: 10.1108/JFRC-02-2020-0016

GlobeNewswire. (2025, April 10). *Generative AI market size expected to reach USD 1,005.07 Bn by 2034*. https://www.globenewswire.com/news-release/2025/04/10/3059463/0/en/Generative-AI-Market-Size-Expected-to-Reach-USD-1-005-07-Bn-By-2034.html

Golinelli, G. M., Barile, S., Saviano, M., & Polese, F. (2012). Perspective shifts in marketing: Toward a paradigm change? *Service Science, 4*(2), 121–134. DOI: 10.1287/serv.1120.0015

Gong, Y., Zhang, X., Li, H., Zhang, X., He, S., & Miao, Y. (2021). A comparison of the growth status, rainfall retention and purification effects of four green roof plant species. *Journal of Environmental Management, 278*, 111451. DOI: 10.1016/j.jenvman.2020.111451 PMID: 33120092

Goutte, S., Guesmi, K., & Saadi, S. (2021). Cryptofinance: A New Currency for a New Economy. In *Cryptofinance: a New Currency for a New Economy*. DOI: 10.1142/12353

Govindaraj, M., Gnanasekaran, C., Khan, P., Gnanamanickam, S. V., & Hoang, S. D. (2024). Humanizing the digital touch: Strategies for balancing automation in modern marketing. In *Balancing Automation and Human Interaction in Modern Marketing* (pp. 175–202).

Govindaraj, M., Gnanasekaran, C., Krishnan, R., Khan, P., & Hoang, S. D. (2024). Retail supply chain management: Ensuring product availability and reducing out-of-stock incidents in India. In *Omnichannel Approach to Co-Creating Customer Experiences Through Metaverse Platforms* (pp. 116–141).

Goyal, K., & Kumar, S. (2021). Financial literacy: A systematic review and bibliometric analysis. *International Journal of Consumer Studies, 45*(1), 80–105. DOI: 10.1111/ijcs.12605

Grand View Research. (2024). *Artificial intelligence (AI) market size, share & trends analysis report.* https://www.grandviewresearch.com/industry-analysis/artificial-intelligence-ai-market

Gupta, M., Abdelsalam, M., Khorsandroo, S., & Mittal, S. (2020). Security and privacy in smart farming: Challenges and opportunities. *IEEE Access : Practical Innovations, Open Solutions, 8*, 34564–34584. DOI: 10.1109/ACCESS.2020.2975142

Gupta, S. e., Leszkiewicz, A., Kumar, V., Bijmolt, T., & Potapov, D. (2020). Digital analytics: Modeling for insights and new methods. *Journal of Interactive Marketing, 51*(1), 26–43. DOI: 10.1016/j.intmar.2020.04.003

Guyo, K., & Kero, C. A. "Mediation of Marketing Intermediaries and AI Adoption Between Livestock Products Marketing and Economic Status of Pastoralist in Ethiopia," *2023 International Conference on Communication, Security and Artificial Intelligence (ICCSAI)*, Greater Noida, India, 2023, pp. 311-316, https://doi.org/DOI: 10.1109/ICCSAI59793.2023.10421261

Haber, S., & Stornetta, W. (1990). How to Time-Stamp a Digital Document. In *Advances in Cryptology-CRYPTO' 90* (pp. 437–455). Springer.

Habib, F. (2021). *A Critical Analysis of Bitcoin from an Islamic Legal Perspective. Book Chapters. Fintech, Digital Currency and The Future of Islamic Finance Strategic*. Regulatory and Adoption Issues in The Gulf Cooperation Council.

Hadi, R., Melumad, S., & Park, E. S. (2024). The Metaverse: A new digital frontier for consumer behavior. *Journal of Consumer Psychology, 34*(1), 142–166. DOI: 10.1002/jcpy.1356

Hahn, A. e. (2017). *Smart contract-based campus demonstration of decentralized transactive energy auctions. 2017 IEEE power and energy society innovative smart grid technologies conference, ISGT 2017*. Institute of Electrical and Electronics Engineers Inc.

Hanafi, S. F., & Rahman, S. A. (2019). Regulating digital currency: taming the unruly. In *Emerging issues in Islamic finance law and practice in Malaysia* (pp. 265–280). Emerald Publishing Limited. DOI: 10.1108/978-1-78973-545-120191021

Haque M.A.; Shoaib M., (2023), e —The digital currency in India: Challenges and prospects *BenchCouncil Transactions on Benchmarks, Standards and Evaluations* DOI:DOI: 10.1016/j.tbench.2023.100107

Hariyani, D., Hariyani, P., Mishra, S., & Kumar Sharma, M. (2024). Stakeholders' perspectives and performance outcomes of sustainable market-focused manufacturing system in Indian manufacturing organizations. *Cleaner Logistics and Supply Chain, 13*(May), 100178. DOI: 10.1016/j.clscn.2024.100178

Hasan, M. R., Islam, M. Z., Sumon, M. F. I., Osiujjaman, M., Debnath, P., & Pant, L. (2024). Integrating artificial intelligence and predictive analytics in supply chain management to minimize carbon footprint and enhance business growth in the USA. *Journal of Business and Management Studies, 6*(4), 195–212. DOI: 10.32996/jbms.2024.6.4.17

Hewett, N., Lehmacher, W., & Wang, Y. (2019, April). Inclusive deployment of blockchain for supply chains. World Economic Forum.

Hong, Y., Al Mamun, A., Masukujjaman, M., & Yang, Q. (2024). Significance of the environmental value-belief-norm model and its relationship to green consumption among Chinese youth. *Asia Pacific Management Review, 29*(1), 127–140. DOI: 10.1016/j.apmrv.2023.10.002

Horvath, D. (2023). Money in the Digital Age: Exploring the Potential of Central Bank Digital Currency with a Focus on Social Adaptation and Education. *Sustainable Futures : An Applied Journal of Technology, Environment and Society, 6*, 100136. Advance online publication. DOI: 10.1016/j.sftr.2023.100136

Hou, L., Hsueh, S. C., & Zhang, S. (2021). Digital payments and households' consumption: A mental accounting interpretation. *Emerging Markets Finance & Trade, 57*(7), 2079–2093. DOI: 10.1080/1540496X.2021.1887727

Hoyer, W. D., Kroschke, M., Schmitt, B., Kraume, K., & Shankar, V. (2020). Transforming the customer experience through new technologies. *Journal of Interactive Marketing, 51*(1), 57–71. DOI: 10.1016/j.intmar.2020.04.001

https://www.forbesindia.com/

Hughes, L. D., Dwivedi, Y. K., Misra, S. K., Rana, N. P., Raghavan, V., & Akella, V. (2019). Blockchain research, practice and policy: Applications, benefits, limitations, emerging research themes and research agenda. *International Journal of Information Management, 49*, 114–129. DOI: 10.1016/j.ijinfomgt.2019.02.005

Hur, W. M., Ahn, K. H., & Kim, M. (2011). Building brand loyalty through managing brand community commitment. *Management Decision, 49*(7), 1194–1213. DOI: 10.1108/00251741111151217

Hye, A., Miraz, M., Sharif, K., & Hassan, M. (2020). Factors affecting logistic supply chain performance: Mediating role of block chain adoption. *Test Eng. Manag.*, *82*, 9338–9348.

Ibañez, J. I., Ladda, A., Tasca, P., & Aldred, L. (2024). The Unintended Carbon Consequences of Bitcoin Mining Bans: A Paradox in Environmental Policy. *arXiv preprint arXiv:2411.07254.*

Ilham, R. N., Fachrudin, K. A., Silalahi, A. S., & Saputra, J. (2019). Comparative of the supply chain and block chains to increase the country revenues via virtual tax transactions and replacing future of money. *International Journal of Supply Chain Management, 8*(5), 1066–1069. https://www.scopus.com/inward/record.uri?eid=2-s2.0-85078321329&partnerID=40&md5=1b001cb243e57d10404d84d56d4ef4e3

IMF. (2021). *The rise of public and private digital money.* International Monetary Fund. Retrieved from https://www.imf.org/en/Publications/fandd/issues/2021/03/the-rise-of-digital-money

IMF. (2022). *Global Financial Stability Report: Navigating the high-inflation environment.* Retrieved from https://www.imf.org/en/Publications/GFSR

Inder, S., Aggarwal, A., Gupta, S., Gupta, S., & Rastogi, S. (2021). An integrated model of financial literacy among B–school graduates using fuzzy AHP and factor analysis. *The Journal of Wealth Management, 23*(4), 92–110. DOI: 10.3905/jwm.2020.1.126

Investor's Business Daily. (2025, April). *AI stocks: Saudi Arabia's AI expansion could boost Nvidia, AMD.* https://www.investors.com/news/technology/ai-stocks-saudi-deals-nvidia-amd-supermicro/

J. Koroma et al. Assessing citizens' behavior towards blockchain cryptocurrency adoption in the Mano River Union States: mediation, moderation, role of trust and ethical issuesTechnol. Soc.(2022) [1]

Jabo, B., & Kant, S. "Impact of Technical CRM on Ethiopia Bank Human-Computer Interface and Competitive Advantage as Mediators of Performance," *2024 IEEE International Conference on Computing, Power and Communication Technologies (IC2PCT)*, Greater Noida, India, 2024, pp. 679-682, https://doi.org/DOI: 10.1109/IC2PCT60090.2024.10486237

Jabo, D., Kant, S., & Borji, B. (2025). Customer Orientation and Ethiopian Bank Performance With Mediation of Competitive Advantage. In *Leveraging AI for Effective Digital Relationship Marketing* (pp. 459–482). IGI Global., DOI: 10.4018/979-8-3693-5340-0.ch015

Jaime, F. J., Muñoz, A., Rodríguez-Gómez, F., & Jerez-Calero, A. (2023). Strengthening Privacy and Data Security in Biomedical Microelectromechanical Systems by IoT Communication Security and Protection in Smart Healthcare. *Sensors (Basel)*, *23*(21), 8944. Advance online publication. DOI: 10.3390/s23218944 PMID: 37960646

Jin, Z. (2022). Long-Term and Short-Term Integrated Learning-Based Price Forecasting for Virtual Currency. *Proceedings - 2022 2nd Asia-Pacific Conference on Communications Technology and Computer Science, ACCTCS 2022*, 438–442. DOI: 10.1109/ACCTCS53867.2022.00095

Joseph, J. (2023). *Digital Currencies and Cross-Border Payments: An Overview. December 2019*, 1–2. https://www.usitc.gov/publications/332/executive_briefings/ebot_digital_currency.pdf

Jothi, C. A., & Gaffoor, A. M. (2017). Impact of social media on online shopping. *Journal of Management Studies*, *3*(3), 576–586.

Jun, J., & Yeo, E. (2021). Central bank digital currency, loan supply, and bank failure risk: A microeconomic approach. *Financial Innovation*, *7*(1), 81. Advance online publication. DOI: 10.1186/s40854-021-00296-4 PMID: 35024292

Kar, A. K., & Navin, L. (2021). Diffusion of blockchain in insurance industry: An analysis through the review of academic and trade literature. *Telematics and Informatics*, *58*, 101532. DOI: 10.1016/j.tele.2020.101532

Kassociation, R. R., Zhang, J. Q., & Athaide, G. A. (2021). Measuring experience of customer management and its influence on financial performance. *European Journal of Marketing*, *55*(3), 840–867. DOI: 10.1108/EJM-07-2019-0592

Katz, E., Blumler, J. G., & Gurevitch, M. (1973). Uses and gratifications research. *Public Opinion Quarterly*, *37*(4), 509–523. DOI: 10.1086/268109

Kaur, M. (2019). Digital Currency and its Implications for India. *The Management Accountant Journal*, *54*(11), 64. DOI: 10.33516/maj.v54i11.64-67p

Keshav, A., & Sinha, A. R. (2024). Digital Money in the Indian Context: An In-depth Exploration of its Evolution, Implications, and Future Prospects within the Framework of Central Bank Digital Currency. *Journal of Electrical Systems, 20*(1), 350–361. DOI: 10.52783/jes.686

Khosravi, A., & Säämäki, F. (2023). Beyond Bitcoin: Evaluating energy consumption and environmental impact across cryptocurrency projects. *Energies, 16*(18), 6610. DOI: 10.3390/en16186610

Kiff, J., Alwazir, J., Davidovic, S., & Farias, F. (2020). *A survey of research on retail central bank digital currency.* International Monetary Fund. https://www.imf.org/en/Publications/WP/Issues/2020/06/26/A-Survey-of-Research-on-Retail-Central-Bank-Digital-Currency-49517

Kochergin, D., & Yangirova, A. (2019). Central bank Digital Currencies: Key Characteristics and Directions of Influence on Monetary and Credit and Payment Systems *Finance. Theory into Practice, 23*(4), 80–98. DOI: 10.26794/2587-5671-2019-23-4-80-98

Koemtzopoulos, D., Zournatzidou, G., Ragazou, K., & Sariannidis, N. (2025). Cryptocurrencies Transit to a Carbon Neutral Environment: From Fintech to Greentech Through Clean Energy and Eco-Efficiency Policies. *Energies (19961073), 18*(2).

Koemtzopoulos, D., Zournatzidou, G., & Sariannidis, N. (2025). Can Cryptocurrencies Be Green? The Role of Stablecoins Toward a Carbon Footprint and Sustainable Ecosystem. *Sustainability (Basel), 17*(2), 483. DOI: 10.3390/su17020483

Köhler, S., Bager, S., & Pizzol, M. (2022). Sustainability standards and blockchain in agro-food supply chains: Synergies and conflicts. *Technological Forecasting and Social Change, 185*, 122094. DOI: 10.1016/j.techfore.2022.122094

Kohli, V., Chakravarty, S., Chamola, V., Sangwan, K. S., & Zeadally, S. (2023). An analysis of energy consumption and carbon footprints of cryptocurrencies and possible solutions. *Digital Communications and Networks, 9*(1), 79–89. DOI: 10.1016/j.dcan.2022.06.017

Komalavalli, C., Saxena, D., & Laroiya, C. (2020). Overview of Blockchain Technology Concepts. In *Handbook of Research on Blockchain Technology* (pp. 349–371). Academic Press. DOI: 10.1016/B978-0-12-819816-2.00014-9

Konieczna, P. (2025). Exploring the Relationship Between Complementary Currencies and Sustainable Development: A Comparative Study. *Sustainability (Basel), 17*(8), 3627. DOI: 10.3390/su17083627

Koohang, A., Nord, J. H., Ooi, K. B., Tan, G. W. H., Al-Emran, M., Aw, E. C. X., & Wong, L. W. (2023). Shaping the metaverse into reality: A holistic multidisciplinary understanding of opportunities, challenges, and avenues for future investigation. *Journal of Computer Information Systems*, *63*(3), 735–765.

Kostrikova, N. (2021). Assessment of Blockchain Technology Adoption Factors and Scenarios Within the Economy of Latvia. *Lecture Notes in Networks and Systems*, *183*, 714–729. DOI: 10.1007/978-3-030-66840-2_54

Kotha, T., Amadae, S., & Rossi, M. (2024). Engaging consumers in sustainable behaviors using blockchain applications. In *Scandinavian Conference on Information Systems*. Association for Information Systems. DOI:https://research.aalto.fi/en/publications/engaging-consumers-in-sustainable-behaviors-using-blockchain-appl

Kotler, P., & Keller, K. L. (2016). *Marketing management* (15th ed.). Pearson Education.

Kraus, N. M., Kraus, K. M., & Andrusiak, N. O. (2020). Digital cubic space as a new economic augmented reality. *Science and Innovation*, *16*(3), 92–105. DOI: 10.15407/scine16.03.092

Krishnamurthy, N. (2023). Improving Sustainability: A Cryptocurrency-Based Reward Scheme for Reducing Carbon Emissions. *International Journal on Recent and Innovation Trends in Computing and Communication*, *11*(4), 413–419. Advance online publication. DOI: 10.17762/ijritcc.v11i4.9852

Krishnan, R., Mahesan, S. S., Manoj, G., Elantheraiyan, P., & Kandasamy, L. (2024). Navigating the crossroads: Stakeholder perspectives in healthcare innovation. In *Revolutionizing the Healthcare Sector with AI* (pp. 238–261).

Krishnan, R., Perumal, E., Govindaraj, M., & Kandasamy, L. (2024). Enhancing logistics operations through technological advancements for superior service efficiency. In *Innovative Technologies for Increasing Service Productivity* (pp. 61–82). DOI: 10.4018/979-8-3693-2019-8.ch004

Ku-Mahamud, K., Bakar, N., & Omar, M. (2018). Blockchain, cryptocurrency and Fintech market growth in Malaysia. *J. Adv. Res. Dyn. Control. Syst.*, *10*, 2074–2082.

Kumar, K., Rama Krishna, V., Govindaraj, M., Sathyakala, S., & Viswanathan, R. (2025). Characteristics determining customer's preferences for OTT video streaming: A multivariate analysis. *Entertainment Computing*, *52*, 100746. DOI: 10.1016/j.entcom.2024.100746

Kumar, V., Lahiri, A., & Dogan, O. B. (2019). A strategic framework for a profitable business model in the sharing economy. *Industrial Marketing Management, 69*, 147–160. DOI: 10.1016/j.indmarman.2017.08.021

Kumar, V., Rahman, Z., Kazmi, A. A., & Goyal, P. (2021). Evolution of sustainability as marketing strategy: Beginning of new era. *Sustainability, 13*(13), 7670. DOI: 10.3390/su13137670

Kumhof, M., & Noone, C. (2018). *Central bank digital currencies—Design principles and balance sheet implications*. Bank of England Staff Working Paper No. 725. DOI: 10.2139/ssrn.3180713

Kuner, C. (2003). *European data privacy law and online business*. Oxford University Press.

Lambert, T., Liebau, D., & Roosenboom, P. (2022). Security token offerings. *Small Business Economics, 59*(1), 299–325. DOI: 10.1007/s11187-021-00539-9

Laroiya, C., Saxena, D., & Komalavalli, C. (2020). Applications of blockchain technology. In *Handbook of research on blockchain technology* (pp. 213–243). Academic press., DOI: 10.1016/B978-0-12-819816-2.00009-5

Lee,Y., Son,B., Park,.S Lee, J., Jang, H., (2021), A Survey on Security and Privacy in Blockchain-based Central Bank Digital Currencies journal of Internet Services and Information Security (JISIS), volume: 11, number: 3 (August 2021), pp. 16-29 DOI:DOI: 10.22667/JISIS.2021.08.31.016

Le, T., Tran, S., Nguyen, D. Q. A. T., & Ngo, T. (2023). The degrees of central bank digital currency adoption across countries: A preliminary analysis. *Economics and Business Letters, 12*(2), 97–104. DOI: 10.17811/ebl.12.2.2023.97-104

Levashenko, A. D., Ermokhin, I. S., & Koval, A. A. (2019). Prospects of legal regulation of crypto economy and ICO in Russia and other countries. *Ekonomicheskaya Politika, 14*(5), 80–99. DOI: 10.18288/1994-5124-2019-5-80-99

Li, M., Jiang, D., Xu, S., Liu, Y., Gao, X., Guo, S., & Qi, F. (2024). A multi-factor real-time monitoring mechanism for the "mining" behavior of blockchain networks. *IEEE International Symposium on Broadband Multimedia Systems and Broadcasting, BMSB*. DOI: 10.1109/BMSB62888.2024.10608287

Lin, H. F. (2011). An empirical investigation of mobile banking adoption: The effect of innovation attributes and knowledge-based trust. *International Journal of Information Management, 31*(3), 252–260. DOI: 10.1016/j.ijinfomgt.2010.07.006

Liu, D. e. (2019). Anonymous reputation system for IIoT-enabled retail marketing atop PoS blockchain. *In IEEE transactions on industrial informatics: 15 IEEE. Computers & Society*, •••, 3527–3537.

Liu, X., Liu, Z., & Dong, X. (2025). Research on Countermeasures for the Governance of Virtual Currency Crimes in the Digital Economy Era. *Journal of Systems Science and Information*, *13*(1), 61–81. DOI: 10.21078/JSSI-2024-0046

Lotfi, R., MohajerAnsari, P., Sharifi Nevisi, M. M., Afshar, M., Reza Davoodi, S. M., & Ali, S. S. (2023, November). MohajerAnsari, P., Sharifi Nevisi, M. M., Afshar, M., Reza Davoodi, S. M., & Ali, S. S. (2024). A viable supply chain by considering vendor-managed-inventory with a consignment stock policy and learning approach. *Results in Engineering*, *21*, 101609. DOI: 10.1016/j.rineng.2023.101609

Luo, S., Yimamu, N., Li, Y., Wu, H., Irfan, M., & Hao, Y. (2023). Digitalization and sustainable development: How could digital economy development improve green innovation in China? *Business Strategy and the Environment*, *32*(4), 1847–1871. DOI: 10.1002/bse.3223

Mackey, T., Kuo, T., Gummadi, B., Clauson, K., Church, G., Grishin, D., Obbad, K., Barkovich, R., & Palombini, M. (2019). "Fit-for-purpose?"-Challenges and opportunities for applications of blockchain technology in the future of healthcare. *BMC Medicine*, *17*(1), 68. DOI: 10.1186/s12916-019-1296-7 PMID: 30914045

Madakam, S., Mark, S., Lurie, Y., & Revulagadda, R. K. (2023). The role of cryptocurrencies in business. *International Journal of Electronic Finance*, *12*(3), 238–262. DOI: 10.1504/IJEF.2023.131771

Maden, A., & Alptekin, E. (2020). Evaluation of factors affecting the decision to adopt blockchain technology: A logistics company case study using Fuzzy DEMATEL. *Journal of Intelligent & Fuzzy Systems*, *39*(5), 6279–6291. DOI: 10.3233/JIFS-189096

Madhani, P. (2010). Resource Based View (RBV) of Competitive Advantage: An Overview. ... *BASED VIEW: CONCEPTS AND ACTIVITIES, Pankaj ..., March*, 2–22. https://papers.ssrn.com/sol3/papers.cfm?abstract_id=1578704

Maesa, D., & Mori, P. (2020). Blockchain 3.0 applications survey. *Journal of Parallel and Distributed Computing*, *138*, 99–114. DOI: 10.1016/j.jpdc.2019.12.019

Mahajan, A., & Issa, T. (2020). Australian users' perspective of green blockchain technology adoption in businesses. In *Green Energy and Technology*. Springer.

Manohar, S. (2024). Cryptocurrency as a Slice in Investment Portfolio: Identifying Critical Antecedents and Building Taxonomy for Emerging Economy. *Asia-Pacific Financial Markets*, •••, 1–26. DOI: 10.1007/s10690-024-09490-7

Manohar, S., & Kapur, G. (2019). Measuring perceived service innovation typologies in retail industry. *Journal of Industrial Integration and Management*, *4*(2), 1850019. DOI: 10.1142/S2424862218500197

Manohar, S., Mittal, A., & Marwah, S. (2020). Service innovation, corporate reputation, and word-of-mouth in the banking sector: A test on multigroup-moderated mediation effect. *Benchmarking*, *27*(1), 406–429. DOI: 10.1108/BIJ-05-2019-0217

Mansfield-Devine, S. (2017). Beyond bitcoin: Using blockchain technology to provide as-surance in the commercial world. *Computer Fraud & Security*, *2017*(5), 14–18. DOI: 10.1016/S1361-3723(17)30042-8

Manyanga, W., Makanyeza, C., & Muranda, Z. (2022). The influence of experience of customer, customer satisfaction and word of mouth intention on customer loyalty: The moderating role of consumer demographics. *Cogent Business & Management*, *9*(1), 2082015. DOI: 10.1080/23311975.2022.2082015

Marin-Garcia, A., Gil-Saura, I., & Ruiz-Molina, M. E. (2022). Do innovation and sustainability influence customer satisfaction in retail? A question of gender. Economic Investigation-. *Ekonomska Istrazivanja*, *35*(1), 546–563. DOI: 10.1080/1331677X.2021.1924217

Marin, O., Cioara, T., Toderean, L., Mitrea, D., & Anghel, I. (2023). Review of blockchain tokens creation and valuation. *Future Internet*, *15*(12), 382. DOI: 10.3390/fi15120382

Marsh. (2021). *Crypto Insurance Solutions: Managing Risk in the Digital Asset Ecosystem*. Retrieved from https://www.marsh.com/us/industries/financial-institutions/insights/cryptocurrency-insurance.html

Mastilak, L., Suchy, R., Kostal, K., & Kotuliak, I. (2023). Blockchain-Based Sustainable Retail Loyalty Program. *IEEE Access : Practical Innovations, Open Solutions*, *11*, 75063–75075. DOI: 10.1109/ACCESS.2023.3296914

Mentari, T., Setiawan, R. Y., Wiriatmaja, N. U., Hutauruk, J. R., Muhyiansyah, A. R., & Rahman, N. (2024). The Influence of Financial Technology and Virtual Customer Service on Customer Satisfaction. *International Journal of Business, Law, and Education*, *5*(2), 2694–2614. DOI: 10.56442/ijble.v5i2.916

Miatton, F., & Amado, L. (2020, April). *Fairness, transparency and traceability in the coffee value chain through blockchain innovation. In 2020 international conference on technology and entrepreneurship-virtual (ICTE-V)*. IEEE.

Miernicki, M. (2024). Cash, accounts, and central bank digital currencies: a legal view on the introduction of account- and token-based digital central bank money Law and Financial Markets Review https://doi.org/DOI: 10.1080/17521440.2024.2308800

Miernicki, M., & Ying, H., (2024), Artifcial intelligence and moral rights *AI & SOCIETY* (2021) 36:319–329 https://doi.org/DOI: 10.1007/s00146-020-01027-6

Mi, J., Yao, C., Zhao, X., & Li, F. (2024). Research on the diffusion mechanism of green technology innovation based on enterprise perception. *Computational Economics*, *63*(5), 1981–2010. DOI: 10.1007/s10614-023-10391-6

Mikhaylov, A. (2021), Development of Friedrich von Hayek's theory of private money and economic implications for digital currencies. http://dx.doi.org/DOI: 10.18522/2073-6606-2021-19-1-53-62

Mikołajewicz-Woźniak, A., & Scheibe, A. (2015). Virtual currency schemes–the future of financial services. *Foresight*, *17*(4), 365–377. DOI: 10.1108/FS-04-2014-0021

Miraz, M. H. (2020). Factors affecting implementa- tion of blockchain in retail market in Malaysia. *International Journal of Supply Chain Management*, *9*(1), 385–391.

Mishchenko, V., Naumenkova, S., Mishchenko, S., & Tishchenko, I. (2025). Formation And Functioning Of Financial Metaverse Platforms. *Financial and Credit Activity: Problems of Theory and Practice*, *1*(60), 111–122. DOI: 10.55643/fcaptp.1.60.2025.4689

Mishra, D., Gunasekaran, A., Papadopoulos, T., & Dubey, R. (2018). Supply chain performance measures and metrics: A bibliometric study. *Benchmarking*, *25*(3), 932–967. DOI: 10.1108/BIJ-08-2017-0224

Moncada, R., Ferro, E., Fiaschetti, M., & Medda, F. (2024). Blockchain tokens, price volatility, and active user base: An empirical analysis based on tokenomics. *International Journal of Financial Studies*, *12*(4), 107. DOI: 10.3390/ijfs12040107

Mora, H., & Mollá-Sirvent, R. (2019). Enhancing business innovation through IoT and big data analytics. *Journal of Business Research*, *96*, 189–201.

Mora, H., Morales-Morales, M. R., Pujol-López, F. A., & Mollá-Sirvent, R. (2021). Social cryptocurrencies as model for enhancing sustainable development. *Kybernetes*, *50*(10), 2883–2916. DOI: 10.1108/K-05-2020-0259

Morales, J., Cornide-Reyes, H., Rossel, P. O., Sáez, P., & Silva-Aravena, F. (2023, July). Virtual reality, augmented reality and metaverse: experience of customer approach and user experience evaluation methods. Literature review. In International Conference on Human-Computer Interaction (pp. 554-566). Cham: Springer Nature Switzerland. DOI: 10.1007/978-3-031-35915-6_40

Mu, J., & Liu, W. (2023). The Impact Mechanism of Blockchain Technology on Financial Risk. *Lecture Notes in Electrical Engineering, 1031 LNEE*, 774–779. DOI: 10.1007/978-981-99-1428-9_95

Mudrika, S., Suharjo, D., Deni, D., & Wiadi, I. (2024). Sustainability in Marketing: Exploring the Influence of Green Marketing on Environmental Concern and Customer Satisfaction. *International Journal of Multicultural and Multireligious Understanding, 11*(2), 97–112. DOI: 10.18415/ijmmu.v11i2.5431

Mujkić, Z., Qorri, A., & Kraslawski, A. (2018). Sustainability and optimization of supply chains: A literature review. *Operations and Supply Chain Management, 11*(4), 186–199. DOI: 10.31387/oscm0350213

Muneeza, A., Arshad, N. A., & Arifin, A. T. (2018). The application of blockchain technology in crowdfunding: Towards financial inclusion via technology. *International journal of management and applied research, 5*(2), 82-98.

Murinde, V., Rizopoulos, E., & Zachariadis, M. (2022). The impact of the FinTech revolution on the future of banking: Opportunities and risks. *International Review of Financial Analysis, 81*, 102103. DOI: 10.1016/j.irfa.2022.102103

Murray, A., Crandall, R., & Vargo, D. (2021). Blockchain in the supply chain: A review of the literature and proposed framework for future research. *Journal of Business Logistics, 42*(1), 45–67. DOI: 10.1111/jbl.12270

Naini, S. R., Mekapothula, R. R., Jain, R., & Manohar, S. (2024). Redefining green consumerism: A diminutive approach to market segmentation for sustainability. *Environmental Science and Pollution Research International, 31*(9), 12916–12932. DOI: 10.1007/s11356-023-31717-9 PMID: 38180668

Nair, A. J., & Manohar, S. (2024). Green Service Consumption: Unlocking Customer Expectations on Technological Transformations Enhancing Purchase Experience in Retail Store. *International Journal of Information Management Data Insights, 4*(2), 100277. DOI: 10.1016/j.jjimei.2024.100277

Nair, A. J., Manohar, S., & Mittal, A. (2024). Reconfiguration and transformation for resilience: Building service organizations towards sustainability. *Journal of Services Marketing, 38*(4), 404–425. DOI: 10.1108/JSM-04-2023-0144

Nakamoto, S. (2008). *Bitcoin: A peer-to-peer electronic cash system.* Retrieved from https://bitcoin.org/bitcoin.pdf

Nakamoto, S. (Online). Available: (2008), https://bitcoin.org/ bitcoin.pdf. Accessed 15 May 2020

Nakamoto, S. Bitcoin: A Peer-to-Peer Electronic Cash System (2008);

National Centre for Financial Education (NCFE). (2022). *Financial literacy and inclusion survey report.* https://www.ncfe.org.in/

National Payments Corporation of India (NPCI). (2024). *UPI statistics.* https://www.npci.org.in/

Nexus Mutual. (2023). *Protocol Documentation.* Retrieved from https://nexusmutual.io/

Nguyen, L. T., Hoang, T. G., Do, L. H., Ngo, X. T., Nguyen, P. H., Nguyen, G. D., & Nguyen, G. N. (2021). The role of blockchain technology-based social crowdfunding in advancing social value creation. *Technological Forecasting and Social Change, 170,* 120898. DOI: 10.1016/j.techfore.2021.120898

Nian, L. P., & Chuen, D. L. K. (2015). Introduction to bitcoin. In *Handbook of digital currency* (pp. 5–30). Academic Press. DOI: 10.1016/B978-0-12-802117-0.00001-1

Nilson, K., & Tuvlind, A. (2020). Carbon offsetting and sustainable aviation: a study of contemporary and future sustainable aviation via carbon offsetting.

Nuseir, M. T., El Refae, G. A., Aljumah, A., Alshurideh, M., Urabi, S., & Kurdi, B. A. (2023). Digital marketing strategies and the influence on experience of customer: A systematic review. The Influence of Information Technology on Business and Marketing Intelligence Systems, 21-44.

Nyabadza, B. (2020). Search engine marketing and social media marketing predictive trends. Journal of Digital Media & Policy.

O'Dair, M. (2018). Distributed creativity: How blockchain technology will transform the creative economy.

OECD. (2022). *Financial Literacy and the Future of Digital Finance.* Organisation for Economic Co-operation and Development. Retrieved from https://www.oecd.org/finance/financial-education

OECD. (2023). *Crypto-Asset Reporting Framework and Amendments to the Common Reporting Standard*. Organisation for Economic Co-operation and Development. Retrieved from https://www.oecd.org/tax/exchange-of-tax-information/crypto-asset-reporting-framework-and-amendments-to-the-common-reporting-standard.htm

Ojha, N., Gohil, D., & Vaish, A. (2024). Cyber Ecosystem and Digital Currency: Review and Current Status. In *Fintech for Esg and the Circular Economy* (pp. 63–92). DOI: 10.1002/9781394234035.ch5

Omeish, F., Al Khasawneh, M., & Khair, N. (2024). Investigating the influence of AI on improving experience of customer through social media marketing: An analysis of Jordanian Millennials. *Computers in Human Behavior Reports*, *15*, 100464. DOI: 10.1016/j.chbr.2024.100464

Omotubora, A. (2024). 2024 Same Naira, More Possibilities! Assessing the Legal Status of the eNaira and Its Potential for Privacy and Inclusion. *Journal of African Law*, *68*(2), 1–18. DOI: 10.1017/S0021855324000044

Onat, N., Jabbar, R., Kucukvar, M., & Fetais, N. (2021). Bitcoin and global climate change: Emissions beyond borders.

Osterwalder, A., & Pigneur, Y. (2010). *Business model generation: a handbook for visionaries, game changers, and challengers* (Vol. 1). John Wiley & Sons.

Ovchinnikov, A. I., Kravchenko, A. G., Mamychev, A. Y., & Fatkhi, V. I. (2019). Virtual currency as an object of civil rights in Russia. *Humanities and Social Sciences Reviews*, *7*(6), 148–153. DOI: 10.18510/hssr.2019.7630

Packard, L., Singh, A. K., & Oguntoye, O. (2022). Crypto has an emissions challenge: Here's what leaders can do about it. *Future Technology, 1*(3), 06-13.

Page, M. J., McKenzie, J. E., Bossuyt, P. M., Boutron, I., Hoffmann, T. C., Mulrow, C. D., ... & Moher, D. (2021). The PRISMA 2020 statement: an updated guideline for reporting systematic reviews. *bmj, 372*.

Panigrahi, A., Pati, A., Sahu, B., Das, M. N., Nayak, D. S. K., Sahoo, G., & Kant, S. (2023). En-MinWhale: An ensemble approach based on MRMR and Whale optimization for Cancer diagnosis. *IEEE Access : Practical Innovations, Open Solutions, 11*, 113526–113542. DOI: 10.1109/ACCESS.2023.3318261

Park, S., Han, N., & Kim, E.-J. (2011). A Study on the Green Finance and Carbon Finance. *Muyeog Yeon'gu*, *7*(4), 345–363. DOI: 10.16980/jitc.7.4.201112.345

Parmentola, A., Petrillo, A., Tutore, I., & De Felice, F. (2022). Is blockchain able to enhance environmental sustainability? A systematic review and research agenda from the perspective of Sustainable Development Goals (SDGs). *Business Strategy and the Environment*, *31*(1), 194–217. DOI: 10.1002/bse.2882

Parssinen, M. A. (2018). Is blockchain ready to revolutionize online advertising? *In IEEE access. Institute of Electrical and Electronics Engineers Inc.*, *6*, 54884–54899.

Pattnaik, D., Hassan, M. K., Kumar, S., & Paul, J. (2020). Trade credit research before and after the global financial crisis of 2008–A bibliometric overview. *Research in International Business and Finance*, *54*, 101287. DOI: 10.1016/j.ribaf.2020.101287 PMID: 34173403

Paul, J., Lim, W. M., O'Cass, A., Hao, A. W., & Bresciani, S. (2021). Scientific procedures and rationales for systematic literature reviews (SPAR-4-SLR). *International Journal of Consumer Studies*, *45*(4), O1–O16. DOI: 10.1111/ijcs.12695

PayPal. (2022). *Annual report and cryptocurrency update*. Retrieved from https://investor.paypal-corp.com

Pelagidis, T., & Kostika, E. (2022). Investigating the role of central banks in the interconnection between financial markets and cryptoassets. *Economia e Politica Industriale*, *2022*(49), 481–507. DOI: 10.1007/s40812-022-00227-z

Peterson, M., Minton, E. A., Liu, R. L., & Bartholomew, D. E. (2021). Sustainable marketing and consumer support for sustainable businsses. *Sustainable Production and Consumption*, *27*, 157–168. DOI: 10.1016/j.spc.2020.10.018

Precedence Research. (2024). *Decentralized finance market size, share, growth 2024 to 2034*. https://www.precedenceresearch.com/decentralized-finance-market

Presthus, W., & O'Malley, N. O. (2017). Motivations and barriers for end-user adoption of bitcoin as digital currency. *Procedia Computer Science*, *121*, 89–97. DOI: 10.1016/j.procs.2017.11.013

Preukschat, A., & Reed, D. (2021). *Self-Sovereign Identity: Decentralized Digital Identity and Verifiable Credentials*. Manning Publications.

Priyanka, N., Sethi, S., Sahai, A., Srivastava, A., Sambathkumar, M., & Boopathi, S. (2024). Reality for human experience in AI in the digital economy. In *Multidisciplinary Applications of Extended Reality for Human Experience*. Christodoulou, I., Rizomyliotis, I., Konstantoulaki, K., Nazarian, A., & Binh, D. (2024). Transforming the remittance industry: Harnessing the power of blockchain technology. *Journal of Enterprise Information Management*. DOI: 10.4018/979-8-3693-2432-5.ch016

Przhedetskiy, Y., Przhedetskaya, N., Borzenko, K., & Bondarenko, V. (2019). Blockchain technologies in healthcare institutions: Focus on security and effective cooperation with the government. *Int. J. Econ. Bus. Adm.*, *VII*(Special Issue 2), 92–99. DOI: 10.35808/ijeba/373

PwC. (2023). *Cryptographic assets and tax treatment under IFRS.* Retrieved from https://www.pwc.com/gx/en/services/audit-assurance/assets/ifrs-cryptographic-assets.pdf

Qian, Y. (2019). Central Bank Digital Currency: Optimization of the currency system and its issuance design. *China Economic Journal*, *12*(1), 1–15. DOI: 10.1080/17538963.2018.1560526

Quarterly, F. I. (2020). *The crypto effect on cross border transfers and future trends of cryptocurrencies.* https://doi.org/DOI: 10.2478/fiqf

Quernheim, N., Winter, S., Arnemann, L., Wolff, S., Anderl, R., & Schleich, B. (2023). Concept for the Evaluation and Categorization of Sustainability Assessment Methods and Tools. In *Lecture Notes in Mechanical Engineering*. DOI: 10.1007/978-3-031-28839-5_81

Raftowicz, M., Solarz, K., & Dradrach, A. (2024). Short Food Supply Chains as a Practical Implication of Sustainable Development Ideas. *Sustainability (Basel)*, *16*(7), 1–14. DOI: 10.3390/su16072910

Rahardja, U., Hongsuchon, T., Hariguna, T., & Ruangkanjanases, A. (2021). Understanding influence sustainable intention of s-commerce activities: The role of experience of customers, perceived value, and mediation of relationship quality. *Sustainability*, *13*(20), 11492. DOI: 10.3390/su132011492

Rahmanzadeh, S. P., Pishvaee, M. S., & Rasouli, M. R. (2020). Integrated innovative product design and supply chain tactical planning within a blockchain platform. *International Journal of Production Research*, *58*(7), 2242–2262. DOI: 10.1080/00207543.2019.1651947

Rai, P., Gupta, D., & Gupta, M. (2025). Cryptocurrencies and Their Economic Implications: Analyse the Impact of Cryptocurrencies Like Bitcoin on Traditional Financial Systems, Including Their Potential to Disrupt Traditional Banking and the Role of Blockchain Technology in Creating Decentralised Economies. *Lecture Notes in Networks and Systems, 977 LNNS*, 131–142. DOI: 10.1007/978-981-97-2671-4_10

Ram Mohan Rao, P., Murali Krishna, S., & Siva Kumar, A. P. (2018). Privacy preservation techniques in big data analytics: A survey. *Journal of Big Data*, *5*(1), 33. Advance online publication. DOI: 10.1186/s40537-018-0141-8

Rane, N., Choudhary, S., & Rane, J. (2023). Metaverse marketing strategies: enhancing experience of customer and analysing consumer behaviour through leading-edge Metaverse technologies, platforms, and models. Platforms, and Models (November 3, 2023).

Ratinaud, P. (2014). IRaMuTeQ: Interface de R pour les Analyses Multidimensionnelles de Textes et de Questionnaires (Version 0.7 alpha 2). En ligne: http://www. iramuteq. org (consulté le 8 janvier 2024).

Raza, S. A., Ahmed, M., & Aloui, C. (2022). On the asymmetrical connectedness between cryptocurrencies and foreign exchange markets: Evidence from the non-parametric quantile on quantile approach. *Research in International Business and Finance*, *61*, 101627. Advance online publication. DOI: 10.1016/j.ribaf.2022.101627

Razi, Q., Devrani, A., Abhyankar, H., Chalapathi, G. S. S., Hassija, V., & Guizani, M. (2024). Non-Fungible Tokens (NFTs) - Survey of Current Applications, Evolution, and Future Directions. *IEEE Open Journal of the Communications Society*, *5*, 2765–2791. DOI: 10.1109/OJCOMS.2023.3343926

Reinert, M. (1990). Alceste une méthodologie d'analyse des données textuelles et une application: Aurelia De Gerard De Nerval. *Bulletin of Sociological Methodology. Bulletin de Methodologie Sociologique*, *26*(1), 24–54. DOI: 10.1177/075910639002600103

Rennie, E., & Steele, S. (2021). Privacy and emergency payments in a pandemic: How to think about privacy and a central bank digital currency. Law. *Technology and Humans*, *3*(1), 6–17.

Reserve Bank of India (2023). Concept Note on Central Bank Digital Currency.

Reserve Bank of India (RBI). (2022). *Concept Note on Central Bank Digital Currency*. https://www.rbi.org.in/Scripts/PublicationReportDetails.aspx?UrlPage=&ID=1210

Reserve Bank of India. (2023). *Concept note on Central Bank Digital Currency*. https://www.rbi.org.in

Risius, M., Breidbach, C. F., Chanson, M., Von Krannichfeldt, R., & Wortmann, F. (2023). On the performance of blockchain-based token offerings. *Electronic Markets*, *33*(1), 32. DOI: 10.1007/s12525-023-00652-5

Rogers, E. M. (1962). Diffusion of innovations the free Press of Glencoe. *NY, 32*, 891-937.

Rogers, E. M. (2003). *Diffusion of innovations* (5th ed.). Free Press.

Rouhizadeh, M.. (2021). Blockchain technology and the sustainable supply chain: Theoretically exploring adoption barriers. *International Journal of Production Economics.*

Rugeviciute, A., & Mehrpouya, A. (2019). Blockchain, a Panacea for Development Accountability? A Study of the Barriers and Enablers for Blockchain's Adoption by Development Aid Organizations. *Front. Blockchain, 2*, 15. DOI: 10.3389/fbloc.2019.00015

Ryan, R. M., & Deci, E. L. (2020). Intrinsic and extrinsic motivation from a self-determination theory perspective: Definitions, theory, practices, and future directions. *Contemporary Educational Psychology, 61*, 101860. DOI: 10.1016/j.cedpsych.2020.101860

Saberi, S. K., Kouhizadeh, M., Sarkis, J., & Shen, L. (2019). Blockchain technology and its relationships to sustainable supply chain management. *International Journal of Production Research, 57*(7), 2117–2135. DOI: 10.1080/00207543.2018.1533261

Sadeghi, M., Mahmoudi, A., & Deng, X. (2022). Adopting distributed ledger technology for the sustainable construction industry: Evaluating the barriers using Ordinal Priority Approach. *Environmental Science and Pollution Research International, 29*(7), 10495–10520. DOI: 10.1007/s11356-021-16376-y PMID: 34528198

Saheb, T., & Mamaghani, F. (2021). Exploring the barriers and organizational values of blockchain adoption in the banking industry. *The Journal of High Technology Management Research, 32*(2), 100417. DOI: 10.1016/j.hitech.2021.100417

Sarmiento A., (2022), Seven lessons from the e-Peso pilot plan: The possibility of a Central Bank Digital Currency Latin American Journal of Central Banking https://doi.org/DOI: 10.1016/j.latcb.2022.100062

Schär, F. (2021). Decentralized finance: On blockchain- and smart contract-based financial markets. *Review - Federal Reserve Bank of St. Louis, 103*(2), 153–174. DOI: 10.20955/r.103.153-74

Scheidegger, G., & Raghubir, P. (2022). Virtual currencies: Different schemes and research opportunities. *Marketing Letters, 33*(2), 351–360. DOI: 10.1007/s11002-022-09620-z PMID: 35502346

Schonebeck, L., & Pöllinger, T. (2020). *Stakeholder Management as a Tool for the Implementation of Sustainable Supply Chains in SMEs in the German Food Industry.* https://www.diva-portal.org/smash/record.jsf?pid=diva2:1481264%0Ahttps://www.diva-portal.org/smash/get/diva2:1481264/FULLTEXT01.pdf

Schulze, M., & Janssen, M. (2024). Self-determined or non-self-determined? Exploring consumer motivation for sustainable food choices. *Sustainable Production and Consumption*, *45*, 57–66. DOI: 10.1016/j.spc.2023.12.028

Schulz, G. (2016). *The green and virtual data center*. CRC Press. DOI: 10.1201/9781420086676

Schwiderowski, J., Pedersen, A. B., & Beck, R. (2024). Crypto tokens and token systems. *Information Systems Frontiers*, *26*(1), 319–332. DOI: 10.1007/s10796-023-10382-w

SEC. (2021). *Tesla Inc. Form 10-K Annual Report*. U.S. Securities and Exchange Commission. Retrieved from https://www.sec.gov/ix?doc=/Archives/edgar/data/0001318605/000156459021004599/tsla-10k_20201231.htm

Serttaş-Yırtıcı, Z., Balkaç, C., Alkaç, M., Alturjman, S., & Al-Turjman, F. (2024). Developing and Implementing a Gamification-Supported Adaptive Learning Environment in an Ai-Based Teaching System: The Example of Sudoku and Puzzle. *Sustainable Civil Infrastructures*, 855–870. DOI: 10.1007/978-3-031-78276-3_83

Sethaput, V., & Innet, S. (2023). Blockchain application for central bank digital currencies (CBDC). *Cluster Computing*, *26*(4), 2183–2197. DOI: 10.1007/s10586-022-03962-z PMID: 36686339

Shafik, W. (2024). Data-driven future trends and innovation in telemedicine. In *Improving Security, Privacy, and Connectivity Among Telemedicine Platforms* (pp. 93–118). IGI Global. DOI: 10.4018/979-8-3693-2141-6.ch005

Shan, S., Yang, S., Becerra, V., Deng, J., & Li, H. (2023). A Case Study of Existing Peer-to-Peer Energy Trading Platforms: Calling for Integrated Platform Features. *Sustainability (Basel)*, *15*(23), 16284. DOI: 10.3390/su152316284

Shao, H., Cheng, J., Wang, Y., & Li, X. (2022). Can digital finance promote comprehensive carbon emission performance? Evidence from Chinese cities. *International Journal of Environmental Research and Public Health*, *19*(16), 10255. DOI: 10.3390/ijerph191610255 PMID: 36011889

Sharma, N., & Manohar, S. (2024). Unlocking the Metaverse and Navigating Legal Implications in the NFT Landscape. In *Exploring the Use of Metaverse in Business and Education* (pp. 193–209). IGI Global., DOI: 10.4018/979-8-3693-5868-9.ch011

Shayan, N. F., Mohabbati-Kalejahi, N., Alavi, S., & Zahed, M. A. (2022). Sustainable Development Goals (SDGs) as a Framework for Corporate Ethic Responsibility (CSR). *Sustainability (Basel)*, *14*(3), 1–27. DOI: 10.3390/su14031222

Singh, S., Gupta, D., Kumar, R., & Balusamy, B. (2025). Pre-and Post-COVID Autonomous Finance: Global Perspective. *Computational Intelligence for Autonomous Finance*, 269-288.

Singh, A., Rupeika-Apoga, R., & Jangir, K. (2023). Does Previous Experience with the Unified Payments Interface (UPI) Affect the Usage of Central Bank Digital Currency (CBDC)? *Journal of Risk and Financial Management, 16*(6), 286. Advance online publication. DOI: 10.3390/jrfm16060286

Singh, S., Sharma, P. K., Yoon, B., Shojafar, M., Cho, G. H., & Ra, I. H. (2020). Convergence of blockchain and artificial intelligence in IoT network for the sustainable smart city. *Sustainable Cities and Society*, *63*, 102364. DOI: 10.1016/j.scs.2020.102364

Singh, V., & Yadav, M. (2025). User adoption of digital currency: A systematic review and future agenda using TCCM approach. *Central Bank Review*, *25*(1), 100183. DOI: 10.1016/j.cbrev.2024.100183

Siripurapu, S., Darimireddy, N. K., Chehri, A., Sridhar, B., & Paramkusam, A. V. (2023). Technological Advancements and Elucidation Gadgets for Healthcare Applications: An Exhaustive Methodological Review-Part-I (AI, Big Data, Block Chain, Open-Source Technologies, and Cloud Computing). *Electronics (Basel)*, *12*(3), 750. Advance online publication. DOI: 10.3390/electronics12030750

Song, S., Xiong, H., Lin, Y., Huang, M., Wei, Z., & Fang, Z. (2022). Robust three-phase state estimation for PV-Integrated unbalanced distribution systems. *Applied Energy*, *322*, 119427. DOI: 10.1016/j.apenergy.2022.119427

Sood, M., Aggarwal, A., Gupta, S., & Rastogi, S. (2021). Identifying factors of indian health system and their influence for providing good customer care. [IJHISI]. *International Journal of Healthcare Information Systems and Informatics*, *16*(4), 1–17. DOI: 10.4018/IJHISI.20211001.oa13

Srivastava, A. P., Yadav, M., Yadav, R., Singh, B., & Dewasiri, N. J. (2023). Exploring digital agility and digital transformation leadership: A mixed method study. [JGIM]. *Journal of Global Information Management*, *31*(8), 1–23. DOI: 10.4018/JGIM.332861

Srouji J., Torre D., (2022), The Global Pandemic, Laboratory of the Cashless Economy? *International Journal of Financial Studies*https://doi.org/DOI: 10.3390/ijfs10040109

Statista. (2023). *Public Attitudes Toward Cryptocurrency Usage in the U.S.* Retrieved from https://www.statista.com/statistics/

Stripe. (2022). *Company blog and Bitcoin payment integration.* Retrieved from https://stripe.com/blog

Stubbs, W., & Cocklin, C. (2008). Conceptualizing a 'sustainability business model'. *Organization & Environment, 21*(2), 103–127. DOI: 10.1177/1086026608318042

Subramanian, H. (2020). Security tokens: Architecture, smart contract applications and illustrations using SAFE. *Managerial Finance, 46*(6), 735–748. DOI: 10.1108/MF-09-2018-0467

Sun, J., Sarfraz, M., Khawaja, K. F., & Abdullah, M. I. (2022). Sustainable Supply Chain Strategy and Sustainable Competitive Advantage: A Mediated and Moderated Model. *Frontiers in Public Health, 10*(May), 1–10. DOI: 10.3389/fpubh.2022.895482 PMID: 35664096

Sveriges Riksbank. (2023). *The e-krona pilot – Phase 2.* Retrieved from https://www.riksbank.se/globalassets/media/rapporter/e-krona/2023/the-e-krona-pilot-phase-2.pdf

Swartz, L., & Westermeier, C. (2023). The money tree: Exploring central bank digital currency blockchain imaginaries. *Anthropology Today, 39*(4), 13–16. Advance online publication. DOI: 10.1111/1467-8322.12827

Szewczyk, R., Zieliński, C., & Kaliczyńska, M. (2019). *Advances in Intelligent Systems and Computing 920 Progress in Automation, Robotics and Measurement Techniques.* https://www.springer.com/series/11156

Tabatabaei, M. H., Vitenberg, R., & Veeraragavan, N. R. (2023). Understanding blockchain: Definitions, architecture, design, and system comparison. *Computer Science Review, 50*, 100575. DOI: 10.1016/j.cosrev.2023.100575

Tang, Y. M., Lau, Y. Y., & Ho, U. L. (2023). Empowering digital marketing with interactive virtual reality (IVR) in interior design: Influences on customer satisfaction and behaviour intention. *Journal of Theoretical and Applied Electronic Commerce Research, 18*(2), 889–907. DOI: 10.3390/jtaer18020046

Tapscott, D. a. (2016). *Blockchain Revolution: How the Technology behind Bitcoin is Blockchain Revolution: How the Technology behind Bitcoin is.* Portfolio- Penguin Books.

Tapscott, D. a. (2016). *Blockchain Revolution: How the Technology behind Bitcoin is Changing Money, Business, and the World, Portfolio.* Penguin Books.

Tapscott, D., & Tapscott, A. (2016). *Blockchain revolution: How the technology behind bitcoin is changing money, business, and the world.* Portfolio.

Tapscott, D., & Tapscott, A. (2017). *Blockchain revolution: How the technology behind Bitcoin is changing money, business, and the world.* Penguin.

Tolooee, K., Budaghi Khajeh Noubar, H., Gharehbiglo, H., & Ramazani, M. (2024). Providing a model of purchase intention and experience of customer on customer behavior in virtual networks. Journal of value creating in Business Management, 4(3), 274-297.

Tran, V. L., & Leirvik, T. (2020). *Efficiency in the markets of crypto currencies.* Finance Research ScienceDirect. DOI: 10.1016/j.frl.2019.101382

Tripathi, G., Ahad, M., & Paiva, S. (2020). S2HS- A blockchain based approach for smart healthcare system. *Health Care, 8*, 100391. PMID: 31753750

Tripathi, S. (2023). Impact of Cryptocurrency on the Environment. *Indian J. Integrated Rsch. L., 3*, 1.

Tripoli, M. a. (2018). *Emerging Opportunities for the Application of Blockchain in the Agri-Food Industry.* FAO and ICTSD, Rome, IT and Geneva.

Truby, J. (2018). Decarbonizing Bitcoin: Law and policy choices for reducing the energy consumption of Blockchain technologies and digital currencies. *Energy Research & Social Science, 44*, 399–410. DOI: 10.1016/j.erss.2018.06.009

Tsang, Y. P., Fan, Y., Lee, C. K. M., & Lau, H. C. W. (2024). Blockchain sharding for e-commerce supply chain performance analytics towards Industry 5.0. *Enterprise Information Systems, 18*(4), 2311807. Advance online publication. DOI: 10.1080/17517575.2024.2311807

Tseng, J. H., Liao, Y.-C., Chong, B., & Liao, S. (2018). Governance on the drug supply chain via gcoin blockchain. [MDPI AG.]. *International Journal of Environmental Research and Public Health, 15*(6), 15. DOI: 10.3390/ijerph15061055 PMID: 29882861

Urdea, A. M., Constantin, C. P., & Purcaru, I. M. (2021). Implementing experiential marketing in the digital age for a more sustainable customer relationship. *Sustainability (Basel), 13*(4), 1865. DOI: 10.3390/su13041865

Vafadarnikjoo, A., Badri Ahmadi, H., Liou, J., Botelho, T., & Chalvatzis, K. (2021). Analyzing blockchain adoption barriers in manufacturing supply chains by the neutrosophic analytic hierarchy process. *Annals of Operations Research, 327*(1), 129–156. DOI: 10.1007/s10479-021-04048-6

Valtakoski, A. (2020). The evolution and impact of qualitative research in Journal of Services Marketing. *Journal of Services Marketing, 34*(1), 8–23. DOI: 10.1108/JSM-12-2018-0359

Venkatesh, V., Morris, M. G., Davis, G. B., & Davis, F. D. (2003). User acceptance of information technology: Toward a unified view. *Management Information Systems Quarterly, 27*(3), 425–478. DOI: 10.2307/30036540

Verma, S. (2024). Study on Blockchain-Based Framework for Central Bank Digital Currency Design Opportunities, Risk, and Challenges. In *Artificial Intelligence Solutions for Cyber-Physical Systems* (pp. 432–438). DOI: 10.1201/9781032694375-25

Verma, N., Dhiman, B., Singh, V., Kaur, J., Guleria, S., & Singh, T. (2024). Exploring the global landscape of work-life balance research: A bibliometric and thematic analysis. *Heliyon, 10*(11), e31662. DOI: 10.1016/j.heliyon.2024.e31662 PMID: 38828335

Vinuella, C., Sapena, J., & Wandosell, G. (2020). The Future of Money and the Central Bank Digital Currency Dilemma. *Sustainability (Basel), 12*(22), 9697. DOI: 10.3390/su12229697

Virijević Jovanović, S., Pijevac, V., & Filipović, V. (2018). *Sustainable Marketing Strategy - the Way To Gain Profits on Worldwide Markets. January 2018*, 542–550. DOI: 10.31410/eraz.2018.542

Vogue Business. (2023). Vogue Business Index: Innovation intersects with sustainability as resale and blockchain adoption rise across luxury. https://www.voguebusiness.com/technology/ innovation intersects-with-sustainability-as-resale-and-blockchain-adoption-rise-across-luxury (Accessed May 23, 2025).

Vohra, S., & Davies, G. (2020). Investor regret, share performance and the role of corporate agreeableness. *Journal of Business Research, 110*, 306–315. DOI: 10.1016/j.jbusres.2020.01.013

Voramontri, D., & Klieb, L. (2019). Impact of social media on consumer behaviour. *International Journal of Information and Decision Sciences, 11*(3), 209–233. DOI: 10.1504/IJIDS.2019.101994

Wamba, S. F. (2020). Blockchain in the operations and supply chain management: Benefits, challenges and future research opportunities. . *Journal of Information Management*, 52.

Wang, L., Luo, G. L., Sari, A., & Shao, X. F. (2020). What nurtures fourth industrial revolution? An investigation of economic and social determinants of technological innovation in advanced economies. *Technological Forecasting and Social Change, 161*, 120305.

Wang, Y. J.-D., Han, J. H., & Beynon-Davies, P. (2019). Understanding blockchain technology for future supply chains: A systematic literature review and research agenda". *Supply Chain Management, 24*(1), 62–84. DOI: 10.1108/SCM-03-2018-0148

Weil, A. R. (2018). Diffusion of innovation. *Health Affairs, 37*(2), 175–175. DOI: 10.1377/hlthaff.2018.0059 PMID: 29401033

Wenzel, M., Koch, J., Cornelissen, J. P., Rothmann, W., & Senf, N. N. (2019). How organizational actors live out paradoxical tensions through power relations: The case of a youth prison. *Organizational Behavior and Human Decision Processes, 155*, 55–67. DOI: 10.1016/j.obhdp.2019.03.001

Wessels, B. (2014). Exploring the Dimensions of Change. *Exploring Ethic Change, January 2005*, 50–68. DOI: 10.1007/978-1-137-47142-0_4

Wibowo, A., Chen, S. C., Wiangin, U., Ma, Y., & Ruangkanjanases, A. (2020). Customer behavior as an outcome of social media marketing: The role of social media marketing activity and experience of customer. *Sustainability, 13*(1), 189. DOI: 10.3390/su13010189

Williams, S. (2022). Central Bank Digital Currency: Welfare and Policy Implications. *Journal of Political Economy, 130*(11), 2829–2861. Advance online publication. DOI: 10.1086/720457

Wolfson, A., Khaladjan, G., Lurie, Y., & Mark, S. (2025). The Greater Sustainability of Stablecoins Relative to Other Cryptocurrencies. *Journal of Risk and Financial Management, 18*(3), 161. DOI: 10.3390/jrfm18030161

World Bank. (2020). *The Global Findex Database 2017: Measuring financial inclusion and the fintech revolution*. World Bank.

World Bank. (2022). *Global Findex Database 2021: Financial inclusion, digital payments, and resilience in the age of COVID-19*. Retrieved from https://www.worldbank.org/en/publication/globalfindex

World Economic Forum. (2020). *Digital Currency Governance Consortium White Paper Series*. Retrieved from https://www.weforum.org/reports/digital-currency-governance-consortium-white-papers

World Economic Forum. (2022). *Digital transformation: Accelerating sustainable business models*. Geneva: World Economic Forum.

Wu, H., Wen, H., Li, G., Yin, Y., & Zhang, S. (2024). Unlocking a greener future: The role of digital finance in enhancing green total factor energy efficiency. *Journal of Environmental Management, 364*, 121456. DOI: 10.1016/j.jenvman.2024.121456 PMID: 38875989

Xiao, Z., Cui, S., Xiang, L., Liu, P. J., & Zhang, H. (2023). The environmental cost of cryptocurrency: Assessing carbon emissions from bitcoin mining in China. *Journal of Digital Economy, 2*, 119–136. DOI: 10.1016/j.jdec.2023.11.001

Xia, W., Chen, X., & Song, C. (2022). A framework of blockchain technology in intelligent water management. *Frontiers in Environmental Science, 10*, 909606. DOI: 10.3389/fenvs.2022.909606

Xu, C., & Jin, B. (2022). Digital currency in China: Pilot implementations, legal challenges and prospects. *Juridical Trib., 12*, 177.

Xu, C., Qin, B., & Rawlings, D. (2022). Motivational crowding effects of monetary and nonmonetary incentives: Evidence from a common pool resources experiment in China. *Ecological Economics, 202*, 107597. DOI: 10.1016/j.ecolecon.2022.107597

Yadav, M., & Yadav, R. (2018). Impact of spirituality/religiousness on cyber bullying and victimization in university students: Mediating effect of emotional intelligence. *Journal of Religion and Health, 57*(5), 1961–1979. DOI: 10.1007/s10943-018-0637-8 PMID: 29790079

Yadav, R., Yadav, M., & Mittal, A. (2022). Effects of gain-loss-framed messages on virtual reality intervened fitness exercise. *Information Discovery and Delivery, 50*(4), 374–386. DOI: 10.1108/IDD-04-2021-0051

Yang, Q., Zheng, M., & Wang, Y. (2023). The role of CBDC in green finance and sustainable development. *Emerging Markets Finance & Trade, 59*(15), 4158–4173. DOI: 10.1080/1540496X.2023.2185096

Yermack, D. (2022). Bitcoin and the future of digital payments in emerging markets. *The Journal of Economic Perspectives, 36*(2), 145–166. DOI: 10.1257/jep.36.2.145

YouGov. (2024). *CBDC awareness and public sentiment survey—India*. https://yougov.in/

Yuriev, A., Dahmen, M., Paillé, P., Boiral, O., & Guillaumie, L. (2020). Pro-environmental behaviors through the lens of the theory of planned behavior: A scoping review. *Resources, Conservation and Recycling*, *155*, 104660. DOI: 10.1016/j.resconrec.2019.104660

Zaid, S., & Patwayati, P. (2021). Influence of experience of customer and customer engagement on satisfaction and loyalty: A case Investigation in Indonesia. *The Journal of Asian Finance, Economics and Business*, *8*(4), 983–992.

Zeng, Y., Dong, P., Shi, Y., Wang, L., & Li, Y. (2020). Analyzing the co-evolution of green technology diffusion and consumers' pro-environmental attitudes: An agent-based model. *Journal of Cleaner Production*, *256*, 120384. DOI: 10.1016/j.jclepro.2020.120384

Zetzsche, D. A., Arner, D. W., Buckley, R. P., & Barberis, J. N. (2020). Decentralized finance (DeFi). *Journal of Financial Regulation*, *6*(1), 172–203. DOI: 10.1093/jfr/fjaa010

Zetzsche, D. A., Arner, D. W., Buckley, R. P., & Börner, C. (2021). The future of crypto regulation: A comparative analysis. *Journal of Financial Regulation*, *7*(2), 345–374. DOI: 10.1093/jfr/fjab007

Zhang, M., Wu, Y., & Su, H. (2025). The Influence of Green Finance on" Dual Carbon" Goals: Analyzing the Functions of Government and Market. *Sustainability (2071-1050)*, *17*(3).

Zhang, Y., Gong, H., Jiang, X., Lv, X., Xiao, R., & Huang, B. (2021). Environmental impact assessment of pavement road bases with reuse and recycling strategies: A comparative study on geopolymer stabilized macadam and conventional alternatives. *Transportation Research Part D, Transport and Environment*, *93*, 102749. DOI: 10.1016/j.trd.2021.102749

Zhang, Y., & Wen, J. (2017). The IoT electric business model: Using blockchain technology for the internet of things. *Peer-to-Peer Networking and Applications*, *10*(4), 983–994. DOI: 10.1007/s12083-016-0456-1

Zhang, Y., Xie, J., & Xu, Z. (2020). The role of social media in the cryptocurrency market: Evidence from sentiment analysis. *Applied Economics Letters*, *27*(18), 1489–1494. DOI: 10.1080/13504851.2019.1704674

Zhao, J. L., Fan, S., & Yan, J. (2016). Overview of business innovations and research opportunities in blockchain and introduction to the special issue. *Financial Innovation*, *2*(1), 1–7. DOI: 10.1186/s40854-016-0049-2

Zhao, X., Zhang, S., Ahmad, N., Wang, S., & Zhao, J. (2024). Unlocking Sustainable Growth: The Transformative Impact of Green Finance on Industrial Carbon Emissions in China. *Sustainability (Basel)*, *16*(18), 8253. DOI: 10.3390/su16188253

Zharikov, M. V. (2022). The Model of a Shared Interest Rate for a Group of Countries to Circulate a Digital Currency: Featuring the BRICS. *Journal of Central Banking Theory and Practice*, *11*(2), 187–208. DOI: 10.2478/jcbtp-2022-0019

Zhong, Z. Z., & Zhao, E. Y. (2024). Collaborative Driving Mode of Sustainable Marketing and Supply Chain Management Supported by Metaverse Technology. *IEEE Transactions on Engineering Management*, *71*, 1642–1654. DOI: 10.1109/TEM.2023.3337346

Ziolo, M., Bak, I., & Cheba, K. (2021). The role of sustainable finance in achieving sustainable development goals: Does it work? *Technological and Economic Development of Economy*, *27*(1), 45–70. DOI: 10.3846/tede.2020.13863

Zohar, A. (2015). Bitcoin: Under the hood. *Communications of the ACM*, *58*(9), 104–113. DOI: 10.1145/2701411

Zook, M. (2018). Information flows, global finance, and new digital spaces. In *The New Oxford Handbook of Economic Geography* (pp. 575–590). DOI: 10.1093/oxfordhb/9780198755609.013.35

Zwitter, A., & Boisse-Despiaux, M. (2020). Blockchain for humanitarian action and development aid. *Journal of International Humanitarian Action*, *5*(16). Advance online publication. DOI: 10.1186/s41018-020-00072-3

About the Contributors

Arjun J. Nair is working as a Professor with St. Lawrance College, Ontario, Canada. He has completed a Master of Science degree in Hospitality and Tourism Management from Madurai Kamaraj University, an MBA in Human Resources and Finance Management from the National Institute of Business Management in India, a Bachelor's Degree in Hotel Management from Calicut University in India and a Diploma in Hospitality Management from the American Hotel and Lodging Association in the United States. He holds professional memberships in several organizations, including the International Management Research and Technology Consortium in New York, the International Association of Innovation Professionals, the American Management Association, the National Human Resources Association and the Institute of Research Engineers and Doctors (Senior Member of the Universal Association of Arts and Management Professionals). With over 15 years of practical work experience in a variety of industries, such as education, exporting, hotel food and beverage, restaurant management and management training, he offers expertise in curriculum development, project management, lecturing, tutoring, general management, business administration, business development, staff management and public relations. He is a strategic thinker who has made significant contributions to training and facilitation, business development and the operations and management aspects of various organizations.

Sridhar Manohar currently works at the Doctoral Research Center of Chitkara Business School, Chitkara University, Rajpura, Punjab. They completed their doctorate in the area of services marketing from VIT Business School, VIT University and hold a bachelor's degree in technology and dual master's degrees in business administration and organizational psychology. The author is also certified with FDP at IIM-A and possesses expertise in service marketing, innovation and entrepreneurship, scale development process, and multivariate analytics. Their interests lie in teaching business analytics, innovation and entrepreneurship, research methodology, and marketing management. The author has published around 20 research papers that include Scopus-listed and ABDC-ranked international journals such as Society and Business Review, Benchmarking: An International Journal, Electronics Market, Corporate Reputation Review, International Journal of Services and Operations Management, and International Journal of Business Excellence. They have also presented papers and ideas in numerous international conferences.

Yam B. Limbu, Ph. D. is a Professor of Marketing at Montclair State University. His research interests include consumer behavior, marketing ethics, services, internet marketing, and healthcare marketing. His publications have appeared in various journals, including Industrial Marketing Management, European Journal of Marketing, Journal of Consumer Affairs, Journal of Research in Interactive Marketing, International Journal of Advertising, International Journal of Bank Marketing, Journal of Business & Industrial Marketing, British Food Journal, Health Communication and Social Science & Medicine. Dr. Limbu has co-authored a book and book chapters. Dr. Limbu has served as Editor-in-Chief for the International Journal of Business and Emerging Markets. He has been a guest editor and co-edited special issues for several journals. He also serves on the editorial boards of various journals. Dr. Limbu has served as vice president of the Academy of Global Business Research & Practice (AGBRP) (2019-2021), formerly known as the Society for Global Business & Economic Development (SGBED) (2013-2018). He has served various professional associations. Dr. Limbu has served as Keynote Speaker, Plenary Speaker, General Chair, Program Co-Chair, Track Chair, Proceedings Editor, Session and Meet the Editors and Doctoral Workshop Panel Members for conferences and symposiums. He has conducted research workshops and seminars with faculties and doctoral students. He serves as a visiting faculty at various institutions.

Bruce A. Huhmann (Ph.D., University of Alabama, 1999) is Professor and Chair of the Department of Marketing in the School of Business at Virginia Commonwealth University. He has previously served as Interim Chair of the Department of Finance, Insurance, and Real Estate at Virginia Commonwealth University, Wells Fargo Professor and Director of the Daniels Fund Ethics Initiative at New Mexico State University, and F. Ross Johnson Fellow and Assistant Professor of Marketing at the University of Manitoba. His research focuses on advertising executions and information, advertising and consumer welfare in health and financial services, and the impact of technology on sales. His publications have appeared in the Journal of the Academy of Marketing Science, Journal of Consumer Research, Journal of Business Research, Journal of Advertising, International Journal of Advertising, European Journal of Marketing, Psychology & Marketing, Journal of Consumer Affairs, Journal of Public Policy & Marketing, and several other journals and scholarly books.

***

Metasebia Adula is an Assistant Professor, Department of Management, Bule Hora University - (Ethiopia)

Tamire Ashuro is a Lecturer with the Department of Logistics and Supply Chain Management, Bule Hora University, Ethiopia

Sanjeev Kumar Bansal is doing industrial teaching, research and administrative experience of 25 years.

Stefano Bresciani received a Ph.D. in Business Administration in 2003 and worked as a Research Scholar in the ESCP-EAP, London. He is currently Associate Professor in Business Management at the School of Management and Economics, University of Torino, where he teaches Business Management and Innovation Management. He undertakes research integrated with the Department of Management of the University of Torino; and his main areas of research include business, innovation and strategic management. He is further, the Country Director for Italy of the EuroMed Research Business Institute (EMRBI) and Chairman of the EMRBI Research Group on "Multinational enterprises and corporate governance".

Himani Devi is a PhD candidate in Commerce at Graphic Era Deemed to be University, Dehradun. Her research focuses on corporate governance, sustainable business practices, and the intersection of technology and finance. She holds a Master's in Commerce from Punjab University and a Bachelor's in Commerce from Shri Guru Ram Rai College, Dehradun. Himani has authored multiple research papers, with two under review in international journals and two book chapters indexed in Scopus. She has presented at international conferences, covering topics such as AI-driven marketing and social media's role in shaping brand image. She is also a reviewer for IGI Global Scientific Publishing. Her expertise includes research design, data analysis, financial planning, and marketing strategies. Proficient in tools like VOSviewer and RStudio, she applies advanced analytical techniques in her work. Committed to academic excellence, she actively participates in faculty development programs and collaborates on emerging research initiatives. Beyond academia, she enjoys dancing and reading books.

Narayanage Jayantha Dewasiri, Ph.D., is a Chartered Manager at the Chartered Management Institute, UK. He conducts research at the Open University of Sri Lanka and the Sri Lanka Institute of Marketing. He is the founding Editor-in-Chief of the South Asian Journal of Marketing. His research interests are in corporate social responsibility, corporate governance, marketing and sales, management, and finance. He is working as the Head of Field Force at the HMD Global Inc., Sri Lanka. He also serves as a senior lecturer at University of Sabaragamuwa, Sri Lanka. He can be reached at dnjay@ou.ac.lk

G. Chamdramowleeswaran is currently working as Assistant Professor in Department of Commerce and business administration, VelTech Rangarajan Dr. Sagunthala R&D Institute of Science and Technology (Deemed to be University), Avadi, Chennai. He has more than 11 years 5 months of industry experience and 1 year and 11 months of teaching experience with specialization in HR and Marketing. He Holds a B.Com., M.B.A., M. Phil., and Ph.D. in Management from Bharathidasan University, Trichy

Shaju G.M. started their teaching career in the beginning of 2010 with 2 years of Industrial experience. Worked as Management Lecturer, Coordinator, Head of the Department, Dean and currently in the position as the Registrar of MIANZ International College.

Anmol Gulati is a Senior Research Fellow at the Doctoral Research Centre, Chitkara Business School, Chitkara University, Punjab, India. Her research interests encompass personal finance, behavioral economics, fintech, and well-being. She brings a strong research background, with multiple publications in prestigious journals like the International Journal of Consumer Studies, Marketing Education Review, etc. She is proficient in conducting systematic literature reviews and performing statistical analysis. Demonstrating exceptional research caliber, she is proficient in advanced software such as SPSS, SmartPLS, Bibexcel, Biblioshiny, Vos Viewer, Gephi, and Pajek. She is the corresponding author and can be contacted at: gulatianmol303@gmail.com

Geshwaree Huzooree serves as the Programme Leader for BA Business Management and lecturer specialising in Strategy and Project Management within the MBA Programme at Edinburgh Napier University. Before joining the faculty at Edinburgh Napier, she held the position of Senior Lecturer at Curtin Mauritius for a commendable eight years. Driven by her passion for the field, she brings seven years of valuable experience in the IT industry, focusing on software application development and project management. Her academic achievements include a Ph.D. in Computer Science (2020), an MSc in Software Engineering Projects and Management (2014), and a BSc in Computer Science and Engineering (2007), all earned from the esteemed University of Mauritius. Dr. Geshwaree's professional reach extends globally, fostering close collaborations with various universities and institutions. Her research pursuits encompass diverse areas such as project management, remote working, the future workforce, health informatics, and digital technologies. She is dedicated to conducting innovative research that addresses national challenges, contributing to a better future.

Amar Johri has been an Assistant Professor in the College of Administrative and Financial Sciences at Saudi Electronic University, Kingdom of Saudi Arabia, since September 2019. He has more than 17 years of academic experience. He obtained his doctorate (PhD) from Graphic Era University, Dehradun, Uttarakhand, India. His research interests include financial services, financial markets, banking, investment, accounting, and general management. He has published around 60 research papers in national and international journals (including Scopus Q1, Q2, Q3, and Q4 indexed journals, Web of Science: SSCI, SCIE, Q1, Q2, Q3 & ESCI Q2 journals, ABDC A and ABS Rank 1 category journals, and Proceedings of International Conferences of repute) and has presented around 30 research papers in national and international conferences. He has completed two research projects as a principal researcher and one as a co-researcher. He is also working on a few more research projects. He has been chair of the technical sessions and honored as a chief guest (valedictory session) at the international conference. He delivers and conducts sessions on financial planning, financial literacy, investment decisions, corporate finance, accounting information systems, corporate accounting, and Microsoft Excel and its use in account, finance, and statistics calculations. He is the reviewer and article editor of various reputed journals, including Web of Science and Scopus-indexed journals, and has reviewed more than 50 research papers. He has also published two patents.

Shashi Kant is an Assistant Professor with the College of Business and Economics, Department of Management, Bule Hora University, Ethiopia.

Amit Kumar Uniyal has more than 20 years (approx.) of experience. He has worked as a faculty member for around more than eighteen years and has taught more than twelve different courses to MBA/ MIB/ PGDM/ BBA/ MCA/BCA/ Ph.D. students., Has done M.Sc. (Statistics), MBA-HR, PGDBM-HR, PhD. in Statistics (Appled Science). He has got certification from University of London and SOAS and University of Illinois. He has got a number of publications in Web of Science, SCI and Scopus indexed journals, also published one patent. Presented and attended a number of national and international conferences and workshops, also has got two books under his credit (Management subjects). He had delivered a couple of expert lectures on "Research Methodology". Got life time membership of (Statistics) DDU University – Gorakhpur and London Journal Press-London.He has been a registered and a regular reviewer of the Elsevier and Springer Journals. He is working as Associate Professor at Graphic Era Deemed To be University for the last seven years. He is Guide to five Ph.D. scholars at Graphic Era Deemed to be University- Dehradun.

Vaibhav is Assistant Professor in Faculty of Commerce, Banaras Hindu University, Dr Vaibhav is UGC-NET qualified, and he holds B. Com (Gold Medalist), M. Com and M.B.A, MI (IIM Bangalore) and URM From University of London (UK). He is Python expert. He followed Stock Market Operations as his Doctoral pursuit. Besides finance, he has been teaching research methodology at P.G. and Ph. D level and specializes in Financial Econometrics. He has sixteen years of teaching and administrative experience in BHU. He commands 65 national papers and 17 internationals papers as well as has presented papers in more than 100 national and international seminars. He has travelled abroad and presented various papers which were highly acclaimed. He has also served as rapporteur, coordinator, session chair, key note speaker and also organized various seminars/conferences and workshops. To his credit are several awards and recognitions at university level for his co-curricular and philanthropist assignments. Currently he is also serving as NSS officer and looking after student's placement work for the faculty.

Olivier Niyompuhwe is currently associated with the Department of Forestry and Nature Conservation, University of Rwanda. His research interest lies in sustainability, services marketing, and supply chain management.

Nitin Pathak is a Professor and HOD-Commerce in University School of Business-Chandigarh University. He uses participatory and innovative teaching methodologies for imparting knowledge capsules on the course curriculum. His forte is Accounting & Finance, and he has mentored research work on many topics from this domain for papers, case studies, chapters in books and several publications in referred journals. Dr Pathak is the mentor for several research scholars who are pursuing research on various topics in the domains of financial inclusion and entrepreneurship development. Dr Pathak has devoted 22 years as a profound academician, holding decision making positions in various committees, teams and clubs focused on making the institution a center of excellence. He has special techniques of assessment, and he is known to prepare questions and assignments that challenge the total classroom and self-study done by those being appraised

Navaneetha Krishnan Rajagopal is a passionate researcher and academic contributor, actively engaging in national and international conferences as a keynote speaker, resource person, and guest lecturer. His research interests include artificial intelligence, business intelligence, supply chain management, and sustainable development. He has delivered insightful talks on AI, research publications, and organizational growth across institutions in India, Nigeria, Oman, and the U.S. Additionally, he plays a key role in faculty development programs, fostering academic excellence. Committed to bridging academia and industry, Navaneetha Krishnan

Rajagopal aims to drive impactful research, mentor future scholars, and contribute to global knowledge through innovation and interdisciplinary collaboration.

Veda Varsha Reddy B is currently pursuing a Ph.D. and holds a postgraduate degree (MBA) from Anna University, where she graduated with an impressive CGPA of 9.02 and earned the distinction of being a University Rank Holder in 2021. Her academic and professional interests are rooted in the fields of Marketing, Branding, Consumer Behavior, and Advertising. As a dedicated researcher, she is actively engaged in exploring these areas to contribute to the advancement of knowledge. She is presently serving as an Assistant Professor, where she imparts her expertise and enthusiasm for these subjects to her students. Her scholarly contributions include a diverse array of publications in SCOPUS Indexed journals, as well as the development of case studies and book chapters.

Tanya is an Assistant Professor in the Department of Commerce at Chandigarh University, currently pursuing a PhD in Commerce. She holds a Master's in Commerce from IGNOU and a Bachelor's from Shoolini University. With teaching experience at reputed institutions, she actively participates in academic and administrative responsibilities, including conferences and student mentorship. She has presented research on Central Bank Digital Currency and is UGC NET qualified in Commerce. Her skills span Tally, MS Office, and data analysis using R.

Mohit Yadav is an Associate Professor in the area of Human Resource Management at Jindal Global Business School (JGBS). He has a rich blend of work experience from both Academics as well as Industry. Prof. Mohit holds a Ph.D. from Department of Management Studies, Indian Institute of Technology Roorkee (IIT Roorkee) and has completed Master of Human Resource and Organizational Development (MHROD) from prestigious Delhi School of Economics, University of Delhi. He also holds a B.Com (Hons.) degree from University of Delhi and UGC-JRF scholarship. He has published various research papers and book chapters with reputed publishers like Springer, Sage, Emerald, Elsevier, Inderscience etc. and presented research papers in national and International conferences both in India and abroad. He has many best paper awards on his credit too. He is reviewer of various international journals like Computers in Human Behavior, Policing etc. His areas of interest are Organizational Behavior, HRM, Recruitment and Selection, Organizational Citizenship Behavior, Quality of work life and role.

Index

E

F

G

I

L

M

S

T

V

www.ingramcontent.com/pod-product-compliance
Lightning Source LLC
LaVergne TN
LVHW080605300926
849162LV00005B/1050